D0443589

174080

ALSO BY RICHARD GOLDSTEIN

America at D-Day

Desperate Hours: The Epic Rescue of the Andrea Doria

Spartan Seasons: How Baseball Survived the Second World War

Mine Eyes Have Seen: A First-Person History of the Events That Shaped America

Superstars and Screwballs: 100 Years of Brooklyn Baseball

Ivy League Autumns

You Be the Umpire

An American Journey (with Jerry Coleman)

HELLUVA TOWN

THE STORY OF NEW YORK CITY
DURING WORLD WAR II

RICHARD GOLDSTEIN

FREE PRESS

New York   London   Toronto   Sydney

WILLISTON COMMUNITY LIBRARY
1302 DAVIDSON DRIVE
WILLISTON, ND 58801-3894

FREE PRESS
A Division of Simon & Schuster, Inc.
1230 Avenue of the Americas
New York, NY 10020

Copyright © 2010 by Richard Goldstein

All rights reserved, including the right to reproduce this book or portions thereof
in any form whatsoever. For information address Free Press Subsidiary Rights Department,
1230 Avenue of the Americas, New York, NY 10020

First Free Press hardcover edition April 2010

FREE PRESS and colophon are trademarks of Simon & Schuster, Inc.

For information about special discounts for bulk purchases,
please contact Simon & Schuster Special Sales at 1-866-506-1949
or business@simonandschuster.com

The Simon & Schuster Speakers Bureau can bring authors to your live event.
For more information or to book an event contact the Simon & Schuster Speakers Bureau
at 1-866-248-3049 or visit our website at www.simonspeakers.com.

Manufactured in the United States of America

1   3   5   7   9   10   8   6   4   2

Library of Congress Cataloging-in-Publication Data
Goldstein, Richard.
Helluva town : the story of New York City during World War II /
Richard Goldstein.
p.   cm.
Includes bibliographical references.
1. New York (N.Y.)—History—1898–1951. 2. World War, 1939–1945—New York (State)—New York.
3. New York (N.Y.)—Social life and customs—20th century. 4. New York (N.Y.)—Social conditions—
20th century. 5. City and town life—New York (State)—New York—History—20th century.
6. Popular culture—New York (State)—New York—History—20th century. 7. Popular culture—
United States—History—20th century. I. Title. II. Title: Hell of a town.
F128.5.G64 2010
974.7'041—dc22
2009051105

ISBN 978-1-4165-8996-9
ISBN 978-1-4165-9302-7 (ebook)

For Nancy

CONTENTS

CONTENTS

PART IV   THE STAGE   127

PART V   THE NIGHT   181

PART VI   THE TENSIONS   205

PART VII   THE HOMECOMING   235

INTRODUCTION

In the south of England, soldiers, sailors, and airmen of the Allied forces massed for the long-awaited invasion of northern France. On the American homefront in this first week of June 1944, tensions rose as D-Day neared. But in Times Square, the Broadway theaters, the movie palaces and the nightclubs played on. Mary Martin starred at the 46th Street Theatre as a statue come to life in *One Touch of Venus*. Harry James brought his orchestra to the Astor Roof. Imogene Coca drew the laughs at the supper club Le Ruban Bleu. Servicemen were everywhere, looking for girls, and war-plant workers flush with cash were looking for night spots to empty their wallets.

Carlos Romulo, the Pulitzer Prize–winning Filipino journalist who fled Corregidor with General Douglas MacArthur's staff in the early months of the war, had arrived in Manhattan soon afterward to find "a city living apparently in a state of fiesta."

"I came from the battlefield into the Starlight Room of the Waldorf where men and women in evening clothes were dancing to Cugat's music," Romulo would recall. "Everyone was out having fun, and only the paper hats and horns were lacking to make every night a perpetual New Year's Eve."

As a native New Yorker intrigued by the city's history, as someone who had written on World War II combat, I had wondered: Was there really a war on so far as Brooklyn and the Bronx could tell?

Indeed there was. In seeking to answer this question, I came upon a story of scientific brilliance, artistic genius, a generous spirit, and the courage of ordinary men and women.

Times Square hosted a nightly frenzy, but why not? The more than three million servicemen who passed through it between Pearl Harbor Sunday and V-J Day were racing against time. Like the three sailors of Broadway's *On the Town* looking for love on a twenty-four-hour pass, they were on their final flings before facing an uncertain fate.

In recalling the show's signature number "New York, New York," Betty Comden and Adolph Green, who wrote the book and lyrics and became one of its three couples, were convinced that "New York *was* a helluva town."

> There were nine daily newspapers, you could buy a hot dog for a nickel, adventure in the streets may have been raffish but not necessarily fatal, and you could see a Broadway movie for 40 cents before 1 p.m., and it might have been Betty Grable or Hutton corn, but not porn.

New York was going to show the men and women headed overseas a good time before shipping them out. And it dispatched their armaments from its magnificent harbor while the Brooklyn Navy Yard built the battleships and aircraft carriers to avenge Pearl Harbor.

The city's popular culture became an arsenal of democracy of another sort. On the Broadway stage, Lillian Hellman, Robert Sherwood, Maxwell Anderson, and John Steinbeck championed the democratic cause, Irving Berlin's *This Is the Army* and Moss Hart's *Winged Victory* paid tribute to the armed forces with their all-servicemen casts, and Rodgers and Hammerstein's *Oklahoma!* buoyed American optimism at a time of national testing. Broadway's leading actors and actresses performed at the Stage Door Canteen in Midtown and at bases and military hospitals around the world.

And New York became a haven for the scientists, artists, journalists, and playwrights fleeing Nazi-occupied Europe.

Laura Fermi, the wife of the Nobel Prize–winning physicist Enrico Fermi, remembered the morning of January 2, 1939, when she arrived with her husband and two children in New York from Southampton, England, aboard the steamship *Franconia* on the final leg of their journey from fascist Italy:

> The New York skyline appeared in the gray sky, dim at first, then sharply jagged, and the Statue of Liberty moved toward us, a cold, huge woman of metal, who had no message yet to give me. But Enrico said, as a smile lit his face tanned by the sea: "We have founded the American branch of the Fermi family."

Enrico Fermi became part of an unseen New York.

Fermi joined with his fellow émigré Leo Szilard to conduct pioneering experiments in nuclear fission at Columbia University leading to creation of the atomic bomb, the Manhattan Project having been named for the place where it all began. The FBI, meanwhile, chased after Nazi spies in the city, Navy intelligence enlisted the Mafia to avert sabotage at the mob-run docks, and the British mounted a vast intelligence operation from obscure offices in Rockefeller Center.

Long before 9/11, New Yorkers felt vulnerable to a foreign foe. The city was assumed to be "Target Number One" if the Germans could send bombers into America's skies or shell the coastline from U-boats. Some 400,000 New Yorkers served as air-raid wardens while antiaircraft guns ringed the city. New Yorkers bought war bonds, donated blood, planted Victory Gardens, and collected metal scrap for conversion to armaments. Lest nostalgia get the best of us, this was also a time of racial and ethnic tensions. Racism and poverty spawned a riot in Harlem. A national rise in anti-Semitism brought attacks upon Jewish youngsters on New York streets.

Finally, this is a story of New York's transformation at war's end. The more than 800,000 New Yorkers who served in the armed forces came home to a city that was emerging as the world capital. New York surpassed Paris in art and fashion, London in financial prowess—its international clout underscored when the newly created United Nations voted to establish its permanent headquarters along the East River.

After ten years' absence from New York, the British writer J. B. Priestley passed through the city in 1947 on his trip to Mexico for a meeting of the United Nations Economic and Social Conference.

Speaking on the BBC when he came home, Priestley took notice of New York the world city.

Its huge cosmopolitanism—it has more Jews than Palestine and more Italians than Naples—is untouched in the history of man. And this gives its little shops and restaurants and odd corners a unique charm. The ends of the earth are gathered together down one New York side street. You can dine, drink and amuse yourself in three continents. The New York that O. Henry described forty years ago was an American city, but today's glittering cosmopolis belongs to the world, if the world does not belong to it.

PART ONE

THE THREAT

CHAPTER 1

WORLDS OF TOMORROW

The images endure. In his twelve years as the greatest mayor of the world's greatest city, he smashed slot machines with a sledgehammer, donned a fireman's raincoat at the first whiff of smoke, and, most famously, narrated Dick Tracy's exploits on the radio when a newspaper strike deprived youngsters of their comic strips.

But on the afternoon of Sunday, April 30, 1939, the colorful and charismatic Fiorello La Guardia went formal. Wearing a top hat, a cutaway morning coat, and striped trousers; swinging his arms vigorously; and bowing to the cheering crowds, the mayor strolled down the center aisle of the Court of Peace in the parade opening the New York World's Fair at Flushing Meadows, Queens. A garbage dump had been turned into 1,216 acres of technical genius, futuristic architecture, offerings of foreign culture and cuisine, and high- and low-brow entertainment.

La Guardia brimmed with pride over his fair and his city. To the mayor, the fair was all about New York. It celebrated the 150th anniversary of George Washington's inaugural in Lower Manhattan as the first president, but it was conceived by business and financial interests headed by Grover Whalen, the city's official greeter. And it propelled Parks Commissioner Robert Moses's vision of a magnificent park on the Flushing Meadows site.

In his speech welcoming visitors, a prelude to President Franklin D. Roosevelt's address formally opening the fair, La Guardia viewed New York as a model for democracy, a place where seven and a half million people of diverse national and racial strains lived together in harmony.

New York was no exception to the racial and ethnic divisions of the time, but La Guardia hoped the world could emulate its better nature. As he put it: "The City of New York greets The World of Tomorrow."

Consolidated Edison's City of Light diorama at the fair, a three-dimensional architectural model that depicted a twenty-four-hour cycle in New York's life, portrayed it as the "wonder city of the modern world."

Elected mayor in 1933, when New York was in desperate shape at the depths of the Depression, plundered by Mayor Jimmy Walker and Tammany Hall, La Guardia had melded boundless energy and the New Deal's money to transform New York into a well-governed, modern city.

The son of Italian immigrants, he was born in Greenwich Village but had grown up in the American West where his father, Achille, was a bandmaster on Army posts. His father was Catholic (though he ultimately renounced Catholicism), his mother, the former Irene Coen, was Jewish, and Fiorello became an Episcopalian, the ultimate triple for New York politics. Standing just over five feet tall, his wide frame suggesting he was even shorter, La Guardia was nonetheless an overpowering presence, hardworking and incorruptible, with a profound sympathy for the underdog. Coming to the mayoralty after a stint as an Army flier in World War I and a tenure as a liberal Congressman, nominally a Republican but more of a maverick, he oversaw the creation of public housing in slum-ridden neighborhoods and the creation of social welfare programs, parks, highways, and a nonpolitical civil service.

The effects of the Depression lingered, but the New York of 1939 was the manufacturing, financial, and cultural capital of America with a modernistic skyline. The Empire State Building, the Chrysler Building, Rockefeller Center, the Lincoln Tunnel, the Triborough Bridge, and the George Washington Bridge were all less than a decade old. La Guardia Field was built off Flushing Bay in Queens in 1939 to replace the outmoded Floyd Bennett Field in Brooklyn as the city's municipal airport.

But the looming involvement of America in another world war overshadowed all.

In the fair's two seasons, nearly 45 million people marveled at Democracity, the General Motors Futurama, and the signature Trylon and Perisphere, whose crystal ball envisioned peace and prosperity in "The World of Tomorrow." Prosperity would return to New York and to America, but it would be fueled by war.

By the time the fair was into its second spring, Nazi Germany had overrun Poland, the Low Countries, and much of France. The Soviet Union's pavilion, perhaps the most impressive among the foreign buildings, had been torn down. The Dutch abandoned their pavilion, and the British and the French mounted war displays. America debated intervention on behalf of the British, who stood alone against Hitler. The fair's Parachute Jump would ultimately be an emblem of the American paratroopers who jumped into Normandy four years later.

When the fair closed in October 1940, the 4,000 tons of steel in the Trylon and Perisphere were purchased by Bethlehem Steel for tanks, ships, shell cases, and gun forgings. Plumbing fixtures from fifty-nine buildings at the fair were installed in new naval stations along the Eastern seaboard.

While the fair was promising a blessed "World of Tomorrow," another world emerged—the age of atomic energy, the unlocking of the elemental forces of the universe to bring about previously unimaginable destruction.

Back in 1936, John Dunning, a physicist at Columbia, directed the design of its cyclotron in Pupin Hall. It weighed thirty tons, stood seven feet high and twelve feet wide, and its arms held a huge electromagnet to guide subatomic particles in spiral paths at speeds up to 25,000 miles per second before smashing them into their targets.

By 1939, Enrico Fermi and Leo Szilard were working at Columbia, utilizing the cyclotron in separate teams for pioneering research. The urgency of their work was underlined in January 1939 when the Danish nuclear physicist Niels Bohr, newly arrived in New York, confirmed that German scientists had achieved atomic fission: Hitler was evidently on the path toward developing an atomic bomb.

Fermi had split the atom in an experiment at the University of Rome in 1934, though he hadn't realized it at the time. He received the Nobel Prize in Stockholm for his nuclear research in 1938.

The evening of January 25, 1939, brought a milestone in the road toward a nuclear bomb. That afternoon, Fermi and Dunning met at lunch in Columbia's Faculty Club to discuss their work. Fermi took a train to Washington afterward to attend a scientific conference. Hours later, Dunning, along with Herbert Anderson, a graduate student studying under Fermi, and fellow physicists placed a thin sheet of solid uranium in the cyclotron's chamber along with a beryllium-radium mixture as the radioactive agent to bombard it.

Wavy green lines appeared on the screen of the cyclotron's oscilloscope, a device that measured the amount of energy given off by a substance under bombardment.

Dunning had never seen anything like it. "God!" he exclaimed. "This looks like the real thing."

After a series of tests to make certain the cyclotron was working properly, the physicists convinced themselves that uranium atoms had indeed been split for the first time in America.

On March 3, 1939, Szilard and Walter Zinn, a Canadian physicist, huddled over an oscilloscope in a seventh-floor laboratory at Pupin Hall, awaiting the outcome of their own experiment, months in the making. Szilard, a native of Budapest, had taught physics in Berlin during the 1920s, then went to England after Hitler's rise to power. He came to New York in 1938 with a reputation as an extraordinary theorist.

Would Szilard and Zinn see flashes signifying the emission of neutrons in the fission process of uranium on that March day? If that happened, as

Szilard would tell it, "the large-scale liberation of atomic energy was just around the corner."

Szilard and Zinn watched as the picture tube heated up. They saw nothing. Szilard, shuddering at the thought of atomic weaponry, felt a sense of relief. Then Zinn noticed something. These brilliant scientists had forgotten to plug the screen in.

It was finally connected, and then, as Szilard remembered it: "We saw the flashes. We watched them for a little while and then we switched everything off and went home. That night there was very little doubt in my mind that the world was headed for grief."

Szilard felt compelled to bring the results of the Columbia research to the White House. As dreadful as the prospect of America wiping out cities with a nuclear weapon might be, an atom bomb in Hitler's hands meant catastrophe.

On July 12, 1939, Szilard and a fellow physicist from Hungary, Eugene Wigner, drove from the King's Crown Hotel in Morningside Heights, where Szilard was living, to visit Albert Einstein, the most renowned of the émigré physicists, who was spending the summer at a friend's home in Peconic, Long Island. When their 1936 Dodge coupe crossed the Triborough Bridge, Szilard and Wigner surely saw the grounds of the World's Fair. The world they were unlocking would be very different from the "World of Tomorrow" prophesied at Flushing Meadows.

Einstein was receptive to making an approach to Roosevelt, and Szilard followed up by drafting a letter that Einstein signed on August 2. It was delivered to Roosevelt in October by a Wall Street investment banker, Alexander Sachs, who had privately advised the president during the New Deal.

Citing "recent work by E. Fermi and L. Szilard," the letter stated "it may become possible to set up a nuclear chain reaction in a large mass of uranium" that could bring about "extremely powerful bombs." It noted that the Germans were conducting just that sort of experimental work.

The Einstein letter ultimately spawned the Manhattan Project that built the atomic bomb.

Important work continued at Columbia well before the Manhattan Project got under way. In 1940, Dunning played a leading role in isolating the relatively rare uranium 235 isotope, which could readily be split in two, suggesting the possibility of a controlled chain reaction to release huge quantities of energy. Fermi and Szilard worked on creating it, and they got help in the fall of 1941 from beefy Columbia students who lugged the graphite blocks and uranium chunks used in their cyclotron experiments.

As Fermi recalled it, George Pegram, the head of Columbia's physics department and dean of the graduate school, noted there was "a football squad at Columbia that contains a dozen or so of very husky boys who take jobs by the hour just to carry them through college." Pegram suggested that Fermi hire them, and, as Fermi put it, "it was a marvelous idea," the football players "handling packs of 50 or 100 pounds with the same ease as another person would have handled 3 or 4 pounds."

But for all the excitement in stretching the frontiers of science, Fermi was troubled. One day, he was standing at his office window high in Pupin Hall. George Uhlenbeck, a physicist who shared the office, saw Fermi cup his hands as if he were grasping a ball as he glanced down at Manhattan Island. "A little bomb like that," he said, "and it would all disappear."

Early in 1942, the efforts to create a nuclear "pile" were shifted to the University of Chicago. On December 2, 1942, on a squash court underneath Stagg Field, the university's football stadium, Fermi, Szilard, and their team created history's first nuclear chain reaction.

The Manhattan Project had outposts throughout New York. It established its first headquarters, from June to September 1942, at 270 Broadway in Lower Manhattan, the offices of the North Atlantic division of the Army Corps of Engineers, which oversaw the vast atomic bomb project under the direction of General Leslie Groves. The Baker and Williams Warehouses, three buildings on West 20th Street in Manhattan, housed processed uranium. The Archer Daniels Midland warehouses on Staten Island stored almost 1,250 tons of high-grade uranium ore obtained from a mine in the Congo.

The bomb-building project got its name from its origins in the city, but more important from the need to avoid even a hint at its purpose. The Manhattan Project was a vast national enterprise with industrial facilities in Tennessee, Washington State, and elsewhere beyond the testing grounds at Los Alamos, New Mexico. Manhattan as an identifier hid all that.

General Groves proposed the term Manhattan Project in August 1942, following the custom of naming Army Engineer districts for the city in which they were located. The Army's general order approving the name was bland enough. There would be "a new engineer district, without territorial limits, to be known as the Manhattan District . . . with headquarters at New York, N.Y., to supervise projects assigned to it by the Chief of Engineers."

While the scientists were harnessing the power of the atom, important figures in New York's legal and financial establishment went to Washington to run the war.

Henry Stimson, named by FDR as secretary of war in 1940, was a native New Yorker who had gained prominence long before with the Manhattan law firm of the influential Republican Elihu Root. Stimson had been appointed by Teddy Roosevelt as the United States Attorney in Manhattan before serving as secretary of war under William Howard Taft and Secretary of State under Herbert Hoover.

Three of Stimson's four assistant secretaries of war came from New York's power circles. Robert Lovett, who oversaw the Army Air Forces, had been a partner in the Brown Brothers Harriman investment bank. Robert Patterson, who managed procurement for the Army, had been a federal district court judge in New York and then a member of the United States Court of Appeals for the Second Circuit, based in the city. John McCloy, handling many matters for Stimson, was recruited from Wall Street's Cravath law firm. James Forrestal, assistant secretary of the Navy and then the secretary following Frank Knox's death in 1944, had been president of the Dillon, Read investment house.

While the debate between isolationists and interventionists raged in the spring and summer of 1940, prominent figures in New York's intellectual and cultural worlds who were members of the Century Association, one of the city's most venerable and prestigious private clubs, gathered there to pursue the cause of aiding Britain in what became known as the Century Group. FDR and Stimson were Centurions, as members of the Century called themselves, and so was internationalist Republican Wendell Willkie, Roosevelt's opponent in his bid for a third term. So the voices of the international-minded Century Association members who gathered at their Stanford White–designed building on West 43rd Street, off Fifth Avenue, would be heard.

The Fight for Freedom Committee and the Committee to Defend America by Aiding the Allies, calling for the United States to stand with Britain, had strong ties to the Century Group. And the group persuaded General John J. Pershing, the esteemed commander of the Allied Expeditionary Forces in World War I, to make a national radio address in August 1940 backing FDR's quest to provide overage destroyers to Britain. On March 28, 1941, Willkie, speaking at the Century Association nearly five months after he was defeated by Roosevelt, told his fellow Centurions that he would work to build public sentiment behind FDR's foreign policy so the president "would become the most famous occupant of the office from George Washington on." The club's library rang with applause.

The isolationist cause displayed its fervor in May 1941 when Charles Lindbergh spoke before an America First rally at Madison Square Garden. It drew a capacity crowd of 22,000 with perhaps another 14,000 people outside listening over loudspeakers. Lindbergh told the crowd that if America entered the war in Europe its losses were "likely to run into the millions" and "victory itself is doubtful."

In the fall of 1940 and spring 1941, Americans were watching newsreel images of London ablaze in the Blitz and listening to the eyewitness accounts of Edward R. Murrow on CBS.

The prospect of an Axis attack on America's East Coast nonetheless seemed remote. Congress was not about to appropriate significant funds for civil defense as long as America wasn't in the war. But the Army staged war games in New York, and in April 1941 it unveiled a low-tech response should a bombing raid cut all communications: the use of homing pigeons to carry messages. Two Army pigeons took the subway from Rockefeller Center to Kew Gardens, Queens, with their handler, Private Felix Orbanoza, who turned them loose in a vacant lot. One arrived back in Rockefeller Plaza twenty-four minutes later, and the other one checked in afterward.

New York got its first air-raid shelter in April 1941, when the Allerton House for Women on Manhattan's East 57th Street reinforced the walls and ceiling of its subbasement, 45 feet below street level. The hotel's chief engineer, Samuel Lea, getting some ideas from the *Illustrated London News*, stocked the shelter with beds, desks, medical supplies, kerosene lamps in the event of a power failure, and Saltines and Sanka. A small banner on one wall read "God Bless America."

A modern-furniture shop on East 49th Street named Artek-Pascoe sold indoor shelters made of wood blocks for placement in cellars or basements to protect against falling beams or masonry. One of the shelters, resembling an igloo, could be had for $135, plus $10 for shipping and installation. A store display outfitted the shelter with a double mattress and bedding; an ax, shovel, and crowbar; a first-aid kit; a stirrup pump; pails for water and sand; an oil lantern; a flashlight; asbestos gloves; a helmet; and canned foods.

Abercrombie & Fitch, Hammacher Schlemmer, and Altman sold Garinol, a colorless liquid that was said to turn ordinary glass into nonshatterable safety glass. In a demonstration at Rockefeller Center's Museum of Science and Industry, the manufacturer hurled a simulated bomb against a Garinol-coated window pane, a blow that would have produced countless slivers in ordinary glass. The Garinol glass gently and harmlessly collapsed, remaining in one piece. And a powder called Instant A-Z was billed as just the thing for smothering fires started by incendiary bombs. Lewis & Company sold it in two-and-a-half-pound tubes.

La Guardia was looking far beyond New York and its embryonic defense preparations. In February 1941, he testified before the Senate Foreign Relations Committee in support of the Lend Lease plan to aid Britain.

In April, La Guardia, who headed the American-Canadian Permanent Joint Board on Defense, an agency considering ways to defend North

America in the event of an Axis attack, presented Roosevelt with a plan for a cabinet-rank director of civil defense. He proposed a vast bureaucracy that would not only engineer defense drills but deter sabotage, mount home-front propaganda against the Axis, and oversee local public health agencies, and he suggested he was the man to run it. La Guardia had already created a secret "sabotage" squad in the New York police department, 180 officers trained to infiltrate subversive organizations.

Roosevelt named La Guardia as the nation's first director of civilian defense in May 1941. This was an unpaid post that did not have cabinet rank, but La Guardia would be allowed to attend cabinet meetings.

Amid skepticism he could manage the national civil defense effort and still run New York effectively—the *New York Times* and *Newsweek* both questioned La Guardia's unbridled ambitions—the mayor tore into his new role with his customary verve. He typically spent midweek in Washington meetings or trips around the country. He proposed the issuance of 50 million gas masks for residents of the East, West, and Gulf coasts, creation of a guard force for railroad beds and defense plants, and emergency plans for defense of cities, none of which had a chance of being financed.

Perhaps hoping to ingratiate himself with Roosevelt, who was growing irritated at La Guardia's self-importance, according to the presidential adviser Bernard Baruch, La Guardia named Eleanor Roosevelt as codirector of the OCD in September, placing her in charge of its vaguely defined propaganda and morale-boosting tasks. But La Guardia seldom confided in Mrs. Roosevelt, and Republicans in the House of Representatives took swipes at the president by criticizing his wife for her do-good, social engineering plans as a civil defense official.

La Guardia could be patronizing toward Mrs. Roosevelt, as happened when he was victimized by her Spartan ways. After having lunch with her at a small apartment she kept in Greenwich Village, he remarked to her on leaving: "My wife never asks me where I have been, nor whom I saw, nor what I did, but she always asks me what I had to eat. Today I can truthfully say I did not have too much."

In November 1941, La Guardia was elected to a third term. But his volatility—he initiated a nasty political spat with the popular New York governor, Herbert Lehman—and questions over his ability to continue running the city effectively while trying to amass national power cut into his margin. His victory over the Democrat William O'Dwyer was a bit more than 130,000 votes, the closest in a New York mayoral election since 1905.

A newspaperman nevertheless congratulated La Guardia on yet another mayoral victory. "Thanks," he said, "but the next four years will be hell."

CHAPTER 2

PEARL HARBOR SUNDAY

President Roosevelt was having lunch in the Oval Office at the White House with his aide Harry Hopkins. On Constitution Avenue, Secretary of the Navy Frank Knox was meeting with Admiral Harold Stark, the chief of naval operations. It was nearing 2 p.m. when a communications officer burst into the naval meeting with a startling message from Hawaii: "Air Raid on Pearl Harbor—This Is Not Drill."

In New York City, events far removed from the Japanese attack were at hand on this Sunday, December 7, 1941. There was a pro football game to be played, and for the more aesthetically inclined, a New York Philharmonic concert at Carnegie Hall.

This was Tuffy Leemans Day at the Polo Grounds. Before the National Football League's New York Giants played the Brooklyn Dodgers on a cold, windy afternoon before a crowd of 55,051, the Giants presented Leemans, their star running back, with $1,500 in defense bonds.

In the Polo Grounds press box, the Associated Press ticker reported a score from Chicago—Cardinals 7, Bears 0—and then it broke in with the words "cut football running" to report that America was at war.

The Polo Grounds public address announcer paged the Army officer who would later direct clandestine war actions as head of the Office of Strategic Services. "Attention please. Here is an urgent message. Will Colonel William J. Donovan call operator 19 in Washington immediately."

Wellington Mara, the twenty-five-year-old son of the Giants' founder and owner, Tim Mara, had been watching from the sidelines. "Late in the second quarter, there were public address announcements for military people to call Washington, but I didn't pay much attention to it," he would recall. "Then at halftime Father Dudley, our chaplain, told me, 'The Japanese bombed Pearl Harbor.'"

George Franck—or Sonny Franck as he was known—the Giants' speedy rookie halfback and a former All-American at the University of Minnesota, bruised his pelvis early in the game. At halftime the Giants put him in a taxi and sent him to a hospital.

"Somebody had said that all of the commanders with a lot of stars on were being asked to leave the stands at about the same time," Franck remembered. "They said something was going on but we didn't know what it was."

Franck was hearing news reports on the taxi's radio. "I said to the taxi driver, 'Why don't you turn on the football game?' He said, 'This *is* the football game.' I said, 'What the hell are they talking about?' He said, 'The Japanese bombed Pearl Harbor this morning.'"

The radio bulletins were spreading the word as the Giants and Dodgers played on in the final Sunday of the N.F.L.'s regular season. The Mutual Broadcasting System broke into the play by play: "We interrupt this broadcast to bring this important bulletin from United Press. Flash! The White House announces Japanese attack on Pearl Harbor."

Some listeners were distraught not so much by the Japanese attack but the interruption of the football broadcast. One caller to the Mutual switchboard, remembering the panic stirred by the Orson Welles *War of the Worlds* radio play of 1938, told the Mutual operator: "You got me on that Martian stunt. I had a hunch you'd try it again."

But Sonny Franck knew what lay ahead for him. He had enlisted in the armed forces and was waiting to be called up.

Seymour Wittek, a twenty-year-old from the Bronx, was in the radio audience for that football game. He had been working in Manhattan's fur district and pondering his immediate future as 1941 neared its end. His father had died when he was a youngster and he was essentially raised by his grandparents. As a boy, he shined shoes in a pool parlor while his mother worked in a steamy laundry in the basement of the Hotel Commodore on East 42nd Street. By December 1941, Wittek's cousins and friends had joined the military, and he was eager to join as well, though it meant leaving his mother alone.

But on Sunday, December 7, romance was uppermost in his mind. On Wednesdays, Fridays, and Sundays, he would visit his girlfriend, Anne Cooperman, at her home in Brooklyn. They hoped to be married before long.

"Since the Giants were playing, I was going to get to Brooklyn early so I could listen to the game," Wittek remembered. "I was at her house when they interrupted it to announce Pearl Harbor. It was complete disbelief."

On the fourth floor of the RCA Building in Rockefeller Center, Robert Eisenbach, an editor in the National Broadcasting Company's news department, heard the clanging on the Associated Press teletype machine at 2:27

p.m., signaling an item of the highest priority. Reading the Pearl Harbor flash, he phoned the network's master control room, ordering it to cut off all programming. The Red Network silenced Sammy Kaye's *Sunday Serenade* and the Blue Network halted the *Great Plays* presentation of Gogol's *The Inspector General.*

Eisenbach had never been on the air. But now he picked up the newsroom's emergency microphone. He was the sole voice on the 246 stations affiliated with the two NBC networks, and he reported that America had been plunged into war. Two minutes later, when NBC had its regular station break, a fourth chime sounded after the familiar cadence tolling *N-B-C.* That was a code telling personnel at home to contact headquarters for instructions.

The skaters at the Rockefeller Center ice rink, the crowds waiting to see Cary Grant and Joan Fontaine in Alfred Hitchcock's *Suspicion* at Radio City Music Hall, watched paper airplanes descend from the Time and Life magazine offices, each inscribed by newsmen with the words "we are at war with Japan."

At the 44th Street Theatre, Sono Osato, dancing as the Lilac Fairy in the Ballet Theatre's *Princess Aurora*, was in a state of panic. Her father, Shoji Osato, was a Japanese native who had come to America just after the turn of the century. Her mother, Frances Fitzpatrick Osato, was of Irish and French-Canadian background. Dancing for the Ballet Russe de Monte Carlo and then performing with the Ballet Theatre, Osato had noticed that her Japanese heritage was invariably mentioned in press notices.

On Pearl Harbor Sunday, "I came out the stage door after the matinee," she recalled, "and I heard something about the Japanese, an attack."

She was scheduled to appear in *Princess Aurora* before an evening audience as well.

"My heritage had never been hidden. I thought, 'Oh, my God, people in the audience who had a child in Hawaii. What if someone gets up and yells something? What if someone throws something at me? What's going to happen if they hiss me when I come on stage?'"

Osato's boyfriend and future husband, Victor Elmaleh, an architect awaiting Army service, tried to calm her, and she came back to the theater for the evening performance. As she stood in the wings before an audience of 400 while the orchestra played the overture, she told Pat Dolin, a coach for the dancers, that she feared going on stage. "Nonsense," he told her, "don't be silly."

She danced in a daze, but "nothing did happen."

At Carnegie Hall, Artur Rubenstein was performing the Chopin E minor piano concerto with the New York Philharmonic-Symphony Orchestra before an audience of 2,200 and a CBS Radio hookup. The audience response was so enthusiastic that when Rubenstein completed the work, he beckoned the conductor, Artur Rodzinski, from the podium to share in the acclaim. While the applause was still resounding, Warren Sweeney, the CBS announcer for the concert, came to the stage and told of the Japanese attack.

Selwyn Hirsch, seated in the audience, recalled how "there was a stunned silence until the orchestra began to play 'The Star-Spangled Banner.' The entire audience stood and sang. It was just like a scene from the movies. I remember thinking that the world would never be the same again."

*Robert Satter, a Rutgers University graduate in his first year at Columbia Law School, may have been one of the last New Yorkers to learn of the Japanese attack.

"I had a job as a guard at the Planetarium, and in the afternoon I noticed that hardly anybody was there. I finished about 6 o'clock and walked across a little park toward Broadway. I had my supper at a restaurant. I was the only one in there. I walked across Broadway to get the subway up to Columbia. I hadn't heard. I saw these blaring headlines in The New York Enquirer, but I didn't believe what they said because I never believed the Enquirer.

"I got up to Columbia and went into Furnald Hall, the law school dormitory. Across from my room, a door was open and a radio was blasting. My friend across the hall was sitting with his head in his hands and he told me about Pearl Harbor. And then he said his brother was in the service on Guam."

Kay Travers, a couple of years out of Prospect Heights High School in Brooklyn, was riding with friends to Packanack Lake in New Jersey for a Sunday outing.

I was with a fellow I was dating and a couple of other people. The boy whose car we were in was showing us his new red convertible. He was a wealthy boy and his father had given it to him, probably for his 21st birthday. We insisted on leaving the top down so everyone could see us. We were freezing. He put the radio on and someone announced there had been a bombing at Pearl Harbor. There were about six of us. Everyone in that car was a bright person. Most of the boys were halfway through college. But nobody except the fellow who was driving knew where Pearl Harbor was. The only reason he knew was because his family had visited Hawaii.

Everybody was stunned. Then they started talking about us going to war. We were all making such fun. "Imagine Jack in a uniform . . . imagine this one." We thought it was hysterical. It was all sort of light-hearted. We couldn't absorb it. It was such a shock.

The dimensions of the Japanese attack could indeed be hard to process.

Dr. Benjamin Spock was at his home in New York, where he had been practicing pediatrics since 1933. His wife, Jane, and his oldest son went to see the Disney movie *Dumbo* and had urged him to come along, but he had too much desk work to do. He was listening to music on the radio—just some soothing background—when he heard the bulletins. He found it difficult to continue with his work.

"After a while Jane and my son came back from the movies," he recalled, "and my wife said, 'oh, you should have gone, it was wonderful.' And I said: 'Do you know what has happened? Since you've been away the Japanese have bombed Pearl Harbor.' And she said, 'You really should have come.' "

For New York's Chinese community, whose homeland had been invaded by Japan and victimized by atrocities, the Pearl Harbor attack represented hope.

"They've committed national hari-kari," said Tom Lee, a life-insurance executive known as the Mayor of Chinatown. "They're rats and double-crossers. With the help of America and American munitions, China will win this war in no time."

The writer Marcia Davenport and her husband, Russell, the managing editor of *Fortune* magazine, were at home on Manhattan's Upper East Side. The Davenports had been ardent interventionists as Hitler's armies marched across Europe. They were active members of the Committee to Defend America by Aiding the Allies, and Marcia Davenport had spoken at rallies of British War Relief. And the Davenports were friends of the renowned conductor Arturo Toscanini, who had helped emigre musicians find work in New York.

On Saturday night, the Davenports had been at Toscanini's NBC Symphony concert. Sunday's Philharmonic concert held no special attraction for them but they had tuned to the broadcast. Russell Davenport was listening while Marcia was elsewhere in their apartment when the Pearl Harbor bulletin arrived, and he called to her in what she remembered as a "high, tense voice."

" 'Japan?' we asked each other. 'Japan?'" The Davenports had been so bound up with the war in Europe that the threat of war with the Japanese had held no immediacy for them. That evening, the Davenports invited friends for supper. They expected Hitler to launch a sneak attack on the East Coast timed with the Japanese bombing, and that brought the war very close as Marcia pondered the day's catastrophic events so far away. Military men who had visited with the Davenports in recent months had noticed the five long windows in their drawing room overlooking the East River and its bridges and had concluded, "What a target."

The dinner group sat talking in low voices, each of the guests seeking to remain calm, when an air-raid siren began to wail. "We stopped talking and looked round the table with raised eyebrows," Marcia Davenport remembered. "Was there really an air attack approaching New York?" She turned on a radio and turned off the apartment lights. Some time later they learned it was only a test.

La Guardia rushed from his apartment to City Hall for a conference with police and fire officials in midafternoon, then went on the radio to warn New Yorkers to be ready should "murder by surprise" arrive from the skies. He banned gatherings by the city's thousand or so Japanese nationals, and the police closed the Nippon Club, a social group on West 93rd Street.

Amid stepped-up security at vital installations, policemen arrived at the International Building in Rockefeller Center while the Japanese consul general, Morito Morishima, and his staff were preparing to leave their thirty-sixth-floor offices. The police left a guard there and escorted Morishima to his home. Three Japanese men emerged from the building with trunks, suitcases, and briefcases, presumably containing documents, and departed in a limousine.

By nightfall, FBI agents and the police began rounding up German, Japanese, and Italian aliens who were evidently on a Justice Department list of security threats. By the predawn hours of Monday, more than sixty Japanese had been taken to the Barge Office in Lower Manhattan for transfer via ferry to detention on Ellis Island. A Park Avenue physician identifying himself as E. Espy, who had been picked up at his home, said he had been in America for thirty-five years and had not been in Japan since 1917. "This is an unfortunate situation," he remarked.

Roosevelt called a meeting of his cabinet for Sunday night, and the White House's chief switchboard operator, Louise Hackmeister, was trying to round up its members.

Frances Perkins, the secretary of labor, and her stenographer had been working through the afternoon in a room at the Cosmopolitan Club in Manhattan, drafting a report on relations with Latin America. They called out for soup and sandwiches and had seen no one else. Then came a phone call from a Labor Department chauffeur in Washington: "Miss Perkins, they say on the radio that the cabinet's been called in for tonight." Perkins said she was usually skeptical of what she heard on the air, but would check and call back. Moments later, Hackmeister phoned, telling Perkins to be at the White House by 8 o'clock.

"What's the matter, Hacky?" Perkins asked. "Why the cabinet meeting tonight?"

"Just the war, what's in the paper," Hackmeister replied, and hung up.

None of the club's officers had heard any unusual news, but the taxi driver taking Perkins to La Guardia Field reported how "they said on the radio there was shooting somewhere."

Vice President Henry Wallace was also in Manhattan that afternoon. So, too, was Postmaster General Frank Walker, who had watched his children perform at a Sunday School concert. Wallace and Walker were at the airport when Perkins arrived there, but neither knew much more than she did. They boarded a charter flight for Washington.

Treasury Secretary Henry Morgenthau had completed work on a new bond offering Friday night, and he was in Manhattan as well. Weary from wrestling with financial matters and the war news from Europe and Asia, he was planning a brief vacation in Arizona. After lunch with family members, he received the news of Pearl Harbor from his chauffeur. Secret Service agents told him that Roosevelt had been trying to reach him for the past two hours. He boarded a plane that had been waiting to take him to Tucson. It headed for Washington instead.

Sonny Franck was among a handful of rookies on that Giants football team of 1941. Jack Lummus, a Texan from Baylor University in Waco, was another first-year player.

"We had three or four real excellent ends and he was one of them," Franck recalled. "Lummus blocked well. He acted real sure of himself. He was a little bit cocky but he could do everything he said he could do. He had Texas pride—self assurance. He was a typical Texas swashbuckling cowboy kind of guy."

After completing his naval flight training, Franck joined the marines, piloting a Corsair fighter in the Pacific, then serving as a ground observer guiding air strikes. Lummus also entered the Marine Corps following the 1941 season and he became a platoon leader—a lieutenant in the 27th Marines, Fifth Marine Division.

On February 19, 1945, Sonny Franck and Jack Lummus came ashore at a place that barely an American alive on December 7, 1941, had heard of—an eight-square-mile speck of volcanic ash in the Pacific called Iwo Jima. They were among 75,000 marines ordered to seize the island from 21,000 Japanese soldiers dug into caves and tunnels and prepared to fight to the last man.

On March 8—thirteen days after the flag-raising on Mount Suribachi created an enduring image of embattled Americans—Lummus stormed Japanese positions on the northern coast of Iwo Jima, moving ahead of his men. Wounded twice by exploding hand grenades, he continued to press forward until his legs were blown away by a land mine. He ordered his men to keep moving. Inspired and enraged, the marines swept ahead and reached their coastal objective.

Lummus was carried to a field hospital. "I guess the New York Giants have lost the services of a damn good end," he told Lieutenant E. Graham Evans, one of the surgeons. He died that day at age twenty-nine. On May 5, 1946, Jack Lummus was posthumously granted the Medal of Honor, the nation's highest award for valor.

CHAPTER 3

DECEMBER JITTERS

Within hours of the Pearl Harbor attack, young men began lining up at Army, Navy, and Marine recruiting stations in the city. Some 2,500 applied for enlistment by Monday evening. At Prospect Park in Brooklyn and Fort Totten in Queens, crews manning antiaircraft guns watched the skies. But La Guardia flew to Washington Monday morning after conferring with his aides, turning to his duties as the national civilian defense director. He met with Roosevelt that evening, then flew to the West Coast for a five-city tour to inspect preparedness efforts.

If New Yorkers needed bucking up, it would come from others—someone like Mary Read, a beloved figure at Grand Central Terminal. Read had been serenading travelers since 1928, when she borrowed an organ from a department store and brought it to the North Balcony. In the Depression, she was featured at Grand Central in performances of the Manhattan Concert Band, a New Deal WPA project providing work for unemployed musicians. During the evening rush hour of Monday, December 8, she played "The Star-Spangled Banner," the strains from the balcony bringing the terminal to a halt. But a stationmaster was displeased. People had to make their trains. The national anthem should not become a daily habit, he told Read.

At Columbia University, some faculty members viewed the war much as the stationmaster had. It was an inconvenience that must not be allowed to disturb routine.

Robert Satter, the law student who had been guarding the Planetarium Sunday afternoon, found that his Columbia professors were unwilling to allow Pearl Harbor to disrupt their lessons.

His first Monday class, at 9 a.m., was civil procedure with Professor McGill.

As Satter remembered it: "The professor called on somebody for a case—unprepared. Another guy for a case—unprepared. Another—unprepared. Finally, somebody was prepared. The professor went through four cases, called on maybe twenty people to get them. At the end of the class he said,

'Gentlemen'—it was all men at the time—'if you're going to be in class on Wednesday, I expect you to be prepared. Good day.' It was idiotic of him to have shown no awareness of this world-shaking event. These were guys who were 21, 22 years old, all of us expecting to go into the service.

"But even more outrageous," Satter recalled, "was Professor Julius Goebel, who was teaching Development of Legal Institutions, starting with the year 1066. On December 8 we were up to the 1300s maybe. The class went from 11:20 to 12:10. When we went to him and asked to be excused at 12 o'clock to hear Roosevelt address Congress about declaring war, he refused. When one of us asked whether we could bring a radio to class, he also refused.

"So a couple of us said, 'Professor Goebel, go to hell,' and we went down to the Hotel Pennsylvania bar and heard the president address the nation, the Day of Infamy speech."

La Guardia's Office of Civilian Defense was said to have 950,000 people enrolled nationally, including air-raid wardens, the firefighting auxiliary, and the medical corps. But it was woefully short of equipment and training, as would quickly become clear in New York.

The city had more than 115,000 wardens, but it possessed not a single air-raid siren. If word were to come from the Army fighter base at Mitchel Field, Long Island, that enemy planes were arriving, sirens on the city's fire engines and police patrol cars would sound the alarm. Fire Commissioner Patrick Walsh explained that the fire engines would move out in front of their houses, and for a five-minute period they would sound one long blast following by one short blast in a continuous sequence. Police cars would sound the same signal, wherever they were. Upon receipt of an all-clear, the fire engines and police cars would sound a series of staccato blasts for five minutes.

City officials didn't have to wait long to test the makeshift alarms. Two days after the Pearl Harbor attack, authorities at Mitchel Field ordered a pair of air-raid alerts following a report that enemy planes were 200 miles out over the Atlantic, heading for New York.

The sirens on the fire engines and police cars were indeed wailing. But they could barely be heard over the city's working-day din. At the Army Building at 39 Whitehall Street in Lower Manhattan, recruiting officers didn't know an alert was on until newspaper reporters told them about it. And New Yorkers shrugged when air-raid wardens and police officers pleaded with them to get indoors.

On the roof of the Paramount Building in Times Square, wardens were poised with fire carts containing sand, stirrup pumps, asbestos gloves, and long-handled shovels in the event incendiary bombs rained down. But in the streets below, pedestrians gawked at the Times Tower electronic bulletins, then glanced at the sky, saw no bombers, and decided there was no reason to seek shelter. Near City Hall, a policeman ordered two busloads of passengers to flee into a building, but they ignored him. After a five-minute standoff, he screamed at the drivers to get the buses out of his sight.

The average New Yorker clearly wasn't about to panic, but a selling wave hit Wall Street, sending stock prices plunging hundreds of millions of dollars, the worst slump since the collapse of France in June 1940.

On Wednesday, Army officers acknowledged that the air-raid alarms of the previous day were simply a product of jitters—their own. The first one had resulted from an Army officer on Governors Island in New York Harbor calling Mitchel Field to inquire about an unsubstantiated report of enemy planes in sight. The second one was attributed to confusion over a plane crash or a small fire at Mitchel Field.

Wednesday morning brought another air-raid alarm in New York, this one beginning at 8:41 a.m. and ending twenty minutes later. Once again, New Yorkers ignored the wardens and the police trying to herd them indoors, and once more the fire and police sirens were inaudible. And for the second straight day, it was all an Army snafu. Radio beams from Mitchel Field had detected 150 planes out over the Atlantic, evidently heading for Long Island. It wasn't until the alarm had been sounded that the Army discovered these were United States Navy planes on a routine patrol.

In Brooklyn's Bedford-Stuyvesant section, Sid Frigand, a student at Boys High School, experienced a terrifying moment.

"We were in the gymnasium. We had a gym teacher named Harry Kane. He came in and he was near hysteria and he said 'we just had a siren alarm. It's the real thing. You guys gotta get out of here and go home.'

"I didn't bother to change my clothes though I only had gym shorts on and a T shirt, and it was in the winter. I sprinted all the way home from Boys High, which was two or three miles from our house. At first I was running full speed. My mother was there alone and I wanted to make sure I could take care of her. As I'm running, I'm looking around. Trolley cars are moving, traffic is moving, people are walking on the streets—in fact, they were looking at me. By the time I got home I realized it was a drill. I was really chagrined but it was a frightening feeling that it was a real thing."

In Monday's early hours, FBI agents arrived at the Park Avenue apartment of Louis Berizzi, an Italian national who imported raw silks for a company based in Bergamo. Berizzi's family epitomized Upper East Side sophistication, but the father had retained his Italian citizenship so he could travel back to Italy easily on business. Now he would fall victim to the federal government's haphazard and callous treatment of aliens who posed no threat to America.

The FBI roused Berizzi and his family from sleep. He was told to get dressed—he was being taken away. No explanation was given and the agents wouldn't say where he was going. They remained in Berizzi's bedroom as he got out of his pajamas, and family members were given no time to speak with him privately. He could not take his personal effects, even his toiletries.

Three days later, Berizzi's family received a telegram from him asking that personal items be taken to the office in Lower Manhattan where barges departed for Ellis Island.

Berizzi's office in Rockefeller Plaza was locked by the office of the Alien Property Custodian and his assets were blocked. When it came time for his son's tuition at Lehigh College to be paid, the family was required to petition the custodian's office to unfreeze some of the father's funds.

In January, Berizzi and a business associate, also an Italian national, were allowed a hearing on Ellis Island. Only family and friends were permitted to speak on his behalf, vouching for his character. The family was not allowed legal representation, and Berizzi's wife, desperate to secure her husband's release, became hysterical. Berizzi was ordered to remain in custody, his family allowed to make weekly visits while the government decided what to do with him.

Berizzi's daughter, Lucetta, personified the image of a cultured and well-educated New Yorker. She had graduated from the Spence School, had studied German at the Lenox School, and had been taught French by a governess. Her language skills had been put to good use at Saks Fifth Avenue, where she helped non-English-speaking European customers.

"The FBI showed up at Saks one day and I was called up to the personnel office," she remembered. "The meeting did not take very long, but I was subsequently fired. I guess they found what I was doing suspicious."

She became an office manager at the United States Cane Sugar Refiners' Association, whose director, Ellsworth Bunker, better known a generation later as the ambassador to South Vietnam during the Vietnam War, was in charge of the nation's allocations of sugar, a rationed item. So the daughter of the interned alien held a sensitive post. But, as she would put it, "the FBI didn't seem to mind that."

Late in 1942, Louis Berizzi was transferred from Ellis Island to Fort Meade, Maryland, where Italian aliens were held behind barbed wire. When his family met with him he had lost weight and wore Army fatigues inscribed PW, for prisoner of war. "He was a pretty crushed guy," his son, Albert, recalled. The family, its finances stretched, had meanwhile moved into a small apartment.

Although his father remained in detention, Albert Berizzi was clearly deemed no security risk. He entered the Army and was trained in military intelligence at Camp Ritchie, Maryland, then served in the Italian campaign with the Office of Strategic Services. The Berizzi family finally went to Washington with a lawyer, arguing for the father to be freed. On March 4, 1943, the family received a telegram from Fort Meade: "Internee Louis Berizzi to be released."

Ezio Pinza, the Metropolitan Opera basso and a veteran of Europe's greatest opera houses, found his celebrity status to mean nothing in the government's hunt for potentially dangerous enemy aliens. But the Justice Department didn't get around to holding Pinza, a native of Rome, until mid-March 1942, when he was sent to Ellis Island. It wasn't clear whether the government had any particular reason to detain Pinza, other than his Italian nationality, but his wife, the former Doris Leak, an American, said at the time that he was suspected of having been friendly with Mussolini, an allegation she called "ridiculous." Pinza was released from Ellis Island in May 1942. He continued to perform at the Metropolitan Opera, and in January 1944 he donated his two Dalmatians, Boris and Figaro, for training with the Army's K-9 Corps at Fort Robinson, Nebraska. In 1950, he stepped away from opera to assume what would become his best-remembered role, as a glamorous lover in Broadway's *South Pacific*.

In the first hours of war for America, the Pearl Harbor attack claimed a casualty on the Broadway stage. *The Admiral Had a Wife*, a comedy about Navy officers and their wives on Pearl Harbor, had been scheduled to open at the Playhouse on Wednesday night. The coproducers, Jose Ferrer and Ruth Wilk, announced its cancellation, lest it be "misinterpreted as disrespectful."

The Broadway columnists were focusing on some peculiar concerns. Cholly Knickerbocker (real name Maury Paul) of the *Journal-American* told of a rumor that Japanese bombs had hit the lawn of the Doris Duke Cromwell estate in Hawaii. Nancy Randolph of the *Daily News* also picked up the story, telling of the heiress's exasperation in trying to reach her caretaker on the telephone. And Cholly Knickerbocker devoted 400 words to musing on whether the society figure Mrs. Frederick Payne should discard her nickname Tokio.

La Guardia caught up with all this in Seattle, continuing his West Coast swing while Newbold Morris, the City Council president, tried to keep track of all those air-raid alarms as acting mayor. "Am I embarrassed? Am I humiliated?" La Guardia fumed, holding up a wirephoto showing New Yorkers milling around during the alarms. "Won't somebody catch hell about this when I get home."

When La Guardia returned, he ripped up the interior of City Hall: Its main floor was about to become a headquarters for civil defense volunteers. Changes in public buildings required approval from the Municipal Art Commission, but La Guardia didn't bother to consult it. On the mayor's orders, workmen chopped holes in the marble floor of City Hall's main corridor to install iron fences as barriers to his office. They broke through walls for telephone and electrical circuits and assembled cubbyholes for the defense staff.

Twenty women working as messengers and receptionists turned up in the ground floor rotunda, clad in blue-gray uniforms with brass buttons and gold epaulets. In their first day on the job, they had nothing to do except stand guard outside La Guardia's office, salute each other when relieved of their shifts, and salute the mayor when he left to witness a test of a Consolidated Edison air-raid siren. They became known as The Palace Guard.

The siren, a large foghorn device placed atop Con Ed's East Side plant and designed to sound over a wide area, proved as much a fiasco as the fire engine and police sirens had been. Standing expectantly on the Brooklyn side of the Brooklyn Bridge for the test, La Guardia listened in vain for the siren's wailing.

The mayor, meanwhile, got into a fight with the Democrats who controlled the City Council when he proposed fines of $500 and jail sentences of six months for New Yorkers who ignored air-raid instructions. Councilmen denounced the penalties as "unconstitutional and hysterical" and smacking of "totalitarianism," and the mayor agreed to clarify its provisions. At any rate, since few wardens had armbands it was hard to know who was really authorized to bark commands.

Ready or not for an air raid, city officials permitted the customary New Year's Eve celebration in Times Square. A million revelers gathered and tin horns sounded as the lighted ball slid down the flagpole of the Times Tower, proclaiming an emblazoned "1942." Lucy Monroe sang the national anthem over a loudspeaker, standing at the statue of Father Duffy, a legendary figure of New York's Fighting 69th Regiment of World War I. The crowd sang along with her, and the radio networks broadcast the spectacle. Newsreel cameras captured the scene for the nation's movie theaters.

More than 2,000 policemen, an unprecedented number for the annual celebration, stood guard, assisted by 1,600 air-raid wardens who had been briefed in a ballroom of the Hotel Astor. Fire trucks and ambulances were poised for action should the Luftwaffe show up. Black-and-white signs directed the partying throng to "leave Times Square" and "WALK—do not run" if bombs began to fall.

A large sign behind the Father Duffy statue proclaimed "Remember

Pearl Harbor." Underneath it, in huge letters, New Yorkers were exhorted to "Buy Defense Bonds."

On New Year's Day, La Guardia was sworn in for a third term. In a radio address from City Hall, he flew into a rage, denouncing critics of his civil defense preparations as "two-by-four editors," "swivel chair scribes," and "liars." He said he had been pleading with Congress for funds to protect communities on the East and West coasts since becoming the civilian defense director in May 1941 but acknowledged it would take "months and months" for the equipment to be purchased.

New Yorkers and their fellow Americans could only wonder whether it might arrive too late.

CHAPTER 4

IN THE EVENT OF AN AIR RAID . . .

Charles Feldman was working at his desk on the thirty-seventh floor of the Equitable Building in the heart of the Wall Street area—just another routine March 1942 day as a purchasing agent for Kennecott Copper—when it struck him that Friday the 13th was indeed going to be his unlucky day.

What he would describe as "three or four very rapid explosions" followed by a rushing or whistling sound startled him. Seconds later, a projectile hurtled into the wall of the building at 120 Broadway, just missing Feldman's window. He smelled smoke, or perhaps it was the whiff of burned powder.

A light rain of stone fragments, a mist of gray stone dust and bits of metal hit the pavement, sending pedestrians scrambling for shelter. Feldman, who happened to be an air-raid warden, grabbed his flashlight and prepared to lead an exodus to the thirtieth floor, designated as a safe haven if the Equitable Building were to come under attack. But he paused, evidently fearful of creating a panic. Police cars and fire engines were soon on the scene, and Lieutenant James Pike of the bomb squad picked up what he instantly recognized as a shell.

The Army's first response? "Not us."

A military spokesman, finding no immediate evidence of shells being fired from antiaircraft posts ringing the city, suggested that a piece of the Equitable Building simply "fell off," perhaps the result of "some tremor."

But an hour and a quarter after the assault on the financial district, the explanation arrived. An Army officer in charge of an antiaircraft battery alongside the East River Drive phoned the Clinton Street police station in Lower Manhattan to report that one of his guns had accidentally discharged eight 37-millimeter shells, each of them seven inches long with a range of more than 2,500 yards.

Seven shells evidently fell into the river. Damage from that eighth shell was limited to a few bricks, and nobody was hurt, but for a while it seemed that the long-feared enemy attack on New York had finally arrived. Excited callers to newspapers wondered whether the Brooklyn Navy Yard had been bombed. Or perhaps the Brooklyn Battery Tunnel, in the early stages of construction, had been blown up.

By early 1942, some 60,000 volunteers of the Auxilary Aircraft Warning Service, mostly men, were stationed at 600 observation points in the New York area in a program overseen nationally by the American Legion. They scanned the skies to note the configuration and course of any plane not clearly a commercial airliner.

Plotters, who took phone calls from the observers concerning suspicious planes, used long pointers to place markers on a large table indicating the whereabouts of the aircraft. The Army was to send fighters aloft to confront planes that hadn't been accounted for. Most of the plotters were women, among them the Broadway actress Emeline Roche, who received a medal for 500 hours of service. They held down responsible positions but they could not escape patronizing attitudes toward women, even when accompanied by a compliment from Eleanor Roosevelt.

Under the headline "As Others See Us," *The Target*, the publication of the New York area warning service, reprinted an item from one of Mrs. Roosevelt's "My Day" newspaper columns: "I visited the information center of the Aircraft Warning Service yesterday. There is just one point I would like to stress, namely, that ladies are never considered to be able to keep a secret. Yet all over the nation these centers exists and complete secrecy about them is maintained."

In springtime 1942, in what was evidently a typical antiaircraft unit, soldiers were in position on a two-acre site in Brooklyn that was formerly a dump. The GIs set up a battery of 90-millimeter guns and machine-gun emplacements. The big guns were capable of being directed at a common aerial target by a master control. The men slept in dugouts with room for twenty soldiers apiece, and a telephone switchboard and two power plants were constructed underground. Newly planted hedges graced the paths, and iris and pansy plants were flowering to camouflage the antiaircraft position as a minipark.

But the outpost was no secret to the neighbors, who had brought the soldiers food soon after they arrived, while one man backed up a truck to their fence and dumped a load of blankets over it. A donation of another sort came from Harry Glantz, the first trumpeter of the New York Philharmonic—recordings of Army bugle calls, including his version of "Reveille."

The Empire State Building, built in the depths of the Depression, symbolizing American optimism in the face of adversity and soaring 1,250 feet to its dirigible mast, was envisioned as a prime target for a bombing attack.

Early in 1942, the building's management undertook detailed preparations for an air raid. A retired police department inspector named John Hennessy, who was overseeing civil defense preparations for Schenley Distillers, the building's largest tenant, with 800 employees, also became its civil defense director. Hennessy enlisted 1,200 volunteers, giving them identification shields with ranks like floor director, group captain, and monitor. The volume was stepped up on fire-alarm bells. Pails of sand and shovels were placed on each floor. Firefighting asbestos suits were stored, ready for transport via elevator to any spot in the building. Surprise drills were held weekly, and on the 86th floor observatory American Legion volunteers looked for enemy bombers.

Fire Commissioner Patrick Walsh became the fire defense coordinator for New York. A broad-shouldered 200-pounder, Walsh had battled countless blazes over the years. At age sixty-eight, he had vivid memories of the horrific Triangle Shirtwaist fire of 1911, when he was among the first firemen on the scene. His wartime task: to prepare for a far greater calamity. As a first step, he oversaw the training of 60,000 auxiliary firemen to back up the department in the event of bombings or other military emergencies. And he sent three fire officers to England to observe its firemen in action during air raids.

But the flurry of false air-raid warnings by the Army in the days following the Pearl Harbor attack, the confused state of civil defense preparations in the city, and the lack of sirens and firefighting equipment made it clear that little had been accomplished in New York beyond the massing of volunteers and the bluster on the need for vigilance.

In January 1942, Roosevelt named James Landis, dean of the Harvard Law School, to head the national Office of Civilian Defense administrative functions, effectively cutting into La Guardia's authority and paving the way for his removal. La Guardia was already frustrated in his job and under Congressional fire, along with Mrs. Roosevelt, for seemingly frivolous social projects like the appointment of the movie actor Melvyn Douglas to direct theatrical activities and naming of the rhythmic dancer Mayris Chaney, a protégé of Mrs. Roosevelt, to oversee programs for children during air raids. He quit as OCD director on February 10.

In his resignation letter to Roosevelt, he made no mention of the criticism, saying only that he had completed his organizing work and awaited an order from the president "to serve in any capacity for the defense of our country"—an order that would never come. Landis replaced La Guardia, and soon after that Mrs. Roosevelt left the agency as well.

La Guardia kept his post as civil defense director for New York, and when he stepped down from his national job the city had more than 210,000 air-raid wardens.

Just about every family tried to do its share for the war effort. Youngsters collected tin for conversion into weaponry, women contributed the grease from cooking, which supposedly could be converted into explosives, and men beyond the draft age, or 4F, volunteered as air-raid wardens.

Maury Allen, a youngster in Brooklyn's Bensonhurst section, a predominately Jewish and Italian area with many small homes, teamed up with his mother and father.

"I collected tin cans. You'd crush the cans and put them in a cardboard basket and pile up twenty or thirty and bring them down somewhere. My mother fried everything. In those days nobody knew it was bad for you. When the pot was filled with this grease, she put it into a big can. I remember putting them in our car. My father was a salesman. He had an A ration card. That meant you could get more gasoline than other people because you were using the car for business. She would also drive down to these different places and drop off the grease."

We were living in a private home—we rented it—and outside we had a little porch and I raised tomatoes. My mother would buy American cheese in a wooden box and take the cheese out and give me the box. I would get dirt and put it in there and get tomato seeds and the tomatoes actually grew. We called them Victory Tomatoes. My mother would cut them up. My favorite sandwich happened to be bacon and lettuce and tomato—a nice Jewish boy having that. We could use the tomatoes and get the grease from the bacon. That was sort of a doubleheader victory effort.

My father had been in the Navy in World War I and he was a very patriotic guy. In the late 1930s he was very active in the American Legion and I was given a Legion cap. I used to walk in the neighborhood parades on Memorial Day and July 4th; they were a big deal. When World War II started he was too old for the draft, he was in his forties, so he joined the air-raid wardens. He had a white helmet and a big flashlight, and I would go out with him every so often when they had blackouts. He would knock on the door of people's houses if their lights were on and remind them to put them out. Most people were incredibly cooperative. They'd come to the door and say, "Oh, sorry."

But in the war's first months, the wardens had no gas masks, and many had no armbands or helmets.

On Manhattan's Upper East Side, the Stolba Funeral Home, owned by a Czech immigrant, designed armbands it distributed free of charge to wardens. It placed the official red-and-white striped triangle within a blue circle on a background of its best heavy white silk, otherwise earmarked for the lining of coffins.

A week after leaving his Washington post, La Guardia faced a headache at home: 530 air-raid wardens in Queens signed petitions asking Congress to give the War Department direct responsibility for civil defense in New York. The wardens claimed that La Guardia had kept them busy drawing maps and performing other "nonsensical tasks" instead of putting them on patrols. And they maintained he had turned them into garbage collectors by ordering that they collect waste metal for conversion into war materiel.

A pair of air-raid wardens on Staten Island, Ernest Frederick Lehmitz and Erwin Harry De Spretter, weren't wasting their time on garbage collection. They were arrested in June 1943 on charges of conspiring to commit espionage. The following September, they pleaded guilty in Brooklyn Federal Court to trying to send information to Germany about ship movements in New York Harbor through invisible ink letters mailed to neutral drops in Portugal and Spain, and they were sentenced to thirty years in prison.

Lehmitz, a native of Hamburg, had come to the United States in 1908, worked for the German consulate, later returned to Germany, then trained to be a spy before coming back to America in 1941. He had lived quietly on Oxford Place in the Tompkinsville section of Staten Island and, according to one neighbor, John Burke, seemed beyond reproach. "He never missed a blackout," Burke said. "Kept insisting that everyone on the block live up to even the smallest regulations."

Federal authorities described Lehmitz as not only a zealous air-raid warden but one of the most enthusiastic tenders to Victory Gardens in Tompkinsville. But when he wasn't busy planting seeds, he had stationed himself in the attic of his home on a hill overlooking the Narrows, a few blocks from busy piers, keeping track of convoys. He also worked in waterfront bars, gleaning information on troop movements from drunken or loose-lipped sailors.

In one of his letters earmarked for Germany between January and April 1942, Lehmitz wrote: "Still no air-raid shelters. Protection against raids completely inadequate. Complete confusion."

Some of the police prose in directives to wardens indeed personified obfuscation. One command read "above designated switches are not to be operated only in an alarm." Another read, "bombs must not be allowed to be dropped until warning is given." One evening, all the wardens in one Manhattan zone—1,790 of them—were summoned to a police station-house for a lecture on how to use a screwdriver to turn off street lights during an air-raid drill.

March 1942 brought the artificial-fog fiasco. A company called Duo-

Spray introduced a mixture of oil and water into a steam boiler at a laundry near the Brooklyn Navy Yard and vaporized it at 750 degrees to create a fog that it hoped would hide vital military installations during an air attack. Army and Navy officials and representatives of the police and fire departments turned out for the test, only to see the artificial fog dispersed by wind before it had traveled a single city block.

The city's cultural institutions, meanwhile, were taking no chances with their treasures.

An Army antiaircraft detachment was deployed in Bryant Park, across from the main branch of the New York Public Library. But the library nonetheless evacuated its most valuable books, prints, and manuscripts.

Irreplaceable possessions like a Gutenberg Bible, the original manuscript of Washington's Farewell Address, and the first edition of Poe's "The Murders in the Rue Morgue" were secretly transferred to vaults of the Guaranty Trust Company of New York and the Bank of Manhattan. Less valuable but important items, together with rare books from the Morgan Library, were sent via moving vans, under police escort, to the Hall of Springs, a solidly built, well-guarded building in Saratoga Springs, New York. Some 27,000 New York Public Library items valued collectively at $20 million were involved in the exodus, and they weren't returned from their hiding spots until November 1944. The Metropolitan Museum of Art sent 15,000 of its most prized works out of town.

Early in 1942, the city began conducting blackout drills to prepare for air raids.

The first blackout came in late March, covering a five-square-mile area below 23rd Street, with 9,000 wardens turning off the street lights and the police halting traffic. But New Yorkers had been given warning of the drill and it was conducted without air-raid sirens—there still were none available.

Manhattan was blacked out from Greenwich Village to 124th Street in Harlem, river to river, for twenty minutes on the night of April 30, but a party atmosphere prevailed. The Times Square streets were jammed since the police hadn't told anyone to remain indoors. Nightclub revelers played on under blacked-out skylights on the Astor Roof and in Rockefeller Center's Rainbow Room. At Madison Square Garden, the circus clowns continued clowning.

The next day, La Guardia crowed how New Yorkers "stayed in off the streets, even the children," only to learn that Police Commissioner Lewis Valentine reported that a huge crowd had milled around in the theater district, gawking at the moon. Valentine had described the scene as "like election night or New Year's Eve without lights." La Guardia fumed that if that were an actual air raid there might have been a "wholesale slaughter."

When La Guardia raced through the streets to inspect blackout operations, he did it with a flourish. In April 1942, he put away his six-year-old limousine, a move billed as saving gasoline for the war effort, and switched to a small two-seat car. But the understated look went only so far. The car was painted green and white to resemble a police vehicle and it was adorned with five white enameled stars and an NYC logo on the hood. Oversized fire-engine-type red headlights were mounted above the regulation headlights. Luminous blackout paint coated the front and rear bumpers to provide visibility during air-raid drills. A red-lensed sign on the roof flashed MAYOR when La Guardia threw the appropriate switch. In May, La Guardia and his wife, Marie, gained an eye-catching residence as well. They left the East Harlem tenement where they had lived since the late 1920s and moved into Gracie Mansion along the East River, designated as the official mayoral residence.

June and July 1942 brought two citywide blackouts for New York, the first one going smoothly but the second one putting La Guardia on the defensive over an unforeseen complication—cigarette smoking at the Polo Grounds, the site of major league baseball's All-Star Game, played that night.

The game ended at 9:28 p.m., two minutes before the blackout was to begin, when Ernie Lombardi of the Cincinnati Reds flied out to Tommy Henrich of the Yankees. As the teams sprinted to their center-field clubhouses, the field was plunged into darkness. The players waited out the twenty-minute blackout before shedding their uniforms.

When someone lit a cigarette in the National League clubhouse, a warden stationed outside shouted a command to put it out. But that was hardly the only glow of the evening in the ball park. The crowd of more than 33,000 had been asked to remain in the seats until the blackout ended. With La Guardia looking on from his seat behind home plate, hundreds of fans lit up, and the mayor raised no objection. Criticized the next day by the Army for tolerating the smoking, La Guardia maintained that no enemy pilot could see a lit cigarette from the air.

On the final night of July, New York had its first "surprise" blackout, though a warning of sorts had been issued. Two days earlier, La Guardia had announced there would be a drill within the week. The city finally had a complement of air-raid sirens to signal the start of the drills—408 regular sirens and a giant siren atop the RCA Building. That siren, designed by Bell Telephone Laboratories and powered by an eight-cylinder Chrysler industrial engine, produced its whine when a six-bladed rotary chopper interrupted a flow of air delivered by a blower at a speed of more than 370 miles an hour. The siren swung in a circle to distribute the blast evenly and could be heard ten miles away.

The city eventually bought 500 air-raid sirens and it equipped public buildings with 32,000 fire-fighting cabinets with pumps, pails with water and sand, and first-aid kits. Some 1.6 million identification tags kept track of schoolchildren during drills.

For Dave Anderson, a student at Our Lady of Angels grammar school in Brooklyn's Bay Ridge neighborhood, near the Narrows, the war seemed exceedingly close to home.

"The left side of our classroom was on 74th Street, just below Fourth Avenue, and that faced the east. If the Nazi planes ever came, they'd come from the east right towards us. For some reason, they had an air-raid drill in the middle of the day. It sounded much more important, because usually they were at night. Sometimes you'd see searchlights in the sky. I remember the teacher—one of the nuns—left the room, which made us think it might be the real thing. I remember standing up and looking out the windows toward the ocean, which was not 20 blocks away."

The fear of an enemy air attack eventually receded, but there were a few frightening incidents reminiscent of the Equitable Building fiasco.

In May 1943, three .50-caliber machine-gun bullets tore through the roofs of homes in the Park Slope section of Brooklyn and another bullet landed in a street. At one home, a twenty-one-year-old woman was working in her kitchen when a bullet lodged in the couch of her living room. The police thought at first that the bullets had been fired from a plane, but it turned out that a machine gun at an antiaircraft post had accidentally touched off a salvo.

Two mishaps in February 1944 brought nervous moments but little damage and no injuries. Grymes Hill and Ward Hill, two venerable residential neighborhoods on Staten Island, came under a fifty-shell barrage from an antiaircraft gun mounted on a freighter anchored in the Upper Bay, two miles away. A gunner had been removing a canvas storm cover from the gun when it accidentally went into action. A week later, two shells were accidentally fired during a gunnery exercise aboard a ship berthed in the Hudson River off West 56th Street. They slammed into a brick chimney of the nearby IRT subway power station.

In October 1943, a bomber buzzed Yankee Stadium during the opening game of the World Series between the Yankees and the St. Louis Cardinals. The Germans couldn't be blamed for that—this was a four-engine Army Air Forces B-17 Flying Fortress. It made three passes over the stadium, at one point clearing the three-deck roof by about ten feet, drowning out the radio broadcast. La Guardia demanded punishment for the pilot, and the Army said it would investigate.

By the following July, the pilot, Jack Watson, was keeping himself busy

WILLISTON COMMUNITY LIBRARY
WILLISTON, ND 58801-3894

bombing German convoys. On one mission, his bomber *Meat Hound* lost two engines, one to mechanical failure and another to enemy fire, but he brought it back to a British base, barely averting a crash, after the other nine crewmen bailed out. "I wonder whether Mayor La Guardia will forgive me now," he remarked.

La Guardia dispatched a cable reading: "All is forgiven. I hope you never run out of altitude."

By late 1944, when Allied troops were on the move toward German soil, air-raid precautions waned. The blackout drill of September 5, the city's twenty-first since early 1942, proved to be the last one, though the powerful siren atop the RCA Building continued to be tested on Saturdays at noon. The wardens' ranks had numbered 290,000 at their peak in September 1943, with a total of 400,000 New Yorkers, 80 percent of them men, having volunteered at one time or another. But the warden corps was greatly reduced as the war entered its final months.

The possibility of New York being hit by Germany's V-1 "buzz bombs" like those that struck London, bringing heavy casualties, could not, however, be ruled out. While in the city to report on the homefront for GIs overseas, Sergeant Andy Rooney, an Army correspondent for the *Stars and Stripes* newspaper in Europe, picked up a rumor that a V-1 bomb had been fired at New York on election day 1944 from a U-boat somewhere offshore. The missile had supposedly been shot down by coastal patrol planes or fallen short.

Rooney checked with the Associated Press, which said it also heard the rumor, then went to Mitchel Field on Long Island and asked a colonel in intelligence about it.

The bewildering response: "Look, where did you hear this silly story? Don't ever repeat it. Now get out of here and don't say a word about it to anyone. It isn't true. I don't know a thing about it. I don't even deny it."

Looking back, the fears of an attack on New York seemed the product of panic, and the army of wardens proved a bloated aggregation. A police captain who worked with wardens remarked in December 1944 that the city needed about half as many as volunteered. As he put it: "Now we've got rid of all the lightweights who wouldn't have been any good anyhow."

CHAPTER 5

NAZIS IN NEW YORK

The battle between the isolationists and the interventionists had hardly begun, but the German military spy service, the Abwehr, was hard at work in America while FDR was still pursuing the New Deal.

The spy rings run by Admiral Wilhelm Canaris scored a major triumph in Manhattan. A German national named Hermann Lang stole blueprints for the Norden bombsight, enabling highly accurate bombing regardless of weather conditions, while working at the Norden plant on Lafayette Street in 1937. He passed them on to Canaris.

As war grew closer for America, a new German spy network formed in New York to obtained secret information concerning weaponry, industrial technology, and troop movements. Lang was one of its members, but the Abwehr had recruited another man, William Sebold, a veteran of Germany's World War I army, to put the ring in motion.

Sebold had come to America in 1921 and worked for Consolidated Aircraft in San Diego. He became an American citizen in 1936 and three years later visited Germany to see his mother. Sebold's background in aviation came to the attention of the Gestapo and the Abwehr, and he was pressured to train as a spy at the military intelligence school in Hamburg.

But Sebold became a double agent. He managed to tell officials of the American consulate in Cologne about his recruitment and volunteered to work with the FBI in exposing German agents in America. After training Sebold in code work and radio transmissions, his spy handlers sent him back to the United States in February 1940 under the alias Harry Sawyer, ordering him to contact fellow agents with instructions contained in microphotographs and to set up a transmitter to broadcast information back to Germany.

When Sebold arrived in New York, the FBI set him up in an office at the old Knickerbocker Hotel building on 42nd Street, off Times Square, under the guise of a consulting diesel engineer. He could meet with members of the spy ring there, and everything they said would be captured on a motion-picture camera and still photographic equipment that agents placed in an adjacent room, on the other side of a mirror. The FBI also planted microphones in the walls and furniture of Sebold's office.

On the evening of June 25, 1941, the FBI filmed and recorded a two-and-a-half-hour conversation between Sebold and Frederick Duquesne, a South African native who had been spying for Germany since World War I. Duquesne drew a long white envelope from his left sock containing photographs of tanks, an antitank weapon, and a secret Navy speedboat. While he was doing that, Sebold was eating candy, unwrapping each piece from its paper.

An FBI agent named William Friedman, who filmed the meeting, narrated it at a subsequent federal trial:

Duquesne said that if the candy was broken into two pieces and combustible phosphorus was placed inside it, it would make a very effective though small incendiary bomb. But, Duquense added, a better bomb could be made from Chiclets. He said that by chewing the gum thoroughly, and then folding it around a phosphorus compound, it could be planted in this way on docks through a hole in the pocket of one's coat.

Duquesne said he had set off a Chiclet-aided bomb in the past, but he preferred lead-pipe devices, and he hoped that Sebold could supply him with slow-burning fuses for them. He planned to detonate them at a General Electric plant in Schenectady, New York.

Sebold was a busy man in those days, or so the German secret service thought. He was ostensibly providing industrial and military secrets to the Abwehr through a shortwave radio-transmitting station set up in Centerport on Long Island. But FBI agents were at the keys, providing false or misleading information. The clueless Germans sent 200 messages back.

The FBI arrested Duquesne and thirty-two other suspected German spies. Nineteen pleaded guilty and the other fourteen went on trial in Manhattan Federal Court in September 1941. They included Hermann Lang, the betrayer of the Norden bombsight secret, and a man named Richard Eichenlaub, who operated the Little Casino Restaurant in heavily German Yorkville, a rendezvous site for the spy ring.

The German conspirators presumed that Sebold had escaped the FBI's roundup, only to find that he had been working for the bureau when he showed up in court to testify against them. All were found guilty, but death sentences could not be applied since the crimes were committed before the United States was formally at war. The longest jail terms—eighteen years apiece—were handed out to Lang and Duquesne. The government provided Sebold with a new identity and he disappeared.

Five months later, a young man from Queens performing one of the less glamorous tasks in the Coast Guard became a celebrity, having been startled to find himself a one-man line of defense when the Abwehr tried again.

His name was John Cullen, he was twenty-one years old and a "sand pounder," the term for Coast Guardsmen who spent tedious hours patrolling shorefronts for hints of German sabotage or perhaps a U-boat lurking offshore with rockets ready to fire.

Cullen's background was ordinary enough. The son of a foreman for the Fifth Avenue Coach bus company in Manhattan, he had graduated from Bayside High School in Queens, worked at a World's Fair soda fountain, then got a job as a deliveryman's helper at Macy's in Herald Square. He liked to lindy-hop with his girl at the Glen Island Casino in New Rochelle, sang Irish ballads, enjoyed bowling, and spoke glowingly of his cocker spaniel, Blackie. A personnel employee who hired him for Macy's described him as "a thoroughly wholesome, typically American boy, with a deep wave in his hair which he probably hates, a ruddy complexion, keen eyes, erect bearing and a modest demeanor."

And he was among the thousands of men who vowed to avenge Pearl Harbor.

"He wanted to join the marines," his wife, Alice, recalled. "He was on a line a couple of days before Christmas and a fella in charge said, 'Whoever is ready to go tonight, step up.' But he wanted another two weeks before he went away so he joined the Coast Guard instead."

It was about twenty-five minutes past midnight, Friday, June 13, 1942. Seaman Second Class Cullen, barely out of boot camp on Ellis Island and lifeguard training at Jones Beach, was patrolling a six-mile stretch of sand near the Coast Guard station at Amagansett, Long Island, 100 miles east of Manhattan. He was unarmed, carrying only a flashlight and a flare gun for signaling. As he emerged from a thick patch of fog 300 yards from his station, he spotted a figure in the mist and the shadowy outlines of three others behind him. The man closest to him was fully dressed, the others wearing bathing suits.

"Who are you?" Cullen called out, his Coast Guard insignia visible as he shined a flashlight in the man's face.

No doubt thoroughly panicked but able to maintain his composure, the man replied: "A couple of fishermen from Southampton who have run aground." He identified himself as George Davis.

Just then one of the men in a bathing suit came over, dragging a bag. He shouted something in what Cullen took to be German, angering Davis—

or whatever his real name happened to be. "Shut up, you damn fool," he snapped. "Everything is all right. Go back to the boys and stay with them."

"That jarred me, made me suspicious," Cullen would remember. "And I could see that this fellow was very nervous."

Cullen asked, "What's in the bag? Clams?" knowing there were none to be had on that part of Long Island. "Yes, that's right," said the man in civilian clothes.

Cullen suggested that the men come up to his Coast Guard station and wait for daybreak. The leader of the group refused, and his alarm was mounting. "Wait a minute—you don't know what's going on?" he said. "How old are you?" He asked Cullen if he had a father and mother (who would presumably mourn him) and said: "I wouldn't want to have to kill you."

Then he changed tactics, turning from a threat to bribery. "Why don't you forget the whole thing," he suggested, offering Cullen $100. When Cullen refused to take it, the man offered $300, and Cullen said yes, seeing that as a means of escaping from the four men, who he assumed were armed. And then the man said, "Look me in the eyes." Cullen feared he would be hypnotized, but he did so. "Would you recognize me if you saw me again?" the man asked. Cullen said he wouldn't.

Cullen ran back to his station and reported the incident to the acting officer in charge, Boatswain's Mate Carl Jenette, showing him the money. (He had been short-changed; there was only $260.) Cullen and fellow Coast Guardsmen, each with .30 caliber rifles, ran back to the spot where he encountered the intruders. The men were gone, but the Coast Guardsmen smelled fuel oil and spotted the superstructure of a submarine beginning to move away from shore, its blinker light on. They ducked behind a dune, expecting to be shelled or called upon to repel an invasion, but the sub disappeared.

At daybreak, they made an unnerving discovery in the sand: four waterproof boxes containing brick-sized blocks of high explosives, bombs designed to resemble lumps of coal that could find their way into industrial furnaces with disastrous results, bomb timing-mechanisms of German manufacture, incendiary devices, a gray duffel bag with four soggy German Navy uniforms, and an empty pack of German cigarettes.

The day before the saboteurs arrived, the MGM film *Nazi Agent*, starring Conrad Veidt in the dual roles of German twins—one a loyal, naturalized American and the other a Nazi diplomat who tries to recruit the first twin to spy—opened at the Rialto in Manhattan. (The good twin eventually killed the bad one.) Now the FBI had another quite genuine spy and sabotage plot to deal with, following the Sebold affair.

The saboteurs, who arrived on Long Island in a small boat dispatched from U-boat 202, were the first of two teams sent by German military intelligence to destroy American factories turning out strategic metals—among them the Aluminum Company of America (Alcoa)—and to knock out rail facilities like the coal-carrying Chesapeake and Ohio Railroad, the Hell Gate railroad bridge in New York, and Penn Station in Newark. A second group of four saboteurs arrived by U-boat at Ponte Vedra, Florida, four days later. Two headed for Chicago and the other two for New York.

All eight were to rendezvous in Cincinnati on July 4 to make final plans for carrying out Operation Pastorius—named for Franz Pastorius, who in 1683 led the first German settlement in America, a group of Mennonites who came to Pennsylvania seeking religious freedom.

The saboteurs were all English-speaking German natives who had lived in the United States, holding jobs as tradesmen, factory workers, and the like, before returning to Germany. Two of them, Peter Burger, the man who had called out in German on the beach, and Herbert Haupt, part of the group that came ashore in Florida, were naturalized American citizens.

George Davis's real name was George Dasch. He had come to America in the early 1920s, worked as a waiter in New York, Miami, and California, and then, disillusioned with his failure to advance himself, returned to Germany in 1941. He met a Nazi intelligence officer named Walter Kappe who had been the New York press chief for the neo-Nazi German-American Bund. Kappe recruited Dasch for the Abwehr's spy and saboteur school, Quenz Farm, where he trained with the seven others who joined him in Operation Pastorius.

Dasch and his accomplices made their way to the Amagansett train station after ridding themselves of Cullen and took the Long Island Railroad into Manhattan's Penn Station. Dasch and Burger checked into the Governor Clinton Hotel across from the station while the other two, Heinrich Heinck, who had once worked as a handyman and machinist in New York, and Richard Quirin, once employed as a mechanic in the city, registered at the Hotel Martinique on West 49th Street.

The four men spent the following day on Manhattan's West Side, but had they ventured over to Fifth Avenue they might have been awed by America's patriotic fervor. Some 500,000 marchers, many of them soldiers and sailors, accompanied by tanks and by bombers flying overhead, took part in the New York at War parade. An estimated 2.5 million people turned out to watch.

The saboteurs had been ordered to spend three months preparing to go into action, but they wasted no time in beginning to spend the Abwehr's money. (Dasch had been given $82,000 in American currency by the spy handlers, and the FBI eventually uncovered more than $174,000 handed out to the eight men.)

The New York contingent bought new clothes, and Dasch's three accomplices visited a nightclub on West 52nd Street, known as Swing Street. Drawing on his culinary tastes as a long-time waiter, Dasch recommended some Manhattan restaurants—the Swiss Chalet, the Kungsholm, and Dinty Moore's. The men also had a meeting at a low-budget Automat near Herald Square.

But the spending didn't go on for long. On Sunday morning, some thirty hours after the men came ashore, Dasch lost his nerve. The encounter with the Coast Guardsman on the beach had been wrenching. The FBI was surely in pursuit. And, as Dasch envisioned it, by exposing the plot he would become a hero in America. He sounded out Burger on his thoughts, and Burger agreed that they would turn themselves in and betray their accomplices.

That evening, Dasch phoned the New York office of the FBI from a pay telephone on Manhattan's Upper West Side, giving his name as Franz Pastorius in tribute to the operation's code name. He said he had just arrived from Germany and had important information he would convey only to FBI Director J. Edgar Hoover. While the FBI agent on the other end was trying to figure out if he was talking to a crackpot, Dasch hung up. Four days later he took a train to Washington and checked in at the Mayflower Hotel. He phoned the FBI again the following morning to begin unraveling the plot. FBI agents arrived at the hotel and arrested him. Dasch told the rest of his story at FBI headquarters, but he never got to meet Hoover.

The information that Dasch provided led to the quick arrests of the others. The three men who had come ashore with him and the two who had arrived in New York from Florida were picked up in Manhattan. Two others were arrested in Chicago. Hoover's announcement of the arrests provided few details. The fact that Dasch had betrayed the plot was not revealed, presumably to enhance the FBI's counter-espionage prowess in the eyes of the Abwehr.

Under Roosevelt's orders, all eight men were tried by a military commission consisting of seven generals. The saboteurs' lawyers, a pair of Army colonels, argued before the United States Supreme Court that the trial should be held in a civilian court, where the rules of evidence were stricter, but were rebuffed. The military trial was conducted in Washington, and in secret. Cullen was called as a witness, and he identified Dasch as the man he encountered on the beach.

The defendants were convicted of espionage and sentenced to death. Six were executed in the District of Columbia electric chair on August 8, 1942, but Roosevelt commuted the sentences of the two men who revealed the plot. Dasch received a thirty-year prison term and Burger got life in jail. Both were released in 1948 and deported to West Germany.

While that spy drama played out, John Cullen was snared by the Coast Guard's publicity machine. The commandant, Vice Admiral Russell B. Waesche, promoted him to a coxswain rating in mid-July, and a photograph of the ceremony, together with the Coast Guard's first account of the events on the Amagansett beach, appeared on the front page of the *New York Times* under the headline "Lone Coast Guardsman Put FBI on Trail of Saboteurs."

But Cullen played down the hero angle when he was introduced to reporters and photographers at a Coast Guard news conference in Manhattan. "The German fellow was nervous, but I think I was more nervous," he said of the encounter with Dasch.

The Coast Guard wasn't looking to have its homefront hero out of sight, ferrying marines onto Pacific beaches. It assigned Cullen to a Brooklyn transportation unit where he drove admirals and other VIPs around. He appeared at parades and ship launchings and received the Legion of Merit medal.

The *New York Sunday Mirror* ran a full-color photo of Cullen in uniform, his girlfriend Alice Nelson beside him in a bright dress, under the headline: "Hero on the Home Front. Coast Guard Coxswain John Cullen and His Best Girl." When John and Alice were married at Holy Family Catholic Church in Flushing, Queens, in October 1944, it made the newspapers, and the turnout extended well beyond the invited guests. "There were many people there we didn't even know," Alice Cullen recalled. "People from the neighborhood."

In November 1944, Germany launched another espionage plot. The Army's SS landed two agents from a U-boat at Frenchman's Bay, Maine, near Bar Harbor. One of the men, Erich Gimpel, was an English-speaking German-born radio technician who had undertaken a spy mission in South America during the 1930s. The other man, William Colepaugh, twenty-six years old, was a onetime All-American boy.

A native of Niantic, Connecticut, with German grandparents, Colepaugh had attended Admiral Farragut Academy, a New Jersey military prep school, then applied for Annapolis. When he wasn't accepted, he entered M.I.T. and studied naval architecture before flunking out in 1940. While in Boston, he became friendly with German sailors and consular officials. He later served a three-month stint in the Navy, but was discharged owing to suspicions that he was a German sympathizer. He got a job as a merchant seaman, jumped ship in Portugal in January 1944, and made his way to

Germany, saying he wanted to join Hitler's army. Instead, he was sent to SS schools to become a spy.

Colepaugh and Gimpel came ashore in Maine the night of November 29, 1944; they were ordered to obtain sensitive military information and to organize the sabotage of industrial plants. Colepaugh was expected to help Gimpel deal with situations requiring familiarity with everyday life in America. His motivations would remain unclear. He professed admiration for the efficiency of the German military but he may simply have been an embittered loser in life drawn to what he perceived as the grandeur of a militaristic state.

The men trudged through the snowy Maine woods, carrying a pair of suitcases, until they found a taxi to take them to Bangor, then arrived at Grand Central Terminal two days later. They lived at the Kenmore Hall Hotel on East 23rd Street in Manhattan, then rented an apartment on the Upper Side East's Beekman Place, bringing $60,000 in American money and ninety-nine small diamonds, to be sold if their cash ran out.

Over the next few weeks, Gimpel sought to set up a shortwave radio set for transmissions to Germany. Colepaugh was more interested in spending the SS spy service's cash at nightclubs, bars, and restaurants.

"Billy was enjoying the whiskey, the generous supply of pocket money and the willing attentions of the sort of girls whom one can buy anywhere in the world for round about two and a half dollars," Gimpel would recall.

On December 26, Colepaugh, after shaking off his accomplice and deciding he was in big trouble, surrendered to the FBI and led its agents to Gimpel, who was arrested at a Manhattan newsstand a few days later. Hoover announced the arrests on New Year's Day but supplied no details.

Once more, an instant hero emerged in the New York newspapers. This time, it was a seventeen-year-old Boy Scout from Maine named Harvard Hodgkins. Back in 1942, Coast Guardsman Cullen had actually confronted saboteurs and raised an alarm. In the case of young Hodgkins, the heroics were dubious.

In an interview with the United Press news agency after Hoover's announcement of the Gimpel-Colepaugh arrests, the boy said he had been driving home from a school dance when he noticed two men in topcoats walking through woods. He thought it odd that they were wearing relatively light clothing for a Maine winter, and, mindful of longstanding warnings that spies might come ashore, he said he left his car and followed the men's tracks in the snow to the water's edge. He claimed that he notified his father, a deputy sheriff, who called the FBI, who was soon interviewing him, his tip leading the bureau to the spies' ultimate arrest.

But the FBI said it was already questioning people on the Maine coast about a possible landing by German agents before it came upon Hodgkins and a woman named Mary Forni, who, while returning home from a card game, had also glimpsed two men in the woods. That FBI inquiry evidently resulted from the sinking of the Canadian freighter *Cornwallis* by a German sub off the Maine coast and the belief that the sub, being so close to land, might have dispatched spies. In fact, U-1230, which sank that freighter two days after Colepaugh and Gimpel arrived in New York, was indeed the submarine that had transported them.

Despite the FBI's unwillingness to accord Harvard Hodgkins a semblance of glory, the *New York Journal-American* saw a chance to sell papers. It brought Hodgkins and his family to New York in early January 1945. Seventy-five fellow Boy Scouts greeted the teenager at La Guardia Field, his first airplane trip, and he met Governor Thomas Dewey, Joe Louis, and Babe Ruth. He was given the keys to the city and appeared on the *Gangbusters* network radio show.

Gimpel and Colepaugh were convicted of espionage by a military commission in a closed trial at Fort Jay on Governors Island in mid-February 1945 and sentenced to death. The executions were scheduled for April at Fort Jay. But they were postponed by Roosevelt's death, and President Truman commuted the sentences to life imprisonment in late June, more than a month after Germany surrendered. Gimpel was deported to West Germany in 1955. Colepaugh was paroled in 1960.

Colepaugh faded from view following his release from prison, but he was eventually tracked down by would-be interviewers. He had opened a print shop and an office supply business in King of Prussia, Pennsylvania, near Philadelphia, had married, joined the local Rotary Club, and lived unobtrusively—just an average American, it seemed. When approached by reporters, he refused to talk about his time as a German spy.

Harvard Hodgkins, the self-styled boy G-man, returned to his hometown of Hancock Point, Maine, following his celebrity tour of New York. He became a chief engineer in the merchant marine and operated a lobster pound. When he died in 1984, he made the obituaries, hailed once more as a home-front hero, whatever the FBI may have had to say about that so long ago.

While the FBI was pursuing Nazi spies, an Army officer attached to the Office of Strategic Services, the forerunner of the CIA, was dispatched to New York to pursue exotic means of breaking down the psychological defenses of captured enemy agents.

The papers of Lieutenant Colonel George Hunter White, discovered in 1977 and made available to a United States Senate committee studying past mind-control efforts by the CIA, told how he carried a marijuana derivative envisioned as a truth serum to New York from Washington by train in August 1943 under armed guard. In rooms rented by the OSS at the Belmont Plaza Hotel in Manhattan, he tested the derivative, which he identified as tetrahydrocannabinol acetate, on seven commissioned and noncommissioned Army officers. But White's papers did not make it clear whether the officers were aware of the nature of the tests. The drug was also tested on a mob figure named August Del Gracio, an associate of the underworld boss Lucky Luciano. Del Gracio was described as an unwitting subject.

There was no indication from White's papers whether the chemical was actually used during the questioning of enemy agents in the United States or overseas. The FBI was able to round up those Nazi spies in New York, but the CIA's long quest for a truth drug never did succeed.

CHAPTER 6

THE BRITISH, THE RUSSIANS, AND THE DOLL-LADY SPY

In the summer of 1940, a diminutive Canadian named William Stephenson arrived in New York on the liner *Britannic* with a seemingly mundane bureaucratic task. He was to relocate Britain's passport control office from a dingy suite in the Cunard Building off Wall Street to an array of offices on the 35th and 36th floors of Rockefeller Center's International Building. But this wasn't just any passport office. It provided cover for the local representative of Britain's SIS, its Secret Intelligence Service.

Standing alone against Hitler with the fall of the Low Countries and France, Britain was embarking on a huge expansion of its intelligence activities in the Americas. Stephenson had been chosen by Churchill to run it, overseeing the SIS and other British operations in the Western Hemisphere under the code name Intrepid.

A native of Manitoba, Stephenson joined Britain's Royal Flying Corps in World War I and became an ace, reportedly shooting down twenty-six German planes over France before a French pilot downed him by mistake. He was wounded and captured, but escaped and took with him a newly developed German can opener he had come upon while a prisoner. After the war he adapted it and made a fortune selling it around the world. Settling in England in the early 1920s, he pioneered wireless transmission of photographs, produced films, and had interests in construction, steel, and transport. All this brought him in contact with British intelligence operatives and with Churchill.

Known as "the quiet Canadian," a slim man with close-cropped graying hair, Stephenson led without bluster, as Roald Dahl, the future children's book author who worked for British intelligence in Washington during the war, would discover.

"He never raised his voice ever," Dahl once remarked. "He had this extraordinary quality. You knew that in that head of his, as he was listening to you and watching you, something was ticking about twice as fast as it was in your head, and every facet and angle was being weighed up, and then one question would come out which would just about cover the whole lot, and you would answer it."

Stephenson was assigned three formidable tasks in New York: the investigation of enemy activities in the Western Hemisphere, the creation of security measures to avert the sabotage of British shipping and property in the United States, and, probably most important, the swaying of American public opinion to bring the United States into the war.

In May 1941, Britain's director of naval intelligence, Rear Admiral Sir John Godfrey, flew to New York with his aide, Ian Fleming. They expected to arrive without notice, but when they touched down at La Guardia Field aboard Pan American's *Dixie Clipper* from Lisbon, photographers gathered round. They were there to shoot the fashion designer Elsa Schiaparelli, a fellow passenger. The admiral could hardly have been pleased when the next day a newspaper photo of Schiaparelli caught him, dressed in a business suit, in the background, his anonymity gone if anyone recognized him.

Stephenson gave Godfrey and Fleming an office next to his. Fleming would describe the shooting of a Japanese cipher agent in Rockefeller Center in his James Bond novel *Casino Royale*, but that was an embellishment of Fleming's considerably tamer time in New York.

Fleming remembered Stephenson as "a man of few words" with "a magnetic personality and the quality of making anyone ready to follow him to the ends of the earth." Beside that, Fleming once said, "he used to make the most powerful martinis in America and serve them in quart glasses."

Stephenson's operation, known as BSC, for British Security Coordination, housing 1,000 or so agents and support workers at Rockefeller Center, helped crack a Nazi spy ring based in the city.

On a rainy March evening in 1941, a man who stepped off a curb against the light at West 45th Street and Seventh Avenue was struck and killed by a taxi. A policeman brought the man's briefcase to the hospital where he was taken, and when it was opened he found papers referring to espionage activities. The FBI was summoned.

British censors in Bermuda had been intercepting messages to Europe from a man named Joe reporting to his superiors on a spy operation. In one message sent following the accident, Joe said that an accomplice had been killed by a taxi in New York.

Working with his associates in Bermuda, Stephenson turned the messages over to the FBI. The man killed by the cab carried a passport identifying him as a Spaniard, but the FBI determined that he was, in fact, Ulrich von der Osten, a captain attached to German military intelligence. The trail ultimately led to Joe, who was Kurt Frederick Ludwig, an Ohio native who had been educated in Germany, then returned to the United States in spring 1940 to run a spy ring. Ludwig, arrested in August 1941, was convicted of espionage along with five accomplices.

While America was still formally neutral, Stephenson contacted New York newspaper publishers, pressing for treatment sympathetic to Britain and revelations of Nazi intrigue in America. His office used the *Herald Tribune* to expose Gerhard Westrick, a German agent who arrived in New York in spring 1940.

In the guise of a businessman, Westrick sought to convince American industrialists, especially those in the oil industry, that Germany had already won the war. He hoped to obtain their support for the isolationist movement in return for business privileges in German-occupied Europe.

According to the BSC's official history, commissioned by Stephenson at war's end and published long afterward, the agency placed a series of articles on Westrick's activities in the *Herald Tribune,* the stories written by the BSC but printed under a reporter's byline. The series resulted in Westrick's being inundated with threatening phone calls and letters, and Stephenson succeeding in getting the State Department to have him sent back to Germany in August 1940.

To gauge American public opinion toward Britain, and to sway sentiment in favor of British interests, Stephenson called on David Ogilvy, the Englishman who would become a legendary figure on postwar Madison Avenue with the Ogilvy and Mather agency, creating images like the eye-patched Man in the Hathaway Shirt. After working in London at his brother Francis's advertising agency, Mather and Crowther, Ogilvy mastered public opinion research as a member of George Gallup's Audience Research Institute from 1939 to 1942, then joined Stephenson's Rockefeller Center operation. Ogilvy marveled at Stephenson's energy, once observing that "it took eleven secretaries to keep up with him."

Stephenson's office fed items to Walter Winchell, whose columns on New York nightlife, politics, and whatever else caught his fancy appeared daily in the *New York Mirror* and were syndicated to more than 800 newspapers with a readership of more than 25 million. Winchell was well connected. He got White House leaks on occasion and he was buddies with J. Edgar Hoover, having turned the notorious gangster Lepke Buchalter over to the FBI in a prearranged surrender on a Manhattan street back in 1938.

Stephenson used an American lawyer (not identified in the BSC account but probably Ernest Cuneo) with access to Roosevelt to plant stories in Winchell's column that served the interests of both the White House and the British.

The intermediary was said to have received a personal request from Roosevelt at one point to assist in preparing American public opinion for the drafting of women to be trained as Army nurses. It was a chance for Stephenson to publicize Britain's drafting of women at the same time.

As the BSC's official history told it: "A column entitled 'British Women—Orchids to Some Gallant Ladies' was prepared by BSC. It was published by Winchell as it stood."

According to the British agency:

In January 1945, President Roosevelt asked WS's [William Stephenson's] intermediary to assist him in preparing public opinion for the passing of a National Service Act . . . another column was written for Winchell, entitled "Things I Never Knew." It contained a full account of the National Service Act in Britain.

Stephenson was knighted by King George VI in 1945. After the war, President Truman awarded him the Medal of Merit, America's highest civilian award at the time, for his "timely and invaluable aid to the American war effort." Stephenson later pursued business interests and died in Bermuda in 1989 at age ninety-three.

For all the hysteria surrounding the wartime internment of Japanese nationals and Japanese-Americans on the West Coast, they were never found to be a security threat. But Japan did have a lone agent in Manhattan. She was a homegrown American named Velvalee Dickinson, who was born in Sacramento and graduated from Stanford.

Dickinson moved to New York from California with her husband in 1937 after handling brokerage accounts for Japanese investors on the West Coast. In October 1941, she opened a doll shop on Madison Avenue, near East 63rd Street. It catered to wealthy collectors and hobbyists interested in obtaining foreign and antique dolls and it was high-toned enough to be listed in the *New Yorker*'s compilation of noteworthy shops in its issue of November 29, 1941:

"VELVALEE DICKINSON. Among thousands of dolls, antique and modern and from all over the world, look at Princesses Elizabeth and Margaret Rose, dressed in outfits approved by Queen Elizabeth; $15 each. . . . Persian brides, 14-inch 'Arabian Nights' charmers, made in Iran and garbed in gorgeous brocades, blue-veiled turban head-dresses and curly-toed slippers; $15."

Between January and June 1942, Dickinson mailed five letters—seemingly sent by five different people from separate locations—to the same person at an address in Buenos Aires, Argentina. For reasons that never became clear, four of the letters came back undeliverable, "return to sender." The other one was intercepted by British censors in Bermuda and held for investigation because of its suspicious phrasing. The people whose names and return addresses were listed on the envelopes knew nothing of the letters, but they were all clients of Dickinson's doll shop. All the letters eventually came into the hands of the FBI, and its investigation found that they bore code phrases referring to American warships on the West Coast, including ships that had been attacked at Pearl Harbor.

One Dickinson letter (with some strange spellings for a Stanford grad) stated in part: "You wrote to me that you had sent a letter to Mr. Shaw, will I went to see MR. SHAW he distroyed YOUR letter, you know he has been ill. His car was damaged but is being repaired now. I saw a few of his family about. They all say Mr. Shaw will be back to work soon."

According to the federal government, the Mr. Shaw who "distroyed" the letter was a reference to the destroyer *Shaw*, damaged at Pearl Harbor. It had a new bow fitted in Honolulu and had arrived in San Francisco in mid-February 1942.

Dickinson, fifty years old, was arrested in January 1944 and charged with espionage—carrying the death penalty—as well as violation of the censorship laws by sending coded messages overseas. She was scarcely 5 feet tall, perhaps 100 pounds, but was said to have fought fiercely with FBI agents when they seized her at a bank in midtown Manhattan, where agents found more than $15,000, most of it traceable to Japanese sources, in her safe deposit box. She claimed the money belonged to her husband, who had died in March 1943, and insisted it was he who did the spying.

But in July 1944, Dickinson admitted to typing the letters to Argentina and obtaining information on American ships during visits to the West Coast though she continued to claim that her late husband was the real traitor. She was allowed to plead guilty to only the censorship violation and was sentenced to a maximum term of ten years in jail. William Stephenson's British spy operation in New York characterized her as "an obvious eccentric, far from representative of the usual agent" and said that she was "reported to have become mentally deranged" after going to prison. She was released from the Alderson penitentiary for woman in West Virginia in 1951.

While British intelligence operated out of Rockefeller Center, America's other great ally, the Soviet Union, was trying to steal the secrets of the atom bomb project.

On December 2, 1944, Army Sergeant David Greenglass, a machinist at Los Alamos, New Mexico, where the atomic bomb was being constructed under extraordinary secrecy, received a visit from his wife, Ruth. She had traveled to New Mexico from their home on Manhattan's Lower East Side at the behest of David's brother-in-law, Julius Rosenberg.

Julius had graduated from City College with an electrical engineering degree in 1939, then married the former Ethel Greenglass. Both were devoted to communist causes, though only Julius was a member of the Communist Party. Julius was hired by the Army Signal Corps as a civilian employee and he worked at Emerson Radio and Phonograph on Eighth Avenue, inspecting electrical components manufactured for the military. He had another calling: In 1942, he began working for the Russian spy service under the code names "Antenna" and "Liberal."

David and Ruth Greenglass took a walk in Albuquerque on that December 1944 day so they could speak without being overheard. In the late 1990s, interviewed by Sam Roberts for his book on the Rosenberg case, David remembered Ruth telling him:

I have a message from Julius. He tells me you're working on a super-secret thing. And he would like this information to be transmitted to our friends. He said the Russians were our allies. We should really help them. It's not fair that the United States should keep it a secret. They're allies. They're fighting on the same side. He said, "If all the nations had the information, then one nation couldn't use the bomb as a threat against another."

David Greenglass, who had joined the Young Communist League as a teenager, said he would do it, and though he had left Brooklyn Polytechnic Institute after only one semester, his machinist's job positioned him to help the Russians piece together a picture of the atomic-bomb project. David was assigned to help fabricate precision molds for high-explosive lenses. Technical people with skills far beyond his were willing to talk about their work, and, as he told it, "I just listened." He said he never broke into files to steal secrets. "Stuff was in the shop; I didn't miss it. I just stored it in my head."

On New Year's Day 1945, Greenglass came home on a furlough and he passed on to Julius Rosenberg all he had learned at Los Alamos beyond what he had already told Ruth—information related to construction of a plutonium bomb, including descriptions of his work in producing devices to measure the explosive power of certain lenses, details on the proving grounds where the lenses were tested, and a list of pro-Soviet scientists at Los Alamos. The Soviet spy service in Moscow received a report on that meeting, presumably passed on by Julius to its agents in New York.

And so began the sensational spy saga concluding with the execution of Julius and Ethel Rosenberg in the electric chair at Sing Sing on June 19, 1953 for conspiracy to commit espionage. Both professed their innocence.

Their convictions, particularly that of Ethel, were based in good part on the testimony of David and Ruth Greenglass, who told the jury that Ethel had typed up Julius's notes on atomic-bomb work at Los Alamos in the Rosenbergs' Knickerbocker Village apartment in Lower Manhattan in September 1945.

(The Venona Project, the postwar decoding by American intelligence of thousands of Soviet wartime espionage messages, still kept secret at the time of the Rosenbergs' trial but revealed in 1995, confirmed that Julius Rosenberg and the Greenglasses had been spies. Deciphered Soviet cables reported that Ethel Rosenberg had recommended recruitment of Ruth Greenglass and that "she knows about her husband's work.")

David Greenglass was imprisoned until 1960. Evidently in return for his testimony, his wife was never prosecuted. When interviewed by Sam Roberts decades later, Greenglass said that he had lied in court, that in fact he had no recollection of his sister having typed up those notes:

> I frankly think my wife did the typing, but I don't remember. You know, I seldom use the word "sister" anymore; I've just wiped it out of my mind. My wife put her in it. So what am I going to do, call my wife a liar? My wife is my wife.

The Greenglasses lived under assumed names in the New York area after David's release from prison. Ruth died in 2008 at age eighty-three. David became a symbol of betrayal. As a character in the Woody Allen movie *Crimes and Misdemeanors* said of a loathsome relative: "I love him like a brother—David Greenglass."

PART TWO

THE HARBOR

CHAPTER 7

SHIPPING OUT

Three centuries earlier, Henry Hudson, the Englishman sailing for the Dutch, dropped anchor in New York Harbor, explored it for a week, then headed up "as fine a river as can be found," as one of his mates described the passage that would bear his name.

New York's harbor became the finest and largest in the world. Its Lend-Lease shipments of World War II served as a lifeline for the British and the Russians, and by the war's end, more than 3.2 million American troops and their vast war materiel had departed from its piers for the British Isles and the European battlefronts.

The harbor extended over 400 square miles of water, it boasted a developed shoreline of more than 650 miles, and it was crammed with 1,800 docks, piers, and wharves. It included thirty-nine shipyards in addition to the vast Brooklyn Navy Yard. Some 1,100 warehouses, with 41 million square feet of enclosed storage space, stocked the armaments and foodstuffs arriving from around the country for shipment to Europe. *Popular Mechanics* magazine, surveying the wartime port, insisted it was "big enough to hold every ship afloat on the globe."

Its winters usually free of ice and severe fog, its tides sometimes tricky but mastered by its 575 tugboat captains, its deep natural channels smoothing the way for oceangoing ships, the harbor extended along the shores of all five boroughs in the City of New York as well as the New Jersey shoreline from Perth Amboy to Elizabeth, Bayonne, Newark, Jersey City, Hoboken, and Weehawken. It included seven bays, most importantly the Upper and Lower bays, separated by the Narrows between Brooklyn and Staten Island; four rivers, most famously the Hudson; and the Harlem and East rivers (technically estuaries), Arthur Kill and Kill van Kull.

Bristling with ocean liners converted to troopships, with transports, freighters, ferries, barges, and tugs, their foghorns sounding, steam rising from their funnels, the wartime harbor became a waterborne spectacular, the scene of a logistical miracle day after day.

GIs arrived from training camps throughout America to be processed for shipment overseas from the New York Port of Embarkation, bureaucratic language for what became known as "Last Stop, USA."

New York sent nearly twice as many troops overseas as San Francisco, the second-largest of the nation's nine wartime Ports of Embarkation.

Most of the soldiers arrived in New York by train. Grand Central Terminal and Penn Station were jammed by GIs carrying duffel bags.

One autumn day in 1942, New Yorkers could spot a newspaper advertisement bearing the likeness of a young man awake in the upper berth of a Pullman, an Army helmet stowed beside him. A long tribute to the boy, and the millions like him, began with the words "It is 3:42 a.m. on a troop train."

It read in part:

> Next time you are on the train, *remember the kid in Upper 4.*
> If you have to stand en route—*it is so he may have a seat.*
> If there is no berth for you—*it is so that he may sleep.*

The bottom of the page read simply "The New Haven R.R."

It was a test message from the New York, New Haven, and Hartford Railroad addressing the flood of civilian complaints over crowded trains, overtaxed dining facilities, and arrivals and departures bearing little resemblance to the printed schedules.

"It was decided to try it once in the *New York Herald Tribune*," Nelson Metcalf Jr., a young advertising copywriter who created the message for the railroad, would recall. "I waited for the result with my heart in my mouth. Finally, three days after the ad broke, the avalanche began and I knew I'd found the answers."

More than 8,000 letters arrived at the railroad's offices from readers touched by the sentiments in the ad headlined "The Kid in Upper 4." The Pennsylvania Railroad asked for 300 posters to display at its stations, MGM made "The Kid in Upper 4" into a movie short, show-business personalities read the ad over the radio, and it was reproduced free by newspapers and magazines throughout the country.

If train seats were at a premium, so too were barracks for all those soldiers to be processed in the New York area before crossing the Atlantic.

In January 1942, the Army began construction of Camp Kilmer on 1,500 acres near New Brunswick, New Jersey, once the home of the poet Joyce Kilmer, who became a sergeant in the 165th Infantry in World War I and was killed in action in France. By midsummer, more than 1,100 buildings and a thousand-bed hospital had been built on the site.

In September 1942, Army officials summoned 130 families with homes, farms, and businesses in the vicinity of Orangeburg and Tappan in New York's Rockland County on the west bank of the Hudson River and told them they would have to move. Some 2,000 acres would be seized to build barracks for the Camp Shanks staging area.

More than 2.6 million men passed through Camp Kilmer and Camp Shanks en route to the New York–New Jersey piers. Their short stays afforded a few frills, like the camp shows put on by show-business celebrities, among them Benny Goodman and Betty Grable, and the chance to sample Times Square nightlife while on liberty. But they were at the camps to be in and out, and on their way to war. The men received their final inoculations at the staging areas and they prepared for the worst at sea, taking part in drills that had them scrambling down ropes to lifeboats resting in a pool of water. Wacs worked as clerks, mechanics, and inspectors checking the rifles and equipment issued to each soldier, while German and Italian prisoners of war helped man mess halls.

"My first look at Camp Shanks was on a cold day in January 1943," a GI named Bernard Kelly would recall. "Raw wood frames covered with composition paper made up most of the buildings, and I was assigned one in Area 7, which was comfortably warmed with a coal-fired space heater. The latrines and shower were outside, and when you came in it was sinfully comfortable to warm up to the space heater."

Within twelve hours of the order to move out and head for the piers, the GIs were put on "Alert." They removed their division patches to preserve troop-movement security and their helmets were chalked with a letter and a number indicating their seats in the trains taking them directly to the docks or to ferries that would transport them to their ships.

Oftentimes, the men were roused in the dead of night.

For Barbara Herman, a member of the Women's Army Corps contingent at Camp Shanks, those moments became a "haunting remembrance."

She would tell of "being wakened around 2 a.m. by the sounds of tramping feet and whispered commands as platoon after platoon filed past in the darkness.

"WACS would often stand by the roadside to wave at the troops as they passed. Low whistles mingled with the tramping and the hoarse whispers as the men spotted the women."

The GIs carried their rifles, gas masks, full field pack, and duffel bags with them to the ships. Red Cross volunteers handed out coffee and doughnuts as they waited to ascend the gangplanks.

The soldiers departing in the predawn hours had no idea where they were in the vast assemblage of piers stretching from Manhattan's great West

Side ocean-liner terminals to Brooklyn's Fort Hamilton (which was also a staging area) and the Brooklyn Army Base, to Piermont Pier four miles from Camp Shanks, to the New Jersey waterfront. They didn't know the name of the ship that would carry them across the Atlantic, they weren't told of their destination, and they certainly had no clue as to when or where they would be sent into combat.

According to Lieutenant General Brehon Somervell, the commander of the Army Service Forces, a ton of ammunition, food, clothing, and medical equipment was required to keep a soldier in combat for a single month. The Port of New York became a launching point for that industrial engine fueling America's military machine in Europe.

In the first four months of 1942, more than 114,000 railroad cars with war supplies were unloaded in the port for transfer to ships. In 1944 and through the first six months of 1945, the port's busiest wartime period, it shipped 28 million tons of cargo and 30.6 million tons of petroleum products abroad. For the entire war period, the Port of New York handled 25 percent of the nation's trade.

The Brooklyn Army Base (later the Brooklyn Army Terminal) housed a pair of concrete warehouses that stored vast amounts of supplies loaded onto freighters, and Brooklyn's Bush Terminal also served as a major supply depot. Sometimes the weaponry arriving from war plants overflowed the warehouse space. Howitzers were placed row upon row in the open, awaiting storage. Cranes lifted fighter planes, sixty-five-ton diesel locomotives, and Jeeps onto transports. Ammunition and petroleum products were shipped from the Army's Caven Point in Jersey City.

On one day in 1943, the harbor brimmed with 543 oceangoing merchant ships.

Dave Anderson would recall the images that impressed themselves upon a schoolboy from his family's apartment overlooking the Narrows.

"We lived on Ridge Boulevard, which had some height to it, so you could look down into the bay. Some evenings, it looked like there'd be ships you could walk across to Staten Island on. The bay was filled with ships. They were gathering for a convoy. The next morning they were all gone."

All that harbor traffic posed an everyday threat of collisions. On the morning of February 6, 1945, the American tanker *Spring Hill*, loaded with 120,000 gallons of aviation gasoline and anchored 1,000 yards off Stapleton, Staten Island, exploded and caught fire when it was struck by the Panamanian tanker *Pan Clio*. The Norwegian tanker *Vivi*, passing by when the collision occurred, was set afire by burning oil splattered on its deck. The three-way accident left 19 dead and 122 injured.

Beyond the danger of accidents that could clog the harbor, the prospect of shellings by German submarines worried military authorities, particularly in the war's early years. Big guns ringed the harbor at five fortresses: Brooklyn's Fort Hamilton and Staten Island's Fort Wadsworth on opposite sides of the Narrows; Fort Totten on the north shore of Queens and Fort Tilden in the borough's Rockaway section to the south, and Fort Hancock, across the bay on Sandy Hook in New Jersey.

At Fort Tilden, along the bottom of a spot called Battery Harris East, a large arc of concrete resembling a Greek amphitheater opened toward the sea. Built just before America entered World War II, it was designed to prevent the fort's two giant cannons, capable of firing 2,300-pound shells twenty-five miles out to sea, from being rotated for a salvo on the city if a German raid somehow captured the outpost.

To keep German submarines from entering the harbor, the Navy stretched a "net" and a "boom" parallel to each other, running from South Beach, Staten Island, to Brooklyn's Coney Island. The net, a few hundred feet from the boom and made of heavy steel cables with mesh about three feet wide, was designed to prevent the passage of torpedoes and mines as well as U-boats. It was supposed to wrap itself around a submarine that tried to go through it, pinning it to the bottom. The boom was a row of wooden floats six yards apart connected by steel cables and held in place by anchored buoys. The floats, cables, and buoys were armed with sharp steel spikes to rip apart a boat that tried to enter the harbor on the surface of the water.

The net and boom were always closed at night unless a specially designated ship was entering or leaving the harbor. If that happened, a pair of barges would haul on cables designed to swing the net and boom open, then close them again after creating a thousand-foot-wide passage.

No U-boats were known to have breached the net and boom, but in the winter of 1942 German submariners got a glimpse of the New York skyline.

The captain of U-123, Reinhard Hardegen, wasn't even supposed to be in the submarine service. While a flier in the German navy, he had suffered injuries in a crash leaving him with a shortened right leg. But he managed to hide that disability, and in the early hours of January 14, 1942, he maneuvered his submarine to a spot off the eastern tip of Long Island. While on the ocean's surface, under the cover of darkness, he torpedoed the Panamanian tanker *Norness*, sinking it in shallow waters. Her bow was still sticking out when the American destroyer *Ellyson* rescued twenty-four survivors the following day.

After lying on the ocean bottom, Hardegen brought his submarine to New York Harbor's outer reaches that night—close enough to see the glow of Lower Manhattan's lights. He invited fellow crewmen to the deck to behold that spectacle, among them a photographer who was aboard to shoot propaganda images. But the skyline was too far away, and it was too dark, to get any photos. (Later in the war, fabricated still photos and movie images of New York's lights, supposedly shot from that submarine, were shown to German audiences, which evidently accepted them as genuine.)

Hardegen took his submarine into deeper waters off Long Island after getting his glimpse of Manhattan, and in the early hours of the following day U-123 torpedoed the British tanker *Coimbra*, bound for Halifax, Nova Scotia. The attack left thirty-six men dead, with six survivors.

Those two sinkings alarmed military authorities responsible for protecting the coastline. The Army sent planes to search for the submarine and the Navy dispatched small craft and blimps, but Hardegen escaped.

To safeguard the harbor and protect shipping in the North Atlantic, the Navy and law-enforcement authorities looked beyond aircraft and patrol boats. They turned to the men who ran the New York docks—the Mafia bosses.

In March 1942, officers from naval intelligence met with Frank Hogan, the successor to Thomas E. Dewey as the Manhattan District Attorney, over concerns that criminal elements in the United States might have provided information to German sources on the movement of ships out of New York, accounting for at least some of the numerous sinkings of freighters and tankers by U-boats.

To get some answers, the Navy and Hogan's office first enlisted the help of Joseph "Socks" Lanza, the underworld figure who ran the Fulton Fish Market and had contacts with Italian fishermen from Maine to Virginia. Lanza evidently received no promises that he would receive any favors, and he wasn't paid for his services. Acting out of a sense of patriotism, so far as is known, he asked his sources if they knew anything about fishing boat captains resupplying German submarines lurking offshore. No evidence of that was uncovered, and after a while Lanza suggested that the Navy go higher up in the mob by asking for help from the Mafia kingpin Lucky Luciano.

Luciano was serving a thirty-to-fifty-year term at Great Meadow Prison for organizing prostitution rings in the 1930s. So the Navy went there to meet with him, bringing along Lanza and the underworld figures Meyer Lansky and Frank Costello. Luciano agreed to put out the word that dock workers should keep their eyes open for sabotage on the New York piers. The Mafia also supplied Navy intelligence agents with union cards allowing them to pose as longshoremen and truckers in their antisabotage efforts. For the rest of the war, the Port of New York remained free of enemy activity, and the mob-dominated longshoremen's unions refrained from calling strikes that would tie up cargo going to the warfronts.

The Mafia's cooperation extended beyond the city. When American forces invaded Sicily, Italian-speaking Navy intelligence officers from New York were with them, armed with information from underworld sources back home enabling them to establish contact with Sicilian Mafia figures who might have information on German positions.

In their final stages of questioning Luciano, law-enforcement authorities were curious about a matter that seemed to have a Mafia link but extended beyond waterfront issues. They asked Luciano if he knew who killed Carlo Tresca, a legendary figure of the American left shot to death while walking with an associate near Union Square the evening of January 11, 1943.

Tresca, the editor of a small newspaper named *Il Martello*, had long been a vocal opponent of both fascism and communism and a champion of organized labor. He held a special enmity for Generoso Pope, the New York businessman and politically well connected publisher of *Il Progresso*, the nation's largest Italian-language newspaper, and a backer of Mussolini until the fall of 1941. Carmine Galante, a mobster with a long criminal record, had been suspected of murdering Tresca, but he was never charged, and with all the enemies Tresca had made over the years it wasn't clear who might have hired Galante to gun him down. But Luciano claimed that he knew nothing about the murder, and it was never solved.

The first public references to the wartime links among the Navy, the Manhattan District Attorney's office, and Luciano and his Mafia associates came in 1946, when Thomas Dewey, having become governor of New York, commuted Luciano's sentence, resulting in his deportation to Italy. In his commutation message, Dewey said that Luciano, whom he had prosecuted when he was a rackets-busting district attorney, had evidently aided the war effort, but Dewey supplied no details.

Luciano's release became a hot political issue since he was among the most unsavory of the Mafia bosses, and there were rumblings that somebody had received a bribe to allow his freedom. The questions were still lingering in 1954 when the New York State investigations commissioner, William Herlands, who had served in a similar post with the La Guardia administration, conducted an inquiry into the Luciano affair at Dewey's request. Herlands found no bribery or other wrongdoing on the part of public officials, but his report was not made public, at the request of naval intelligence, which maintained that its release could jeopardize future operations and could cause "embarrassment to the Navy public relations wise."

The Herlands report was deposited in Dewey's papers and remained secret until 1977, six years after his death, when Rodney Campbell, the editor of his memoirs, was permitted to use them for his book *The Luciano Project*.

A retired lieutenant commander named Maurice Kelly, who had been part of the Navy intelligence team seeking the Mafia's wartime cooperation, told the Herlands investigation that the mob had indeed helped ensure the security of the port.

"There was no idle or careless talk on the part of the loaders, shippers, longshoremen of the type of supplies that were going aboard these ships, and the destination," Kelly said. "That was very important because enemy agents were trying to find out what was going on certain ships and it was our job to see that there was no careless talk."

A civilian intelligence officer for the Navy, identified as Agent X, testified before the Herlands inquiry that stevedores and truckers on the docks had cooperated "because 'the Big Boss' as they called him, or 'Charlie Lucky,' had asked for their help."

Agent X said the alliance among the Navy, the district attorney, and the mob had been no secret while it remained active—though the authorities were not exactly putting out press releases. The agent cited his contacts with a onetime Tammany Hall district leader and Manhattan county clerk named Albert Marinelli, who had been accused of mob ties by Dewey back in the 1930s.

As Agent X told it:

Practically the entire city of New York knew that the underworld was cooperating with the District Intelligence Office, and this I got particularly in person from Albert Marinelli, who was a very influential political leader in New York City at one time, and whenever I used Albert Marinelli as an informer, he would tell me, "I understand the boys are doing very well."

While the "boys" of the underworld were doing their bit, the boys going off to war were boarding their ships.

Staff Sergeant Robert Tessmer of the 100th Infantry Division had been waiting at Camp Kilmer for the word to go overseas, and on the night of October 5, 1944, it finally came. A train transported Tessmer and his buddies to a ferry that took them to a pier somewhere in the New York Port of Embarkation.

"We were herded like cattle, struggling under the weight of 100-pound duffel bags, packs with bed rolls, rifles and steel helmets into a gaping hole in the side of the towering ship," Tessmer remembered. "In the dark of night required for operational security, we never did get a look at her before boarding."

It was the Army transport *George Washington*, Tessmer would learn, and it carried almost 7,000 soldiers in a convoy of eleven troop ships bound for Marseilles, France, the jumping-off point to fight the Germans dug into the Vosges Mountains in Lorraine and Alsace.

A GI named Guy Charland was among the men of the 90th Infantry Division taken to a New York pier at 4 o'clock in the morning, March 3, 1944, and loaded onto the British cargo ship *Dominion Monarch*. Three months later, Charland took part in the invasion of Normandy, going ashore at Utah Beach. But he had no idea where his ship was heading that winter's night in New York Harbor.

"We boarded the ship in total secrecy," Charland recalled. "No lights, no noise or fanfare. Sometime later we were allowed up on deck. We were surrounded by other ships in a convoy. As we looked out to sea we could see faintly the lights of the Port of New York far off on the horizon. I got a sick feeling in the pit of my stomach. God knows when I would see New York City again and the Statue of Liberty with that upraised torch. God knows, maybe never."

CHAPTER 8

THE GREAT NAVY YARD

The Senator from Missouri was in a hurry.

As a brisk wind battered Brooklyn's Wallabout Bay on a Saturday afternoon in January 1944, Harry S. Truman had a speech to make, and not much time to deliver it. The occasion: the christening and launching of the USS *Missouri,* the most powerful battleship in the history of the United States Navy.

A crowd of 30,000 had gathered at the Brooklyn Navy Yard for a warship that some day might avenge the loss of a battleship built in Brooklyn during World War I. The *Missouri's* keel had been laid on January 6, 1941. Almost precisely eleven months later, the *Arizona,* launched at the Brooklyn Navy Yard in 1915, had been sent to the bottom of Pearl Harbor.

Superlatives abounded at the *Missouri's* launching. She was 880 feet from bow to stern, and like her sister ship, the *Iowa,* the longest ever built for the Navy. At sea, she could displace enough water to flood forty-six acres. Her electric plant could power a city the size of Santa Fe, New Mexico. She had ninety miles of piping and 1.135 million rivets. Her main battery bristled with sixteen-inch guns and her antiaircraft armament boasted scores of 20- and 40-millimeter guns. Some 10,000 Navy Yard workers had pledged to donate a pint of blood for the men of the *Missouri* and her fellow ships.

Truman was to deliver the principal address at the *Missouri's* launching on January 29, 1944, and his nineteen-year-old daughter, Margaret, a student at George Washington University, was to swing the christening Champagne bottle.

Before that could happen, the Navy Yard's commandant, Rear Admiral Monroe Kelly, addressed the crowd, and messages were to be read from Admiral William F. Halsey, the Third Fleet commander, and Admiral Ernest J. King, chief of naval operations. As Kelly finished his remarks, he got a hurry-up signal. Wind and tide conditions had required that the launching time be moved up. The messages from Halsey and King were dispensed with, and Truman was compelled to race through his address.

"When Dad finally got to the microphone, he had about three minutes to deliver a fifteen-minute speech," Margaret would recall. "I never heard him talk so fast in my life."

Truman urged that the *Missouri* become "an avenger to the barbarians who wantonly slaughtered the heroes of Bataan."

"The time is surely coming," he said, "when the people of Missouri can thrill with pride as the *Missouri* and her sister ships, with batteries blazing, sail into Tokyo Bay."

Margaret lifted her magnum of Champagne (well, not truly Champagne, since it was made from pressed Missouri grapes) encased in a sterling silver jacket, and she bashed the *Missouri's* bow. But nothing happened. She playfully put her hand on the bow and gave the battleship a gentle shove. Still nothing. By then she was getting a shower, the winds having sprayed the Champagne, or a facsimile thereof, over her dress and the whites of Admiral Kelly.

One minute later, the *Missouri* finally began to move. As it hit the water, the sun emerged, the only time during the ceremony that it would appear. Whistles blew and sixteen tug boats crowded around the battleship, poised to escort her back to her pier for the final steps in her outfitting.

Truman had become a highly respected member of the Senate as chairman of a committee investigating shoddy Pentagon work and profiteering by defense contractors. To hear Truman and his daughter, Margaret, tell it later, that Senate investigation had not been forgotten by embarrassed admirals. According to the Trumans, shifting wind and tides notwithstanding, the Navy had exacted vengeance by letting the *Missouri* ceremony drag on until the senator's time had essentially run out when he got up to speak.

For all the tiffs consuming politicians and the military brass, for all the grandiose promises of retribution in christening speeches, a certain solemnity pervaded the yard as the war wound on. That mood was captured at the *Missouri's* launching by a master shipfitter named H. P. Connor.

Writing in a Navy Yard newsletter, Connor recalled how, earlier in the war, there had been something of a party atmosphere at the major launchings. No more.

How different then was the launching of the USS *Missouri*. The hilarity generally prevalent, the usual jovial attitude of those present, these were missing. It was, no doubt, the quietest launching of the past decade, yet it was comforting to know that those in attendance realized the purpose of this ship. As this mass of protectiveness began slowly to slide towards the water, a spontaneous cheer went up and as she smoothly cut her way out into the stream, the crowd, to a man, was again silent. If these were not war times, she could be looked upon as a thing of beauty. For the time being, we shall be content to consider it as a potent weapon and a comforting asset.

General Douglas MacArthur would accept the surrender of Japan aboard the *Missouri* in Tokyo Bay. But the age of the battleship had been dealt a huge blow at Pearl Harbor when Japanese air power destroyed or severely damaged the *Arizona*, the *California*, the *Oklahoma*, and the *West Virginia*. The aircraft carrier, not the battleship, would prove decisive in the Pacific.

The Brooklyn Navy Yard built both. It launched the battleships *North Carolina* and *Iowa* before sending the *Missouri* down its way, and it launched the aircraft carriers *Bennington*, *Bon Homme Richard*, *Franklin D. Roosevelt*, and *Kearsarge*. Work was continuing on another carrier, the *Oriskany*, at war's end. Eight LSTs—landing ship, tanks for beach assaults— were launched at the yard as well.

But the yard was much more than a shipbuilding giant. More than 5,000 ships of the Allied nations damaged by bombs and torpedos limped into New York Harbor for repairs in Brooklyn. The yard also converted some 250 ships from civilian to military use. By V-J Day, the Brooklyn Navy Yard (officially the New York Naval Shipyard) had become the world's largest shipyard with 75,000 workers crammed into a land parcel that could fit four times into Central Park.

Its roots could be traced to 1637 when a Belgian Huguenot, or Walloon, named Joris Jansen de Rapelie bought 335 acres on the site from the Canarsie Indians. His farmland lay astride a crescent-shaped bay at the Brooklyn neighborhood now known as Fort Greene. When the British seized New Amsterdam from the Dutch, they called the bay Wallabout. In the Revolutionary War, George Washington anchored his left flank there during the Battle of Long Island. A civilian shipyard was built on the site after the Revolutionary War, and in February 1801, the Navy bought the property.

As America's entry into World War II neared, the yard expanded from its original 40 or so acres into a complex of nearly 400 acres with dry docks, huge storehouses, furnaces, and forges. Some 300 buildings were connected to the edge of the bay by thirty miles of railroad track.

The first of the trumpeted World War II launchings came on June 13, 1940, when the 35,000-ton battleship *North Carolina* slid into Wallabout Bay as 50,000 onlookers cheered. But the extravaganza was not without slip-ups. After receiving a nineteen-gun salute, the State of North Carolina's governor, Clyde Hoey, inspected the ship's band by mistake before turning around and inspecting the honor guard. Rear Admiral C. H. Woodward's speech referred to the battleship as the *South Carolina*. When the governor's daughter, Isabel, let fly with the Champagne, she sprinkled New York's official greeter, Grover Whalen, and his Palm Beach suit in the process.

The next big event came on August 27, 1942, when the *Iowa*, with a standard displacement of 45,000 tons (52,000 tons while fully loaded), the largest battleship ever built in America, slid down the Navy Yard ways, seven months ahead of schedule. Ilo Browne Wallace, the wife of Vice President Henry Wallace, an Iowan, performed the Champagne honors. The Navy Yard Band played the usual martial selections, paying tribute to all the branches of the armed forces, but the Shipfitter Shop band—a civilian workmen's outfit—provided a lighter touch. Its numbers included "Jingle, Jangle, Jingle" and "I Left My Heart at the Stage Door Canteen."

Arthur Miller, rejected for military service because of poor eyesight, was writing patriotic plays for radio at the war's outset. But he left that cushy job to become a workman at the yard. It gave him a greater sense of contributing to the war effort and, as it developed, provided material for his plays touching on waterfront life.

Working thirteen out of fourteen nights at a stretch, from 4 in the afternoon until 4 in the morning, Miller entered a world populated mainly by Italian-Americans from Brooklyn's tougher neighborhoods.

Miller would remember his boss, Ipana Mike, "so called because he had no front upper teeth," a Sicilian who wore his cap sideways and was partial to Bond bread spinach sandwiches, usually devouring at least six of them by the time midnight arrived on his nightly shifts. Ipana Mike had a wife and at least two girlfriends, one of them a packer on the night shift at Macy's. He would send Miller outside the yard to phone her and help arrange their trysts.

"From her hot arms he would hurry home to his wife, who was keeping his bed warm, and sometimes by noon he was sniffing up a third woman on her lunch hour from the Abraham and Straus department store," Miller recalled. "Mike was a busy man, apart from helping win World War II."

Ipana Mike, like many of the yard's workers, considered malingering an art form, but, as Miller considered it, "his was as much a sign of his realistic appraisal of the Navy's need for his services as a fuck-you attitude, which of course was mixed into it. The yard was vastly overmanned. Planning was often chaotic, and one man more or less in this beehive could not mean too much."

One worker, as Miller told it, had rigged himself a bed in a cruiser's engine room as a pleasant alternative to working his shift only to find upon awakening that the ship had departed. "He did not return to his Red Hook crap game for six weeks."

One time, the yardmaster put up a notice asking workers to avoid wasting imported cadmium, needed for underwater hull areas because it didn't rust. The next night, the workmen were busy filing rings for their wives or girlfriends out of cadmium nuts and making bracelets for them out of cadmium rods.

Miller remembered as well the anti-Semitic talk among the yard's workers and how they sometimes beat up British seamen at night in the streets near the yard, angered because Britain had declared war on Italy. The paradox, as Miller observed: "While rooting for Mussolini they were also deeply attached to Roosevelt and the America with which Il Duce was at war."

Given an opportunity to work in jobs never before open to them, women would presumably be a reliable asset for the Navy, and they were not likely to curl up in an overlooked space aboard ship when they were supposed to be working.

Before the war, women employed at the yard were primarily limited to sewing work in the Flag Loft, a warehouselike building that overlooked the dry docks. By August 1940, some 120 women were working eight-hour shifts in the loft, sewing 300 flag designs, hemming officers' tablecloths and napkins, and stitching green baize curtains for officers' quarters.

But everything began to change in September 1941, when the yard started to hire women for skilled craft work. Upon passing civil service tests, a woman could become an arc welder, an acetylene torch burner, or a shipfitter.

Sylvia Honigman and Ida Pollack, friends from the Bronx who had attended Brooklyn College together, were among the first of the female workers, becoming welders. They endured fifty-eight-hour work weeks—ten hours Monday through Friday and an eight-hour "half day" on Saturday—rotating every three months among afternoon, evening, and overnight shifts.

"The men didn't exactly welcome us," Sylvia Honigman Everitt recalled years later:

> There was a lot of sneering, a lot of sly remarks. The first day we came to work in the shop, they had never seen a woman there. The men are standing there with these hostile looks. And the foreman is walking ahead of us with this cap on and a cigar out the side of his mouth. Taylor. Nice man, really nice man. And he says, "Watch your language, these are teachers."

For a while, Honigman worked in a part of the welding shop where the men got their supplies. "This one guy used to come in, and I spoke to him because you try to be friendly. Not much had passed between us, and he walks in one day and wants to know if I'll go away for the weekend with him. If my mouth didn't drop to the floor. He acted like it was perfectly natural—what else is a woman good for?"

But, as she told it, "they began to accept us because we were very good welders."

The women had to battle for equal wages. They were hired at half the pay that inexperienced male workers received, management noting that the women were working only in the shops while the men were engaged in harder labor on the ships. "We told them, 'We're not refusing to go out on the ships. You're refusing to send us,'" Ida Pollack remembered.

Sylvia Honigman and some of the other female workers protested the unequal treatment through the Navy Yard's division of Industrial Union 22. A few of the men supported those efforts, among them a shipfitter named Sam Kramer, and Sylvia and Sam began dating. Sam, the son of a Brooklyn furrier, was drafted in April 1943. Sylvia married him six months later. In October 1944 Sam departed for Europe aboard the steamship *John Erickson* with the 309th Regiment, 78th Infantry Division.

In May 1944—it happened to be Mother's Day—women were finally allowed to work aboard ships. "There were about five of us who walked on the ship, and you would think we came from Mars," Ida Pollack recalled. "Every hole on the deck had a head come up. I don't know how much work was done that day, but they couldn't get used to it."

Pollack's husband was overseas in the armed forces, so she lived with her parents, who were less than supportive. "I would come home very hungry and I'd make breakfast while my father was getting ready to go to work. I'd make bacon and eggs and whatever else, and he constantly lectured me that I wasn't eating right. He irritated me—I always had to defend myself. But one of the things that bothered me all the time was that I was earning more money than he was."

The Brooklyn Navy Yard won six E flags, presented by the Navy to defense facilities for efficiency. Thousands of its workers labored in hot and dangerous plants or endured icy winds aboard the ships, trudging to work on winter days and nights in their mackinaws, earflaps, and steel-tipped shoes.

Solomon Brodsky, who packed supplies for ships, remembered a sense of mission:

For quite a while, we worked at seven days. There was no such thing as time off, except for emergencies. I'm Jewish, and we had the Jewish holidays coming up, Yom Kippur and Rosh ha-Shanah, and the rabbis told us we should work, we were at war. There were days I felt like a zombie. You work; there was a war. I had my kid brother in the war. So you feel like you're working for him.

The sense of patriotism was felt as well in the gritty neighborhood adjoining the yard. As a workman named Henry Tatowicz recalled it: "Every morning when I was leaving the yard after my shift, they had a bugle blow taps and a flag-raising ceremony, and all around the yard, no matter what area, as far as a person could see, all the trains, buses, cars stopped while the taps were going, and people walking the streets stopped to face the area where the flag was."

Safety regulations required that workers wear hard hats, goggles, and visors. The yard's newsletter, *Shipworker*, ran a cartoon strip called "Dopey Dan" to preach safety considerations, Dopey and his shipworker-girlfriend Ann making their points in Brooklynese.

Leo Skolnick, who worked on the *North Carolina*, the *Iowa*, and the *Missouri*, long remembered the conditions. "It was a hard place. I was primarily in new construction, and the closest thing to describe it was like 'Dante's Inferno,' between the noise and the fumes and the welding and everything. I don't think we built a big ship without losing people."

One moment remained vivid. "They were building a ship and they were pulling in the propeller shafts using what they call chain blocks with cables. And one time they strained it, and the cable snapped and just whipped and took one kid's head off."

Years later, a hazard unknown at the time claimed the lives of numerous shipyard workers. Particles of asbestos applied to ships had seeped into their lungs, causing cancer and other respiratory diseases.

The shipworkers went about their daily grind under conditions of high security. Uniformed marines manned the yard's Sands Street entrance, inspecting identification badges and the contents of bags. Cameras were banned, and, as one sign put it, "Be careful—if you are talking someone may be listening."

Just beyond the Navy Yard gates, Sands Street drew shipyard workmen and sailors around the clock. A combination of Broadway and the Bowery, jammed with bars, dance halls, and shops selling Navy gear, it was a town unto itself. The writer Carson McCullers, living at 7 Middagh Street in Brooklyn Heights, told of the "curious traditions" at the Sands Street bars, among them "vivid old dowagers of the street." They included Submarine Mary, whose every tooth was said to be made of solid gold. "There is a saying among sailors that when they die they want to go to Sands Street," McCullers wrote.

The Navy Yard was Brooklyn's largest industrial facility during the war, but companies throughout the borough converted to war production. Mergenthaler Linotype, in the Williamsburg section, known for machines that turned out the "hot lead" metal lines of type for newspapers, designed high-precision tools for the armed forces. Murray Manufacturing, in Bedford-Stuyvesant, which produced radiators and electrical products before the war, made trench mortar shells for infantrymen, hiring women for 90 percent of its 1,800 slots. (In February 1944, the federal War Production Board reported that 134,000 women were employed in New York City's 341 major war plants, nearly 28 percent of the workforce.)

Todd Shipyards, one of the world's largest ship-repair facilities going back to World War I, built and repaired cargo ships on nearly 300 acres along the Brooklyn waterfront. And Brooklyn's Robins Dry Dock & Repair boasted the world-champion riveter. His name was Raymond Davidson, he was twenty-seven years old, weighed 200 pounds, and claimed his title on July 13, 1942, when he drove 3,228 rivets in a seven-hour working day.

"When the whistle blew, and somebody threw a bucket of water over me, and the scorekeeper said three thousand two hundred and twenty-eight, I damned near dropped my machine," Davidson said. "There's nobody ever going to be that good again. The Lord himself couldn't shoot more rivets into a ship shell than my gang and I did today."

Davidson and his fellow Robins shipworkers aside, the Brooklyn Navy Yard remained the focus of the borough's industrial might. On April 30, 1945, the yard launched a 45,000-ton aircraft carrier with the customary fanfare surrounding a signal event. That ship was to have been called the *Coral Sea*, for a pivotal naval battle of 1942. It was renamed the *Franklin D. Roosevelt*, and Eleanor Roosevelt attended the ceremony, her first public appearance since her husband's death on April 12.

In remembering his days as a Navy Yard workman, Arthur Miller marveled at the sight of all those ships, patched together or built from a blueprint, that departed from Wallabout Bay.

As he put it:

Whenever a drydock was finally flooded and a ship instead of sinking floated safely into the harbor and sailed out into the bay, I was not the only one who stared at it thinking it miraculous that out of our chaos and incompetence, our bumbling and goofing off and our thefts and our dedicated moments in the wind, we had managed to repair it. More than one man would turn to another and say, "How the hell'd it happen?" as the ship vanished into the morning mists and the war.

CHAPTER 9

THE *NORMANDIE* ABLAZE

They stood side by side in New York Harbor, the three largest passenger ships ever built, the pride of France and Britain, safe for the moment, 3,000 miles from the yards where they had been christened.

On August 28, 1939, completing her 139th crossing of the Atlantic, the glorious *Normandie* arrived at Pier 88 off West 49th Street. She was scheduled to leave for France two days later, but with war in Europe looming orders arrived from home canceling the trip. On September 5, two days after Britain and France declared war on Germany following the invasion of Poland, the *Queen Mary*, camouflaged in battleship gray with U-boats prowling the Atlantic, arrived in New York. She tied up on the south side of Pier 90, some 100 feet from the still resplendent *Normandie* in her peacetime garb of black hull, white superstructure, and three red funnels. On March 7, 1940, the *Queen Elizabeth* drew into the north side of Pier 90.

The French and Cunard lines had always scheduled their jewels for alternate sailings, and so the *Normandie*, the *Queen Mary*, and the *Queen Elizabeth* had never before been berthed in any port at the same time. Now they were together.

Crewmen from the *Normandie* and the *Queen Mary* enjoyed some camaraderie. Monsieur Magrin of the *Normandie* and Mr. Marty of the *Queen Mary*, the once-rival chefs, went ashore one evening to have dinner together. Their seamen spent a boisterous night toasting each other at the Anchor Bar on Twelfth Avenue. The owner, Meyer Oppenheimer, offered free beer and hamburgers, and a *Queen Mary* stewardess stood with one arm around a *Queen Mary* oiler and the other around a *Normandie* dishwasher as the English and French joined in "God Save the King."

The *Queen Mary* departed for Sydney, Australia, and conversion to a troopship soon after the *Queen Elizabeth*'s arrival in New York. In mid-November 1940, the *Queen Elizabeth* followed her to Sydney. Unlike the British queens, the *Normandie* had no commonwealth nation to welcome her. And so she remained at her Manhattan pier.

There had never been a liner to rival the *Normandie*. She was the first to exceed 1,000 feet in length, the first to cross the Atlantic at better than thirty knots. Her Art Deco appointments, sumptuous cuisine, flaring prow, and rounded sides bespoke unparalleled luxury and elegance. She had been awash in superlatives since that noontime in spring 1935 when she steamed out of Le Havre, bound for New York, a crowd of 200,000 gaping from the banks of the Loire.

But the *Normandie* became a ghostly presence at her Hudson River pier. Some 1,200 crewmen returned to France soon after war arrived in Europe, leaving only 115 to tend to her daily upkeep. The *Normandie*'s gangway remained slung out, but there were no passengers to come aboard. The walls of the half-lit corridors were swathed in gray-white cloth, the floors covered with canvas. The silverware, packed in wooden boxes, rested in a fireproof vault below decks. Blankets were placed in mothballs while fine china and rugs were secured in airtight rooms.

But the *Normandie* was kept ready to steam off once more, though no one could say when that might be. Workmen greased the machinery daily and applied fresh coats of paint to prevent rust. One of the four propulsion engines remained under steam at all times in a rotation schedule. And perhaps most important, the skeleton crew guarded against fire, the alarm system operating as if the *Normandie* were still in service. A master control room with an illuminated panel linked to smoke detectors throughout the ship was manned at all hours. Firemen patrolled the ship, reporting back to the control-room monitor at twenty-minute intervals.

On May 15, 1941, the Coast Guard sent 150 men aboard the *Normandie* to guard against sabotage while allowing the remnant of her crew to maintain the boilers and the machinery. But time ran out for the crewmen when the Japanese attacked Pearl Harbor. The United States Maritime Commission took possession of the *Normandie* five days later, and the Coast Guard removed her staff captain, Herve Le Huede, and the last of his crew.

Like the *Queen Mary* and the *Queen Elizabeth*, the *Normandie* was envisioned as a troopship. The Navy took control of her, and Robins Dry Dock & Repair received a contract to do the work. It was to have the liner ready to leave for Europe with 10,000 soldiers by February 1, 1942.

Workmen streamed aboard, stripping the sumptuous interior and installing 10,000 canvas berths. They removed the gold letters inscribing *Normandie* on her hull. She was renamed the USS *Lafayette*, a tribute to the Frenchman who became an American hero for aiding George Washington's army in the Revolutionary War.

All through January the welders, electricians, carpenters, and plumbers worked at a frenzied pace. Some 3,000 men might be aboard the ship on a given day, most of them civilian workers, the rest Navy personnel and Coast Guardsmen. But the February 1 deadline passed, the work incomplete. Robins was given another two weeks to finish the job.

On the afternoon of Monday, February 9, a bright, cold day, the city whipped by a northwesterly wind, a welder named Clement Derrick was turning his acetylene torch to the last of four lighting stanchions he was cutting down in the Grand Salon. His back rested on burlap-wrapped bales of kapok life preservers. As he was finishing the job just after 2:30 p.m., sparks from his torch ignited the lint surface of the burlap. Flames raged through the hundreds of bales in the salon, then spread to passageways cluttered with debris.

Charles Collins, an eighteen-year-old ironworker, and a fellow workman, Leroy Rose, tried to beat the flames out with their hands. Rose's clothes caught fire and Collins carried him out, then collapsed from smoke inhalation. A fire hose in the salon spurted briefly, then went dry.

Another ironworker, Jack Panuzzo, ran up to the Sun Deck, where he knew malingering workmen were sleeping. He roused them, then went back to the salon, where he spotted the stricken Collins. He carried him off the ship on his back, then made four more rescue trips.

Fifteen minutes after the flames erupted the first fire engines arrived, the firemen dragging their hoses across Twelfth Avenue. The boiler-room engineers, overcome by smoke, left their posts, and the lights went out. An announcement on the battery-powered public-address system bellowed: "Get off the ship."

Frank Trentacosta, a thirty-six-year-old physiotherapist and the trainer of the St. Francis of Brooklyn college basketball team, had been working as a fire watcher on the *Normandie,* earning $80 a week to supplement his income. He hoped that his wife, Gemma, could quit her office job with the International Ladies Garment Workers Union. They wanted to have a baby.

Trentacosta and another fire watcher, George Deighan, were racing down a ladder, fleeing the flames, when a blast, probably the explosion of a tank feeding the acetylene torches, threw Trentacosta to the floor unconscious. Deighan carried him off and he was placed in an ambulance. The driver, Albert de Marco, happened to be Trentacosta's brother-in-law. De Marco also drove for top officials at the Todd Shipyards, overseer of the *Normandie* conversion, and it was he who had gotten Trentacosta his job on the ship.

On a lower deck, a carpenter named Arnold Christofferson had been working on paneling. "A few of us whiffed this smoke. I looked out the port to see what was what. Two fellas are on the pier. They holler 'the ship's burning' and they point way over my head. I smiled. I thought it was kind of a gag. Then one of the men on the pier crosses his heart and I see he means it."

Christofferson ran up to a spot two decks higher and tried to get through a smoke-filled corridor, a moist handkerchief covering his nose and lips. In the shock of the moment, he was still gripping his hammer, screwdriver, and a ruler. The corridor burst into flames. A sailor with a hose tried to flush down the floor, and the water rose to Christofferson's ankles. He made it to an outside deck and he saw men pulling hoses over the side. He dropped his tools and lent a hand. "We smashed windows and we stuck the hose through and we kept playing it on the flames. I stayed put until my overalls got so stiff with ice I could hardly move my legs or my arms." A sailor wrapped Christofferson in a white blanket and told him, "You can't do any more." He was taken to Bellevue Hospital.

Another rescue effort bordered on the bizarre.

Stanley Franks, an eighteen-year-old sailor from Port Marion, Pennsylvania, who had enlisted exactly one month after Pearl Harbor Sunday, had been bunking at Pier 92, its top level converted into sleeping quarters, the bottom level a mess hall, while assigned to load ammunition on barges and ships. He had also been standing guard at the *Normandie* over the past couple of weeks. "We'd walk up and down with our rifles, four hours at a time."

Franks was just out of boot camp and had never been aboard a ship, let alone the most magnificent liner of the age. As he recalled it:

The alarm went off and we went over there, a bunch of us seamen, after it had been burning for quite a while. I was standing there with two other seamen and they said "you three go in" and they told us where the captain's cabin was. "Get his trunk and his hat and get it off."

The three of us went up—it was really plush inside that ship. Oh man, there were still chandeliers hanging and beautiful rugs on the decks. We went up to the captain's cabin. The other two seamen grabbed his trunk and I grabbed his hat and we hurried. I remember looking in his hat—it had a San Diego address.

As he went down the gangplank, Franks could feel the ship rolling and he feared the gangplank would snap loose, spilling him into the Hudson. "The ship was listing then and the ropes were really tight. We got off that ship just in time because I looked in the river below us. It was ice floating around."

Franks and his mates returned to Pier 92 with the captain's belongings, and then Franks looked back. "Now you could see the smoke coming out toward the back part of the ship. It was sort of real dark gray and black at times."

Amid the commotion and the confusion, an intrepid adventurer didn't necessarily have to be a fireman or a Navy man or a Coast Guardsman to get aboard the burning ship—to the delight of a teenager named Coleman Schneider and his friends.

Schneider had joined the Sea Scouts, a nautical version of the Boy Scouts, in 1939, when he was fifteen years old, growing up in West New York, New Jersey. He learned to sail, tie knots, and splice lines at Friday night meetings aboard an old barge called the *Ranger,* docked on the Hudson River in North Bergen.

The day the *Normandie* blazed, Schneider and his friends had worn their Sea Scout outfits to classes at Memorial High School, in West New York, to celebrate Boy Scout Week. Their uniforms "looked very much like those the enlisted Navy men would wear," as Schneider recalled it.

The boy had been fascinated by the great ocean liners. "Memorial High School overlooked the skyscrapers and passenger terminals in Manhattan, and we always saw the ships come and go."

When school let out at 3 p.m., the *Normandie* had been afire for more than twenty minutes.

"We noticed the large plume of smoke," Schneider remembered. "Six of us decided to cross the river to get a better view. It was five cents for the bus to the ferry, and ten cents to cross. The dock was within two blocks of the ferry entrance. We walked through the police and Navy lines. I guess we looked like them in our uniforms."

Soon Schneider and his pals were doing their part to fight the fire. "We helped by carrying hoses with firemen into the grand lounge," but finally "the smoke was so thick we were told to leave."

At any rate, there were other things for teenage boys to do. "It was time to go anyway. Some of us had part-time jobs."

The dozens of firemen had a daunting task just to get aboard the ship. Lugging their hoses up the six gangways, they found their paths blocked at times by fleeing workers. Two dozen ambulances were dispatched, most of them from Manhattan but some from the hospital near the Brooklyn Navy Yard. Doctors and nurses treated workmen for burns and smoke inhalation. More than fifty men plunged into the icy Hudson and were plucked from the water. Another 200, trapped high on the *Normandie,* were taken down eighty-five-foot-high fire ladders.

Across Twelfth Avenue, thousands of onlookers converged, held back by soldiers with rifles and bayonets. Graham McNamee, the prominent NBC broadcaster, reported from the pier on a national radio hookup. Navy and Coast Guard planes circled overhead, taking photos.

La Guardia had been at the city's radio station, WNYC, in Lower Manhattan, that afternoon, assuring New Yorkers that the sacred nickel subway fare would remain intact. Handed a note telling him of the fire, he cut his broadcast short, arriving at the pier in his black, corduroy-collared fireman's raincoat and a black homburg.

By 3:15 p.m., the *Normandie's* three top decks—her superstructure—had essentially been gutted. With the exception of the theater, her public rooms had been swept by flame.

All the while, water had been pouring into the *Normandie's* port side from a growing assemblage of fireboats. By 3:30 p.m., seven boats had converged on the *Normandie*—the Fire Department's *James Duane, John J. Harvey,* and *Fire Fighter,* and four private fireboats. Their torrents of water began to tilt the *Normandie,* whose starboard side faced the pier. Her gangways started to pull away from the pier, finally swinging loose and crashing against her hull, tossing some firemen into the Hudson. The gangways were refastened, but then came another ominous sign: The mooring lines, slack that morning, had grown exceedingly tight.

Fire Commissioner Patrick Walsh didn't know much about the structure of the *Normandie.* Neither did Admiral Adolphus Andrews, the commander of the Third Naval District and the officer formally in charge of the ship. But the Navy officer overseeing the details of the *Normandie's* conversion to a troop carrier, Captain Clayton Simmers, had studied her blueprints and stability characteristics, and he was growing worried.

Simmers knew that the ship wouldn't be burning much longer, in view of all that water pouring in from the fireboats. And the *Normandie* was made of steel, its integrity in no danger. The engine rooms didn't seem to be threatened by fire or water. So the liner could quickly be refitted for its troop-carrier mission, Simmers believed, and the blaze might even be a blessing of sorts. It would allow for more significant alterations, and the disappearance of the fire-wracked superstructure might make for greater stability.

But Simmers feared the slowly increasing list to portside. If that were not corrected, the *Normandie* could capsize. Simmers tried various maneuvers to correct the list, but they all failed. He considered trying to open the sea cocks and scuttling the ship—letting it come to rest in the shallow mud, allowing for a relatively easy salvage operation—but the smoke and lack of specially trained crew to do the job made it impossible.

While Simmers labored frantically to reverse the list, the man who had designed the *Normandie* and knew the ship intimately was only a few blocks away. But he may as well have been in France.

Vladimir Yourkevitch, a Russian naval engineer who emigrated to Paris in 1922, had won the contest to fashion the *Normandie's* hull. He left France for the United States late in 1939 and opened a marine engineering office in Manhattan, where he was working when he received a phone call from a friend. "Your *Normandie* is burning. I am watching it from my office window. The smoke is coming out thick and black."

Yourkevitch set out for Pier 88 in a taxi, then got out when it became stuck in traffic and alternately walked and ran the last few blocks. He tried to tell the policemen manning the barriers who he was, but he was turned away. He saw a Navy officer, insisted he could help, but was assured the Navy had everything under control. He finally gave up and went to his apartment at Riverside Drive and West 99th Street. From his window, he could witness the final hours of his magnificent creation.

The fireboats continued to pour water into the *Normandie*'s port side as the afternoon waned, worsening the list. Firemen on the pier trained their hoses on the starboard side as a counterbalance, but those efforts were largely unsuccessful. Simmers wanted the fireboats to stand down, but Fire Commissioner Walsh insisted on carrying out his prime duty—extinguishing the blaze. Walsh finally ordered the fireboats to halt operations, but they ignored the department's cease-pumping signals. It took a radio telephone call from La Guardia to end the pumping sometime before 7 p.m.

The fire had been declared under control at 6:15. Some three hours later, F.B.I. men investigating the possibility of sabotage came onto the ship to sift through the Grand Salon, the fire's origin point, and to question the workmen.

At 10:37 p.m., low tide arrived, and the *Normandie*'s port side hit bottom. But the ship stabilized at a list of 20 degrees. At 11:30, the engine room began taking on water, and at midnight the list reached 23 degrees. An hour or so later, Admiral Andrews ordered the few remaining Navy officers and firemen aboard to abandon ship. Soon the list reached 33 degrees, and then came the "death rattle"—anything that hadn't been tied down tumbled onto the port-side plating or into the Hudson.

The last two men off the *Normandie* stumbled onto the pier at 2:15 a.m. Father Baptist Duffee and Dr. Edward Maloney of St. Vincent's Hospital had climbed down to the engine room, looking for men who may have been trapped. The *Normandie*'s final lurch threw them against the generators. Duffee injured his stomach and back, and Maloney suffered cuts when his eyeglasses shattered.

At 2:37 a.m., almost precisely twelve hours after the sparks from welder Clement Derrick's torch had brushed a burlap life preserver, the *Normandie* fell quietly onto her side as searchlights continued to play upon her.

The fire claimed two lives.

Frank Trentacosta, the physiotherapist working as a fire watcher, died of a fractured skull and internal injuries at Roosevelt Hospital at just about the time the fire was declared under control. His wife, Gemma, was at his bedside. Another workman, Larry Trick, died of his injuries two days later. At least 300 workmen, Navy personnel, and Coast Guardsmen were treated for injuries, burns, smoke inhalation, and exposure.

When morning arrived, 30,000 New Yorkers converged on Pier 88 to glimpse the inconceivable. Thousands gawked from office or apartment windows. "It was as though the Empire State Building had slowly teetered and fallen sideways into the street," wrote John McClain of the *Journal-American*.

But this was much more than the loss of a glamorous icon from the otherwise drab Depression. A ship that could have carried 10,000 troops to Europe on a single voyage had been rendered a wreck. As the *New York Times* put it in an editorial: "It is not alone a ship that has been damaged. Men may have to die on the other side of some ocean because help cannot now get to them in time. The investigation should be relentless."

The FBI, the Navy, the United States Senate and the House of Representatives, the New York City Fire Department, and Manhattan District Attorney Frank Hogan launched inquiries.

FBI agents ruled out sabotage. A Navy court of inquiry blamed the workmen from the Robins company for "gross carelessness and utter violation of rules and common sense" in touching off the fire. It also faulted two midlevel officers, one from the Navy and the other a Coast Guardsman, for inadequate supervision of the workers. But this court of high-ranking officers declined to hold Admiral Andrews, the man formally in charge of the *Normandie*, or anyone else among the Navy's top brass responsible.

Congressional committees faulted Washington's rush to have the conversion completed within weeks and cited confusion among naval and civilian authorities. "There was no overall command," a House Naval Affairs subcommittee concluded. It blamed the fireboats' relentless pouring of water onto the ship's port side for the capsizing, but the Fire Department absolved itself of any responsibility for the ship's demise.

District Attorney Hogan's conclusion said it all: "There is no evidence of sabotage. Carelessness had served the enemy with equal effectiveness."

But it seemed that the *Normandie*—or the USS *Lafayette*, as the Navy insisted upon—might rise again. Naval engineers and divers, working with the salvage company Merritt, Chapman & Scott, undertook a massive effort to refloat the liner. Elsewhere in Manhattan, the ship's fine wines, Champagne, and what remained of her furnishings were sold at auction.

By fall 1943, the salvage job had been completed. The *Normandie* was again at even keel. She was taken to the Brooklyn Navy Yard and then to a dry dock off Columbia Street in Brooklyn while the Navy considered converting her into a combination troopship and aircraft carrier. But there was no need for her by then, and when V-J Day arrived the *Normandie* was still in Brooklyn.

The United States Maritime Commission put the *Normandie* up for sale as scrap in July 1946. A junk firm, Lipsett, Incorporated, bought her for $161,680, and the hull that once been emblazoned with the gold letters *Normandie*, then repainted *Lafayette*, was painted once more. The white letters read "Lipsett."

On Thanksgiving Day 1946 a dozen tugboats towed the *Normandie* hulk to Port Newark, New Jersey, for wrecking. In October 1947, a crane lifted a seventy-five-ton section of the *Normandie*'s bottom, the last remnant of the great liner, and loaded it onto a railroad car for shipment to a steel company in Coatesville, Pennsylvania. The *Normandie* was no more.

CHAPTER 10

THE PORT IMPERILED

They were called the Subway Sailors.

While Coast Guard coxswain in the Pacific were bringing marines onto invasion beaches in the face of Japanese fire, the men of the Coast Guard at Caven Point in New York Harbor could ride the subway in their off-duty hours to visit girlfriends or sample the honky-tonk nights in Times Square.

It was 5:30 in the evening, Saturday, April 24, 1943, the "subway sailors" awaiting supper at their barracks. Their week's work—loading bombs, ammunition, and gasoline onto freighters at Caven Point, a Jersey City weapons depot, for shipment to the European battlefronts—was done. They were planning to go on liberty for the Easter weekend.

But there would be no supper, no liberty. At that moment, a fire erupted on an old Panamanian freighter, the *El Estero,* berthed at Caven Point's long pier. An oil-fed pipe had burst in the bilges, igniting fuel oil. Flames engulfed the boiler room and licked at its metal walls. Crates with highly volatile cargo were on the other side of those walls, which were growing hotter by the minute.

The *El Estero* was packed with 1,500 tons of explosives, including ten one-ton bombs, along with highly flammable gasoline for planes and jeeps. Two ships similarly loaded were near the freighter, and railroad cars at Caven Point held even more ammunition and bombs.

Hardly anyone beyond the Subway Sailors and the longshoremen who worked alongside them had heard of the *El Estero.* But if her explosives were to blow and touch off the ammunition and bombs on the ships and railroad cars nearby, disaster loomed for stretches of Lower Manhattan, Staten Island, Jersey City, and Bayonne.

Memories of the Halifax, Nova Scotia, inferno of World War I remained fresh. On December 6, 1917, the French freighter *Mont-Blanc,* en route to Europe from New York and carrying 5,000 tons of TNT, collided in Halifax's outer harbor with the Norwegian steamship *Imo.* The *Mont-Blanc* caught fire, touching off its explosives. The blast killed more than 1,600 people, injured 9,000, destroyed 3,000 buildings, and incinerated the ship.

As a result of that disaster, the United States Coast Guard was assigned to provide security, law enforcement, and safety measures at all major American ports in World War II. Coast Guardsmen supervised the loading and stowage of explosives and military ammunition at Caven Point although the Army ran the facility.

Seymour Wittek, the young man from the Bronx who had been visiting his girlfriend in Brooklyn when he heard the Pearl Harbor bulletins, joined the Coast Guard soon afterward. Now he was a seaman second class, and at the outset of Easter weekend April 1943 he had been loading the dangerous cargoes at Caven Point.

"We were at our Jersey City barracks located on the Morris Canal. The alarm bell rang and we all ran. They said, 'There's a fire on the *El Estero*, we need men to go.' The bosun's mate, who was the ranking guy, said: 'I haven't time to pick. Whoever wants to go, come on. Let's go.' About 60 of us stepped forward. Nobody looked to the left, nobody looked to the right, nobody twisted their heads around to see what anybody else was doing."

Most of the time, the Coast Guardsmen stationed in Jersey City were ferried to Caven Point in whaleboats that were roomy but slow. This time, they were crowded into trucks and rushed to the pier. Wittek remembered:

> The Coast Guardsmen who were already on the *El Estero*, with the help of soldiers and some of the *El Estero* crewmen—though a lot of them had been hustled off the ship—started trying to put water on it. When we got there they had already started opening some of the holes to get water into the engine room. Those holes would normally be closed with wooden planks, and then tarpaulin would be put over them to make them watertight.
>
> Black smoke was coming up like crazy. We started putting pumpers up to put more water on the ship but we weren't really accomplishing much. And everyone knew the ship could explode at any moment. We understood the nature of the beast.

Aboard the *El Estero*, Coast Guardsman Tom Joyce had been watching carpenters below deck boarding up cargo. Then he heard running overhead. Glancing up, he saw smoke. He tried to avert a panic.

"Okay, you guys, quitting time," he called to the carpenters. Then someone came running over and yelled, "Fire, fire." The carpenters gathered around the ladder, and a scramble seemed at hand.

"There's no fire, that guy's crazy," said Joyce, casually throwing a leg over the edge of a hatch. "Bring your tools with you. It's quitting time."

The men followed his instructions, remaining calm as they ascended the ladder.

The Coast Guard's munitions officer in charge of the *El Estero*, Lieutenant Commander John Stanley, told his men to fight the fire the best they could. But he was in his first day in that job. "We were fortunate since the commanding officer of the detail I was assigned to, a man named Pfister, had been high up in the New York City Fire Department and he really had great knowledge," Wittek recalled. "He was directing us."

The Coast Guardsmen who had rushed to the *El Estero* from their barracks had no gas masks, but they grabbed hoses and axes, seeking to gain access to the engine room.

Getting water on the fire proved a daunting task. Coast Guardsman Tom Savoury dragged a hose to the top deck but when he raced back to turn the water on, there was no pressure. Fellow Coast Guardsmen brought hoses aboard from their trailer pumpers.

Locked steel boxes containing cases of antiaircraft shells for guns on freighters had to be moved away from the top deck, since they were sitting atop the blazing boiler room. But the Navy gun crew had taken the keys upon leaving some time earlier. Joyce popped the locks with his ax handle. Coast Guardsmen carried the cases to the bridge, then slid them down a greased plank to the foredeck.

Coast Guardsman Bill Ryder, just out of boot camp, was ordered to feel with his hands for hot spots on the afterdeck. When he found the most vulnerable areas, they were sprayed with water. Finally, the heat became too much for him. "Sir, I can feel it through the soles of my shoes now," he shouted. He was ordered away and went to the top deck to help with the hoses.

The New York City fireboats *Fire Fighter* and *John J. Harvey*, veterans of the *Normandie* fire, were summoned. Fireman Harry Biffar, a member of the department for nine months, was polishing brass on the 134-foot *Fire Fighter* at the Hudson River's Pier 1 in Lower Manhattan when the *El Estero* alarm came in. The *Fire Fighter* set out for Caven Point and pulled up on one side of the *El Estero* while the *Harvey* got in position on the other side, each boat in gray camouflage paint as an air-raid precaution.

"We were ordered by the chief to stretch a line to the engine room," Biffar remembered. "The fire was confined to it. We opened the engine room door and it was like an inferno, like a furnace. The flames came right at us. My rubber coat was burned and my eyebrows were singed."

The fireboats poured foam on the *El Estero* in the hopes of smothering the flammable liquid and removing oxygen from the fire while cooling down the surface.

"But we just couldn't extinguish it," Biffar recalled. "It was spreading."

As for the peril facing the firemen, "We knew it was an ammunition ship, but you just do it like it was another job."

Three hours after the fire began, the Coast Guard and the Fire Department saw they could not win their battle. Their only alternative was to sink the freighter.

The New York City Police Department asked radio stations to tell listeners that "a large vessel is afire containing an explosive cargo" and to advise them to keep their windows slightly open and to stay away from them. A police teletype to precincts in the Bay Ridge and Fort Hamilton areas of Brooklyn and the Tompkinsville neighborhood of Staten Island, the spots closest to the blazing freighter, warned "there is imminent danger of an explosion." Policemen were told to go to homes in those areas and personally deliver the instructions being broadcast.

But the announcement also brought several hundred gawkers to waterfront areas at Jersey City and Bayonne, Staten Island, and Brooklyn. Patrol cars were dispatched to shoo them away.

The Army had rejected sinking the *El Estero* at its pier since that would tie up vital space there. So the freighter had to be towed into the harbor before it could be scuttled. The tugboats *Margaret Olsen* and *Ola G. Olsen* took hold of the freighter, still aflame and spewing black smoke, and began to pull it away from the pier. Coast Guard officers asked for volunteers to stay aboard. So many men agreed to remain with the *El Estero* that a few had to arbitrarily be left behind.

The pressures of the moment spawned bizarre conduct. A young crewman pointed to an emergency lamp carried by Coast Guardsman Homer Nagy. "This lamp belongs on the ship," he said. "You put it back when you finish. Don't forget." A Jersey City fireman, remaining aboard, poked around with his flashlight, asking everyone he saw whether they had spotted his favorite crowbar.

Soon after the freighter got under way, some of the Coast Guard volunteers were taken off.

"I was told to leave the ship when we were not too far from shore because they realized they had too many men," Wittek remembered. "Everything that could be done had been done. They didn't want to imperil everyone. The bosun said 'you get the hell off, you're going to be married in a few weeks.'

"There was a picket boat. I went down a Jacob's ladder, and as I did that one of my friends said to me: 'Seymour, take my wallet. If anything happens, at least they'll know I was there.' The Coast Guard volunteers had been assembled so quickly at their barracks that there was no time to take names."

As the freighter was being towed, two police launches from the city's harbor precinct warned river traffic away. The fireboats played water on the *El Estero,* causing her to list sharply to starboard, and she was finally anchored in forty feet of water, 400 yards off Tompkinsville, Staten Island. At 9:15 p.m., the *El Estero* sank from the weight of the water poured into it, a portion of the superstructure still visible. Not a single bomb or shell had exploded.

"We felt that any minute we might be gone, and thank God we got through it safely," La Guardia told New Yorkers in his weekly radio talk on Easter Sunday.

Lieutenant Commander Stanley received the Legion of Merit for his leadership in battling the blaze. Lieutenant Commander Arthur Pfister received the Navy and Marine Corps Medal. Bayonne held a parade to honor the Coast Guardsmen who helped save the city, and officials presented them with medals. But neither the Coast Guard nor the City of New York accorded special recognition to those Subway Sailors. When Wittek approached officials at City Hall decades later seeking belated honors for the men, he got nowhere. Then came a column in the *New York Times* on the 2008 Memorial Day weekend recounting the bravery of Wittek and his fellow Coast Guardsmen. The following Veterans Day, the Coast Guard made amends. Wittek was presented with the Coast Guard Commendation Medal by Vice Admiral Robert J. Papp Jr. aboard the Intrepid Sea, Air, and Space Museum in New York Harbor.

Harry Biffar became the commander of the Fire Department's marine division in 1962. The fireboat *John J. Harvey,* commissioned in 1931 and named for a fireboat pilot killed in the line of duty a year earlier, was taken out of service in 1994. Five years later it lay rusting in the Brooklyn Navy Yard when preservationists took it over and created the John J. Harvey Museum. It was added to the National Register of Historic Places.

When the World Trade Center's twin towers fell on September 11, 2001, the Lower Manhattan water mains and fire hydrants were crushed. In a desperate search for water to pour on the smoldering ruins, fire officials summoned the *Harvey* back to duty. Its volunteer crew evacuated workers from Lower Manhattan and joined with the still active *Fire Fighter* and the fireboat *John D. McKean* to stand off Battery Park City and play water on the wreckage.

Seymour Wittek was married to his Brooklyn girlfriend, Anne Cooperman, seven weeks after he fought the *El Estero* blaze. The Coast Guardsman who had given Wittek his wallet as identification attended the wedding. When that man was married, Wittek was his guest. The Witteks had been married for sixty-four years when Anne died.

Looking back on the *El Estero* blaze more than six decades later, Seymour Wittek reflected how "if she blew I knew what would come down immediately: The Statue of Liberty, the Bayonne Navy Yard. But we didn't think about it. We had a job to do."

But the threat to New York posed by explosives in the harbor had not ceased when the *El Estero* slipped beneath the waves. Eight months after that near disaster, the city was again imperiled.

Windows shattered by the hundreds along a 15-mile stretch of Staten Island, all the way from Tottenville to Mariners Harbor. At Coney Island, the Boardwalk and Surf Avenue were littered with glass. Houses on Atlantic Beach in the Rockaways seemed to sway. In northern New Jersey, towns as far inland as Belleville, twenty-five miles from shore, felt a shudder.

On 241st Street in the northern tip of the Bronx, a homeowner named Paul Rowan awoke to a wind whistling through his bedroom. His picture frames rattled, his Scottie barked, and her seven pups whined. "I thought it was our oil burner blown up," he said. "I put on the light and went to the window, and all around me, as far as I could see, other people were up, putting on their lights. Some people thought it was an earthquake."

It was 6:15 in the morning, Tuesday, January 3, 1944, and a wind-whipped snow was falling.

In the Lower Bay, a few miles south of the Rockaways and east of Staten Island, some three and a half miles from the Ambrose Channel lightship, a beacon for ships entering and leaving the harbor, the 1,700-ton Navy destroyer *Turner* had lain at anchor.

Named for Daniel Turner, a New Yorker and a Navy captain in the War of 1812, the *Turner* had arrived the previous night after helping escort a convoy of freighters from Casablanca. Its captain, Commander Henry S. Wygant Jr., thirty-seven years old and a Naval Academy graduate, anticipated moving on to the Brooklyn Navy Yard in the afternoon, then granting liberty for his crew of 292.

Wygant seemed on track for a fine career. Back in 1934, only four years out of Annapolis and a lieutenant on the destroyer *Gilmer*, he dove into the ocean in an effort to save a pilot from the aircraft carrier *Lexington* who had gone down. A shark hovered, but Wygant struggled to find the trapped flier. His efforts were in vain, but he received a commendation from the secretary of the navy.

As Wygant prepared to take his destroyer on to the Navy Yard to complete his Atlantic crossing in this first week of 1944, the *Turner*'s crew assembled for breakfast.

And then the blackness of a winter's morning dissolved. First came a rumble, then the flashing of a brilliant yellow ball of fire. A huge explosion originating in an ammunition storage area blew up the *Turner's* bridge and the foremast and ripped a V-shaped gash in the hull. The crew's main mess hall and the officers' ward room on the main deck were ablaze and filled with dense smoke. Crewmen were enveloped in flame and smoke, many trapped in the rubble.

John McDonald, a ship's baker from Milwaukee, had just left the mess hall, anticipating a reunion with his wife, Alice, who was living on Staten Island.

"I was gonna get shut eye because I'd worked all night," he recalled. "I was going up a ladder. I was just about at the top when that thing went off. It threw me up against a bulkhead and it burned all the clothes off me. It burned all the hair off my head. I tried for the one hatch and it evidently jammed and I couldn't get out. So I went over to the other side and I could feel the cold—it was snowing. I couldn't hear and I couldn't see and I was crawling on the deck. It was hot as a stove. And then I passed out."

Another sailor came to McDonald's aid and attended as well to two other injured sailors while the other warships from the convoy, also anchored for the night, headed toward the stricken destroyer.

"The bigger ships wouldn't go near us because everything was on fire or exploding," McDonald remembered. "They sent in their motor whaleboats—they're 26 feet or something like that. This guy found some life jackets. He put them on the three of us and threw us over the side so the small boats could pick us up."

McDonald was rescued by a whaleboat from the destroyer escort *Inch*, and he was taken to the Brooklyn Navy Hospital.

Robert Freear, a motor machinist's mate, had filled his breakfast plate and was about to take a seat in the *Turner's* main mess compartment when another sailor pushed past him and sat down. Freear moved on to a forward mess area. "I had taken one bite of a piece of toast and was thinking how nice liberty in New York would be," he remembered. "Then the lights went out. I came to five to ten minutes later. Two men were lying on top of me, and I pushed them off, shook them, but there was no response. I heard screams of men who were trapped in the wreckage and burning to death."

Freear fell down a ladder while scrambling from the wreckage, his body burned, one eye blistered shut. But he made it to the main foredeck. He learned later that the explosion had originated in the destroyer's main magazine below the main mess hall. As he told it: "The man who pushed past me inadvertently saved my life and lost his because in the next minutes everyone in the main mess compartment would die."

Freear was among forty sailors who slid down a line thrown from a Coast Guard boat on antisubmarine patrol that had tied up to the *Turner's* port bow. But fifteen sailors, many badly burned, had leaped into the water to escape the flames, and they were floundering. Leon Frederick, a coast-guardsman who stood six feet five inches tall and weighed 220 pounds, fished them out.

"I laid out flat on the deck and another crew member held my legs to keep me from sliding into the water," Frederick remembered. "I didn't actually see the faces of any of them and I know they didn't see mine. There was only one thought—grab them in."

One of the sailors didn't make it. "I grabbed his arm and it slid out of my grasp, leaving only a handful of burned flesh. The sailor slid back into the ocean."

Jack Paulson, a Navy fireman, was blown into the water and lay floating on a mattress. Seaman Gustave Dellanoyd dove into the icy water and pulled Paulson toward a Coast Guard boat that picked up both sailors.

Chief Machinist's Mate Rene Pincetl, who had been in the engine room when the *Turner* exploded, stepped onto a Coast Guard cutter at 7:05 a.m. as the last man to leave the destroyer. "The ship was listing badly to starboard," he recounted. "The last explosion split her in two and she went down . . . fuel oil blazing, ammunition exploding."

The second blast came at 7:20 and the final and, evidently, largest one, at 7:51.

The Coast Guard took many of the survivors to the Fort Hancock Army Hospital at Sandy Hook, New Jersey. They needed immediate transfusions of blood plasma, but the hospital's supply was running out.

The snow had grown heavy, grounding small planes that might have brought in blood and slowing military and Red Cross vehicles trying to reach the hospital with plasma supplies.

The scene was set for a pioneering achievement: the first military helicopter rescue mission.

On the morning of December 7, 1941, Frank Erickson, a Coast Guard aviator and the naval air station duty officer at Ford Island, astride Pearl Harbor, was watching a marine color guard march to a flagpole when he heard the sounds of bombs exploding and saw a Japanese plane drop a torpedo that struck the bow of the battleship *California*.

Erickson ran to Ford Island's control tower, and from that vantage point he could see American sailors swarming from the wreckage of their ships onto the harbor's oil-coated burning waters. There was nothing he could do to save them.

A few months earlier, Erickson had read an article in the magazine *Aero Digest* describing a helicopter that had been developed at Igor Sigorsky's plant in Connecticut. Erickson became convinced that the helicopter would be an ideal craft for Coast Guard rescues, and as he watched the Pearl Harbor carnage he thought how he might have been able to pick up those sailors if only he could have reached them in a helicopter.

A husky man with a thick neck and a square face topped by a thatch of blond hair, known to his friends as Swede, Erickson proved a hard-charging figure zealous in his determination to create the age of the helicopter.

He learned to fly helicopters at the Sikorsky plant and became the Navy's first helicopter pilot (the Coast Guard being part of the wartime Navy). But he was bucking the Navy's traditional devotion to fixed-wing planes, which had much longer ranges and far larger load capacities than helicopters. Erickson offered a few arguments of his own, hailing the helicopter's flexibility of control and its ability in operate in severe weather with limited visibility and low ceilings. In December 1943, he got a chance to prove his point when he was named commander of the world's first helicopter training base, on the grounds of the Coast Guard Naval Air Station at Floyd Bennett Field in Brooklyn.

When the *Turner* blew up, the Navy put aside its skepticism, if not hostility, toward Commander Erickson and his helicopter dreams. Erickson had never flown a helicopter in the conditions prevailing that day, a twenty-five-mile-an-hour northwesterly wind whipping snow and sleet, and no one else had either. But Admiral Stanley Parker, the Third Naval District commander, desperate to get blood plasma to his burned sailors, phoned him at Floyd Bennett Field to ask if he could fly to the Battery's barge office in Lower Manhattan, pick up a plasma supply, then fly it on to Sandy Hook.

Erickson had no doubts. "Yes, sir," he said.

Piloting a dark blue Navy helicopter—the only crewman was his copilot, Ensign Walter Bolton, who had qualified to fly the craft only three days earlier—Erickson struggled with shifting winds and visibility so low that "we practically had to feel our way around the ships in Gravesend Bay."

But he made a successful steep approach over shoreline pilings and landed in Battery Park. Bolton left the helicopter to make room for two cases of blood plasma strapped to the landing floats, and Erickson took off again, backing out since trees blocked his way forward. Steadily keeping the shaking helicopter in place as the winds battered it, Erickson climbed, backed out over the pilings, then headed downwind. He arrived on a Sandy Hook beach fourteen minutes later with his lifesaving blood plasma.

The explosions that rocked the *Turner* sank the ship, taking the lives of Captain Wygant, fourteen of his sixteen officers, and 138 crewmen. A Navy court of inquiry was unable to determine the cause of the first explosion, but concluded it was not due to enemy action (a German submarine attack) or sabotage. The Navy Bureau of Ordnance did offer a possible explanation.

It suspected that improper defusing of Mark 131 rockets had touched off the initial blast, the others resulting from the spread of the fire.

But the *Turner* had been far enough away from the other convoy escorts and their own ammunition stores to avert a catastrophic chain reaction. As in the *El Estero* episode the previous April, the city had been spared.

Frank Erickson continued his crusade for the helicopter all through the war, and he wasn't averse to a publicity stunt. At a Fourth of July bond rally in 1944, he arranged for two Navy helicopters to fly over the Statue of Liberty. "I suggested that one helo line up just back of and slightly above the torch so it would appear that the torch was actually supporting the helo. They came back with a remarkable photo which I thought had been made according to my suggestion."

The Army was not amused.

As Erickson told it: "The colonel who was responsible for the protection of the statue threatened to have me court-martialed for endangering the Statue of Liberty."

CHAPTER 11

FROM EUROPE'S SHORES

He was among the intellectual elite of Europe, a celebrated playwright and poet, and once he was a wealthy man with a sixteenth-century chateau outside Paris and a modern, Renaissance-style castle on the Riviera. He still had his family, his reputation, his title of Count, bestowed by King Albert of Belgium on his seventieth birthday, and his automobile, but all else was gone. When the Greek liner *Nea Hellas* arrived in Hoboken, New Jersey, on July 13, 1940, Maurice Maeterlinck, acclaimed for his exploration of mysticism and a Nobel Prize winner for literature, was another refugee fleeing Hitler.

Maeterlinck was a month shy of his seventy-eighth birthday, a black net draped over his shock of unruly gray hair, as he came down a gangplank to meet reporters. He pronounced himself "a very old man," a weary survivor of the catastrophe unfolding in Europe.

"I had my money in a bank in Brussels," he said. "The Germans occupied Belgium. I had my house and belongings in Nice. The Germans have occupied France. All I have, I have with me."

He was accompanied by his French actress wife, Renée Dahon, thirty-two years his junior, her father, and her blind mother, thirty-two pieces of luggage, two Pekinese dogs, and two parakeets. The Paris château was in German hands, its extensive library with first editions and Maeterlinck's own French-language manuscripts taken away. The home in Nice, Orlamonde, had been looted. Hollywood had made a movie out of Maeterlinck's most celebrated work, *The Blue Bird*, written in 1908, but his wife shuddered at what had been done to it: "There is nothing but the title—there is no Maeterlinck in it."

Maeterlinck carried the scripts for two plays on his voyage to America, and he hoped they would be produced. But for the time being the small royalties he received from the movie version of *The Blue Bird* would have to tide his family over. And customs officials confiscated his parakeets. "Perhaps it's for the best," he would say. "Bluebirds are the symbol of happiness."

Maeterlinck had fled France for neutral Portugal, fearing that he would have been shot by the Nazis in retribution for a play he wrote on the German occupation of Belgium in World War I. In the aftermath of France's capitulation to Germany in June 1940, the Maeterlincks turned on their radio at their refuge in Portugal, hoping for news they could believe. Only German communiqués were coming through. But they were able to leave, and when they arrived in the Port of New York they knew little about the fate of France.

The Maeterlincks moved into a small apartment at the Hotel Esplanade on Manhattan's West Side. Maeterlinck found only six of his books and plays in the original French at New York libraries. If he wished to see his other works, he would have to read the English translations. But the Maeterlincks still had their cream-and-red roadster with its Paris license plate, having carried it aboard their ship, and they tooled around New York with it. Maeterlinck marked his seventy-eighth birthday with a cocktail party his manager, Saul Colin, gave for refugee writers at the Rockefeller Club in the RCA Building. But he found only frustration in pursuing his craft in New York. He had written a play about Joan of Arc but could not get it produced.

Maurice Maeterlinck was among perhaps 30,000 refugees who fled France and arrived in the United States during World War II, most coming between the summer of 1940, when the Germans marched into Paris, and the spring of 1941. The majority settled in New York or elsewhere in the Northeast. They came directly from France or, more likely, had first gone to England or to Portugal.

From the art world came Salvador Dali, Marc Chagall, Max Ernst, Jacques Lipchitz, Yves Tanguy, Marcel Duchamp, André Breton, and Fernand Léger. From the literary world, the theater, and journalism came Maeterlinck, André Maurois, Jules Romains, Antoine de Saint-Exupéry, Henry Bernstein, Saint-John Perse (the pen name for the former French department of foreign affairs head Alexis Léger), Erwin Piscator, Jacques Schiffrin, Geneviève Tabouis, Robert Goffin, and Jacques Deval. The philosopher-theologian Jacques Maritain, the anthropologist Claude Lévi-Strauss, and the physicist Jean Perrin found refuge in New York as well.

The British journalist Alistair Cooke observed how "New York is more than ever the home of the homeless," how a passerby "caught the nervous chatter at Fifth and Fifty-Ninth of the wealthy refugee French, and, it seemed, the entire unscathed population of the Riviera."

The refugee artists and intellectuals were in sharp contrast to the Ellis Island immigrants of years past, as the journalist Simeon Strunsky noted.

Strunsky wrote of a hypothetical stranger, a "grey-haired little woman with the brave voice and conciliatory smile" asking for directions to a subway stop in the Bronx.

One hates the thought of sending her off on the wrong train. It is the voice and smile which recently have become more and more familiar in New York, in conjunction with a foreign accent, a bookish turn of phrase, and good clothes that have seen very hard use. It is the refugee's voice and smile in their latest American version. The voice is cultured. The clothes are well-cut.

The inquirer does not hold out a slip of paper with a street address for the native to decipher, as millions of earlier refugees on American transportation lines have done. This later arrival speaks and reads our language with fair ease. It is simply a question of telling her which train she should take.

The influential French journalist Geneviève Tabouis, the niece of a former ambassador to Washington, may not have been asking for subway directions. But when she arrived in New York late in 1940 after fleeing to England, she felt lost. It was not only her exile from the political and cultural life of Europe but the demise of free France. She had long warned of the consequences of fascism in her dispatches, and it all had come true. As she would remember it:

Numerous reporters are on the huge pier in New York, awaiting the arrival of the boat. They all ask me the same questions at the same time. For the first time, I hear those brutal words "The Collapse of France." But in their pressing questions, I detect such a real love for France, such distress at its defeat, that it seems as if this immense America is somehow in harmony with my pain!

That first night in New York, in my hotel room, seeing some of the photos taken that morning, I looked at myself several times without recognition! An expression of anguish has turned me into another person, and I note that in a few weeks, my hair has gone completely white.

I am haunted by longing for my loved ones; I am shamed by the attitude of the new French leaders towards Germany. The suffering beginning for the tens of thousands of French patriots, so innocent of what is happening, overwhelms me.

In the face of her anguish, Tabouis plunged into a host of activities. She became a correspondent for British and Argentine newspapers and undertook a national lecture tour appealing for American support for France's ultimate liberation. In 1942 she helped found and became a major contributor to *Pour la Victoire*, the eight-page tabloid-sized newspaper published in New York by French exiles. With a circulation exceeding 33,000 by 1943 and contributions from the leading intellectuals among the French émigrés, the paper covered the war news in general but it also told of Free French activities around the world. It reported on French communities throughout America and presented articles on French culture.

In the spring of 1942, Jacques Surmagne, formerly the director of France Presse, wrote a series of features in *Pour la Victoire* telling of the churches, clubs, cultural, and educational facilities in New York for the French refugees and he wrote of the people who didn't make the headlines, like the physicians working as waiters while preparing to take New York licensing exams. The title of the articles: "New York est-il Francais?"

For a journalist like Geneviève Tabouis, opportunities to write and be read abounded. But the New York theater world offered few opportunities for émigrés like Maurice Maeterlinck and Henry Bernstein, whose style might not translate into appeal on Broadway.

Bernstein (he shunned the French spelling Henri) was a popular contributor to the Paris stage, having had more than two dozen plays produced. Most of them explored the relationships between the sexes, but his last play reflected the times: *Elvire* dealt with the despair of refugees fleeing the Nazis. It ran until the Germans closed in on Paris, and then Bernstein fled to Bordeaux, got on a boat to England, and sailed for New York a few days later.

Bernstein was a grandson of William Seligman of the Wall Street firm of J. and W. Seligman, his father having married Seligman's daughter Ida in Paris. The father was a businessman and art connoisseur, and when Henry was six, Manet painted his portrait. The Bernsteins and the Manets were summertime neighbors at Versailles.

An impressive figure at six feet three, Bernstein become a social lion among New York's French émigrés, giving grand parties at his luxurious Waldorf-Astoria apartment graced by the paintings of Toulouse-Lautrec, Manet, and Courbet. A white-gloved valet attended to the guests.

While he wasn't entertaining his fellow refugees, Bernstein picked fights with some of them over the fate of France. In a series of articles in the *Herald Tribune* in June 1941, he attacked France's collaborationist Vichy government of Marshal Pétain, writing that its anti-Semitic and generally repressive measures "were all taken spontaneously, not under pressure from the Nazis."

He castigated André Maurois for his defense of the Vichy regime early on, Antoine de Saint-Exupéry over his disdain for De Gaulle, and Jules Romains for his sympathy for pacifism.

Maurois, Romains, and Saint-Exupéry continued to flourish during their exile in New York, publishing in French with translations into English.

Maurois lived at the Ritz Tower on Park Avenue, wrote books and articles, and lectured at Columbia University and other colleges around the country. Romains's publisher, Alfred Knopf, gave him a suite at the Mayflower Hotel overlooking Central Park. He made radio broadcasts to France for the BBC from its New York offices, published in 1941 as *Messages aux Francais.*

But Bernstein was stymied in reaching the American theater audience. His first English-language play, *Rose Burke*, written for Katharine Cornell, who played a glamorous sculptress, was headed for a Broadway opening in 1942, but closed during its tryout in Toronto.

Saint-Exupéry, the aviator and author and something of a legendary figure for surviving air crashes, arrived in New York on December 31, 1940, on a boat from Portugal that also carried the film director Jean Renoir. He was an instant celebrity.

Saint-Exupéry's *Wind, Sand and Stars*, published in 1939, an account of his harrowing years as a mail pilot flying over the Andes and the Sahara, and focusing on his improbable survival of a crash in the Libyan desert in 1935, was a classic adventure tale. He received the National Book Award for it in 1941 at a Hotel Astor luncheon that drew 1,500 guests.

Flight to Arras, Saint-Exupéry's account of his reconnaissance mission with the French air force over the town of Arras during the German invasion of May 1940, spoke to the spirit of his now-crushed countrymen. Through Supreme Court Justice Felix Frankfurter, whom he knew socially, Saint-Exupéry had the book, published in New York in February 1942, sent to the White House as evidence that the French had not capitulated to the Germans without resistance. He inscribed it "For President Franklin Delano Roosevelt, whose country is assuming the immense task of saving the world."

And during his two years in New York, interrupted by trips to California and Montreal, Saint-Exupéry wrote what became his best known book, *The Little Prince*, a fantasy about an urchin's interstellar travels that satirized the ways of the adult world.

Saint-Exupéry was buffeted, meanwhile, by the political wars among the exiles.

On November 29, 1942—three weeks after Operation Torch, the American invasion of French North Africa—he called on his countrymen to put aside their differences. In "An Open Letter to Frenchmen Everywhere," printed in the *New York Times Magazine* and broadcast by Saint-Exupéry in French (he refused to learn English, lest his views be misconstrued), he called for an end to recriminations over the past misdeeds of the Vichy government, and the cessation of feuds over allegiance to Charles De Gaulle.

For all Saint-Exupéry's eloquence, that appeal was seen by some émigrés as an attack on De Gaulle. Henry Bernstein, who had been stripped of his French citizenship in absentia by the collaborationist Vichy government, felt that Saint-Exupéry had let the Pétain regime down too lightly. "We cannot, however touching the appeal, by however brilliant a writer, by however courageous an aviator, by however nice a man, say mildly, 'we'll let bygones be bygones,' " Bernstein wrote in a letter to the *Times*.

Saint-Exupéry yearned for a return to the war and an end to the ceaseless political arguments consuming the French intellectuals in New York. On April 14, 1943, he stepped over the hull of the *Normandie*, lying on its side at its West Side pier, a symbol of the lost glory of France, and boarded the steamship *Stirling Castle*, bound for Algiers and aerial combat with the Free French. On July 31, 1944, overweight and beset by old crash-related injuries, he took off from Corsica in a Lightning P-38 reconnaissance plane. He never returned.

The French exiles in New York presumably put their factional wars aside on June 6, 1944, when the Allies stormed the beaches of Normandy in the long-awaited D-Day invasion. That afternoon, Major Jean de Lustrac of the French Military Mission to the United States, Lieutenant Georges Rossel of the French Navy, and six French sailors marched down Madison Avenue, bearing the Cross of Lorraine on the flag of the Free French. Some 50,000 New Yorkers assembled in Madison Square Park for the city's official D-Day observance. La Guardia opened the ceremonies by reading Eisenhower's Order of the Day, prayers were offered, and a singer named Lily Djanel, her arms outstretched, intoned "La Marseillaise."

For many an émigré intellectual and cultural figure, The New School for Social Research in Greenwich Village provided a chance to exchange views with colleagues and to teach.

Claude Lévi-Strauss, a native of Belgium from a Jewish family, studied at the University of Paris in the 1930s, taught in Brazil and undertook anthropological research expeditions there for the remainder of the decade, then returned to France in 1939. After the French capitulated to Germany, he was dismissed from an academic position under the racial laws and fled to America.

Arriving in New York in spring 1941, living in a small apartment in Greenwich Village, Lévi-Strauss wandered the city streets, savoring the flavor of Manhattan and what he called the "immense disorder" of its skyline. Coming upon cultural artifacts from all over the world, he found New York appealing to his instincts as a collector. "The whole substance of the artistic patrimony of humanity was present in New York in the form of samples; washed about over and over as the tide does with driftwood, following the unpredictable rhythm of the rise and fall of societies, some objects still adorned living-rooms or had gone towards the museums, while others piled up in unexpected corners."

In fall 1941, Lévi-Strauss began teaching a course on the sociology of Latin America at the New School. He also joined with fellow émigrés to found the Ecole Libre des Hautes Etudes, where more than ninety professors taught more than 200 courses, all in French.

Lévi-Strauss broke from traditional thought in anthropology by refusing to view western civilization as privileged. He looked at all cultures on their own terms rather than comparing them to the West. During his time in wartime New York, he found a kindred thinker in Franz Boas, the German-born professor emeritus of anthropology at Columbia University who had explored the "race question," debunking the idea of the "blond superman" as "Nordic nonsense" even before World War I. Lévi-Strauss was seated alongside Boas at a luncheon in the Columbia men's Faculty Club on December 31, 1942, when Boas collapsed in his arms and died of a heart attack at age eighty-four.

After a stint as a cultural attaché to the French embassy, Lévi-Strauss returned to Paris in 1948. He was celebrated as a French national treasure over the years, and on his hundredth birthday, in November 2008, he was honored in Paris at the Musée du Quai Branly, which he had inspired.

The director and producer Erwin Piscator, a founder of Germany's leftist political theater of the 1920s, came to New York from France in 1939 with his wife, Maria Ley, a dancer, and founded the New School's Dramatic Workshop, whose students included Marlon Brando, Harry Belafonte, and Elaine Stritch.

A small man with flowing silver hair, formal in his approach to his students and known as a disciplinarian, Piscator did not fare well with Brando, who chafed at authority.

Brando, who regarded the renowned dramatic teacher Stella Adler as "the soul" of the Dramatic Workshop, recalled the time Piscator took his students to Sayville, Long Island, for several productions.

"A lot of unbridled fornication occurred during the summer of 1944, and I was in the thick of it. One day Piscator lifted up the trapdoor to the loft where I was sleeping above a garage, found me with a girl, and said I had to leave because I'd broken the 'Rules of Summer Stock.' "

It was a fortunate turn of events for Brando. "Because I was expelled I got my first acting job about three weeks later in 'I Remember Mama.'"

The émigrés of Europe's art world found a welcoming in New York, thanks in good measure to the bohemian and fabulously rich American expatriate Peggy Guggenheim, who returned to the city after a quarter century abroad.

Guggenheim's West Side modern-art gallery, Art of This Century, provided a showplace for many of the European modernists who fled occupied France, playing a role, as the art critic Hilton Kramer once observed, "in establishing New York as the nerve center of the international avant-garde, and thus the successor to Paris as the artistic capital of the modern movement."

The gallery also presented the first public showings of the American Abstract Expressionist painters Jackson Pollock, Robert Motherwell, and Mark Rothko.

Peggy Guggenheim was a granddaughter of Meyer Guggenheim, who started out as a peddler and amassed a fortune in copper mining, and the banker James Seligman, a brother of Henry Bernstein's grandfather William Seligman. Peggy's father, Benjamin Guggenheim, who died in the sinking of the *Titanic*, had taken her to Europe every summer. She made her debut in 1916 and moved to Park Avenue, but the staid and proper life was not for her. James Seligman had been a founder of Temple Emanu-El in 1845 and had been its president, but Peggy spent one Yom Kipper shopping for furniture, scandalizing her mother, who refused to pay for it.

After inheriting a fortune in 1919, Peggy went to Europe, where she met some of the famous figures of the age—James Joyce, Isadora Duncan, Ezra Pound, and Emma Goldman. She lived in London and Paris and had two children from a stormy marriage to a painter named Lawrence Vail and a fling with the Irish playwright Samuel Beckett.

In 1938, she opened a London gallery she called Guggenheim Jeune to display modern art. It was unprofitable, and she closed it. She hoped to open an art museum and began amassing a large collection of contemporary art, on which she was advised by the British critic Herbert Read. But the war thwarted that, and she went to Paris. When the Louvre refused to take her paintings in order to safeguard them from the Germans, she shipped them to America as household goods.

While in Paris, she met Max Ernst, a leading figure of the Dada and Surrealist movements. Born in Cologne to a Roman Catholic family that he eventually disowned, Ernst settled in Paris in the 1920s. When Hitler came to power, he warned of a looming catastrophe in Europe. His 1933 painting *Europe After the Rain* prophesied a disaster on the Continent that could be likened to a flood tide of filth. When war came, the French interned Ernst as an enemy alien, but he got out of detention. He fled to Portugal with his son, Jimmy, and Peggy Guggenheim. All three came to New York on a Pan Am Flying Clipper in July 1941. Max and Peggy were married in December, living in a spacious, remodeled brownstone mansion on Beekman Place.

Guggenheim opened Art of This Century on West 57th Street in October 1942 with a benefit for the American Red Cross. The museum's designer, Frederick Kiesler of Columbia University's School of Architecture and the scenic director of the Juilliard School of Music, created novel touches. Many of the paintings were suspended in air, without frames, but with a device enabling visitors to rotate them. A revolving wheel that showed seven works by Paul Klee went into motion when a visitor stepped across a beam of light, and the paintings swung by, one by one, remaining in the spotlight for ten seconds, then disappearing.

Soon after the museum's opening, Ernst went to New Orleans for a show of his works and Peggy began an affair with the artist Marcel Duchamp, whom she had known for twenty years.

The following January, as a supplement to the museum's permanent collections, Guggenheim displayed the works of thirty-one female artists, including one very unlikely exhibitor. The *New York Times* art critic Edward Alden Jewell reported that the gallery's elevator operator told him on his way up that he had given the place "an extra thorough cleaning" because Gypsy Rose Lee was expected there later in the day to publicize her "self-portrait." According to Guggenheim, the superintendent of the gallery was a jealous sort and fired the elevator boy for getting his name in the paper, leaving Jewell feeling guilty.

Lee's artwork was a "paste-up" or collage. Jewell wrote that "Miss Lee's face makes several appearances, once surmounting a form manifestly not her own, dressed in a Victorian bathing suit." In another section, Jewell noted, she pasted a photo of a dog's head "where one would expect to find hers," but "the form this time is unmistakably authentic, teasing along toward the strip."

The artists recruited for Guggenheim's all-women show included Dorothea Tanning, a painter from Galesburg, Illinois, who had been living in New York for several years. Tanning would recall how Max Ernst came to her apartment during the 1942 Christmas season to discuss the prospective show, how they began playing chess there nightly and how he moved in with her soon afterward.

As she put it: "He lived in me, he decorated me, he watched over me."

Guggenheim's marriage with Ernst collapsed, and Ernst married Tanning in 1946. She became a noted Surrealist painter, a sculptor, and a poet as well, and their marriage endured until Ernst's death in 1976.

Guggenheim's visitors at Art of This Century included Eleanor Roosevelt, who viewed a photograph exhibit, The Negro in American Life, and wrote about it in her newspaper column, "My Day." But Guggenheim was irked by Mrs. Roosevelt's lack of interest in her prized artwork.

"Before she left I did my best to make her go into the Surrealist gallery, but she retired through the door sideways, like a crab, pleading her ignorance of modern art."

When the war ended, Guggenheim shut down her gallery and went to Venice, housing her collection in her eighteenth-century palazzo on the Grand Canal. She eventually left the collection and her home to the New York museum named for her uncle Solomon Guggenheim.

Like most of the émigré artists, Fernand Léger, a principal figure in the cubist art movement, returned to France after the war. But his warm feelings for America endured.

Léger had first visited the United States in 1931 and was enthralled by the skyline, describing it in a French art magazine as "the most colossal spectacle in the world." And his bold coloring reflected his delight at New York's dazzling neon signs.

He painted prolifically during his years in wartime New York, his work including murals for Nelson Rockefeller's apartment. He also taught at colleges and was known for the parties he gave at his apartment on East 42nd Street, being an excellent cook. He sampled the city in all its variety, attending a sailors' ball at the Paradise dance hall near the Brooklyn Navy Yard and visiting the Savoy Ballroom in Harlem. His mural Composition With Two Parrots was shown at the Museum of Modern Art.

After returning to France in December 1945, Léger titled a canvas Adieu New York and painted those words on it. He created stained-glass projects for churches along with murals and a mosaic that he completed in 1950. A tribute to the nation that had sheltered him, the mosaic was placed in a crypt constructed that year in Bastogne, Belgium, honoring the American soldiers killed in the Battle of the Bulge.

In September 1998, fifty-four years after Antoine de Saint-Exupéry disappeared, a fisherman off Marseilles found a silver bracelet in his net bearing the names of Saint-Exupéry and his wartime New York publisher, Reynal & Hitchcock. Divers later found the remains of Saint-Exupéry's plane, but his body was never recovered. In 2006, a former German fighter pilot named Horst Rippert said he believed he had shot Saint-Exupéry down over the Mediterranean. If his suspicions were true, he had ended the life of his idol: As a youngster in the 1930s, Rippert had been enthralled by Saint-Exupéry's adventure tales from the early days of flight.

Dorothea Tanning would remember a dimmed-out winter's evening in 1943 when she accompanied Max Ernst for a visit with Saint-Exupéry, whom she called Tonio, and Saint-Exupéry's wife, Consuelo, at the Sutton Place apartment that Consuelo maintained.

"The talk tarries behind drawn curtains and Max and Tonio play chess in the lamplight. It may have been his last chess game, for we heard the news some time later: flying his reconnaissance plane over the Mediterranean, flirting with German U-boats as Icarus flirted with the sun, he dips and swings once too often, and is heard from no more."

PART THREE

THE UNIFORMS

CHAPTER 12

CAMPUS NAVIES

On a cold, sunny morning in December 1942, a young man named Willie Keith kissed his mother good-bye at Broadway and 116th Street and entered Columbia University's Furnald Hall, formerly a dorm for law students. Willie had pursued comparative literature at Princeton, graduating in 1941, but he had majored in partying. Now he was leaving the good times and his girlfriend, May Wynn, behind. He was joining the Navy's V-7 program, which turned college boys into officers within four months.

Thus began the Pulitzer Prize–winning novel *The Caine Mutiny.* Willie Keith, destined for an epic confrontation with Captain Queeg, existed only in the imagination of Herman Wouk.

Wouk was a genuine V-7 recruit, and Columbia's Morningside Heights campus became his first step toward World War II service aboard a minesweeper. He was among more than 23,000 collegians who received Navy commissions in New York.

On September 1, 1940, the Navy opened three training schools to produce thousands of ensigns for a looming war with Japan. It began recruiting unmarried men between ages nineteen and twenty-seven, with two years of college, to become officers and presumably gentlemen in programs at Columbia, Northwestern University outside Chicago, and Annapolis itself in a course apart from United States Naval Academy regimen.

The New York program had its first headquarters aboard a mothballed battleship once known as the *Illinois* and built during the Spanish-American War. The ship had been disarmed in the mid-1920s and converted into a training vessel with construction of a large wooden shed that replaced almost the entire superstructure. It had mainly been used by the New York Naval Militia for semiweekly drills, but with the arrival of the V-7 program it was converted into a cluster of classrooms, dormitories, and mess halls. Moored at the Hudson River and 135th Street, about a mile from the Columbia campus, the ship was remained the *Prairie State* early in 1941 when a new vessel christened the *Illinois* joined the fleet.

Upon surviving fifteen-hour days studying fleet tactics, navigation, signaling, the use of torpedoes, the rescue of airplane crews at sea, first aid, and the more prosaic knot tying, the V-7 recruits became deck officers or engineers.

Early on, classes were held aboard the *Prairie State* or at a nearby building owned by the New York Central Railroad. To gain a taste of sea life and a modicum of proficiency with a weapon, the officer candidates were also taken on all-day cruises aboard a Navy sailing ship, the *Sylph*. Tied up at a pier south of the *Prairie State,* it was once the yacht *Intrepid,* owned by Walter P. Murphy, a Chicago railway-equipment manager, who sold it to the government for a dollar. Forty men went out on the *Sylph* at each sailing, busying themselves with firing rifles at crates and boxes being towed.

As for the creation of gentlemen, instructors from the Arthur Murray dance school visited the *Prairie State* on occasion. "The captain believes that dancing is desirable in a naval officer's education," explained Lieutenant Commander W. D. Austin, an aide to the ship's skipper, Captain John J. London.

When the Navy stepped up its production of virtually instant ensigns in 1942, the program expanded beyond the *Prairie State.* Columbia University leased Furnald Hall, John Jay Hall, and Johnson Hall to the Navy for V-7 dorms, it opened classroom space at the Journalism Building and East Hall, and it made South Field available for drills.

Robert Satter, joining the officer program in 1942 out of Columbia Law School, found no respite from a challenging academic environment.

> It was a pretty rigorous program. Classes every day on navigation, on ordnance, a whole bunch of things. I remember one guy from Texas who was having a terrible time—he was a football player; though all of us were college graduates—and we helped him with the math and with the other academic studies. I heard about a year later the poor guy was killed on a destroyer.

Every Saturday, Satter remembered, the recruits paraded at South Field. "We used to march over from the *Prairie State* to Columbia. I remember a guy from Iowa who used to sing, 'We're from Iowa, best state in the land, that's where the long tall corn grows.' We all used to sing it. On November 11, which was Veterans Day, we marched down Fifth Avenue as part of a big parade. Our class had one famous guy, Richard Nye. He had played the husband of Mrs. Miniver in the movie."

Edward Keyes, who entered the program in April 1943 with twelve fellow graduates of Springfield College in Massachusetts, recalled how the gathering of rambunctious young men under military regimentation created a frat-house atmosphere.

There was, for example, the great sit-up competition. A trainee from Keyes's company who became known as Myro the Gyro laid claim to being unbeatable in sit-ups, having knocked off sixty at a clip. Another company had a would-be champion as well, so a "shootout" was arranged. Myro the Gyro took his place on a lower bunk and his opponent was poised on an upper bunk, recruits from their respective companies crowding into a twelve-by-fifteen-foot room to cheer and razz.

As Keyes recalled it:

Myro was in good form and was making the room shake with his contortions. The chap on the upper level lay there thumping his arms on the bed while his counters called out the score. When Myro was about to give out, the challenger began some real sit-ups and racked up a dozen or so more than Myro's counter had reported. The phony bets paid off made this a truly memorable scam. Myro fell from popularity to where he was before; just another midshipman. To the best of my knowledge he never got an inkling that the contest was faked.

On Sunday evenings, the midshipmen went to religious services, the Protestant recruits singing as they marched to Riverside Church, a few blocks from the Columbia campus. "The girls from Barnard would lean out the widows and give us the eye," Keyes remembered. "Occasionally, one of the brethren would come back from liberty a little under the influence and would be held by the elbows to and from the church."

The Rover Boys atmosphere notwithstanding, the young men were soon off to war. Robert Satter, who served in the Pacific, his ship narrowly missed by a kamikaze pilot, felt that he had been well prepared.

The V-7 program trained reserve officers who became every bit as good as the regular officers. In fact, except in the highest command, the ships were operated by V-7 officers who had been trained in these midshipmen programs. They took college graduates who had analytical abilities and gave us some basic training and we applied it to the tasks we had.

The New York training center, the largest in the Navy's V-7 program, graduated 23,550 men in its twenty-six classes by the time it closed in December 1945, and it furnished 6 percent of all Navy officers ashore or afloat. Some 350 graduates of that program were killed or reported missing in action.

Prairie State–Columbia officers were aboard the battleships *Arizona*, *Oklahoma*, and *California* during the attack on Pearl Harbor, the cruiser *Houston* when she was sunk off Java and the submarine *Shark* when it was lost in the Pacific.

Seven of the twenty-six ensigns cited for courageous conduct at Pearl Harbor were from the New York program, among them Stanley Caplan, a University of Michigan alumnus who graduated from V-7 school in February 1941. In the absence of superior officers who were ashore on leave, Caplan was the senior officer aboard the destroyer *Aylwin* when the Japanese attacked. Caplan took the *Aylwin* from its anchorage to its emergency station in the channel, ordered its machine guns to fire at the Japanese planes, and directed the dropping of depth charges against what were believed to be two Japanese submarines. The *Aylwin*'s guns were reported to have downed three planes and perhaps damaged the subs without a single casualty.

Herbert Charpiot Jones, the son of a Navy officer, joined the first class at the *Prairie State*, graduating in November 1940. Serving as an antiaircraft officer aboard the *California* when the Japanese attacked Pearl Harbor, he took command of a crew manning a five-inch gun. When the *California*'s power system was knocked out, the ammunition hoists from the hold stopped running. Jones went below and organized a chain of men to pass ammunition up from the magazines, all of them nearly suffocating from smoke and cordite fumes. Then a Japanese bomb exploded near the powder room, grievously wounding Jones and starting a fire. He ordered his fellow sailors to go topside. When two of them tried to carry him up a ladder, he refused their help, fearing that would imperil their own escape. Jones died alone in the hold of the *California* at age twenty-three. He was posthumously awarded the Medal of Honor.

While the Navy turned out ensigns at Columbia, more than 80,000 Waves and several thousand female members of the Marine Corps (known simply as women marines) and the Coast Guard (the SPARs) were trained at Hunter College's Bronx campus. Informally known as the USS *Hunter*, the facility prepared women for a host of jobs to free up men for combat duty, an undertaking that proved highly successful but fraught with controversy in the early going.

During World War I, more than 11,000 women served in the Navy, but no formal organization had been created for them. When the war ended the Navy went back to being all male. There were few champions among the Navy's top brass and the more hidebound members of Congress for female enlistments a generation later.

Virginia Gildersleeve, the dean of Barnard College and a key figure in establishing the Waves, would recall how Thomas Walsh of Montana, the chairman of the Senate Committee on Naval Affairs, "used to roar at any woman who mentioned the subject of a women's reserve . . . violently opposed to calling women into the Navy because he thought that this would tend to break up American homes and would be a step backward in the progress of civilization."

When Kay Travers, living at home in Brooklyn, told her parents she was giving up her job as secretary to the vice president of a Wall Street shipping company to join the Hunter program, they were none too thrilled.

I had to wait until I was 21 because my family wasn't as enthusiastic as I was about joining the Navy. I went in during September '44. I told my mother in August that I had signed up for the service, but I wasn't sure if I'd be accepted. She never made a remark. I don't think she believed it. She thought, well, I was just talking. The day before I was to report to Hunter I was throwing a few things together. She said, "what are you doing with the suitcase?" I said, "I joined the Navy, remember." She looked at me like, "what, what?" The next morning she actually had to wake my father up to say goodbye. They weren't emotional people and she obviously wasn't too crazy about the idea and maybe thought "better not to say anything."

When I went back home that last weekend of training for an overnight stay and I stepped into the subway with my uniform on, I got attention. Everybody's head turned. I wasn't sure whether it was in a complimentary way or not. There were a lot of disparaging remarks made about women in the service at the beginning. I don't think any of the young men really liked the idea. This was another invasion of the females, like women going to work, flying planes, all the firsts that women did. This was a big first for the average guy. They didn't talk too much about it but it was there in society. What's more masculine than a guy in uniform serving the country in time of war and here these females are coming in, in uniform.

The women's branch of the naval reserve was established on June 30, 1942, with an initial quota of 10,000 enlisted personnel and 1,000 officers. Elizabeth Reynard, a professor of English at Barnard, designed the Waves program, and Gildersleeve became chairman of an advisory council consisting of prominent female educators from around the country. Mildred McAfee, the president of Wellesley College in Massachusetts, was named director of the Waves, with headquarters in Washington.

It was Reynard who came up with the designation Waves—for Women Accepted for Voluntary Emergency Service. As she told Gildersleeve:

There were two letters which had to be in it, "W" for women and "V" for volunteer, because the Navy wants to make it clear that that this is a voluntary and not a drafted service. I figured the word 'emergency' will comfort the older admirals because it implies that we're only a temporary crisis and won't be around for keeps.

The small women's officer program was based at Smith College in Massachusetts while Hunter opened the enlisted women's program in February 1943. The Hunter recruits had to have a high school diploma, and virtually all had to be single—if married, the trainee's husband had to be a civilian and they couldn't have any children under age eighteen. And, in the program's first few years, she also had to be white. That was the case as well in the *Prairie State*–Columbia program for Navy officers, but Hunter was a municipal college, raising a touchy issue for the progressive La Guardia administration

Black leaders, including Walter White, executive director of the NAACP, and Adam Clayton Powell Jr. wrote to Frank Knox, the Navy secretary, shortly after the Hunter program got under way, calling for black recruits to be admitted. Knox responded with a vague claim that steps were being taken to improve the status of blacks in the Navy. A group of Hunter College graduates called on the Board of Higher Education, the overseer of the city's municipal colleges, to refuse the use of Hunter to the Navy unless it abandoned racial discrimination. But it wasn't until later in the war that a few black recruits were admitted.

Hunter had a roomy campus with four stone buildings for classrooms and physical training facilities. The nearby Kingsbridge National Guard Armory accommodated drills during poor weather as well as reviews, most notably an appearance by FDR in October 1944, during the final weeks of his campaign for a fourth term. Eleanor Roosevelt and Madame Chiang Kai-shek dropped by as well.

In choosing Hunter, the Navy viewed New York City as a vast recruiting platform for the Waves. The American Women's Volunteer Services distributed enlistment applications at thirty-five booths around the city, and a "Waves at War" display was mounted at Rockefeller Center to catch the eyes of patriotic young women.

Captain William F. Amsden, previously Commodore of Convoys in the Pacific, became the commander of the Hunter program. Amsden "was simply horrified when he heard of this assignment," Gildersleeve remembered, but "he soon grew to love the USS *Hunter* dearly."

The regular Hunter students were transferred to the college's buildings on Manhattan's Upper East Side, but the Navy still had to find housing for the trainees since Hunter was a commuter school with no dormitories. Under authority provided by Congress, naval officials commandeered seventeen five- and six-story apartment buildings in the Jerome Park area of the Bronx, the majority of them on University Avenue. More than 600 families were evicted. City officials promised to assist them in finding new apartments, no easy matter in view of the wartime housing shortage, and the city paid their moving costs. La Guardia acknowledged that many people "may suffer some inconvenience," but he thought they "will have the satisfaction of knowing that they are directly contributing to the prosecution of the war."

Patriotic sentiments notwithstanding, there was no little consternation among the people losing their apartments. Protest meetings were held, to no avail, and at least one tenant, Margaret Tully, who described herself as a "poor woman," appealed directly to the Navy in a letter saying she would be taken advantage of by a prospective landlord since she had to relocate quickly.

The neighborhood people fell victim to the catchall "don't you know there's a war on," and only three weeks after the Navy announced its intention to take over the apartment buildings it had swept the tenants from five of them.

The Waves moving into those apartments slept on double-deck bunks, though their mattresses were thicker and larger and presumably more comfortable than those aboard ships. They were housed two to four to a room, with some of the apartment walls torn down to create dorm-like space, and their furnishings were Spartan: a locker, a chest of drawers, a table, chairs, and lamps.

Converted passenger liners and merchant ships—among them the lamented former *Normandie,* and the *Manhattan* and *America*—provided eighty-five truckloads of furnishings for the apartments and the Navy classrooms at Hunter. Six thousand white unused bedspreads were purchased from the United States Lines.

Navy Lieutenant Herbert Schwab, an Annapolis graduate and a onetime Wall Street lawyer, returned to New York in the winter of 1943 for a new assignment. He had completed sixteen months' duty in the Atlantic, and it seemed that he could now look forward to living at home in Brooklyn with his wife and two sons. His orders designated his new station as "U.S. Naval Training Center, the Bronx, W.R."

As he told it: "I caught a train for home—that's in Flatbush—and about halfway there it struck me that 'W.R.' stood for Women's Reserve. 'Ye gods!' I thought."

Schwab had been designated as the supply officer overseeing furnishings, mess-hall food, and—surely a "first" for the Navy—the purchase of beauty supplies. "Don't think it doesn't make you feel peculiar to be ordering face powder instead of chewing tobacco," he told an interviewer.

On February 8, 1943, designated Waves and SPARs Day by the city, 350 women were sworn in as Hunter's inaugural class at a City Hall ceremony. In a program lasting up to eight weeks (at its peak the women were in and out in four weeks), the recruits were indoctrinated in Navy and Coast Guard tradition and were classified for specialties they would be trained in at advanced programs elsewhere.

A regimental parade was held every Saturday, but the recruits found themselves marching everywhere during the week, a hardy pursuit when wintry winds blew from the Jerome Park Reservoir. As Kay Travers Langan remembered it:

> We got up at 5:30. By 7 o'clock we were dressed and ready to march to breakfast, or mess as they called it. We had classes, then lunch. Every time we moved, we moved as a platoon. We marched up a big wide avenue to wherever we were going, whether to lunch or a class. I loved marching. I was in very good shape—5 feet 4½, 108 pounds, and 32–21½–31.
>
> In the afternoons, we all went into an auditorium and sang. One side of the group sang "Waves of the Navy" and the other side sang "Anchors Aweigh." They had somebody playing piano. It was a high spot in the day for me—I loved to sing.

She also loved the uniforms designed by Mainbocher and supplied by the major Manhattan department stores.

> A lot of women bitched the whole time they were in uniform—"Oh, I've gotta keep wearing this thing." They were beautiful, I thought. They were Navy blue, like a high cut blazer, three or four buttons up the front. For the summer you could buy your own whites, which I did.
>
> They had two kinds of shoes. One had a Cuban heel—they also called it nurses' shoes. Years ago that's the kind of shoe that nurses wore. It was about an inch and a half high, an excuse for femininity. The other was flat, like a man's shoe. If we had known about all the marching we would do, we would have taken two pairs of the perfectly flat. But since we were so feminine we thought, "at least this one has a little heel." We were going from 4-inch heels that we normally wore in civilian life to these flat shoes. I took one of each. The one with the Cuban heels stayed in my locker most of the time.

Olive Osterwise, who arrived at Hunter in 1943 from Uniontown, Pennsylvania, wasn't too fond of those flat shoes, practical as they were. "The shoes were so heavy. My word—traipsing around. Marching was fun, until my back started hurting. I was taken off marching. When basic training was over, I no longer needed the shoes. But they would never wear out."

Marie O'Hare, a Hartford-area native who had been working in a defense job for Pratt and Whitney, became a Hunter classmate of Kay Travers, joining "out of a spirit of adventure, and, of course, patriotism was very high." Years later, Marie O'Hare Walsh most remembered the military discipline and the rushed meals.

All the clothes in the closet had to be regulated. The shoes had to be set side by side, the toes facing the door. Your clothes had to be hung in a certain order. The bedspread had to be so tight. The inspectors would come in with white gloves and look for dust. They would drop a coin on top of your bed, and if it didn't bounce you got a demerit.

In those days, long hair was popular. We had our hair inspected. They would pull down the hair on the back of our neck, and if it would touch your collar, God bless you, you got told that the hair had to be cut. Lots of times on weekends, the girls would be cutting each other's hair.

As Olive Osterwise O'Mara recalled it: "Some of the girls made their beds and slept on the floor because they didn't want to have to get up in the morning and go through the ordeal of 'perfect beds.' "

The recruits were given an average of seventeen minutes to finish a meal. "When we went to breakfast we had to march and we had to eat in our full uniform with our overcoats on, I guess to keep the lines going," Marie O'Hare Walsh remembered. "There were so many to be fed at one time. You were told to eat your food and get out of there because another group was coming in."

Military training meant the loss of privacy. "I remember never being alone. We were always marching. I didn't know what it felt like to walk down the street alone anymore."

And the strange surroundings, the loss of a protected atmosphere at home experienced by many women, could sting.

Before I got into the Navy we'd go into New York on weekends. That was the mecca for my generation. We saw Frank Sinatra and Tommy Dorsey and Jimmy Dorsey and Harry James. My first Saturday night in the Navy, when I was in bed I was thinking, "Oh, my God." This is not the way I envisioned life to be. I wanted to be out dancing to those big bands. You were very conscious of the fact that you didn't have your own world anymore. Sometimes you'd hear the kids crying at night.

Almost 81,000 Waves, together with 3,200 women marines and 1,800 SPARs, had gone through the Hunter program by time the last class graduated in October 1945. The installation was officially decommissioned in February 1946, the ship's bell in front of the Hunter gym tolling six times and a Waves honor guard lowering the colors.

For all the anonymity of boot camp, one recruit at the USS *Hunter* stood apart. She was from Waterloo, Iowa, and her name was Genevieve Sullivan. In November 1942, her brothers George, Francis, Joseph, Madison, and Albert died off Guadalcanal in the torpedoing of the *Juneau,* a destroyer commissioned at the Brooklyn Navy Yard. Their deaths were the heaviest loss suffered by a single family in American naval history, and the tragedy stirred the nation.

On June 16, 1943, Genevieve Sullivan reported to Hunter College after going on a nationwide tour of war plants with her parents, Mr. and Mrs. Thomas Sullivan, and attending the launching of the destroyer *The Sullivans* to honor her brothers. She was greeted by Captain Amsden and she told reporters that she wished to repeat the message her brothers had often conveyed to the family. "If you're a good Navy person, you keep your chin up."

CHAPTER 13

THE COAST GUARD IN BROOKLYN

Once it personified the privileged life of the Gilded Age—luxurious hotels, a delightful waterfront, and even presidential visits. Then came a decline and a new life as a middle-class summer resort. With the arrival of World War II, the Manhattan Beach section of Brooklyn reinvented itself once more.

In the late 1870s, a businessman named Austin Corbin, later the president of the Long Island Railroad, built two grand hotels in Manhattan Beach, originally an unsettled area known as Sedge Bank. Ulysses S. Grant dedicated the Manhattan Beach Hotel in 1877, and three years later another president, Rutherford B. Hayes, dedicated the Oriental Hotel. John Philip Sousa brought his bands to the hotels, entertaining the rich and fashionable, and the setting inspired his "Manhattan Beach March."

A developer, Joseph P. Day, bought the property from Corbin's son, Austin Jr., in 1908 and tore down both hotels. Day divided Manhattan Beach into residential lots and laid out pleasant streets with English place-names like Amherst, Exeter, and Falmouth. He also built four-and five-room summer cottages, locker rooms for bathers, and a ball field. Although lacking the glamour of old, Manhattan Beach offered a respite from the summer's heat.

In February 1942, the Navy Department, which included the Coast Guard, paid Day $2.5 million for fifty acres of his property to create a Coast Guard training center. Martial music would be sounded once more at Manhattan Beach, but this time Sousa marches were played by a Coast Guard band. The cottages were converted to barracks, sixteen men to a building.

The Coast Guard had a surefire asset to publicize its Manhattan Beach base: the former heavyweight boxing champion Jack Dempsey, an icon of the 1920s golden age of sports. Dempsey had traded on his fame to open a popular Times Square area restaurant, but he put his appearances there aside to become a Coast Guard officer, assigned to physical training.

A generation earlier, Dempsey had gone on trial in federal court on charges he dodged the draft in World War I, an accusation leveled by his former wife, Maxine. He was quickly found not guilty, and the slacker image became a promoter's dream. Dempsey defended his title in July 1921 against Georges Carpentier, a French war hero, in the first "million-dollar gate." He battered Carpentier and went on to greater glory.

Dempsey demonstrated hand-to-hand combat to the Manhattan Beach recruits in a curriculum that included old-fashioned, clean boxing but also offered rabbit punching, butting, and the placing of a knee to the groin for a time when these future Coast Guardsmen might come across enemy agents while on waterfront patrols.

"We want our men to be better than commandos because we want them to bring the enemy back alive," Dempsey said. "The saboteurs won't be any good dead. We want information from them."

Dempsey had thirty-two assistants, including prominent former boxers like Lou Ambers, a onetime lightweight champion; Fritzie Zivic; and Marty Servo.

Collingwood Harris was once a Coast Guard mascot at the Manasquan Beach lifesaving station in New Jersey. The Coast Guardsmen let him come up to their tower and share meals with them. But when he joined the Coast Guard and was sent to Manhattan Beach, he found the training—at least so far as physical fitness went—falling short of any idealized vision he had.

Lou Ambers used to walk around the gym with a cigar in his mouth, and first time around the gym, he would say, "Okay you guys, get busy." The second time he would come around the gym, he would say, "You guys take it easy." Third time he would go around the gym he'd say, "Okay, you guys get busy." The fourth time around was, "Okay, you guys take it easy." That was the extent of Lou Ambers's tutelage.

Walter Lafferty, a recruit from Philadelphia, encountered the former pro wrestler Bibber McCoy, another of Dempsey's assistants.

We were awakened every day at 4 a.m. and drilled to 5 a.m. Then breakfast. Later in the morning we went to a huge gym for physical defense instructions. One day, McCoy, a giant of a man about 250 pounds, wanted to demonstrate a move. He picked up my 130 pounds and threw me against a wrestling mat hung on the wall. What an experience.

Dempsey ultimately left all this behind, shipping out to the Pacific to meet servicemen and promote the Coast Guard. He went ashore in the Okinawa invasion.

When the Coast Guardsmen at Manhattan Beach weren't learning to kick saboteurs in the groin or practicing rescue techniques, navigation, the tying of knots, and rowing in sometimes icy waters, they were at times enlisted in "voluntary" programs.

As Collingwood Harris told it: "We had a savings bond drive. The company commander wanted 100 percent enrollment and we didn't do that well. So we marched up and down the street at 2 in the morning three consecutive nights. He said, 'Until there's 100 percent we're going to get up every night at 2 o'clock and march up and down the street.' "

The quota was met.

Jack Dreyfus, later a Wall Street titan as founder of the Dreyfus Fund, had a college degree and he was already working in the financial world when he entered the Coast Guard, so he was invited to take an exam for officer candidate school. He flunked it because of poor mechanical aptitude and was sent to Manhattan Beach as a lowly recruit.

I was assigned to a garbage truck. I was third in charge, although I had the highest position, on top of the truck. One day I got off the base. The three of us had a good load of garbage and were ordered to bring it to the Mineola garbage dump. Not far from Mineola people started waving wildly at us. We thought, "How wonderful." We'd heard how much people appreciated the uniform, but had never experienced it. The people waved, and we waved back, and it felt patriotic.

We were enjoying this when a car, with the words Fire Chief on it, pulled alongside. The driver gesticulated for us to stop. Then we noticed we had a load of burning garbage. The chief ordered us to dump it, and we did. Firemen came, put out the fire, and shoveled the remains back into our truck and we took it to the dump. On the way back to the base nobody waved at us.

Beyond the tips from the best of boxing's yesteryear and the customary travails of a military recruit, important matters were afoot at Manhattan Beach with implications for postwar race relations.

The Coast Guard had a tradition of black enlistment dating back to the nineteenth century. A small group of blacks had manned a lifesaving station at Pea Island on North Carolina's Outer Banks and blacks had served at lighthouses in the Mississippi River Basin and as stewards.

During World War II, the Coast Guard began accepting blacks for regular recruit training and for specialized training. The first group, 150 volunteers, arrived at Manhattan Beach for basic training in springtime 1942. Classes and other duty activities were integrated, but the men were assigned to their own training company, and the sleeping quarters and mess were segregated.

Robert Hammond enlisted in the Coast Guard in Harlem in 1942, but after taking his oath he was told to go home. "This is wartime, why are they sending me home?" he wondered. He was eventually told to report. "It hit me when the bus pulled up to the training center in Manhattan Beach why I was sent home initially. They needed enough blacks to field a company. My bus stopped at a barracks with only black men while all the buildings next to it had white men training."

After a four-week basic course, black recruits who qualified were trained for assignments as coxswains, radiomen, and pharmacists, among various specialties.

Hammond and many of the other black recruits at Manhattan Beach were assigned to the first integrated boat in the Coast Guard, the product of a campaign by an obscure junior officer.

Lieutenant Carlton Skinner was commanding the cutter *Northland* in waters off Greenland when the engine died. The cutter was unable to move, and none of the white mechanics could figure out how to fix it. But a black steward, who was cracking eggs and cleaning heads, made the repairs. The man asked Skinner to be advanced to machinist's mate, and Skinner submitted a recommendation, but he was told that blacks could only be steward's mates.

Skinner decided to do something about his frustrations and the larger issue of black participation in the war. While on shore duty at Coast Guard headquarters in June 1943, he recommended to the commandant that a group of black enlisted men receive seagoing experience in an integrated setting under a sympathetic commander. He contended that a widespread distribution of blacks throughout the Coast Guard's seagoing vessels was no "experiment in social democracy" but "an efficient use of manpower to help win a war."

The plan was rejected by Skinner's immediate superior but approved by the commandant, Admiral Russell R. Waesche. In November 1943, Skinner took command of the *Sea Cloud*, a little-used, German-built yacht that had been converted into a weather-patrol cutter reporting on conditions in remote North Atlantic waters. Waesche arranged for the placement of black apprentice seamen, most from Manhattan Beach, aboard the *Sea Cloud* in groups of about twenty, gradually increasing the numbers each time the boat returned to a home station. Manhattan Beach also trained black women for the SPARs.

With a completely integrated operation, the *Sea Cloud* performed admirably and was credited with helping sink a German submarine in June

1944. Its crew included several black officers, among them Clarence Samuels and Harvey Russell, both having served as instructors at Manhattan Beach before gaining their commissions. Jacob Lawrence, later a renowned artist, was another of the black Coast Guardsmen on the *Sea Cloud*.

Samuels became the first black in the twentieth century to command a Coast Guard vessel in wartime, serving as captain of a lightship and the cutter *Sweetgum* in the Panama Sea Frontier. Russell became executive officer on a cutter operating out of the Philippines, then commanded a racially mixed crew shortly after the war.

A pair of black recruits at Manhattan Beach were part of an integrated singing group that went on to entertain troops in the Pacific, then forged a career in radio and television.

James Lewis, a bass-baritone, had performed on Broadway in *The Hot Mikado* with the black dancer Bill "Bojangles" Robinson. Homer Smith, an Alabama native and a tenor, had been part of an all-black vocal group called the Southernaires.

Lewis and Smith enlisted in the Coast Guard and arrived at Manhattan Beach in springtime 1942. Directed to put a chorus together, Smith brought in a pair of white Coast Guardsmen, Tom Lockard, a Californian and a baritone who had sung with the Los Angeles Opera Company, and Marty Boughan, a tenor from Missouri who had performed with the American Opera Company in Chicago.

Lewis, who was already singing on the Sunday radio program *The Navy Goes to Church*, joined with Smith, Lockard, and Boughan to entertain the recruits in Brooklyn. Calling themselves the Manhattan Beach Quartet, they performed patriotic and pop music as well as spirituals.

"We didn't really think whether we'd be jarring anybody's sensibilities by singing together—two white and two black people—we just did it," Lockard recalled. And the men socialized off base, their families attending dinner at each others' homes and going to restaurants together.

The Coast Guard, deciding that the group's talents should be displayed beyond Manhattan Beach, renamed it the Quartet of the United States Coast Guard and sent the integrated troupe to bond rallies, recruiting drives, and military hospitals on the East Coast and performances with the Coast Guard Band on the CBS radio show *The Coast Guard on Parade*.

The group had been well received in New York—La Guardia welcomed the singers to City Hall—but an unpleasant moment came in Washington, as Lewis told it. The men arrived for an anticipated overnight stay at the Captain of the Port Barracks on the Potomac after having appeared with Army and Navy bands in Washington. "Seeing that we were a racially mixed group, the officer in charge would not by any means countenance blacks sleeping in the same barracks with white Coast Guardsmen," Lewis recalled. "They moved two beds out into the corridor." Those beds were outside the latrine. All four members of the group left, finding accommodations elsewhere in Washington.

When the men were discharged at the war's end, they rechristened themselves the Mariners and appeared on network radio and TV programs hosted by Jack Benny, Fred Allen, Arthur Godfrey, and Ed Sullivan. In 1953, with Nat Dickerson, a Broadway performer, replacing Smith, the Mariners performed at President Dwight D. Eisenhower's inauguration.

As Lewis saw it, the long road from the Coast Guard's World War II recruiting station at Manhattan Beach had culminated in the acceptance of his group as a symbol of racial harmony. "We were the Declaration of Independence," he said. "We epitomized all those words—brotherhood and freedom."

CHAPTER 14

ARMY CAMERAS IN QUEENS

On September 1, 1939, the day Germany invaded Poland and the war in Europe began, the United States Army numbered 174,000 officers and enlisted men, a ranking of no. 17 in the world. It was a force better suited to fight a latter-day Pancho Villa than an Adolf Hitler. But the Army would soon be training millions of men, and it turned to film to help instruct GIs on the art of war and explain why they were being called upon to fight.

By war's end, the Army Signal Corps had produced more than 2,500 films. Its training movies covered everything from *Bridge Destruction* to *Baking in the Field* to *Hasty Sign Making*. It made motivational films for distribution to war plants, and it trained combat cameramen to capture footage for the brass to analyze and for homefront newsreels.

In Astoria, Queens, where the stars of the silent film era once preened, the Signal Corps operated its version of Hollywood, known first as the Signal Corps Photographic Center and then the Army Pictorial Center.

The producers Adolph Zukor and Jesse Lasky opened the Famous Players–Lasky movie studio in Astoria at 36th Street at 35th Avenue in 1920, and Paramount took over the site seven years later. Rudolph Valentino shot scenes from *The Sheik*, W. C. Fields, Lillian Gish, and Clara Bow made movies, and the Marx Brothers cavorted in *Cocoanuts* on those stages. When the motion picture industry moved to Hollywood, the studio went into eclipse. In 1942, Paramount sold it to the Army for $500,000, and during World War II it became one of the world's busiest motion-picture production centers.

The center was staffed by soldiers, many with backgrounds in the film industry. The director George Cukor made training films at Astoria and the future director Sidney Pollack was an assistant cameraman and film editor there.

For impact on the public consciousness, one Astoria film eclipsed all. Its title was *Diary of a Sergeant* and it was the prelude to an Oscar-winning Hollywood film.

Harold Russell, a Nova Scotia native who grew up in Cambridge, Massachusetts, working in a meat market, joined the Army soon after the Pearl Harbor attack. He was trained as a paratrooper and a specialist in explosives. On D-Day, Sergeant Russell was teaching demolition work at Camp Mackall in North Carolina when a block of TNT blew up. It severed both his hands and they were amputated a few inches above the wrists. He was fitted with metal hooks and began convalescing at the Walter Reed Army Medical Center in Washington.

The Army was planning a film showing how servicemen could overcome amputations and their psychological as well as physical consequences. It turned to Russell to become the focus of that movie. *Diary of a Sergeant* dramatized Russell's experiences from the time of his accident to his rehabilitation and finally his going home and entering college. It was shot without dialogue—the actor Alfred Drake provided narration—with the scenes improvised by Russell, who was remarkably agile in using his hooks. (As he would quip, "The only thing I can't pick up is a dinner check.")

After filming began at Walter Reed, the Army transferred Russell to Astoria where most of *Diary of a Sergeant* was shot under the supervision of Captain Julian Blaustein, a former Hollywood story-department executive, and his staff of servicemen with motion picture credentials.

"The point they wanted to make was that amputees had nothing to hide, or be ashamed of, that they could master their prosthetic devices and themselves, and lead sound, fruitful happy lives," Russell recalled. "Instead of being a dry, dead, training-film demonstration of how I handled my hooks, the picture was going to be a miniature drama with me as its hero."

Everything went just fine except for a scene when Russell was supposed to dance with his girlfriend at a bar. He happened to be a poor dancer, and after eight takes he was still stumbling around and being heckled by the director, Captain Joe Newman, a former MGM director. He finally stomped off the set in a rage. "Damn it captain, I'm a soldier, not an actor," he fumed.

But, as Russell remembered it: "Everyone burst out laughing, and when I began thinking about it I couldn't help laughing myself. Then I came back and played the scene the way I should have played it the first time."

Diary of a Sergeant was completed on New Year's Day 1945. Russell was discharged from the Army two days later and entered the Boston University business school. The film premiered at Walter Reed, and then, at the Treasury Department's request, Russell toured with it to spur war bond purchases.

Samuel Goldwyn had been hoping do a movie about the often searing transitions that faced returning servicemen: the travails of the grievously wounded and the emotionally scarred, and troubled reunions with wives and girlfriends.

When the motion-picture director William Wyler saw *Diary of a Sergeant* at a Hollywood bond rally, he knew he had his man for a central role in the movie he would make for Goldwyn telling of the returning veterans. Wyler cast Russell as Homer Parrish, a sailor who had lost his hands in the war, for the 1946 movie *The Best Years of Our Lives*. Believed to be the first person with a visible major disability to appear in a Hollywood film, Russell received an Oscar for best supporting actor and a special Oscar "for bringing aid and comfort to disabled veterans through the medium of motion pictures."

The Best Years of Our Lives got the Oscar for best film and Frederic March won for best actor. Russell went on to raise a family, served as national commander of the Amvets, American Veterans of World War II and Korea, and was the longtime chairman of the President's Committee for Employment of People with Disabilities. But in 1992, he auctioned off his Oscar for best supporting actor for $60,500 to pay family medical bills and retirement expenses. The Oscar for inspiring his fellow wounded veterans remained on the mantel of Russell's home in West Hyannisport, Massachusetts. He died at eighty-eight in 2002.

The Astoria center also turned out entertainment features for servicemen. The Hollywood actress Carole Landis starred in a bathing-beauty feature shot in a swimming pool below the basement level of the sound stages. Ruby Dee played the romantic lead in a movie for the predominately black transportation unit known as the Red Ball Express. Arturo Toscanini conducted for a film shot for the United Nations conference in San Francisco in April 1945.

Astoria became a center as well for training GIs to become movie cameramen and still photographers in combat assignments.

Ray Fisher grew up in Astoria, where his father was a photo finisher, and attended William Cullen Bryant High School. Fisher took photos as a young man, worked as a photo lab technician for NBC, and while stationed at an Army post in Wyoming wrote to the Signal Corps telling of his background and requesting a transfer to the Astoria center. In July 1944, he was back in his old neighborhood.

The Army gave Fisher and his fellow still-photographer trainees Speed Graphics for their four-week course, but the cameras lacked some of the up-to-date attachments—for a reason.

"There was no range finder so we had to guess distances," Fisher recalled. "The idea was that there would be no time in combat to set it. And we had to guess exposures; there were no exposure meters."

The students were sent on assignment in the New York area. "I'd take candid photographs on the subway," Fisher remembered. "I'd sit across from someone who wasn't looking at me, and shoot a picture."

Fisher volunteered once to help put together an outdoor exercise.

There was a mock invasion of Long Island to give experience for troops in training and also to give the students who would be movie combat photographers a chance to learn. They had Eyemos—hand-held motion picture cameras that were spring wound. It was 35 millimeter film, 100 feet to a roll. When they finished a roll, they put it in a can and started another roll. Since I wasn't shooting anything, they gave me a bunch of cans that I put inside my field jacket. A truck came along and someone said: "Who's got the film? We need it to bring back to the lab." I gave it to them. Afterward, the officer commanding my side in the "invasion"— Lieutenant Herb Rau—was looking for the film. I told him who I gave it to, and he said, "You idiot, that's the enemy."

When his classes ended at Astoria, Fisher became a combat still photographer in Europe. He was shot in the leg in an Austrian town three days before the war in Europe ended, but a medic saved his life. He went on to photograph the hanging of nine Nazi war criminals.

After the war, Fisher worked as a photographer for the *Miami Herald* and caught up with the former Lieutenant Rau of the Long Island invasion days. "He became the entertainment editor of the *Miami News*," Fisher recalled. "We used to laugh about it."

Being stationed in Astoria was certainly good duty, but the movie complex was an active Army base. Parts of the upper floors were converted into barracks with double-decker beds, each neatly covered by khaki blankets, though some of the trainees were housed at hotels in mid-Manhattan. Fisher lived at the Hotel Capitol on Eighth Avenue and was given subway passes for commuting to Astoria.

Calisthenics were held daily outside the barracks and "we did a lot of practice shooting in the back lot," recalled Robert Wandrey, one of the trainees. "But it was flooded and frozen for ice-skating during the winter."

When the facility opened in 1942, La Guardia was on hand for the very public ceremonies. But it seemed as if the D-Day invasion was being planned in Astoria from an instructional sheet put out for GIs training to become combat cameramen. If a trainee was approached by "curious civilians" while on a photography assignment in the New York metropolitan area, "he should not answer where he is stationed nor give out any information about the post."

The Army also had a list of "Forbidden Subjects." Students were "not allowed to take pictures of the following":

1. Drunks.
2. Cheesecake (leg art) women in poses unmilitary.
3. Clowning by members of the crew.
4. Any picture that would bring discredit to the Signal Corps or Army in general.

A Hollywood professional who wound up in uniform at Astoria might not take so kindly to cinematic directives from someone whose only "qualifications" were the gold bars on his uniform. Stanley Cortez, a leading cinematographer, who received an Academy Award nomination in 1942 for his work in *The Magnificent Ambersons*, was a private at Astoria. When his commanding officers came to him with a simple request, he engaged in a bit of passive resistance, as Gerald Hirschfeld, a still photographer in New York turned Astoria GI, would remember.

"He had no love for the men heading the camera department. One day, Stanley was called into our captain's office, and the conversation went something like this:

" 'Stanley, we'd like you to teach a lighting class for the new recruits.'

" 'Sir, I don't think I can do that.'

" 'Come on now, Stanley, you'd be doing a great service for the Army. Your reputation will impress these men.'

" 'I'm sorry, but I must refuse.'

" 'Private Cortez, this is an order. You will teach a lighting class, starting tomorrow.'

"The next morning, Stanley appeared at a lower-level stage and saw about fifty young recruits seated and waiting for his class. Standing in the rear were the captain and the lieutenant. Stanley instantly knew that they were there only so they themselves could learn something about lighting from an expert. They didn't really care about the recruits who were going overseas to shoot news footage.

"Smiling broadly and walking tall, Stanley took center stage. 'It might be best to get right to the heart of the subject by answering your direct questions.'

"A hand went up and Stanley nodded to a recruit who asked, 'Will you tell us the main difference between high-key and low-key lighting?'

" 'Ah, a good question. Well, in high-key lighting you raise the main, or key, light as high as you can, and in low-key lighting you keep it low, near the floor sometimes.'

"The teaching lesson was immediately canceled."

On another occasion, Cortez, shooting a black-and-white film, attached red and green gels to the lights on each side of the camera.

"Stan, I don't understand what the colored fill lights are doing," Hirschfeld wondered.

Cortez replied: "Jerry, they're not doing a damn thing to the picture."

Then, as Hirschfeld recalled it: "He gestured to two officers standing in the background. 'Those nosy bastards over there can't figure it out either and they're too stupid to ask.'"

PART FOUR

THE STAGE

CHAPTER 15

VOICES OF DEMOCRACY

It was the little war that made headlines: the Soviet Union's invasion of Finland in the winter of 1939–40. The Finns' courageous but doomed resistance was a prelude to the overrunning of the democracies of Europe. It also provided the inspiration for Broadway's first important play addressing an impending world war.

Robert Sherwood's *There Shall Be No Night*, telling of the stand taken by a cultured Finnish doctor and his son at the cost of their lives, illuminated the stakes for an America stymied by the isolationist movement and loath to stand up to tyranny.

Caught in the battle between the isolationists and the growing sentiment to aid Britain, *There Shall Be No Night* proved highly controversial. But it received the Pulitzer Prize for drama in 1941, and in its wake Lillian Hellman, Maxwell Anderson, and John Steinbeck brought their voices to Broadway in reflecting on the struggle between democracy and fascism.

A product of New York's Westchester suburbs and the son of an investment banker, Sherwood began his literary journey as editor of the *Harvard Lampoon*. He tried to join the Army during World War I but was turned down because he was too tall, at six feet seven inches. He enlisted instead in Canada's Black Watch and was wounded and gassed in France.

By the late 1930s, Sherwood had become an acclaimed figure on Broadway. His play *The Petrified Forest* (1935), bringing Humphrey Bogart to prominence, enjoyed an extended run, and he received Pulitzer Prizes for *Idiot's Delight* (1936), an antiwar play, and *Abe Lincoln in Illinois* (1938).

Although apprehensive over America entering another world war, Sherwood grew increasingly alarmed by the late 1930s. He feared being viewed as a "warmonger," but deplored what he saw as America's equivocal attitude toward the Russo-Finnish conflict. In his preface to the published *There Shall Be No Night*, he wrote that "abject fear" seemed to be at work, and if that were the case, "we had already been conquered by the masters of the slave States, and we must surrender our birthright." He described his play as a protest against the "hysterical escapism" that dominated American thinking and "pointed our foreign policy toward suicidal isolationism," despite all of Roosevelt's warnings.

The Finns had been crushed by the Russians by the time *There Shall Be No Night* opened on Broadway on April 29, 1940. The Germans had invaded Norway and Denmark in early April and they would overrun the Netherlands and Belgium in May. France would fall in June. The Russo-Finnish War may have been a thing of the past for America, but with Europe falling into Hitler's hands, the play's sentiments proved timely.

As Brooks Atkinson, the drama critic of the *Times*, saw it, Sherwood's play "fixes the price everyone must pay for living like a human being."

Its central character, played by Alfred Lunt, who also directed, is Dr. Kaarlo Valkonen, a Finnish neurologist who has just won the Nobel Prize for medical research. His wife, Miranda, portrayed by Lunt's wife and longtime dramatic partner Lynn Fontanne, is American, and they have a son, Erik, of military age, played by Montgomery Clift.

Dr. Valkonen doesn't believe in war and sees no point in Finland's resisting Russia. But when his young son joins the ski troops in the north to fight the Russians, he closes his laboratory and joins the Finnish army's medical service.

Sherwood believed that a passage spoken by the Valkonens' future daughter-in-law, Kaatri, just before Erik goes off to war was the kernel of his message.

Miranda: "I understand one thing, Kaatri. Erik is my son. I want to save his life."
Kaatri: "What good is his life if it has to be spent in slavery?"
(To Erik) "And that's what it would be if he gave in to them. Slavery for us—for all of us. Oh, I know that you Americans don't like to think of such terrible things."

In his review for the *New Yorker*, Wolcott Gibbs wrote of Lunt's "nearly interminable monologues" in a "lush and incendiary manner" that "brings the action to a standstill." But he cited Sherwood's "writing with tremendous sincerity, burning indignation and occasional high eloquence."

Sherwood pursued his convictions beyond the theater. He became a charter member of the Committee to Defend America by Aiding the Allies, wrote newspaper advertisements stating the case for aiding Britain, and contributed $25,000 to have them printed.

There Shall Be No Night went on a national tour in November 1940 after 179 performances. It was to continue that run, after a summer break, until February 1942, then reopen on Broadway. But Hitler's invasion of the Soviet Union in June 1941 put a very different light on matters. The Russians, portrayed as unprincipled aggressors in *There Shall Be No Night*, had become an American ally, and Finland had become an ally of Germany. Sherwood asked that the tour end in mid-December 1941.

Sherwood went on to serve as overseas director of the federal Office of War Information. Lunt and Fontanne did not forsake *There Shall Be No Night* with the conclusion of its national tour. Lunt had spent a summer with family members in Finland when he was a youngster, and Fontanne was British-born. While the interventionist-isolationist arguments were still raging, the Lunts had contributed to Finnish War Relief and worked as volunteers for Bundles for Britain. By springtime 1942 they were devoting many hours to the Stage Door Canteen, but they grew determined to spend the rest of the war in Britain.

They arrived in London in October 1943, became air-raid wardens, then starred in the British production of *There Shall Be No Night* at the Aldwych Theatre where the play was revised to tell of the Nazi invasion of Greece. (The Lunts later took their new play *Love in Idleness* to the Continent, entertaining troops for the USO's Foxhole Circuit.)

One night, the Aldwych came under a German buzz-bomb attack during a performance of *There Shall Be No Night*. The audience remained rapt, and the show went on. With the theater still shaking from explosions, Lunt delivered a speech in the final scene that Sherwood had written more than three years earlier. But its sentiment perfectly caught the moment. "Listen," Lunt said:

> What you hear now—this terrible sound that fills the earth—it is the death rattle. One may say easily and dramatically that it is the death rattle of civilization. But—I choose to believe differently. I believe it is the long deferred death rattle of the primordial beast. We have within ourselves the power to conquer bestiality, not with our muscles and our swords, but with the power of the light that is in our minds.

The issue of comfortable America's complacency in the face of fascism was addressed anew in April 1941, nearly a year after the opening of *There Shall Be No Night*, when Lillian Hellman brought *Watch on the Rhine* to Broadway

Born in New Orleans, in a family of prosperous merchants of German-Jewish background on her mother's side, Hellman had arrived in New York with her family as a youngster when her father suffered business reverses.

She shuttled between Manhattan's Upper West Side and a New Orleans boardinghouse kept by two aunts, then attended New York University. She read manuscripts for a publishing house, was married briefly to the writer Arthur Kobler, then met Dashiell Hammett, whom she would live with intermittently for three decades, becoming the inspiration for Nora in Hammett's *The Thin Man*.

Hellman found success on Broadway in 1934 with *The Children's Hour*, the story of a vicious girl who destroys the lives of two teachers by accusing them of a lesbian affair, a reflection, Hellman said, of the evil power of a slander. Then came *The Little Foxes*, a play about a southern family obsessed with money and power, the outgrowth of her resentment against her mother's family.

Hellman went to Spain in the late 1930s, helped develop the Joris Ivens anti-Franco film *The Spanish Earth*, then returned to speak out for the Loyalists fighting Franco, seeing that conflict as foreshadowing the coming confrontation with the Nazis.

By springtime of 1941, with Hitler supreme in Europe, the forces of isolationism in America might be on the defensive, but they were hardly beaten. Hellman had been devoted to leftist causes and she believed that Soviet communism was showing the way toward a more just world. But in writing *Watch on the Rhine*, she stood against the Communist Party line in the United States that called for support of the nonaggression pact signed by Hitler and Stalin. Her extensive research on fascism in Europe strengthened her view that she must speak out against it.

The play voiced Hellman's conviction that many good people still failed to understand the need to confront barbarism in Europe. By bringing the conflict into the confines of a soft home in America, she spoke of the imperatives of meeting Nazism with force, and the requirement to sacrifice, even at the cost of one's own life.

Watch on the Rhine centers on Kurt Muller, played by Paul Lukas, the Hungarian who came to the role as a familiar mustachioed villain in the movies. Muller is a leader in the anti-Nazi underground who brings his American wife, Sara (Mady Christians), and their three children to the Washington area country house of his mother-in-law in 1940. After years of being on the run, he is eager to leave his family in this peaceful setting before he returns to Germany to fight on against Hitler and face almost certain death. But even here he encounters European depravity. A destitute Romanian count who is a houseguest learns of Muller's underground work and seeks a payoff from him under the threat of betraying him to the German Embassy in Washington. Muller ultimately kills the man and then goes back to Germany alone to plot anew against the Nazis.

Produced and directed by Herman Shumlin, *Watch on the Rhine,* its title taken from a German soldier song, was voted the best play of the 1940–41 season by the Drama Critics Circle. Its cast gave a command performance for Roosevelt at the National Theatre in Washington in January 1942.

Hellman received outstanding notices for her rich characterization, and in her review for *Theatre Arts,* Rosamond Gilder praised Paul Lukas for portraying Kurt Muller's complexity.

"He succeeds in conveying throughout a sense of Kurt's anguish and preoccupation, the fear that haunts him, his desolation at the necessity of going back into a way of life against which his whole soul cries out."

Watch on the Rhine ran on Broadway for 378 performances. The movie version opened in August 1943 at the Strand in Manhattan, the screenplay written by Hammett, Lukas reprising his role as Muller, and Bette Davis replacing Mady Christians as Muller's wife.

In April 1944, Hellman took aim at the prewar appeasers with *The Searching Wind,* the title coming from something a maid who worked for her once said.

"Some mornings when she came, she'd say, 'It's a searching wind today.' She meant one of those winds that go right through to your backbone. I suppose in my title I was thinking of the wind that's blowing through the world."

The Searching Wind begins in wartime Washington at the home of a former American ambassador, then flashes back to Mussolini's march on Rome in 1922, the persecution of the Jews in prewar Berlin, and finally Paris on the eve of the Munich Conference, which came to symbolize appeasement. The former diplomat, Alex Hazen, played by Dennis King, had been stationed in Italy, Germany, and France, and each time failed to confront the rise of fascism. The fruit of his dithering arrives in a very personal way when his soldier son, portrayed by Montgomery Clift, comes home after being grievously wounded at Anzio.

A romantic current is enmeshed with the larger political theme. The ambassador is married to a wealthy, socially ambitious woman (Cornelia Otis Skinner) who is devoid of political ideals, and he also has a longtime girlfriend (Barbara O'Neil) who is highly political and antifascist. In his love life, as in his diplomatic career, Alex Hazen never makes a firm commitment.

The *New York Daily News* praised *The Searching Wind* as a "strong and measured indictment of appeasers who eventually caused WWII" and the *New York World-Telegram* cited Hellman as a "master craftsman." But Hammett, reading the screenplay shortly before the opening, told Hellman "it doesn't seem to me that you make your point," and he worried that the romantic subplot tended to overshadow the historical arguments.

The Searching Wind ran for 318 performances and fell only one vote short of winning the Drama Critics Circle award for 1944 (no award was given for that year), but it didn't match the acclaim accorded to *Watch on the Rhine*.

Like Robert Sherwood's *There Shall Be No Night,* John Steinbeck's *The Moon Is Down,* opening in April 1942, employed Scandinavia as a locale to write of the yearning to remain free in the face of oppression.

Acclaimed for his portrayal of the Depression's Dust Bowl Okies in his Pulitzer Prize–winning *The Grapes of Wrath,* Steinbeck now told of the people in a small Norwegian mining town occupied by the Germans, who have been abetted by a local traitor. (The setting is clear, though not specifically identified.) The colonel in charge of the occupation (Otto Kruger) goes about his duties with the ruthlessness expected of him, but he knows that terror will only increase the townspeople's resistance and ultimately bring about the invaders' downfall.

Steinbeck's belief that the quest for freedom would ultimately prevail and his attribution of a certain amount of sensitivity in the German colonel became matters of much controversy.

The critics' arguments that sank the play were reflected by Clifton Fadiman, who called *The Moon Is Down* a "melodramatic simplification" in his *New Yorker* review of the Steinbeck novel upon which it was based.

> The simplification is based on the notion that in the end good will triumph because it is good and evil will fail because it is evil. Once we get interested in winning the war for our remote posterity, it is half lost. Why not win it for ourselves? And if we are to win for ourselves, we will, I fear, hardly be helped by the noble message in "The Moon Is Down" and in dozens of similar works full of high intentions; we can be helped only by the blood, toil, tears and sweat of which Mr. Churchill has spoken. We no longer need to be told we are in the right, for we know it. We wish to be told only how we may make that right prevail.

The Moon Is Down was made into a movie in 1943, but the play had closed after only fifty-five performances at the Martin Beck Theatre. Ticket sales "withered under the repeated blasting" of critics, said its producer, Oscar Serlin.

The misery of the World War I battlefronts had been memorably portrayed in the Maxwell Anderson–Laurence Stallings 1920s play *What Price Glory?* Its success enabled Anderson, a New York newspaperman, to turn to playwriting full-time, and he received a Pulitzer Prize for *Both Your Houses* (1933) and the New York Drama Critics Circle awards for *Winterset* (1935) and *High Tor* (1937).

Anderson brought his voice to bear on the Second World War with *Candle in the Wind* and *The Eve of St. Mark*.

Candle in the Wind, opening in October 1941, told of a French journalist and naval officer (Louis Borell) who is thrown into a German-run concentration camp outside Paris. His lover, portrayed by Helen Hayes, tries all manner of strategy to get him out. The play, directed by Alfred Lunt, depicts the savagery and utter immorality of the Nazis, but it didn't quite measure up as theater. Nazi depravity was hardly a matter for debate, and, as Brooks Atkinson put it in the *Times*: "Although Mr. Anderson's moral convictions are passionate, his regard for his characters is a little platonic. The candle he has lighted does not burn for them." The play went on tour after only ninety-five performances on Broadway.

The Eve of St. Mark, which arrived on Broadway in October 1942, follows a presumably typical American farm boy from the barracks horseplay of pre-Pearl Harbor training camp to his combat death in the Philippines. The soldier, Private Quizz West (William Prince), his parents, and his girlfriend have no romantic illusions about war. Soldiers have a miserable job to do, but they persevere because the job has to get done.

To get a sense of Army life while writing *The Eve of St. Mark*, Anderson visited Fort Bragg, North Carolina, where he met Marion Hargrove, assigned to the post's public relations office after surviving basic training as a befuddled draftee. Hargrove introduced Anderson to his fellow GIs and showed him columns on his Army misadventures that he wrote for the *Charlotte News*, where he had worked as features editor. Anderson passed the pieces on to the New York publishing house Henry Holt and wrote a foreword to them. *See Here, Private Hargrove* became a No. one best-seller of 1942.

The Eve of St. Mark received generally good reviews and it ran on Broadway for eight and a half months.

The war resonated on Broadway indirectly through the voicing of American ideals and a reprising of great historical moments.

Sidney Kingsley's *The Patriots* told of America's Founding Fathers.

I wrote that play at a time when it looked as though this nation, this democracy, might very well be destroyed. Hitler was marching. Nothing was stopping him. Mussolini had thrown in with him. And then the Soviet Union signed a pact with him. The three of them looked as though they were unbeatable. I thought to myself, "I am just going into the Army. What is this country which I might be called upon to die for?" Eventually it became a play about Jefferson and Washington and Hamilton struggling to make a new world. One thing that the research made clear to me is that this is a continuing and unending struggle.

The role of Thomas Jefferson went to Raymond Edward Johnson, who was making his Broadway debut while spending his Sunday nights as "Raymond," the ghoulish host who turned the creaking door opening episodes of radio's long-running *Inner Sanctum*. Cecil Humphreys played George Washington and House Jameson portrayed Alexander Hamilton. Judson Laire, who would go on to play the Scandinavian papa opposite Peggy Wood in the TV series adapting John Van Druten's *I Remember Mama*, was James Monroe.

Kingsley was an Army sergeant, assigned to an entertainment unit, when *The Patriots* opened on Broadway in January 1943. After going on tour, it arrived in December for a one-week run at the new City Center on Manhattan's West 55th Street, having received the Drama Critics Circle award as the previous season's best play.

La Guardia, always a lover of the arts, had engineered the conversion of the old Mecca Temple into the City Center performing arts auditorium where working-class people could enjoy drama and musical productions at prices below those at the traditional Broadway houses. The City Center had opened earlier in December with a one-week revival of *Susan and God* with Gertrude Lawrence, the tickets priced at $1.65 and below.

The Voice of the Turtle, by the British-born Van Druten, proved the most successful of the romantic comedies touching on the war. Opening in December 1943, it ran for 1,557 performances, closing in January 1948. Taking its title from the biblical reference to spring's arrival when "the voice of the turtle is heard in the land" (the allusion was actually to a turtledove), it told of a young actress from Missouri (Margaret Sullavan) who unexpectedly spends a weekend at her Manhattan apartment with an Army sergeant on a brief furlough (Elliott Nugent). Her decision to sleep with him challenged the more conventional aspects of social morality in America, but wartime was changing the attitude toward fleeting romance.

As Van Druten told it:

The Voice of the Turtle, written and produced during the war, was timed to an audience exactly in the mood to receive it, and I had astonishingly few letters objecting to its morality. In England, a few years later, it met with an audience in a totally different frame of mind. The sense of romance that the war had given the story had disappeared. The appeal was no longer there.

When *Tomorrow the World*, by James Gow and Arnaud d'Usseau, opened in April 1943, D-Day was more than a year away. But the playwrights looked toward the postwar world, asking how German children indoctrinated with Nazism could be taught democratic and humanitarian ideals. Telling of a brainwashed twelve-year-old German boy who remains a stalwart little Nazi even after he is taken to the home of a midwestern professor (Ralph Bellamy) when his anti-Nazi parents die in a concentration camp, it sees patience and kindness as the answer. But Skippy Homeier played the youngster with such malevolence that Lewis Nichols of the *Times* suggested "an audience could see him strangled without a qualm."

Skippy had been working in radio since age nine, appearing on soap operas and Eddie Cantor's programs. Affecting a German accent wasn't too hard for him since he had grown adept at mastering the accents of fellow radio actors. But he memorized his lines under less than optimum conditions at his family's apartment on Continental Avenue in the Forest Hills section of Queens. During the day, he had a tutor. In the evenings, he sometimes wrestled with the dimout and periodic blackouts.

"I learned my part with a flashlight sitting in a closed closet in my home," he recalled. "Everybody was afraid of any light leaks. We were all good citizens and really battening down the hatches."

Tomorrow the World, as he remembered it, "was an extremely electric experience for most audience members. People would come to the dressing room afterward and be emotionally drained."

But when he was away from the theater, Skippy found no pleasure in being a celebrity.

Recognized is not the word. Notorious, I guess, is. I came from a strict Roman Catholic family and it was difficult taking heat as a twelve-year-old from people on the street who would give me static for being a Nazi, which was about as far from my upbringing as you could throw a rock. People don't realize sometimes that the comments they make at a child can be rather cruel, especially when they identify you as an individual with the part that you play.

Tomorrow the World was made as a movie in 1944 with Frederic March replacing Bellamy while Skippy reprised his role. Shortening his decidedly juvenile nickname to Skip or using G.V. (for his given names, George Vincent), Homeier later appeared in many Hollywood movies and he was featured in the 1970s TV series *The Interns*.

Paul Osborn's *A Bell for Adano*, the 1944 Broadway adaptation of John Hersey's novel, also pointed toward the remaking of Europe. It featured Frederic March as Major Victor Joppolo, the American civil affairs officer in the Italian town of Adano, who battles the dictates and insensitivity of the occupying military brass as he seeks to replace fascism with democratic ways.

La Guardia fashioned himself as a more exalted Joppolo, having sought, with no success, to be given a major role in Italy's rehabilitation. But another New Yorker was chosen to help Italy recover. Charles Poletti, who served as governor of New York in the final weeks of 1942, moving up from the lieutenant governor's post when Herbert Lehman was named to oversee relief efforts in Europe, entered the Army and became a popular figure in the reconstruction of Italy with the rank of lieutenant colonel. La Guardia's headquarters remained at City Hall.

CHAPTER 16

HEARTS AT THE STAGE DOOR CANTEEN

Katharine Cornell cleaned tables, Hume Cronyn checked coats, and Alfred Lunt, a master chef, not only cooked but took out the trash. They were among the biggest stars on Broadway, and they were indeed toiling in the heart of the theater district. But their names weren't on a marquee this time. Their nightly calling came at a landmark of wartime New York: the Stage Door Canteen.

As the actress Paula Laurence put it long afterward, the theater people gave their best in activities that were "wondrously therapeutic in relieving the guilt we all suffered because our lives were comparatively undisturbed; we weren't flying bombers or being shipped to crematoriums."

Opening on March 2, 1942, in the basement of the Forty-fourth Street Theatre, the Stage Door Canteen played host to an average of 3,000 Allied servicemen (but no servicewomen) seven evenings a week, between 6 o'clock and midnight. It was a gathering spot for free world-class entertainment, food and (non-alcoholic) drink, and, probably most important for a lonely GI, sailor, or marine, the company of a young woman for a dance and a sympathetic shoulder. And while the canteen bands played "Goodnight, Sweetheart" as the last number each night, that wasn't necessarily a finale. It was against the canteen rules, but a dance with a junior hostess sometimes led to a date.

By war's end, the New York canteen had inspired similar night spots in eight other American cities and in London and Paris as well as a weekly radio program, a Hollywood movie, and Irving Berlin's "I Left My Heart at the Stage Door Canteen."

The canteen was the best-remembered and most popular project of the American Theatre Wing, the service organization that became Broadway's prime avenue for supporting the war effort.

On the eve of America's entry into World War I, prominent Broadway actresses formed the Stage Women's War Relief, which opened a canteen for servicemen, arranged entertainment for troops, sold almost $7 million in war bonds, and collected clothing for the people of Europe.

Soon after Germany's invasion of Poland brought war to Europe again in September 1939, the actress Rachel Crothers, who had helped created the World War I theatrical relief unit, revived it as the Allied Relief Fund. It merged with the British War Relief Society and aided European refugees as well.

When America went to war, the agency dropped its affiliation with Britain and became the American Theatre Wing War Service. Crothers was named president, the Broadway actress and director Antoinette Perry (later honored through the Tony awards) became the chairman and treasurer, and Gertrude Lawrence and Helen Hayes were vice presidents. A men's executive committee included the playwright George S. Kaufman, the producers Lee Shubert, Brock Pemberton, and Billy Rose, and the *Times* drama critic Brooks Atkinson.

The wing refurbished a former basement speakeasy, the Little Club, for the canteen's use. Shubert, who owned the space, loaned it out. Irving Berlin donated a piano. The scenic artists Jo Mielziner and Raoul Pene du Bois painted murals. Union carpenters and electricians who worked on Broadway helped out free of charge. The actresses Jane Cowl and Selena Royle oversaw the daily operations.

The movie *Stage Door Canteen*, its cast including Broadway and Hollywood personalities, raised more than $1 million to help run things. Restaurants and caterers donated food. Radio station WMCA asked studio audiences to donate nonperishable goods. For a $100 contribution, an "angel's table" could be reserved by five civilians for a single night.

Antoinette Perry contributed financing for the theater wing from an unlikely source. As her daughter Margaret told it: "The seed money for many a wing activity or show investment came from my mother's track winnings. Even during wing board meetings, mother played the horses. She'd have her secretary tiptoe in to give her the odds, then place a wager with a bookie."

The canteen was jammed on opening night when Gertrude Lawrence and the cast of *Lady in the Dark* performed numbers from the show. Walter Pidgeon and Tallulah Bankhead turned up, and a conga line wound through the room. One night, Judy Garland and Johnny Mercer dropped by and sang some of Mercer's tunes. Count Basie and Benny Goodman brought their bands, Ethel Merman belted out numbers.

Alfred Lunt and Lynn Fontanne were famously devoted to the canteen, with Alexander Wolcott calling Lunt "the chief cook and bottle washer of the American Theatre Wing." As for Lunt's insistence on emptying garbage cans, in part his way of learning whether the menus should be changed, Katharine Cornell observed that "he's the only man who succeeded in putting glamour into garbage." Lunt, passionate about his calling as an amateur chef, conducted cooking classes for Theatre Wing members at its Fifth Avenue offices—six lessons for ten dollars—for the canteen's benefit.

The Army put on a canteen revue by the theatrical section at Fort Hamilton, Brooklyn, its *General Disorders of 1943* starring Sergeant Bert Parks, better known in the postwar years for "There she is, Miss America." His canteen routines included "The Six Little Goldbricks" and "Thru Channels," telling of the red tape encountered by a private trying to get a new shoestring for the one he had broken running through a commando course.

But no one could top a Coast Guardsman named Frank Piro so far as servicemen entertaining their own at the canteen. Growing up in East Harlem, the son of an Italian-born tailor, Piro was "skinny and ugly," as he told it. To meet girls, he took up dancing at a neighborhood social club called the Green Robins. He dropped out of school at fifteen to help his family, working in construction and plastics, but he continued to dance, winning $20 prizes at the Savoy Ballroom in Harlem. In 1942, he became the first white dancer to win the national jitterbug championship at the Harvest Moon Ball. And then his sinewy frame discovered the Stage Door Canteen. He danced there with Judy Garland and Shirley Booth and with the junior hostesses, his energy knowing no bounds. Early in 1944, he shipped out to man a Coast Guard craft ferrying troops and supplies in the South Pacific. By then he had driven countless young women into exhaustion on the dance floor, bringing him the sobriquet Killer Joe.

For many servicemen, the canteen simply represented a break from anonymity, from wandering through Times Square looking for something to do, someone to talk to. A senior hostess named Christie McDonald told of telling a first-time visitor, "I'm very glad to see you here." The reply: "Really? Will you shake hands with me? I'm from the midwest and I've been in New York for two days. This is the first time since I arrived that anyone seemed glad to see me."

In a letter to the staff, an Army private named Herbert Chersin told how he had been "lonely, wandering" along "a dimmed out Broadway" when he saw the lamp outside the canteen. A hostess beckoned him to sit with her. "I talked. I laughed," he recalled. "And my heart cried, its tears flooding and washing away the unpleasantness and tenseness within me."

Landon Chambliss, a serviceman who had visited the canteen before going overseas, reflected on those evenings while recuperating from broken bones at a hospital at Camp Reynolds, Pennsylvania.

I am writing lying flat on my back with my leg in a cast suspended from mid-air, but I am happy although I miss the canteen a lot. I was there every night I was in New York. The whole time I was in Casablanca I never saw a girl. But I saw my buddies go down one after another, shot down in cold blood. They didn't have a chance and there are only six of us left. I will never forget you.

The junior hostesses who provided a moment's closeness took satisfaction from building servicemen's morale. But some envisioned the Stage Door Canteen as launching a show-business career. Perhaps being so close to the stars of the stage, screen, and radio would lead to an introduction and an audition.

Their ranks included Lauren Bacall, a model and aspiring actress from Flatbush. In the fall of 1940, she had begun studying at the American Academy of Dramatic Arts, next to Carnegie Hall, but she dropped out after a year when she could no longer afford the tuition. She modeled sportswear in the garment district, but her boss fired her. She was too thin and flat-chested. In the summer of 1941, at age sixteen, she had an unsuccessful audition for George Abbott's *Best Foot Forward*, then worked as an usher at Broadway shows. While making the tryout rounds, she ate cream cheese on nut-bread sandwiches at Chock Full O' Nuts.

When the Stage Door Canteen opened, she signed up as a hostess for Monday nights. "I was to dance with any soldier, sailor or marine who asked me—get drinks or coffee for them, listen to their stories," she recalled. "Many of them had girls at home—were homesick—would transfer their affections to one of us out of loneliness and need. It was really very sweet and sad and fun, a natural set-up for a dreamer."

Sometimes she was in the middle of a circle, being whirled by a GI, then passed on to another one "until I thought I would drop."

Amidst the frenzy, the loneliness of her dance partners was palpable. "I overdramatized every situation for myself. A young sailor took a fancy to me—I think I reminded him of his girl. He came in every Monday night for weeks, then one night he told me he was going to sea—didn't know where, of course. He was charming and very homesick. He asked if he could write to me. 'Certainly,' I said, 'I'll let you know what's going on back here.' I didn't know what to say to him—war was a fiction to me, not a reality."

Some of the servicemen were shy and a bit tongue-tied. Mildred Dobin, a junior hostess who was otherwise a John Robert Powers model, told of one GI who walked up to her and said: "Please, miss, the girls here overwhelm me. They're all so pretty. But you're not. Will you dance with me?"

She did.

For some soldiers and sailors, the canteen brought more than a dance and a chat.

Bob Gallagher, an Army corporal at Camp Shanks, New York, awaiting shipment overseas, headed to the canteen the first time he got a pass. Rumor had it that the hostesses were showgirls from Broadway productions. He found that to be something of an exaggeration but he asked one of them, whom he considered pretty enough to be a showgirl, to dance.

"After introductions, the first thing she asked was, 'Did you see the movie *Stage Door Canteen*?' I told her 'yes' and the next thing she said was, 'Wasn't that silly when they said the hostesses here can't date the servicemen?' I took the hint immediately, and we met that evening and every night while I was in the New York area."

The young woman, it developed, was working in a department store while hoping to break into show business. She fixed up some of Gallagher's pals with her friends, and they all had a fine time sampling New York's nightlife. "When our money ran out, they paid some of the expenses," Gallagher remembered.

Servicemen at the canteen were evidently well behaved, but merchant seamen, admitted there early on even though they weren't members of the armed forces, proved a rowdy bunch. Tom Rutherford, a member of the canteen's executive committee, reported to it on how "the junior hostesses have complained bitterly about their language and behavior." The seamen eventually got their own service center in New York, and they were barred from the canteen.

The admission of women serving in the military might have toned the crudity down, but the American Theatre Wing, citing space considerations and wishing to focus on men who were headed to or returning from combat, kept the women out. The wing instead sponsored a weekly Sunday afternoon tea and dance at the Roosevelt Hotel, where men and women in the armed forces could meet.

The issue of making black servicemen feel comfortable arose at meetings of the canteen board. Black women were sought out as hostesses, the prospect of interracial dancing something the canteen's board preferred not to contemplate.

On July 30, 1945, the canteen vacated its basement, located behind the main entrance to the *New York Times* offices, to allow for an addition to the *Times* plant. It moved to the Crystal Room of the Hotel Diplomat, two blocks away, and did it with a flourish, La Guardia leading a parade with cast members from Broadway shows trailing him, carrying the pots and pans.

The strains of "Goodnight, Sweetheart" were heard for the last time on the evening of October 29, 1945. Unable to extend its lease at the hotel, the canteen closed for good, having entertained 3.25 million servicemen over the previous three years and eight months.

On the final night, the cast of *Carousel* and Duke Ellington's band were on hand. But a more personal performance highlighted the finale: June Havoc serenaded the Brooklyn-born Marine air ace Kenneth Walsh, a recipient of the Medal of Honor.

CHAPTER 17

LUNCHTIME FOLLIES

The American Theatre Wing's Stage Door Canteen may be long gone, but passersby on the south side of West 44th Street will occasionally notice a bronze plaque next to the Starlight Deli, at the back of the former *New York Times* building. It was dedicated in 1950 at the canteen's site in honor of "the men and women of the entertainment world who brought cheer and comfort to the soldiers, sailors and Marines of America and her Allies."

As beloved as that smoke-filled, boisterous room below the Forty-fourth Street Theatre had been, the wing and the USO entertained servicemen far beyond its stage.

The wing arranged for shows at more than two dozen military hospitals in the New York area, and its speakers exhorted New Yorkers to buy war bonds. And when the whistles blew for meal breaks at New York's war plants and shipyards, their gritty workshops and smokestacks provided a backdrop for a slice of Broadway—the Lunchtime Follies.

Soon after the Pearl Harbor attack, the playwright Moss Hart, the producers Kermit Bloomgarden and George Weller, and the actress Aline MacMahon spurred creation of the follies, a variation on Britain's Entertainments National Service Association, known as ENSA.

The first presentation came at the Todd Shipyards in Brooklyn in June 1942. Some 150 performers were soon on call at metropolitan-area war plants every day, the headline names working without a fee, the lesser entertainers receiving perhaps $10 a day. Settling for makeshift stages, their audiences sitting on benches, scaffolding, and cranes, eating sandwiches, the troupes sometimes gave three performances at a single plant in a twenty-four-hour period—at noon, 4 p.m., and 4 a.m.

A typical follies entourage showed up one day in August 1943 at a large New York shipyard, left unidentified in a reporter's description of the day in deference to wartime security, but probably the Brooklyn Navy Yard.

At noon, with a few thousand workers filling an open area around the stage, a quartet featuring Howard Da Silva of *Oklahoma!* recited a sketch by Norman Rosten telling the story of the submarine commander Howard Gilmore, who gave his life to save his crew during a Japanese attack in the South Pacific, earning him the Medal of Honor. Da Silva concluded with the admonition: "Give us the ships and subs as strong as the skipper was and we'll finish Commander Gilmore's battle. That's a promise."

The workers shouted and whistled their applause.

The show ended with a satire on dictators titled "He Got His" featuring chorus girls dressed in fishnets. As one of the girls ran up the wooden steps to the stage, she whispered to a reporter, "This old sex always gets 'em."

The Lunchtime Follies became a part of wartime pop culture. One issue of a Black Terror comic book, depicting its hero in hand-to-hand combat with Nazi saboteurs at a war plant, showed scantily-clad chorus girls cavorting on a truck bed used as a stage in the background. A banner below the stage read "Lunchtime Follies."

When the workmen weren't ogling the chorus girls, they were laughing at lines by Milton Berle or George Jessel. But the follies went beyond bucking up worker morale through light entertainment. At the urging of the national War Production Board and industrial leaders, the follies sought to indoctrinate war-plant workers to keep the ships, planes, and tanks rolling off the lines.

A musical number called "On Time," written by Harold Rome and sung by Patti Ryan, employed sexually suggestive lyrics to confront absenteeism: "The man who stays home and lets his pals down/Won't get in my plant to turn my wheels around."

Follies routines also implored workers to avoid on-the-job accidents. The tune "Sloppy Joe" depicted a "flippy, floppy, mopey, dopey" production-line worker forever dropping tools and injuring his co-workers.

Some of the follies sketches paid tribute to the proverbial Rosie the Riveter. Harold Rome's *Solid, Solid, Suzabelle* told of a woman who put aside her everyday concerns to work in a war plant. "She Rolled Up Her Sleeves, She Hitched up her Hose" featured a six-woman chorus line in short skirts high-kicking Rockettes style, underscoring the government's campaign to convince women they would not be compromising their femininity by working on an assembly line.

Rosie the Riveter, her kerchiefed profile gracing magazines, newspapers, and billboards, became a signature image of the Women in War Jobs campaign created through the War Advertising Council, a public service unit mobilized by New York's advertising agencies. The council, chaired in the war's early years by Chester LaRoche, chairman of Young & Rubicam, joined Madison Avenue with newspaper, magazine, and radio advertising people to turn out messages for the government. It created "Smokey

Bear" to warn against carelessly setting off forest fires and "Loose Lips Sink Ships" posters imploring Americans to be security conscious. Its "Buy War Bonds" signs were everywhere.

George S. Kaufman and Moss Hart wrote skits focusing not on the day-to-day problems in war-plant production, like absenteeism and carelessness, but on the larger themes of patriotism and support for the war effort.

Their *Fun to Be Free*, an abbreviated adaptation of a 1940 patriotic pageant written by Ben Hecht and Charles MacArthur, presented vignettes from moments in American history when freedom had been imperiled. "The Man Who Went to Moscow" lampooned Hitler, in the person of the comedian David Burns, who turned up in a military jacket, armband swastika, and fake moustache. The Harold Rome musical number "Gee, But It's Cold in Russia," a part of the skit, underlined the failures of Hitler's army in its attempt to conquer Russia. Although it portrayed Hitler as a ranting maniac with delusions of grandeur, the skit also presented him as a threat to civilization requiring the best efforts of war-plant workers backing the boys overseas.

Presenting Hitler as a buffoon was nothing new—Charlie Chaplin had famously done it in the 1940 film *The Great Dictator*—but the theater wing's Kermit Bloomgarden wondered about overdoing that approach. At a meeting of the wing's board in July 1942, he viewed some of the skits as "quite unfunny" and suggested that Hitler be portrayed as the menace he was.

Another Kaufman-Hart skit, *Washington, D.C,* took a wry look at the alphabet-soup of wartime federal agencies like the WPB, OWI, and WMC. But it suggested that the efforts of the war-plant workers would surmount the red tape and play a key role in stopping Hitler and Tojo.

Kaufman and Hart also combined to write three skits for presentation at Army camps—*The Paperhanger,* another satire of Hitler; *The Ladies,* taking a look at female soldiers; and *Dream On Soldier,* presenting servicemen's fantasies about postwar life that was first staged in a Red Cross benefit at Madison Square Garden, with Kaufman and Hart in the cast.

While the American Theatre Wing was sending troupes to war plants and military hospitals, the United Service Organizations—better known as the USO—sponsored theatrical productions at military bases stateside and abroad. The program received a big boost in June 1941 when General George C. Marshall, the Army chief of staff, unveiled a large USO sign in Times Square with a portrait of FDR and his endorsement "the USO deserves the support of every individual citizen."

USO Camp Shows was overseen by Abe Lastfogel, a top executive of the William Morris talent agency, who helped raise an initial $16 million for the program from private sources. It sent top-line Broadway talent as well as actors and actresses drawn from retirement to perform in the leading plays and musicals. The playwrights and producers waived all rights. Sometimes a contribution involved more than sheer talent. When Olsen and Johnson's Broadway hit *Hellzapoppin'* was about to tour military posts, an important prop was missing: a straitjacket. Emil Friedlander, the head of Dazian's, a century-old theatrical costuming agency, and the man in charge of purchasing equipment for the USO productions, contacted the Bellevue Hospital psychiatric ward. It presented a straitjacket as a gift.

By November 1942, the Camp Shows had been divided into three circuits for stateside military posts: The Red Circuit, visiting the larger Army camps, offered the big shows; the Blue Circuit sent out only a few performers to each post it visited and encouraged audience participation, and the White Circuit presented vaudeville-style entertainment.

Ethel Merman received a special request to perform. Her "stage" would be Fort Hamilton, Brooklyn, where her husband, Bob Levitt, a newly commissioned Army officer, was serving as an aide to the commander, General Homer Groninger.

Merman, three months pregnant, had withdrawn from Broadway's *Panama Hattie* to spend time with her husband. "I was expected to attend parties given by his Army friends," she remembered, but "if there was one role I was never born to play it was the Army wife."

The first time Merman attended an officers' club party with her husband, warm Manhattans were served. She hated Manhattans, whether warm or cold, but belted a few down to help her endure the evening. She was having her entrée when a band began to play and the general's wife asked if she could sing a few numbers.

"I said, 'Get out of my way, Cuddles, or I'll spit in your eye,' and went back to eating. Mrs. Groninger seemed to think I was being funny and we got along fine. She never asked me to sing again though."

When American troops began to be deployed overseas, the camp shows followed them, and by the war's end more than 200 troupes were touring the war fronts.

Katharine Cornell and Brian Aherne took the Victorian literary romance *The Barretts of Wimpole Street* to bases near the front lines, and, despite some trepidation, found that the soldiers were enthralled. Maurice Evans brought an all-soldier show he called *GI Hamlet* to Pacific outposts. Theatrical icons like Helen Hayes, Ethel Barrymore, Judith Anderson, and Frederic March appeared in overseas dramas.

Seventeen USO actors and actresses died overseas during the war, the most searing losses coming in February 1943, when a Pan Am Flying Clipper crashed in the Tagus River, outside Lisbon. The singer and actress

Tamara (the stage name of Tamara Drasin), who had introduced "Smoke Gets in Your Eyes" in the 1933 Broadway show *Roberta*, was among the dead. The singer Jane Froman, who was rescued by the plane's copilot, John Curtis Burn, barely escaped the amputation of a leg. The accordionist Gypsy Markoff also suffered grievous injuries.

Back in the 1930s, Froman had appeared in the Ziegfeld Follies and she had performed in the 1940 Broadway musical *Keep Off the Grass* with Ray Bolger and Jimmy Durante. In November 1943, she returned to the Broadway stage in a motorized wheelchair, appearing in *Artists and Models* with a cast up to her hip, her scars covered by gowns and long gloves. She returned to Europe on crutches in 1945 to entertain the troops. In 1948, she married the copilot who saved her life, and her story was told in the Hollywood movie *With a Song in My Heart*.

Moss Hart toured the Pacific in 1945 with *The Man Who Came to Dinner*—formally known as USO Camp Show No. 453—directing it and playing the role of Sheridan Whiteside. In the first performance, on Johnson Island, Hart wore a silk smoking jacket embroidered with seagulls that Clifton Webb had donned playing Whiteside in the play's Chicago production. It was not a good beginning: Many of the servicemen hooted at the affectation.

Janet Fox, who played Miss Preen, remembered the moment:

Moss was, well, swishy in that jacket, and the boys took one look at him onstage and began to whistle and hoot. They didn't know the play, they didn't know Alexander Woolcott, and they didn't know Moss. All they saw was this rather affected man in a beard and silk jacket covered with seagulls. The play couldn't continue. Finally Moss got out of his prop wheelchair and walked to the edge of the stage and said: "Look, we've come here to do our duty, and your duty is to let us do it. Save your boos for the end. If you don't like it then—fine."

"It quieted them down," Fox recalled. "They seemed to respect him for standing up to them and in the end they liked the play. Moss toned down his mannerisms after that."

The tour proved a physical struggle for Hart. He contracted an ear infection and tropical fungus and he found the heat and the mud difficult to endure. Dorothy Sayers, playing Maggie Cutler, remembered how the cast's visits to military hospitals were too much for Hart: "He told me, 'I have learned to respect my fellow man as never before,' but he had to be forced to pay respect to the wounded. Some of those boys were disfigured or dying and he was frightened and repelled. We all were, but we did it."

Sono Osato, the Japanese-American dancer best known as Miss Turnstiles in Broadway's *On the Town*, was among the dancers from *One Touch of Venus*, in which she had previously appeared, who were organized into troupes by the choreographer Agnes De Mille. They visited Army camps, embarkation centers, and military hospitals.

Osato's father was among the thousands of Japanese nationals and Japanese-Americans, or Nisei, removed from their homes and interned. Her brother was training at Camp Shelby, Mississippi, with the 442nd Combat Regimental Team, the Nisei unit that would display extraordinary bravery in the Italian campaign.

When the bus carrying Osato and her fellow dancers approached the gate of an Army installation, uniformed guards invariable waved it through with little concern about security. As Osato put it long afterward: "How ironic that the same military and governmental red tape that had forbidden my entrance into California was now passing me without a glance into a highly restricted area. The magic of the theatre!"

Mary Martin's rendition of "That's Him" from her starring role in *One Touch of Venus* proved the high spot of the performances.

As Osato reflected: "Seeing the young men's unlined faces looking up at her so wistfully, I felt that she must have embodied all the girls they were leaving behind."

CHAPTER 18

IRVING BERLIN'S ARMY

The Army sergeant reluctantly arose from his cot in his olive drab uniform and wrap-around leggings. He stretched sleepily, looked around, and then, in a creaky voice, began to sing: "Oh! How I hate to get up in the morning."

Irving Berlin, reinvented as a World War I doughboy, captivated the World War II homefront with an all-soldier show that ribbed and paid tribute to the Army of democracy.

On the Fourth of July 1942, Berlin's *This Is the Army*, with a cast of 359 soldiers singing, dancing, and mugging their way through some two dozen acts to aid an Army charity, opened at the Broadway Theatre. Scheduled to run for four weeks, it remained in town for nearly three months. It put on a command performance for President Roosevelt, toured the nation, became a Hollywood movie, then played the warfronts. When it closed on October 22, 1945, in Hawaii, it had raised nearly $10 million for the Army Emergency Relief Fund, aiding needy servicemen and their families, and it had been seen by two and a half million soldiers and civilians.

During World War I, Berlin was stationed with the 77th Infantry Division at Camp Upton in Yaphank, Long Island. Already a celebrity for his hit "Alexander's Ragtime Band," he was putting on camp shows while unhappily contemplating the life of a doughboy and arising at 5 a.m.

Then everything changed. The post's commanding officer, Major General J. Franklin Bell, asked Berlin to write an all-soldier revue to raise funds for a visitors' center at the post. It became the Broadway hit *Yip, Yip, Yaphank*, with a cast of 300 soldiers, and it introduced "Oh! How I Hate to Get Up in the Morning" as a standard every GI could appreciate. Berlin had been promoted to sergeant by the time the show opened at the Century Theatre in the summer of 1918, but he appeared on stage as a private with a mop and pail, singing "Poor Little Me, I'm on K.P."

By the 1930s, Berlin had become a national treasure. In 1938, his "God Bless America," written for *Yip, Yip, Yaphank*, then discarded in favor of the more martial "We're on our Way to France," was introduced by Kate Smith for an Armistice Day broadcast. It became the unofficial national anthem.

Berlin wrote a few patriotic songs—"Any Bonds Today," "Angels of Mercy" (promoting the Red Cross), "Arms for the Love of America" (backing Lend-Lease), "When This Crazy World Is Sane Again"—as war drew closer for America. His "White Christmas," its sentiments of longing for home an enduring theme, in war and peace, would be unveiled in the 1942 movie *Holiday Inn*.

Early in 1942, Berlin phoned Army Chief of Staff Marshall to propose a new soldier show, something in the tradition of *Yip, Yip, Yaphank*. Marshall loved the idea.

Berlin orchestrated a nationwide search for soldiers who had professional show-business credentials or had displayed talent in camp performances. A phone call from Berlin or his chief aides—carrying the imprint of General Marshall—would turn an infantryman into a military song-and-dance man overnight.

In May 1942, Berlin assembled the cast for *This Is the Army* at his old outpost Camp Upton, which had been converted into a Civilian Conservation Corps barracks during the Depression, then reactivated for National Guard training and the processing of Army recruits.

Sergeant Ezra Stone, radio's Henry Aldrich, the mischief-making adolescent whose voice cracked with his signature "Coming, Mother," became the director. Stone was only twenty-four years old, but he was a Broadway veteran. He had appeared in the George Abbott-produced comedies *Three Men on a Horse* and *Brother Rat* in the mid-1930s. *The Aldrich Family* was based on his role in the 1938 Broadway comedy *What a Life*, which ran for more than 600 performances. He had been assigned to the Army's Special Services section, putting on camp shows, when Berlin recruited him.

A core of GIs newly separated from the entertainment world worked closely with Berlin and Stone. Milton Rosenstock, a graduate of the Juilliard School of Music and once a child prodigy on the clarinet, directed the forty-four piece orchestra. The choreographers Bob Sidney, Nelson Barclift, and Fred Kelly, the brother of Gene Kelly, put the dance routines together. John Koenig, a Broadway designer, created the sets. Alan Anderson, a stage director before being drafted and son of the Pulitzer Prize–winning playwright Maxwell Anderson, became a first sergeant, responsible for the troupe maintaining a semblance of military decorum.

The cast included the actor-singer Burl Ives, the actor Gary Merrill, and the comedian Julie Oshins, but most of the GIs came to *This Is the Army* with little or no professional experience.

Phil Kraus, a Bronx boy, was already at Camp Upton when Berlin arrived for his second stint there.

My brother was a professional musician. He worked on the staff at CBS and he was Kate Smith's pianist. He sent me to Juilliard and I played all the Catskill mountain resorts, and by time I was 21, I was on staff at WNEW Radio as a drummer and a vibraphonist. We'd precede and follow *The Make Believe Ballroom* with Martin Block.

In '41 I was drafted and I got into the band at Camp Upton. The band marched every day and brought recruits from the train to the main part of the camp. There was no authorization for an Army band at an induction station so they listed us as cooks and bakers. We used to play every night for the recruits—people would come in and go out the next day— little shows, at a place called the Ol' Opry House. Ezra Stone would put together shows there. Half of that band joined the orchestra for *This Is the Army* and it also gathered people for its orchestra from Fort Dix.

Berlin had one of his four personal pianos delivered to Camp Upton. In a couple of weeks he wrote all the tunes for *This Is the Army*, retaining only a few numbers from *Yip, Yip, Yaphank*, most notably "Oh! How I Hate to Get Up in the Morning." The cast rehearsed every day, having been spared much of the drilling and routine of Army life.

Early in June, Berlin's GIs began final rehearsals at three Broadway theaters. The soldiers got a few dollars a day for quarters and meals, living wherever they could find an affordable apartment.

The day before the first rehearsals, a crisis emerged. Major Simon Ambraz, a former police officer who had become the company commander, posted a decree stating that every morning at 7 o'clock, the cast was to assemble in front of the Broadway Theatre and march to a playground at Fifty-fourth Street and Tenth Avenue for drills. The men were to return at 11:15 a.m. and could have the rest of the day for rehearsals.

The military brass ordered the drills on the understanding that Berlin had once said he didn't want his men "viewed by the public as pampered actors wearing Army uniforms."

With opening night near, and much to do in terms of perfecting the show, an appalled Ezra Stone tried to contact Berlin so he could cancel the drill order, but he was unreachable. And so the next morning, the cast trudged off to play soldier. When Berlin showed up for the afternoon rehearsals, the men were performing listlessly, and when Berlin found out why, he was incensed. He considered phoning General Marshall to nullify the drill schedule, but his phone call to General Irving Phillipson, the commander of the Army's entertainment units for the New York area, countermanded the order.

Two weeks before the scheduled opening, another crisis arose. Berlin became convinced that the show would fall apart, that something wasn't right. He summoned Josh Logan, who had been drafted after directing the Broadway hit *By Jupiter*.

Logan would recall how Berlin was "in a black panic" over the show's prospects and "gave me nine days to take it apart and put it back together into a hit." But after Logan viewed a full rehearsal, he was convinced there was little for him to do.

"I was probably the first outsider to see *This Is the Army*, and the size, emotion, melody and comedy of it left me weak. It was stupefying—bulletproof perfection."

But Berlin's fears weren't eased, and he insisted that Logan fix the show.

Logan watched rehearsals repeatedly, then appeased Berlin with minor revisions in some of the songs, dialogue, and staging. Logan was listed as the "additional director," and Berlin "felt as if I had saved his neck." He soon returned to his regular military duties.

Before opening night arrived, yet another unsettling matter arose—a feud between Berlin and Stone. Berlin had broken a barrier with his decision to include black soldiers in the cast, creating what was evidently the only integrated unit in the Army. But he nonetheless harkened back to the customs of his youth, envisioning a minstrel number like the one he had staged in *Yip, Yip, Yaphank*. Stone was appalled and persuaded Berlin to scrap a minstrel extravaganza, though vestiges of the old blackface routines did remain.

A clash of egos further fueled a deteriorating relationship. Stone was offended by Berlin's vanity and the likelihood that he would become the "star" of the show with the contributions of the servicemen cast almost ignored, to the detriment of those who would resume or embark on show business careers after the war.

Berlin seemed to validate that fear when he posted an edict on a cast bulletin board through his press representative, Sergeant Benjamin Washer. "You are reminded that no one is to talk to the press about the show or their own performance." Any cast member who was approached was to refer the reporter to Washer.

The bickering, the demands of the Army bureaucracy, and Berlin's insecurities aside, *This Is the Army* opened to rave reviews before an audience of military brass, women in evening gowns, ordinary New Yorkers, and a handful of GIs given seats for free. Kate Smith contributed $10,000 to

Army relief for her two seats. Berlin, who worked without pay, bought a pair of boxes for $2,000.

Part vaudeville, part minstrel show, with songs of sentiment and romance and gentle jabs at the military, concluding with a patriotic flourish, *This Is the Army* proved that Berlin remained a master of capturing the American spirit.

Private Henry Jones told of the transformation of a young man into a soldier with "This Is the Army, Mr. Jones." Private William Horne sang "I'm Getting Tired So I Can Sleep," a soldier yearning to dream as a way of reuniting with his love on the homefront, the dream scene featuring GIs in drag. Private Pinkie Mitchell sang and danced in "My Sergeant and I Are Buddies."

Corporal Earl Oxford offered "I Left My Heart at the Stage Door Canteen," the show's leading ballad. Private Alan Manson portrayed Jane Cowl, the Broadway actress in the forefront of the canteen's work. Corporal Nelson Barclift played the dancer Zorina, and Private Julie Ochins impersonated Gypsy Rose Lee in the canteen scene.

Red Hederman, who played a canteen girl, remembered long afterward how servicemen sought introductions to the actors in drag, saying "don't tell me that ain't no girl." As Hederman put it, "Some of those guys were absolutely gorgeous."

Ezra Stone got on stage in a skit with Corporal Philip Truex, son of the actor Ernest Truex, who denounced Private Oshins for his unsoldierly demeanor. Oshins responded with the often-voiced "Break me. Go ahead, make me a civilian." To that, Stone broke into song with "The Army's Made a Man Out of Me," the lyrics belying his cracking voice, a reprise of his Henry Aldrich persona.

"That's What the Well-Dressed Man in Harlem Will Wear," which drew on the show's black GIs, became one of its best-remembered numbers. Corporal James A. Cross, a dancer known as Stump Cross, and Bill Smith, who had danced at Harlem's Cotton Club and performed with Cab Calloway and Duke Ellington, told how the Harlem "dude" sheds his "Lenox Avenue clothes" for a uniform with a "suntan shade of cream/or an olive-drab color scheme." To underline the point, large cardboard figures in striped suits and broad-brimmed hats—the civilian styles discarded for the war's duration—hovered over the dancers.

The soldiers also performed musical tributes to the Navy and the Army's airmen. Then came a mock wedding number, "Mandy," borrowed from *Yip, Yip, Yaphank*. It featured a soldier chorus on risers and several performers in blackface with others in drag.

"Aryans Under the Skin" offered a satiric look at the Germans and Japanese, but Berlin dropped it after the show's second week. With American forces reeling in the Pacific, and Hitler's troops ascendant in Europe, he viewed the tone as inappropriate.

During the opening night's first act, Berlin sat in the fourth row with his wife, Ellin, and their fifteen-year-old daughter, Mary Ellin. Then he went to his dressing room, preparing to go onstage for the show's next-to-last scene, Sergeant Irving Berlin in his World War I uniform singing, "Oh! How I Hate to Get up in the Morning."

Berlin's daughter long remembered the moment.

And then, there he is at last, sitting up sleepily, swinging his legs over the side of a cot and standing up, alone, stage center. A small, black-haired man in an old doughboy's uniform with a high-necked jacket and puttees. It is the first perfectly still moment since the evening began. He looks down, then up, and out at the audience, mouth open, ready to sing. Then the silence is broken by a roar, as sudden as thunder, and the pounding of applause. Everyone around us is rising, cheering now; and we are on our feet, too, applauding furiously—there is no question of family modesty. The demonstration continues for a full ten minutes as my father stands there looking down, looking up, opening his mouth, closing it again. Finally, he is allowed to begin his song.

Mynna Granat, Berlin's secretary, who attended to his immediate needs—she made sure, for example, that his uniform was pressed—would recall Berlin's delight. "I couldn't have a seat because they were so expensive, so I sat on the step backstage. And when he came off he would kiss me and say, 'How did I do?' He loved to sing—he loved it."

Alan Anderson, the unit's first sergeant, remembered how "the suffering and bitterness in the words he had written in 1918 had lost none of their heartfelt resentment. He still hated to get up in the morning."

Berlin returned for the show's finale, standing in front of 150 soldiers in battle gear perched on risers, the green recruits of the opening act now combat ready. Their number "This Time Is the Last Time" expressed the hope the world would never again be plunged into war.

John Chapman of the *Daily News* brimmed with emotion telling of the show's impact on the audience, and he gushed with affection for Berlin.

It was the sort of demonstration that made you want to cry, it was so good. It you had been that little guy, you would have burst right out in tears . . . His is the only voice I ever heard that is at once squealy and husky. But on that night he would have drawn audiences away had

Caruso been singing across the street. The only thing that can stop *This Is the Army* is the end of the war.

This Is the Army offered little in the way of a martial tone. There would be no hit tunes in World War II America in the mold of "Over There," when naïve doughboys headed off to the World War I trenches to make the world safe for democracy.

Richard Watts of the *Herald Tribune* noted how Berlin had caught the national mood with a show "at once delightful and a song of American democracy."

As Watts saw it: "Because *This Is the Army* does not try to capitalize on patriotism it is one of the most truly patriotic works I have ever encountered. Because it always keeps its sense of humor and never tries to be emotional it is one of the most moving events in theatrical history."

During its run of 113 performances, the cast had little time to savor the wonderful reviews. Those drills in the lot on Tenth Avenue that Berlin had averted during rehearsals went forth, four afternoons a week, two hours at a clip.

Ezra Stone would tell how the men marched "in full battle dress with our guns and helmet" along the streets west of Times Square and were treated to "flowers, candies and cookies" from the neighborhood people, who assumed the soldiers they saw each day were successive waves heading to the Hudson River piers to board ships for Europe.

"After two weeks of that we were a snappy looking bunch in spite of the differences in age, height, weight, girth and physical abilities," Alan Anderson recalled. "We hid the clumsy ones in the middle and put the sharp ones on the edge."

When the soldiers weren't onstage or rehearsing, they might be required to watch sex-orientation or training films in the Broadway Theatre.

"We lined up in the alley outside the theater," Bob Lissauer, the GI who helped manage the music publishing arm of the show, recalled. "And then we walked in through the stage door, right across the stage for short-arm inspection. Everyone gets in front of the doctor. You have to unzip yourself and take out your penis and check for venereal disease."

Walter Winchell learned about the exams and told of them in his column.

Even the cast members who were established figures in show business performed lowly Army chores, as Seymour Greene—Corporal Seymour Goldfinger, the show's lead trombone player, back then—would recall.

Greene, a native of Newark, had played spent two years with the trombonist Jack Teagarden's band before being drafted.

I was part of an entertainment unit at Fort Dix. Before *This Is the Army* was formed, the people of the military put together a big show for the City of New York because they were so hospitable to the GIs. It was at the Metropolitan Opera House. I was featured in a number in that.

One day later on I was out in the field, I had my rifle and bayonet, and a messenger comes out, "Report back to the orderly room." They tell me to turn in my rifle and gear and they gave me a train ticket to Camp Upton, Long Island. I had no idea what it was about.

I ended up playing first chair in the orchestra. The second trombone player, Don Madison, came out of Jimmy Dorsey's band. The third trombone player, Herbie Platner, or Herbie Pine then, had been playing in *Hellzapoppin'* on Broadway when he was drafted. And we had the finest bassonist in the country, Lenny Sharrow.

As for those military tasks that no one wanted to do:

I had a hotel room on the East Side and I'd walk over to the theater with my horn to practice in the morning. And Burl Ives comes running out with his guitar, and his manager is at the curb holding a cab door open. Prior to the war he had a daytime radio show called *The Wayfaring Stranger*. He would sing and play; he had a tremendous repertoire of folk tunes. While we were playing in New York he was evidently still doing his morning show.

Burl sees me and says, "Hey, Goldie, I'll give you a ride to the theater." I said, "sure, sure." We get to the stage door and he runs out and goes inside. I get out slowly. His manager paid the fare. I get inside and I see Burl with a mop and a pail. It seems that he might have been late for some shows or something. You know the usual military punishment— they assigned him to cleaning the latrines back stage.

One day in late July, a labor dispute derailed Greene and eighteen of his fellow musicians. They had assembled for the opening of the Times Square Service Men's Center and were waiting for a signal to start playing as backup for a quarter-hour sketch from the show when Local 802 of the American Federation of Musicians intervened.

The city's Defense Recreation Committee had asked the union's permission for the band to play, but a wire arrived from Jacob Rosenberg, the local's president, saying no. The union had allowed *This Is the Army* to be staged on Broadway, even though its GI musicians who were union members were getting Army pay instead of union scale. But Rosenberg wouldn't allow them to work free "for anybody else," including the Defense Recreation Committee.

The ceremony went on without the band. La Guardia gave a talk and Helen Hayes recited "The Star-Spangled Banner." The next day's *New York Times* had a photo of the Army musicians sitting on the bandstand, staring at their sheet music, having been silenced by the union.

Lieutenant Marc Daniels, the immediate commander of the show's soldiers (and future director of TV's *I Love Lucy*), set up eight squads. But the black GIs were all placed in a single section, overseen by a pair of black sergeants, Clyde Turner and Jack Brodnax, prewar entertainers who had experience in infantry units before joining the show.

"We all got along very well," Seymour Greene remembered. "There were never any problems. But there was one incident where one of the fellas of the Harlem group had done something. The lieutenant, Marc Daniels, goes over to Clyde Turner and he tells Clyde to put this guy in his place—to tell him to behave, or whatever."

The black sergeant felt that the lieutenant should have handled the matter himself.

> Clyde's response to the lieutenant was, "Hey, look, he's one of the men in your outfit, you don't treat him separately." The idea was that we were all treated the same.
>
> When we went to various camps, we'd walk in and the commanding officer might say, "The white guys go here and the colored fellas go there." We said: "We don't separate. Our orders were to stay together." When that happened, we all ended in the colored section of the camp. In Liverpool, they had a white Red Cross club and a colored Red Cross club—using the terms they used then—so the whole outfit would stay at the colored Red Cross club.

During the New York run, Eleanor Roosevelt saw *This Is the Army* and was so impressed that she requested a command performance for FDR. Three days after the New York closing, *This Is the Army* appeared at the National Theatre in Washington, the president watching from a box. After touring the nation, the cast made a Hollywood movie that included a romantic plot involving Ronald Reagan, a lieutenant in the Army Air Forces, and Joan Leslie. Kate Smith sang "God Bless America," and Joe Louis, in the Army by then, banged away at a punching bag to introduce the film version of "That's What the Well-Dressed Man in Harlem Will Wear."

In the fall of 1943, a reduced cast headed overseas—Ezra Stone, his relationship with Berlin unrepaired, was among those staying home—and *This Is the Army* premiered at the Palladium in London on November 10, 1943, before King George, Queen Elizabeth, and princesses Elizabeth and Margaret. Berlin wrote a special song for the occasion, "My British Buddy." Eisenhower asked that the show continue on to the European and Pacific battlefronts, and Berlin added a few numbers for those tours, among them "The Fifth Army Is Where My Heart Is" and "There Are No Wings in a Foxhole."

The final performance was held at Honolulu Stadium on October 22, 1945.

At the conclusion, Irving Berlin walked to the front of the stage and spoke of how pleased he was to aid Army relief efforts for a second time.

"It has been a glorious thing for me—to help in the only way I could to win this war. My prayer now is, as a songwriter, I hope to God I'll never have to write another war song."

CHAPTER 19

MOSS HART'S AIRMEN

If Irving Berlin's GIs could charm the home front with *This Is the Army* and raise millions for a military charity, the nation's airmen could presumably put on just as good a show if not better, so far as General Henry (Hap) Arnold, the commander of the Army Air Forces, saw it.

The opening salvo came at the Oak Room of the Plaza. The principals were a thirty-five-year-old junior officer using military service as another rung in his show-business climb and a renowned figure of the Broadway stage epitomizing the ultimate in New York sophistication.

On a spring evening in 1943, Lieutenant Irving Paul Lazar—he had been born Shmuel, or Samuel Lazar, but Irving Paul sounded classier—approached Moss Hart, the man he considered "the glamour, wit and charm of Broadway at its popular best."

Lazar, who was living at the Gotham Hotel in Manhattan while serving in an Air Forces entertainment unit at Long Island's Mitchel Field by day, had become Arnold's emissary to the theater world. He was supposed to find the man to put the airmen on Broadway.

Lazar's roots were far afield from the glamour of the Manhattan theater. He was born on the Lower East Side, notwithstanding his embellished reference in *Who's Who* listing his birthplace as the decidedly tonier Stamford, Connecticut. He grew up in Brooklyn's Brownsville section, where the biggest celebrities were the gunmen of Murder Incorporated. Having escaped that dead-end life, he became an agent at MCA, the Music Corporation of America, and booked performers on Manhattan's West 52nd Street, known as "Swing Street." He later joined the William Morris Agency, handling personalities like Sophie Tucker and Joe E. Lewis.

If Lazar wanted to keep his cushy spot in the Army Air Forces, he needed to move quickly in carrying out Arnold's "Let's put on a show" decree.

As he told it:

I submitted a very carefully worded proposal suggesting that Jimmy Stewart, Clark Gable, Henry Fonda, Josh Logan and a number of other Hollywood stars who were in the Air Force should be asked to participate. I knew none of them. Anyone with any knowledge of show business whatsoever would have realized that it was merely a list of top American talent that any fool could compile. But the general wasn't in show business, and that's what I was banking on.

A few days later, Lazar was summoned to meet Arnold, whom he found to be an impressive man "who looked through you, not at you."

"Lieutenant, do you think you can do this show so it will be a credit to the Air Force?" Arnold asked. Lazar gave Arnold a "yes sir," and he was told he could go anywhere he wanted in order to seek out talented Air Forces personnel as long they weren't training to be pilots, bombardiers, or navigators. But he was on his own in financing the production and renting a theater. The Pentagon wasn't paying for that.

Lazar recruited another lieutenant at Mitchel Field named Benjamin Landis, a former talent agent who once represented Eddie Cantor, as his partner in finding talent. But first, Lazar had to find figures of stature as the show's writer and director.

One evening Lazar was at the Plaza's Oak Room having a drink. Moss Hart was at a nearby table. Lazar introduced himself, told Hart of Arnold's interest in staging a military show, and asked Hart if he would be interested in writing it.

Hart, as he recalled the moment, replied "certainly" with the hope that the young lieutenant would go away happily instead of sitting down and ruining Hart's evening by belaboring him with the details.

When Lazar phoned him a few days later, Hart said he would have to speak directly with Arnold before committing himself. A meeting at the Pentagon was arranged, though just how Hart came to be invited is murky. Lazar would claim that he sent Hart an invitation that he had composed, signing Arnold's name to it. At any rate, Hart was enormously impressed by Arnold but confessed that he didn't know a thing about the Air Forces. Arnold said he would arrange for Hart to visit installations throughout the country.

Best known for collaborating with George S. Kaufman on the comedies *Once in a Lifetime, You Can't Take It With You,* and *The Man Who Came to Dinner*, Hart had already lent his talents to the war effort. Working with the American Theatre Wing, he had written for British War Relief benefits before collaborating with Kaufman on sketches for the Lunchtime Follies.

Hart hated to fly, but three days after his meeting with Arnold he was strapped into an Army bomber and dispatched to an Air Forces base in Fort Worth, Texas, for an introduction to the training regimen. It was the start of a grueling 28,000-mile tour. Shedding his civilian clothes, Hart was given a private's uniform and, nearing age thirty-nine, he posed as a cadet as he flew around the country, hoping to blend in with the trainees and learn of their hopes, their fears, their families, and the planes they would fly.

Hart went to Keesler Field, Mississippi, for basic training, then visited the cadet training program for college students at the University of Missouri. He flew to Santa Ana, California, to take part in intensive tests determining whether a cadet would become a pilot, a navigator, or a bombardier.

In days that began before dawn and might last until 8 o'clock at night, Hart took part in pressure chamber and reflex tests, acrobatics, and night fights, and he ate and drank with the cadets, some of them half his age. It was, he said, "the roughest, toughest" experience of his life.

"I had, of course, traveled back and forth many times across America without ever really seeing it or hearing it," Hart would write. "In eight short weeks in the Air Forces I learned more about my country in terms of people than I had ever learned before."

In June 1943, Hart began working on a script at his estate in Bucks County, Pennsylvania, envisioning something wholly original that would not invite comparisons to Berlin's Army revue. He wrote a play with music and he called it *Winged Victory*.

Lazar and Landis flew to Air Forces installations all over the country, obtaining several thousand applications for the production. *Winged Victory* would have a cast of 210, mostly Army Air Forces personnel, but also their wives and girlfriends and an occasional professional actress; a forty-five-man orchestra, a fifty-member choral group, and a stage crew of seventy.

A few of the airmen-actors had recognizable names in show business or would make their mark after the war, most notably Karl Malden, who portrayed a Nazi in *Counterattack* and a Flying Tiger pilot in *Sons and Soldiers* on Broadway; Red Buttons, Lee J. Cobb, Gary Merrill, John Forsythe, Barry Nelson, Mario Lanza, Ed McMahon, George Reeves, Don Taylor, Martin Ritt, Peter Lind Hayes, Edmond O'Brien, Henry Rowland, and the Blackburn twins, Ramon and Royce.

David Rose, a leading composer-arranger in Hollywood, best known in the postwar years for "Holiday for Strings," became the musical director, although Norman Leyden, a promising arranger, conducted the orchestra for most of the *Winged Victory* run. Glenn Miller, wielding his big-band baton as a captain in the Air Forces, helped recruit the musicians, including Joe Bushkin, who had played the piano with Tommy Dorsey and Benny Goodman. Leonard de Paur, who was the choral director in Orson Welles's all-black production of *Macbeth,* had that duty for *Winged Victory.*

Harry Horner, the designer for Broadway's *Lady in the Dark,* oversaw the complex staging, which included seventeen scenes and five revolving stages. Abe Feder, a well-known Broadway lighting director, supervised five switchboards for more than 250 light cues. Layne Britton, a leading prewar makeup man in Hollywood, performed those chores for the cast. Nat Hiken, later a writer for Phil Silvers as TV's Sergeant Bilko, put out publicity releases.

Ramon Blackburn had been performing in shows, usually dance routines, with his twin, Royce, since they were children.

As Ramon remembered it:

When my brother and I turned eighteen we got our draft notices. We wanted to be flyboys—fighter pilots—we were all fired up. My father said "you gotta go in together or you won't go at all." I failed the Navy test because of my eyes. Then we went to the Air Corps and it was the same thing. That was in Lower Manhattan. After that test, we stood by an elevator on the eighteenth floor. We were dejected. A colonel says, "You fellas are twins, aren't you?" Incidentally, we always dressed alike. He said, "What are you doing now?"

The Blackburns told the colonel they were seasoned Broadway performers and had appeared most recently in Olsen and Johnson's *Sons o' Fun* with Carmen Miranda:

The colonel said, "Oh my God, I saw that. You were dancing with Ella Logan, right?" I said, "That's right."

He took us to a back office, and there was Irving Lazar, and he introduced us. Lazar said: "We want you to be in *Winged Victory.* Allow yourself to be drafted and I'll catch up with you wherever you are." I thought, "Lots of luck, they're gonna find us out of millions of people."

Lazar made good on his promise. After training in Greensboro, North Carolina, the twins joined the cast.

Norman Leyden was conducting the combined bands at the Army Air Forces training center in Atlantic City early in 1943 when he received a surprise visitor.

All of a sudden Glenn Miller showed up. He walked into the headquarters room and said, "I'm Captain Miller." I was the ranking non-com, a master sergeant. He said: "I'm sending my music here. We're going to start rehearsing. Get your men together." He was looking to form a cadre for his own band being organized in New Haven.

It was a real kick. He was my idol. I was trying to imitate him as an arranger. He stayed maybe two weeks and we played in the mess halls at noon time. I played tenor saxophone in the band. He once said, "For a Yale man you don't play bad tenor," kind of a left-handed compliment.

I was in the middle of a rehearsal one morning after that and someone said "there's a call from New York, a Captain Miller." He said: "I've got a job for you. The Air Force is gonna put on a show on Broadway. Your job would be to organize the orchestra. I've got lots of applications. David Rose is coming in to write the music and he's going to conduct for the first week. After that you will conduct the show." It was an opportunity I just couldn't believe.

Having completed his script in six weeks, Hart staged *Winged Victory* in only seventeen days, the rehearsals held at the Forty-fourth Street Theatre, where the play opened.

"He never yelled," Lazar remembered. "If something bothered him he would always go up to the stage, pull the actor aside and speak to him privately and gently, acting out the lines the way he thought they should be delivered. That technique turns a director into a father figure."

The producer Gilbert Miller assembled a committee to secure much of the $100,000 production costs, bringing in Marshall Field, Albert Lasker, William S. Paley, Henry Luce, and Juan Trippe. Hart worked without pay.

Boston was selected for the out-of-town shakedown, and the cast assembled on a Sunday morning outside the Forty-fourth Street Theatre. Then it marched to Grand Central Terminal to catch the train. Don Taylor remembered how when the men crossed Broadway, "this civilian started singing 'Over There.' The whole company joined in, the band struck up the song. Traffic stopped. Men waved their hats, women wiped their tears, saluting us with their damp handkerchiefs, children were hoisted to see the departing soldiers—not off to war but merely catching a train to Boston for a tryout. Naturally, that civilian was Moss Hart."

When the cast returned to New York, it was just another military unit so far as passersby could tell. Eugene Shepherd, who played the violin in the *Winged Victory* orchestra—he had played in a string quartet in Cleveland before entering military service—recalled how "there's a picture of us lined up at Grand Central Terminal after we returned from the Boston tryout. And we had gas masks on our shoulders and they marched us to the hotel."

The Broadway opening, on November 20, 1943, proved a major theatrical event, the curtain rising to a fifteen-minute standing ovation from a celebrity audience.

For Norman Leyden, "my favorite moment was right at the beginning":

The audience was all seated and they dimmed the lights until they were out, like you were in a mine. It was absolutely pitch dark. The audience simmers down. Then you'd hear this drone of about fifty or sixty bombers way off in the distance, a whole squadron taking off. And they'd roar. They brought this roar up until it was almost unbearable. I had a phone on my head and a plastic electric baton. When the sound got to this terribly high level, the stage director would say "hit it" and I would take this baton and go voom. And the band would play David Rose's overture based on the Air Corps song. I loved it.

Winged Victory opened with a scene in Mapleton, Ohio, the town Hart had conceived for *The American Way, Lady in the Dark,* and *The Man Who Came to Dinner.*

Three young men from Mapleton—a chemist, a banker, and a barber—were awaiting letters telling them when to report to the Air Forces, and they were eventually joined by men from Brooklyn, Texas, and Oregon to train as the crew of a bomber christened *Winged Victory.*

The play described the tests the men needed to pass to take part in air combat and conveyed the crushing disappointment of those who "washed out" in the quest to be pilots. It told of the war's impact on the airmen's families, portraying the young wives following their husbands from camp to camp.

In the final scene, the airmen were on an island in the South Pacific. Two members of the crew, exhausted from battle, took their wounded gunner to an aid station. One of the boys from Mapleton sat beneath a palm tree, writing a letter to his newborn son just before departing on yet another mission.

Hart withstood pressure from the Pentagon in telling of the disappointment faced by cadets who dreamt of becoming pilots, but were selected instead to be navigators or bombardiers. After reviewing the script, Major General Barney Giles expressed concern to Hart that the disappointments were "overemphasized" and feared that Hart might contribute to a feeling in the public mind that certain positions on warplanes deserved more recognition than others (which they presumably did). But Hart kept the scene the way he wrote it.

David Rose chose "The Army Air Corps" hymn ("Off we go into the wild blue yonder") as the theme song. He also reprised "The Whiffenpoof Song," "Mademoiselle from Armentiers" (Hart wrote special lyrics), "White Christmas," and "I Can't Give You Anything but Love, Baby" and wrote a couple of original numbers, "Winged Victory" and "My Dream Book of Memories."

There were laughs as well. Sascha Brastoff impersonated the flamboyant Carmen Miranda in a scene depicting a Christmas Eve party in the Pacific, punctuating it with the hot number "Chica-Chica-Boom-Chic." Red Buttons (real name Aaron Chwatt) and the Slate Brothers parodied the Andrews Sisters.

The real war made its presence felt one evening at the Forty-fourth Street Theatre. On December 16, 1943, the 40th anniversary of the Wright Brothers' first flight, a bomber based at Mitchel Field was christened *Winged Victory*. Shortly before its crew members departed for overseas, they were guests of the play *Winged Victory* and met the cast backstage. The pilot, Lieutenant Terence Breidenstein, and the copilot, Lieutenant John Mortenson, promised to drop souvenir programs of the show together with the bombs they released on their first mission.

When they weren't onstage or performing routine military tasks, cast members entertained at nearby military posts and Red Cross benefits. Karl Malden, Martin Ritt, and Peter Lind Hayes couldn't resist a routine that wasn't part of their script at those visits. They would set up a piano and a makeshift public address system. When they had finished their little show, they would pack up the piano and help the cast carry it back to the truck. As Malden told it:

> Part of the shtick was that Hayes would say: "Wait a minute. Ladies and gentlemen, this guy is just moving the piano, but if we could get him to sing for us, it would be great." Then Mario Cocozza would take the stage and sing *Pagliacci*. He brought the house down every time. Later, after the war, he became Mario Lanza.

The cast members who weren't married lived at Manhattan's Narragansett Hotel, where a semblance of military discipline prevailed.

"They wanted the hotel to seem more military so they yanked out all the beds and brought in double Army bunks and we had inspection every week to make us feel that we're still in the Air Force," Eugene Shepherd remembered. "It was rigorous. They would write on our mirrors if we had some problems—'beds not tight enough, clothes not hung up.'"

Just as the cast of *This Is the Army* trekked to a West Side lot to drill, so, too, did the *Winged Victory* airmen project a military image of sorts. As Karl Malden put it: "They didn't want people to be able to say, 'My son has gone off to war and these boys are goofing off on stage.'"

But goofing off they did.

On most mornings, the cast drilled and went through calisthenics at the Young Men's Hebrew Association on the Upper East Side or, when the weather was good, in Central Park.

But, as Malden remembered: "There was simply no controlling this group. The noncom officers would drill us, and half the time when they said 'column right,' everyone just kept on marching straight ahead. It was understood that the first four guys, whoever they were, would not follow directions and the rest of us would just keep following them. Nobody listened. Nobody cared."

When the cast members were summoned to the "Y," blankets were laid out on the basketball court, and they would have to take their rifles apart and put them back together blindfolded. They were also sent to rifle ranges for target practice.

All that wasn't particularly onerous, but for Ramon and Royce Blackburn, service in *Winged Victory* became an especially soft deal. They lived at their parents' home in Great Neck, Long Island, during the play's run, commuting to Manhattan. On one occasion, they were given door-to-door service to and from rifle practice at another village on Long Island's North Shore.

As Ramon Blackburn told it:

There were two colonels. The first one, he looked like an Englishman. He had riding crops. He complained to Hap Arnold: "These boys should be doing more. After all, we're at war." That's why they got us this other colonel and he put the screws on us. He made us go to Central Park and we did close-order drill. But being a dancer, it came easy to me.

One time, the colonel said: "All you guys are gonna go out to Port Washington and learn how to fire. We'll get you buses." There was a firing line out there. They said to my brother and me, "We'll pick you up." So here we are with these three buses in front of our home and the neighbors are saying, "What's going on here?" We fired our carbines and they dropped us off again.

When they weren't fiddling with their rifles at the Y, the men played picked basketball games there with consequences that worried the medical officer, Lieutenant William Cahan, since the cast wasn't exactly in prime shape.

As the doc put it in his "RX" column in the unit's newsletter, *The Gremlin*:

> Let me be the last to dampen the enthusiasm of the 92nd Street Commandos. But too long a trail of the halt leading the blind has formed on sick call, and most of its constituents are a product of "overdoing it."
>
> The two months of rehearsal, Boston, and opening commitments were not devoted to keeping you physically fit. As a consequence the most rugged became flabby and out of condition. Any concerted exertion such as basketball requires a good wind and smoothly functioning and coordinated muscular activity for the long runs, sudden checks, quick cut-ins and body contact. Your warm-up period is managed for you, but the truly hectic, do-or-die games should be delayed until you are physically ready for them.

Winged Victory ran for 212 performances, and Moss Hart received the Donaldson Award as best Broadway director for the 1943–44 season. He wrote to the parents of decorated American pilots, enclosing a silver *Winged Victory* pin and two tickets for any performance of the play.

The cast went to Hollywood in spring 1944 for Daryl Zanuck's 20th Century Fox movie, which added Lon McAllister, a heartthrob for teenage girls. Hart wrote the screenplay but turned the directing over to George Cukor. A six-month nationwide tour after that drew nearly 845,000 theatergoers.

Whatever dramatic merit the play held, it was conceived as a recruiting tool for the Army Air Forces. "It was a very good pep talk for anybody who wanted to join up," Ramon Blackburn recalled. As Norman Leyden put it: "There was a lot of patriotism going around in those days and it hit the nail on the head. You could hardly do anything wrong."

Moss Hart underlined the national mood in a brief opening-night curtail call. "I have just heard on the radio that we have just bombed Berlin again," he told the audience. "That's what this play is all about."

Howard Barnes of the *Herald Tribune* called *Winged Victory* "a great and profoundly moving war play" of "heroic proportions."

Lewis Nichols of the *Times* hailed it as "a stirring, moving, and what is more important, a most human play about the boy next door."

But the *New Yorker*'s Wolcott Gibbs viewed *Winged Victory* as "fundamentally recruiting poster art," although "stunning" in that regard.

Gibbs wrote that Hart provided "tentative references in his play to freedom and tolerance and other abstractions, but the strong, general implication is that not one of the very attractive boys on the stage has the slightest idea of what the war is actually about."

Emery Battis, one of the play's eight assistant stage managers, who appeared in many Shakespearean productions after the war, took a similar view. Battis recalled years later:

> The character roles were very stereotypical. The brash, Jewish Brooklyn boy; the nice boy from the sticks; the boy that got killed; the sad one. It looked great but it was simplistic, simple-minded even, if you will.
>
> But it was at a time when audiences were perfectly willing to accept that kind of thing—a flag-waving production—and I guess that critics for the most part were indisposed to be excessively critical about an enterprise which was making money for Air Force relief. The money we made went back to wives and children of Air Force members.

General Hap Arnold wrote to Moss Hart in 1946 to express appreciation for the play and its fund-raising prowess. "I am sure that it must give you a warm feeling as it does me to realize that these funds will be used to repair the ravages and suffering caused by war among personnel and their families whose efforts and sacrifices saw us through to victory."

As for the brash lieutenant who badgered Moss Hart to carry out Arnold's directive, Irving Lazar became an audacious superagent, a small man in oversized horn-rimmed glasses who threw fabulous Hollywood parties and famously stole his rival agents' clients. One day, as the story went, Humphrey Bogart bet Lazar that he couldn't make three movie deals for him a single day. When Lazar did just that, Bogart called him Swifty, and so he was known for the rest of his years.

CHAPTER 20

BEAUTIFUL MORNIN'
AND SAILORS ON THE TOWN

It's dawn at the Brooklyn Navy Yard. Workmen sing softly and all is drowsiness. And then, at the stroke of six, sailors in their whites bounce down a gangplank and the air is vibrant. To a burst of percussive music, three of the Navy boys break into the exuberant strains of "New York, New York" and they set out for Manhattan and a frantic race against time. They are out to explore the dazzling city, but most of all to find love on a twenty-four-hour pass. It's December 28, 1944, at the Adelphi Theatre, the opening night of *On the Town*.

As America entered its fourth year at war, Jerome Robbins and Leonard Bernstein collaborated on a valentine to New York and a portrait of longing and loneliness in wartime. They did it with an exhilarating blend of music, dance, and lyrics, building on the kind of meld introduced by *Oklahoma!* the previous year.

Broadway musicals had been giving a nod to the war, but the angles were often contrived, even with Cole Porter's imprint.

Back in 1940, Porter's *Panama Hattie* presented Ethel Merman as Hattie Maloney, a nightclub owner in the Canal Zone who while courted by a naval officer becomes entangled in a spy plot threatening vital fortifications.

Porter returned in 1941 with *Let's Face It*, a musical-comedy hit in which wealthy wives, seeking revenge on their unfaithful husbands, try to steal soldiers from their sweethearts. Danny Kaye's "Melody in 4-F," a double-talking takeoff on a reluctant draftee's experiences, provided the highlight.

Something for the Boys (1943), the third Porter musical with a wartime twist, starred Merman as Blossom Hart, who inherits a ranch near San Antonio that she converts into a hotel for wives visiting their airmen husbands stationed nearby. When Merman becomes attracted to a sergeant who is already engaged to a socialite, complications ensue. Merman scored with "Hey, Good Lookin'," and Betty Garrett charmed with the ballad "I'm

171

in Love with a Soldier Boy." At the show's conclusion, an Army bomber appeared on stage, tossed about in a thunderstorm.

The war found its way into the 1944 musical comedy *Follow the Girls*, played out at a serviceman's club called the Starlight Canteen. The forgettable plot centered on a portly civilian (Jackie Gleason) vying with a handsome Navy officer (Frank Parker) for a buxom stripper (Gertrude Niesen).

When *Something for the Boys* opened on January 7, 1943, the *Herald Tribune* called it "bright" but noted "it shares the structural weakness of many large-scale musicals in that its dance numbers are not convincingly integrated in the plot."

Big changes were coming.

Sleet was falling the night of March 31, 1943, but when the curtain rose at the St. James Theatre, an old woman churning butter on the porch of a farmhouse had her labors interrupted by a cowhand's *a capella* baritone refrain: "There's a bright golden haze on the meadow."

Oklahoma!—music by Richard Rodgers, book and lyrics by Oscar Hammerstein II—became a theatrical milestone, melding story, lyrics, music, costumes, lighting, scenery, and dance to an extent never before achieved. And in recounting the transformation of an Indian Territory into a state at the turn of the twentieth century, it blended nostalgia with a much-prized optimism amid the grim headlines of the day.

When he completed the book for *Oklahoma!* Hammerstein concluded "it's a long time since any musical had such an American flavor as this one."

As the farmers and the cowmen sang: "the land we belong to is grand."

"Young people were going out to fight and perhaps to die for this country. What better time to be reminded of the unselfconscious courage of those folks who settled the West?" Celeste Holm, who played Ado Annie Carnes, the girl who "cain't say no," once observed. "People in uniform were always in the audience. People have told me it was the last show they saw before they went overseas and how proud it made them feel to be an American."

Hammerstein's daughter Alice told how "he gave me a job at *Oklahoma!* supervising standing room, with all the rowdy, noisy GIs."

"The first time I heard the score, I believe it was up in the Theatre Guild building, next to the Museum of Modern Art," recalled George S. Irving, who, at age nineteen, was a member of the chorus in the first of his more than thirty Broadway shows.

I recall the marble stairway going up and in a niche was Jo Davidson's bust of George Bernard Shaw. Richard Rodgers was sitting at the piano, impeccably dressed—he was the most elegant man—and he played through the show and he sang it, and I think Oscar sang a little of it. It was just lovely. It was very American and very accessible. The kick-line chorus shows were great fun and very skilled, but this one really got to the people. And it was a score you could hum on your way out of the theater.

But *Oklahoma!* arrived on Broadway with question marks. The play it was based on, Lynn Riggs's *Green Grow the Lilacs,* was a box-office disappointment on Broadway in 1931. Having ended his hugely successful collaboration with Lorenz Hart, Rodgers was working for the first time with Hammerstein, who was coming off a half-dozen Broadway flops. The choreographer, Agnes de Mille, was highly respected but had yet to make a mark on Broadway. The director, Rouben Mamoulian, had directed *Porgy and Bess* on Broadway, but most recently had worked in Hollywood. None of the performers were big names. The best known, Joseph Buloff, who played a peddler, was a veteran of the Yiddish theater.

As for financial backing, "How they got the money is still not completely clear to me," Rodgers once recalled, "for the financial resistance to the show was enormous. First, there was the piece itself. It was a horse opera with no questionable jokes but overdressed women."

The Theatre Guild, overseeing the production, managed to secure $80,000 in backing. Harry Cohn, the head of Columbia Pictures, invested $15,000. The playwright S. N. Behrman invested $20,000 as a payback to the guild for its past support of his work.

They would be well rewarded. George S. Irving remembered how during the Boston tryout "we were at the Colonial Theatre, and up at the Shubert, Mary Martin was trying out a show called *Dancing in the Streets*, and they all thought that would be the great hit. And they were a flop and we were a thunderbolt."

In the hours before *Oklahoma!* opened, there were still seats to be filled. Adding to its uncertain prospects, it was competing with Ethel Merman in *Something for the Boys* and Ray Bolger and Nanette Fabray in Rodgers and Hart's *By Jupiter.*

Before securing her part in *Oklahoma!* Celeste Holm had waited on tables at the Stage Door Canteen, "dancing with these naïve kids from all over the country in their new uniforms who were scared to death, not knowing what they were getting into."

She joined with fellow cast members on a quick trip to the canteen as the opening curtain grew near "and told the boys to come up the street to the St. James to see our show free."

Hammerstein sat in the orchestra while Rodgers paced at the back of the theater. But for all their angst, it was clear from the outset that *Oklahoma!*

held its audience in thrall. "Not only could I see it and hear it," Hammerstein once said, "I could feel it. The glow was like the light from a thousand lanterns. You could *feel* the glow. It was that bright."

Agnes de Mille recalled how "Oh, What a Beautiful Mornin' " brought "a sigh from the entire house that I don't think I ever heard in the theater. Just, 'Aaaah!' Like people seeing their homeland. The Dream Ballet was a sensation, but after 'The Farmer and the Cowman' in act two, the audience was screaming and yelling."

Joan Roberts, as Laurey, fought over by the cowhand Curly (Alfred Drake) and the thuggish ranch hand Jud (Howard Da Silva), had to change hurriedly into her wedding dress for the last scene. She remembered how "I left the stage and was half undressed, but the applause wouldn't stop. So they made me get back into my costume, and as I ran back onstage I was holding my dress together at the back because I hadn't had time to do up the zipper."

Oklahoma! presented a love triangle. Laurey, who lives on a farm with her Aunt Eller, is in love with Curly, and the attraction is mutual, but each seeks to avoid appearing too eager. Laurey, in an attempt to stir jealousy in Curly, agrees to accompany Jud to a box social. But when Jud tries to force himself on her, she fires him. He vows revenge. Laurey and Curly are married, and they join in singing "Oklahoma." But on that wedding day, Jud appears, attacks Curly with a knife, but falls on it and dies. Curly is cleared of wrongdoing and he heads off with Laurey for their honeymoon in their surrey with a fringe on top—a new life in a soon-to-be new state.

The show's elements, when woven together, enhanced the basics of the plot. The songs, orchestrated by Robert Russell Bennett, flowed from the story and the characters, the ambivalence in the relationship between Laurey and Curly underscored most memorably in "People Will Say We're in Love." De Mille ignored the custom of selecting tall, gorgeous chorus girls whose routines generally had a questionable connection to the plot, believing that "the dreamy girls don't deliver the performances." In the dream ballet "Laurey Makes Up Her Mind," conveying Laurey's sexual longings and her fears, de Mille bypassed Alfred Drake and Joan Roberts. Choosing the dancers for their technical skills, she used Marc Platt, formerly of the Ballet Russe de Monte Carlo, and Katharine Sergava of the Ballet Theatre.

Once the rave reviews were in, tickets became exceedingly hard to get, but sometimes a sellout was not quite that, as the theater historian Ethan Mordden noted in recounting his favorite story.

A young couple showed up at the St. James box office, hoping against hope that there might be something—a cancellation, perhaps? Nothing.

The man was in uniform, and he mentioned that he was shipping out for Europe the next day. The ticket seller silently pushed over a pair, fifth row center. They were my parents.

Oklahoma! received a special commendation from the Pulitzer Prize committee in 1944 and it dispatched a troupe for the USO Camp Shows program. It ran until May 29, 1948, its 2,212 performances setting a record for an American musical that endured until *My Fair Lady*. It became a Hollywood film, its national road company toured for more than nine years, and it was presented all over the world, in more than a dozen languages. It launched the Rodgers-Hammerstein collaboration creating *Carousel, South Pacific,* and *The King and I.*

In the wake of *Oklahoma!* wartime Broadway returned to Americana with *Bloomer Girl*, telling of the nineteenth-century suffragette movement; *Sing Out, Sweet Land*, saluting American folk and popular music from the Puritans to World War II; *Up in Central Park*, a remembrance of the battles against the graft of New York's 1870s Tweed Ring, and, most notably, at war's end, *Carousel*, its dark themes played out against life on the carnival circuit.

While *Oklahoma!* was comfortably settled into its run, Jerome Robbins and Leonard Bernstein launched an epic collaboration with their melding of song and dance in the ballet *Fancy Free*, opening on April 18, 1944 at the old Metropolitan Opera House at 39th Street and Broadway.

Robbins, the son of a New Jersey corset maker, had begun to study dance while a chemistry major at New York University in the mid-1930s. At age twenty-three he became the youngest principal dancer in the brief history of the Ballet Theatre of New York. But he was determined to be a choreographer. Bernstein, born in Boston, had gone to Harvard and had studied at the Curtis Institute in Philadelphia, a prestigious musical conservatory. He had attracted mentors like Serge Koussevitzky, Dimitri Mitropoulos, and Aaron Copland, and in the spring of 1943 he became the assistant conductor of the New York Philharmonic. He received sensational notices that November stepping in for the ailing conductor Bruno Walter in a Sunday afternoon broadcast performance.

Robbins had an idea for a ballet—a portrayal of character through dance. It would be a short story, focusing on three sailors on a brief leave in New York vying for the attentions of two girls in a bar, and it sprang from his observations of Navy boys walking the streets of wartime Manhattan. Robbins noticed how "sailors usually went around in threes," their "eyes and mouths open to all the sights."

He envisioned the dancers displaying "typically sailor movements: the swagger, the pose, the slouch, the strut and walk," the steps derived from the boogie, the lindy-hop and the soft-shoe shuffle. He saw his dancers as "warm, tender, human," and "not just tough sailors and girls of easy virtue." And Robbins himself would be one of the sailors.

As Bernstein, who wrote the jazzy score and conducted the orchestra for *Fancy Free*, put it in a program note:

> The curtain rises on a street corner with a lamp post, a side street bar and New York skyscrapers pricked out with a crazy pattern of lights, making a dizzying back drop. Three sailors explode on the stage. They are on a 24-hour leave in the city and on the prowl for girls. The tale of how they first meet one, then a second girl, and how they fight over them, lose them, and in the end take off after still a third, is the story of the ballet.

The "dizzying back drop" sprang from the imagination of a third prodigy, Oliver Smith, the scenic designer for de Mille's *Rodeo* for the Ballet Russe and, like Robbins, a member of the Ballet Theatre. A frantic air prevailed, however, in the moments before the curtain rose on opening night.

The prop man was unable to find the phonograph needed to play "Big Stuff," the opening musical number, a blues song heard on a juke box and recorded by Bernstein's sister, Shirley. Bernstein solved that crisis with help from his friends Betty Comden and Adolph Green, partners in the Revuers, a nightclub act that had played at the Village Vanguard and the Blue Angel. (The Revuers also included a young actress named Judy Tuvim, soon to be known as Judy Holliday.) Comden and Green, who were in the opening-night audience for *Fancy Free*, rushed to Comden's apartment to pick up her table-model phonograph and hustled back with it in a taxi. Robbins, meanwhile, had split the side zipper on his sailor-suit trousers while warming up. The wardrobe mistress quickly repaired it.

Fancy Free, only nineteen minutes long, proved a sensation, producing twenty-two curtain calls. John Martin, the dance critic of the *Times*, called it "just exactly ten degrees north of terrific." The Ballet Theatre's season was extended for two weeks to accommodate ticket demands. The opera house's 3,330 seats were filled for each performance and the standees were three deep.

The dancing, the music, and their melding were brilliant. But *Fancy Free* was more than that. Janet Reed, one of the two girls pursued by the sailors, recalled how the choreography reflected the frantic times.

> It was World War II. The whole attitude of young people was very disoriented. And we were living right in the middle of it. On tour, the Ballet Theatre cars would be hooked up to the troop cars. All these soldiers and sailors and ballet dancers, in strange places and different towns. We

were uprooted, and though we had a very carefree attitude, we were also very tentative about relationships. We were all so very young . . . innocent and rather lonely . . . wanting so much to be close to one another and knowing it couldn't last.

In the afterglow of *Fancy Free*, Robbins proposed a more ambitious project to Bernstein that he envisioned as "a new form for theater and ballet" that employs "three mediums of expression: dance, music and voice." As Robbins saw it, this would be "a real braiding of these three mediums, not a matter of placing them in layers one on top of the other." It would be a full-scale Broadway musical using actors who could also sing and dance, an undertaking even more ambitious than *Oklahoma!*

But Robbins, Bernstein, and Smith faced a formidable obstacle. The moneymen hardly knew them. The sorely needed strong hand of experience came when George Abbott, the writer-director-producer who had overseen numerous Broadway hits, including *The Boys From Syracuse* and *Pal Joey*, took over as director and a father figure. Once Abbott came aboard, the financing fell into place. MGM invested in the show and signed up for a movie deal, and RKO also supplied backing.

On the Town, with book and lyrics by Comden and Green, was a successor of sorts to *Fancy Free*, but with important differences. There would again be three sailors, but this time there would be three girls, not two, and the Navy men, Gabey, Chip, and Ozzie, would cooperate, rather than compete. The show had almost an hour of symphonic dance music but none taken from *Fancy Free*.

The sailors were played by relative unknowns—Cris Alexander as Chip, Adolph Green as Ozzie, and John Battles as Gabey. Nancy Walker, a comedienne who had appeared in Broadway's *Best Foot Forward*, played Hildy Esterhazy, a pushy but warmhearted and man-crazy taxi driver, who latches on to Chip. Betty Comden was Claire de Loone, a zany anthropologist who two-times her naïve fiancé, Judge Pitkin W. Bridgework, and attaches herself to Ozzie. The best-known cast member was Sono Osato, who had performed with Robbins in the Ballet Theatre's *Pillar of Fire* and *Romeo and Juliet* before gaining acclaim in Broadway's *One Touch of Venus*. Osato played Gabey's love interest as Miss Turnstiles.

Gabey falls in love with the image on a poster he spots in the subway—the likeness of Miss Turnstiles, a takeoff on the Miss Subways promotion sponsored by the Transit Authority and Macy's. Miss Turnstiles was, in fact, an everyday New Yorker who had become a celebrity of the month—a singing, dancing and painting student named Ivy Smith. But Gabey sees her as the girl of his dreams and vows to find her. Ozzie, who is simply out for sexual adventure, and Chip, an innocent type armed with his father's 1934 guidebook to New York, agree to help him.

They go their separate ways in search for Miss Turnstiles. Gabey tracks Ivy down briefly at Carnegie Hall, where she is taking voice lessons from her loopy alcoholic instructor Madame Maude P. Dilly (played by Osato's actual singing teacher, Susan Steell). Ozzie becomes entangled with Claire de Loone (he reminds her of the Neanderthals she is studying) at the American Museum of Natural History. Chip, who has high hopes of seeing the aquarium and getting a ticket to *Tobacco Road*, is instead overwhelmed by Hildy when he rides in her taxi.

The sailors' frenzied whirl through wartime New York was something of a farce, but the poignancy of young men and women in their fleeting wartime romances shone in Robbins's choreography, Bernstein's ballads, and the lyrics of Comden and Green.

Gabey, wandering through Times Square, where nobody has time for him, laments his plight in "Lonely Town."

In the "Times Square Ballet," the dancers rush about, meeting and then parting in the "dimout," illuminated only by passing cars and taxis, a representation of the soldiers and sailors and their girls of the moment in their encounters of a wartime night.

When Gabey becomes convinced that Ivy will be his girl, if only for a few precious hours, he exults in "Lucky to Be Me." But when Gabey, Chip, and Ozzie, along with Hildy and Claire de Loone, ultimately head for Coney Island, where Madame Dilly told them they could find the elusive Miss Turnstiles, the sailors and their girls wonder if they will see each other beyond this day and night. They vow that some day "we'll catch up": the poignant ballad "Some Other Time."

They do find Ivy in Coney Island, but Gabey learns that she is nothing like his vision. She is working as a belly dancer, a long, colored handkerchief between her teeth, to pay for her singing lessons. Gabey professes his love nonetheless.

And then the sailors return to the Brooklyn Navy Yard. Their twenty-four hours "on the town" is up, their ship will soon leave. Their girls wave good-bye. Just then, another group of sailors rushes down a gangplank for twenty-four hours in town.

They, too, sing: "New York, New York, a helluva town./The Bronx is up, but the Battery's down."

Comden and Green, who would collaborate for more than six decades and write *Wonderful Town, Bells Are Ringing*, and *Singin' in the Rain*, viewed *On the Town* as conveying "the poignancy of young people trying eagerly to cram a whole lifetime into a day."

From Oliver Smith's perspective: *"On the Town* wasn't about three sailors. It was about the enormous love each of us felt for New York."

On the Town also broke social ground. Robbins wanted to replicate the feel of Times Square, which he saw as the symbol of New York, and in doing it he gave Broadway its first integrated chorus, four white dancers holding the hands of four black dancers, a representation of the faces in a midtown crowd.

To Osato, *On the Town* perfectly mirrored the wartime city.

It was amazing. You would perform on the stage, and when you went out you saw exactly the same things happening in the street. It was filled with soldiers, sailors, and airmen who were on leave for twenty-four hours or three days or whatever. They were children, seventeen, eighteen, nineteen years old, and they'd never been here. There was a lot of innocent wonder at the bigness of the city, the pace of the city, the energy of the city.

But Osato had become Miss Turnstiles with misgivings.

In the ballet I was never cast in an ingénue role, and I never liked coy, little girls who were so innocent, so sweet, who didn't know anything. So I can't say I was enamored with my part. I had one discussion with Betty Comden, and I said, "I don't want a large part, but I would like to have a character that has some guts and spirit, more pep and drive." But she was not interested in changing anything about my part.

Osato was determined that her Miss Turnstiles "was not to be an ingénue," and she tried to make her "just as real and down to earth as possible." She had been startled over her selection for the role.

It was amazing to me that at the height of a world war fought over the vital political, moral, and racial issues, a Broadway musical should feature, and have audiences unquestioningly accept, a half-Japanese as an all-American girl.

While Osato was appearing in *On the Town,* her father, Shoji Osato, who had been living with her mother in Chicago, was swept up in the mass internment of Japanese.

The FBI, or whoever it was, came and took him without telling my mother how long it would be or where he would be. My mother found out later. He was kept in a former stone mansion on the South Side of

Chicago with Germans and Italians for ten months. It was a very painful experience. I visited him and took some *Life* magazines with me, and we were sitting at a card table with an armed guard who shook the magazines to see if there was a weapon or something inside. I felt so badly for my father more so than for myself. He did not express his feelings much but there was an expression of huge pain and embarrassment.

When Osato's father was released from internment, he came to New York to see her perform. Her brother, Tim, was fighting in Italy at the time with the Army's Japanese-American 442nd Regimental Combat Team. One time, Osato encountered some Japanese-American soldiers in New York, preparing to head overseas. "I was not very Japanese in my behavior because I started to cry. I remember being so moved, thinking, 'Well, I guess they have to die to prove they're Americans.' "

On the Town ran for 426 performances, outlasting the war. But for many, it is the 1949 movie adaptation that is remembered, most notably the opening scene when Frank Sinatra, Gene Kelly, and Jules Munchin sing "New York, New York" while prancing on the Brooklyn Bridge. But Bernstein's "Lonely Town," "Lucky to Be Me," and "Some Other Time" were cut by MGM. "Helluva town" was deemed too strong for movie audiences. It became "wonderful town."

By the time the movie was released, it had been four years since sailors were racing against time on shore leaves, then shipping out for an uncertain destiny. The original *On the Town* had been a show for its time. And when Germany surrendered, no one was more joyful than Sono Osato.

Her father was free and her brother had survived the bitter fighting in Italy.

V-E Day, May 8, lit up a sunny matinee day. Between scenes we rejoiced quietly in our dressing rooms, while through the windows of the Martin Beck Theatre, our new home, we saw crowds of men and women, in uniform and out, hugging, dancing and shouting. That day the reality outside in the streets blended gloriously with our glimpse onstage of the preciousness of our todays in the face of our unknown tomorrows. Joy and tearful relief engulfed the theater and the city.

Mayor La Guardia with Eleanor Roosevelt in September 1941, when he named her codirector of the national Office of Civilian Defense, which he had been heading since the previous May. Library of Congress

Mrs. Eddie Rickenbacker (*second from left*), the wife of the World War I air ace, joins civil defense volunteers plotting the locations of unidentified planes flying over New York. Library of Congress

Auxiliary firefighters ride aboard a fire engine painted gray to avoid detection in the event of an air raid and equipped with minimal headlights for operating in a blackout. Library of Congress

Soldiers march up Fifth Avenue in the New York at War parade of June 1942. Library of Congress

Erich Gimpel, a German national, and William Colepaugh (*at rear*), a native-born American, at Fort Jay in New York Harbor, where a military tribunal convicted them of spying for Germany in February 1945. AP/Wide World Photo

Members of the 6888th Central Postal Directory Battalion, the only all-black unit of Wacs to serve overseas in World War II, await departure for Britain at the New York Port of Embarkation's Camp Shanks staging area in February 1945. Front row (*left to right*): Private Rose Stone, Private Virginia Blake, Private First Class Marie Gillisspie. Middle row (*left to right*): Private Genevieve Marshall, Technician Fifth Grade Fanny Talbert, Corporal Callie Smith. Top row (*left to right*): Private Gladys Schuster Carter, Technician Fourth Grade Evelyn Martin, Private First Class Theodora Palmer. AP/Wide World Photo

The once-glamorous French ocean liner *Normandie* begins to capsize at its Manhattan pier after it was swept by fire in February 1942 while being converted to an American troopship. AP/Wide World Photo

The battleship *Iowa,* built at the Brooklyn Navy Yard, moves through New York Harbor in March 1943. The *Iowa* later transported President Roosevelt to and from Casablanca, then saw action in the Pacific. Naval Historical Center

Margaret Truman christens the battleship *Missouri* at the Brooklyn Navy Yard in January 1944 alongside her father, the senator from Missouri, who will be president when the Japanese surrender aboard the ship in Tokyo Bay. United States Navy, Courtesy Harry S. Truman Library

Peggy Guggenheim founded the Manhattan gallery Art of This Century, where modernists arriving from occupied France and the abstract expressionists (also known as the New York School artists) displayed their works in an innovative setting of freely hung, unframed paintings and curved walls. AP/Wide World Photo

French students at L'Ecole Maternelle Française on West 28th Street in Manhattan pay tribute to the Tri-Color on D-Day. Library of Congress

The former battleship *Prairie State*, anchored in the Hudson River, was converted to classroom use with construction of a wooden shed over its hull as part of the Navy's officer-training program at Columbia University. Naval Historical Center

Navy Waves and Coast Guard Spars being sworn in at City Hall Park in February 1943 before joining a vast training program at Hunter College in the Bronx. Naval Historical Center

Harold Russell, a paratrooper who lost his hands in a training accident, demonstrates his use of steel hooks in the film *Diary of a Sergeant,* shot at the Army's photo center in Astoria, Queens, in 1944. Russell went on to receive two Oscars for his performance in the 1946 Hollywood movie *The Best Years of Our Lives.* Copyright Ray Fisher

Servicemen being entertained by Broadway stars at the American Theatre Wing's Stage Door Canteen on West 44th Street. Library of Congress

Irving Berlin, emerging from a tent in his World War I doughboy outfit, sings "Oh, How I Hate to Get Up in the Morning" in his 1942 all-soldier show *This Is the Army.* Billy Rose Theatre Division, The New York Public Library for the Performing Arts, Astor, Lenox, and Tilden Foundations

Joan Roberts as Laurey in Rodgers and Hammerstein's *Oklahoma!*, which saluted the American spirit at a time of national trial. Billy Rose Theatre Division, The New York Public Library for the Performing Arts, Astor, Lenox, and Tilden Foundations.

Cris Alexander as Chip and Nancy Walker as the amorous cabbie Hildy Esterhazy in the Leonard Bernstein–Jerome Robbins production of *On the Town*. Billy Rose Theatre Division, The New York Public Library for the Performing Arts, Astor, Lenox, and Tilden Foundations.

An airman blows Camel smoke rings (actually steam) in Times Square. Library of Congress

Night and day, the lines wound around the Paramount for Frank Sinatra in October 1944, when the crush of bobby-soxers erupted into the "Columbus Day Riot." AP/Wide World Photo

The Copacabana nightclub featured the dancing of the Copa Girls, among them (*left to right*) Betty Carson, Joan Wynne, and Tally Richards. Courtesy of Joan Wynne

The Hitler salute greets the German-American Bund at its February 1939 rally in Madison Square Garden. AP/Wide World Photo

New York synagogues were vandalized and Jewish youngsters attacked in an upsurge of anti-Semitism during the war. On D-Day, the congregation at Emunath Israel on West 23rd Street in Manhattan joined in the prayer services held throughout the city. Library of Congress

A pawnshop at Eighth Avenue and 145th Street was looted in the Harlem riot of August 1943, touched off by the shooting of a black soldier by a white policeman, but fueled by longstanding racial discrimination. AP/Wide World Photo

Firemen examine the wreckage from the crash of an Army bomber into the Empire State Building's 79th floor, where members of a Catholic war-relief agency were working on a rainy Saturday in July 1945. AP/Wide World Photo

General Dwight D. Eisenhower being cheered by 4 million New Yorkers on June 19, 1945, during his triumphant homecoming. Library of Congress

Speaking every Sunday from City Hall on the municipal radio station, Mayor La Guardia gave housewives advice on rationing, vilified black-market racketeers, and, most famously, told of Dick Tracy's exploits when a newspaper strike in July 1945 deprived youngsters of their comics. Library of Congress

An enduring image symbolizing peace: a sailor and a nurse kissing in Times Square on V-J Day. This photo was taken by Lieutenant Victor Jorgensen, a Navy photographer, at a slightly different angle from the image captured by Alfred Eisenstaedt for *Life* magazine. United States Navy, via AP/Wide World Photo

Marlene Dietrich greets servicemen returning from Europe when the troopship *Monticello* docks at a Manhattan pier in July 1945. AP/Wide World Photo

The transport *Joseph V. Connolly* arrives in New York on October 26, 1947, with 6,248 coffins bearing the remains of servicemen killed in Europe. Sailors from the destroyer *Bristol* pay tribute. AP/Wide World Photo

PART FIVE

THE NIGHT

CHAPTER 21

TIMES SQUARE IN SHADOW

In the early months of 1942, U-boats prowled America's East Coast virtually unmolested, sinking scores of oil tankers and freighters bound for Britain. Oil slicks washed up on beaches, the depressing residue of the submarines' victims. On February 28, a German submarine torpedoed the destroyer *Jacob Jones* off Cape May, New Jersey, and only 11 of its 150 crew members survived.

Navy ships and Army planes were getting a late start in confronting the U-boat menace, but there was one step the military could take without firing a shot or dropping a depth charge. The glow from New York City's lights was silhouetting ships offshore, leaving them easy marks for those submarines. At the end of April 1942, the Army ordered a "dimout" of the entire city.

Times Square was no longer the Great White Way. The brilliant neon advertising signs were doused. Neon peanuts no longer cascaded from a huge bag of Planters, urging "a bag a day for more pep." The multicolored electronic fish blowing bubbles in the Wrigley chewing gum sea blew no more.

Office buildings and apartment houses throughout the city were required to veil windows more than fifteen stories high. Stores, restaurants, and bars toned down their exterior lighting. Streetlights and traffic signals had their wattages reduced, and automobile headlights were hooded. The gold-leaf roof of the United States Courthouse in Lower Manhattan was daubed in black paint, lest it gleam in the moonlight. The Statue of Liberty's torch, emblazoned with 13,000-watt lamps, was relegated to a pair of 200-watt bulbs needed to warn away low-flying aircraft. For the first time since its debut on November 6, 1928, when Herbert Hoover was elected president, the *New York Times*'s electronic news bulletins winding around the Times Tower went dark.

Artkraft Strauss, Times Square's leading sign company, and its chief idea man, Douglas Leigh, were undaunted. An Alabama native and the son of a banker—the archetype of the boy from the hinterlands who heads to New York to pursue a dream—Leigh had arrived in the city in the early 1930s, hoping to sell advertising space for a Birmingham sign company. He was a brilliant salesman, but he had a boundless imagination as well. He scored his first creative success in 1933 with his Times Square advertising sign for A&P coffees, featuring an oversized cup of coffee emitting steam through holes in its metal rim.

When war seemed near for America—blackouts or at least lesser measures to curb lighting sure to come—Leigh looked for alternatives to the animated neon signs. His quest for a sign that would be ideal for both day and night display spawned the Camel smoke rings.

Installed by Artkraft Strauss in 1941 on the façade of the Claridge Hotel at West 44th Street and Broadway, the Camel sign featured a smoker's mouth forming a perfect "O." Every four seconds, from 7 a.m. to 1 a.m., he exhaled a "smoke" ring—actually steam from the hotel's heating system.

The face on the sign belonged to Lyman Clardy, a professional model. He was a nonsmoker, but for a $5 fee he spent a morning before a camera in a studio posing with a Camel in his hand, attempting to blow smoke rings. "It sounded nuts to me," he once said. "And I didn't really like cigarettes. But five bucks was five bucks." Later in the war, Clardy was replaced at varying times by the images of a soldier, a sailor, an airman, and a marine. By then he was a Navy officer, serving in the Pacific.

With its sixteen Times Square neon signs blacked out by the war, Artkraft Strauss searched for a way to highlight advertising displays at night without running afoul of the dimout rules. The solution: mosaics of one-inch-square mirrors tinted gold, blue, green, red, and yellow that reflected light from auto headlights and the minimal street lighting still permitted.

While the Times Tower no longer displayed electronic news bulletins, Times Square did have an eye-catcher nearby, a large replica of the Statue of Liberty erected in November 1944 to spur bond sales for the Sixth War Loan Drive with a stage in front for lunchtime performances by top Broadway talent.

The dimout posed no problems at the old Madison Square Garden on Eighth Avenue, where boxing, college basketball, and hockey carried on through the war. An August 1944 nontitle bout between the lightweight boxing champion, Bob Montgomery, and the former titleholder, Beau Jack, both in the army, required a war bond purchase as the price of admission, with tickets scaled from $25 to $100,000. Wounded soldiers from the Normandy and Italian campaigns were given seats in the first three rows in an event that raised $35.8 million for the Treasury Department.

Notwithstanding the dimout, New York wasn't all that dark in compari-

son to the great cities of Europe, so far as Farnsworth Fowle, a war correspondent on home leave, could tell. Having covered the Salerno invasion
and the capture of Rome for CBS Radio, Fowle was in New York during the
summer of 1944, acquainting himself with the CBS newsroom on Madison Avenue.

Ed Murrow's broadcasts from London and the correspondents known
as the "Murrow Boys" had brought CBS preeminence in broadcast journalism, but the New York operation was an uncomplicated affair. "It was just
one floor of a small office tower," Fowle recalled. "CBS News was essentially an ex–United Press operation. The key man was Paul White, who
went directly from U.P. to set up the thing. It was very close knit. Anyway,
in New York I said: 'You guys are pros and I'm strictly an amateur. Give me
some cues on how I should do this microphone stuff.' They said, 'Oh, no,
you guys are reporters, and if you were a little awkward on the microphone,
well that's just more authentic.' They in effect told me to do my own thing."

When he wasn't at CBS headquarters, Fowle had time to sample some
of New York's nightspots, including Café Society Uptown, featuring Hazel
Scott at the piano. He wasn't too impressed with the dimout.

"In Rome it was a complete blackout," he remembered. "You don't really
appreciate Roman Baroque architecture until you've seen it by moonlight.
It was a very striking experience—the moonlight on all those rounds and
curves and irregularities. Architecturally, it was very exciting to see the city
the way it had been originally. But in New York, at the street level it was
all lit."

E. J. Kahn Jr. of the *New Yorker*, home in spring 1943 after Army service in New Guinea, expected Times Square to be "shrouded in hazardous
gloom" only to be disappointed.

I noticed at once, naturally, that the Wrigley fishes had ceased to wriggle
and that curfew had sounded for the electric bar from which those giant
Wilson Whiskey highballs once so inexorably flowed. Below the second-
story level, though, Times Square was still a good deal brighter than any
other place I have recently been in, with the possible exception of Port
Moresby, where, because there is so much more important work to be
done, the lights stay on at night until the sirens announce an uninvited
aerial visitor.

Beyond Times Square, the city's sports and recreational worlds played
on amid the dimout.

Servicemen were admitted free to baseball games, but they wouldn't be
seeing any night games during the early war years. Night baseball at the

Polo Grounds in Harlem and Ebbets Field in Flatbush (Yankee Stadium still had no lights) was banned for the 1942 and 1943 seasons.

Complications ensued. On August 3, 1942, the Giants tried a twilight start when they faced the Dodgers in a game benefitting the Army Emergency Relief Fund. The game, drawing 57,305 to the Polo Grounds, was to end at 9:10 p.m., when the ballpark lights had to be turned off, the glare becoming noticeable at sea as darkness descended. Trailing by 7–4, the Giants had two men on and nobody out in the bottom of the ninth inning when the game was called and the Dodgers declared the winner—9:10 had arrived. When the Fred Waring orchestra and a 150-member choral group went out to second base to conclude the patriotic affair with the national anthem, the furious Giants fans booed. The jeering stopped only when a spotlight was shined on an American flag flying over the roof in center field.

When night baseball returned on May 23, 1944, for a game at Ebbets Field, the Dodgers were sporting their new evening garb: white satin jerseys with royal blue trim. They defeated the Giants, 3–2, before a crowd of more than 23,000, but there wasn't much to see by then. With most of the top talent off to military service, the major league ball clubs carried on with players too young or too old for the draft, or possessors of gimpy knees that didn't keep them from chasing down fly balls but merited a 4-F deferment. The Yankees' Joe DiMaggio, Phil Rizzuto, and Tommy Henrich, the Dodgers' Pete Reiser and Pee Wee Reese, and the Giants' Johnny Mize were all in military service, though playing baseball most of the time for armed forces teams.

A few miles from Ebbets Field, Brooklyn's landmark playground and beach were still thriving by day. Gasoline and rubber rationing, along with a scarcity of parts, cut severely into automobile traffic, but millions poured into Coney Island on the BMT subway.

The shows kept up with the times. A wax museum featured displays on "MacArthur at Bataan" and "The Bombing of London." Soldiers and sailors far from the war worked out their aggression by tossing balls at wooden milk bottles painted with the grimacing faces of Hitler, Hirohito, and Mussolini forming the backdrop. Would-be paratroopers rode the Parachute Jump late of the World's Fair, dismantled and then reassembled at Steeplechase Park.

But Coney carried on in shadow at night. The Parachute Jump was left with a single light, at its top, a beacon for planes. The 800,000 lightbulbs of all colors that had outlined the Ferris wheels, the roller-coaster frames, and the side shows and hot-dog stands were doused. The street lamps on the Boardwalk had their sides blackened, leaving but a candlelike glow downward. The concessions made do with blue night lights.

Sid Frigand, the Brooklyn boy who had run home from Boys High School the day after the Pearl Harbor attack, convinced that New York was about to be bombed, spent late nights at Coney while on leave from Army basic training at Fort Benning, Georgia.

"I got together with a couple of friends who were on leave, or deferred for physical reasons, and our reunion place was Nathan's hot dogs. When we were going on dates we'd take them home and then all meet at Nathan's at 1 o'clock in the morning, and we'd all boast how we made out. And lied. They had to black out the lights that faced the ocean and it was dark and dingy. It had a mysterious air to it, but Coney Island was not fun."

It was less fun after the summer of 1944, when much of the Luna Park amusement area burned down.

In the dim Times Square nights, soldiers and sailors walked the streets. The *New Yorker*'s Robert Coates, reporting on "New York at its boomtown boomiest," watched those servicemen on a Saturday evening a few weeks before D-Day.

"You heard every accent among them except the New York one; they had hit town and they wanted to have a good time, but they were painfully uncertain how to go about it, and their restlessness as they wandered, searching for some hint or happening that would lead them to the excitement they wanted, gave the crowd its peculiar character."

Fewer than half the men had girls with them. The others eyed the display cards in movie theater lobbies and paused at restaurant windows, cut-rate book stores, shops selling cheap jewelry or sheet music, then moved on. Many wandered into the Crossroads (billing itself as "Times Square's largest bar") and the oval bar at Jack Dempsey's restaurant.

When a serviceman sought out a girl, the pickup was often casual. "A fellow would simply pull up alongside a girl and glance at her," Coates noted. "If she smiled, he took her arm. If she didn't, he just walked on."

The *New York Times* feature writer Meyer Berger, surveying a 1944 summer's night in Times Square, stayed around to watch the stragglers and drunks as dawn beckoned:

4 A.M.: A mixed group of American and British servicemen come out of Forty-Fourth east into the square roaring "Roll Out the Barrel." They've switched service caps and join hands in a drunken kind of flying wedge. Couples embrace in doorways. Two very young Navy kids literally throw a much drunker companion into a cab.

The soldiers and sailors looking for love often found venereal disease as well in their encounters with prostitutes and "V-Girls," teenagers seeking a quick thrill. During the first nine months of 1943, a total of 3,662 soldiers reported incurring VD in New York, the highest number for any city in the nation. Speaking out on the issue in January 1944, Charles Taft, a former official with the federal Community War Service Agencies, criticized the La Guardia administration for allowing token fines on pimps and madams while prostitutes were given harsh jail sentences. "This is a health program, not a vice crusade," Taft told the State Bar Association in calling for treatment programs for the girls. La Guardia dismissed the criticism, maintaining that "Charlie didn't know what he was talking about," and he insisted that the city had been cooperating with Army and Navy authorities in dealing with vice.

Lonely GIs looking for girlie magazines could find them at newsstands on West 42nd Street. At a time before porn magazines were openly displayed, a quick under-the-counter sale would yield titles like *Eyeful*, *Titter*, and *Sir*, all newly published to cater to servicemen.

The GIs willing to settle for a couple of hours at a burlesque house would have to look elsewhere. The Lord's Day Alliance, a national evangelical organization, urged La Guardia to shut down the few houses remaining, calling them "obscene, vulgar and perniciously poisonous" as well as a threat to national defense. The Catholic archbishop Francis Spellman, and the Protestant Episcopal bishop William Manning protested as well. La Guardia, always something of a blue nose, had closed many burlesque houses in the 1930s. In February 1942, the city refused to renew the licenses of the three that remained in Times Square—the Eltinge, Republic, and Gaiety—lest the morals of the servicemen passing through New York be undermined.

The influx of servicemen contributed to the underground homosexual activity centered on West 42nd Street, and by 1944, La Guardia had grown so concerned that he ordered the nightly closing of Bryant Park, on 42nd between Fifth and Sixth avenues. The balconies and bathrooms of the West 42nd Street "grinder house" movie theaters, mostly owned by the Brandt chain and showing low-budget action films, were alternate spots for homosexual trysts.

Tennessee Williams would tell of cruising Times Square with another young writer (whom he didn't identify), who "would dispatch me to street corners where sailors and GIs were grouped to make very abrupt and candid overtures, phrased so bluntly that it's a wonder they didn't slaughter me on the spot."

Sometimes they mistook me for a pimp soliciting for female prostitutes and would respond, "Sure, where's the girls?"—and I would have to explain that they were my cruising partner and myself. Then, for some reason, they would stare at me for a moment in astonishment, burst into laughter, huddle for a brief conference, and, as often as not, would accept the solicitation, going to my partner's Village pad or to my room at the "Y."

Williams's anonymity would soon be shed with the 1945 Broadway opening of *The Glass Menagerie*.

But Times Square and the surrounding streets still had something of a neighborhood feel, as George S. Irving, exploring it in his time off from the choruses of *Oklahoma!* and *Lady in the Dark*, would recall.

It was all smaller and shorter. The tallest building was the Paramount Theatre. On Eighth Avenue there was the Happiness Tea Garden, where you got a Chinese lunch for thirty-five cents. Times Square was a little dusty, but it wasn't slovenly. And the Upper West Side had neighborhoods; there was a Japanese enclave and an Irish enclave with their own stores.

War or not, Broadway columnists and press agents could be found at any hour at Hanson's drug store, 51st Street and Seventh Avenue, "the poor man's Stork Club," according to Walter Winchell, who sometimes dropped by.

Winchell was known to have bought a war bond or two from one of the Times Square area characters, Louie the Waiter, or, more formally, Louis Schwartz, a rotund forty-two-year-old fixture at the Sixth Avenue Delicatessen. Louie needed no formal campaign to pitch bonds. "About drives I am ignorant," he once said. "Here every day is a drive going on." Louie persuaded customers who came in for nothing more than a pastrami sandwich to buy bonds as well. By spring 1944 he was orchestrating an average of $7,000 in weekly bond purchases at the deli, earning a congratulatory handshake from Treasury Secretary Henry Morgenthau at his Rockefeller Center office and a pen-and-ink portrait by Al Hirschfeld, an old friend and customer.

Times Square's Runyonesque figures included Swifty Morgan, a peddler of garish neckties with a bulldog as a steady companion, and Broadway Sam Roth, a ticket agent with an ever-present carnation in his lapel, his slogan "a carnation a day keeps oblivion away."

When a corpse turned up, in Times Square or elsewhere in Manhattan, Arthur Fellig, better known as Weegee (from Oujia, for his psychic-like ability to arrive almost instantly at the scene of mayhem), turned up as well with his Speed Graphic. A freelance chronicler of New York's seamy side for the tabloid papers, Weegee lived by the credo "crime is my oyster and I like it." His collection of black-and-white photos in his 1945 book *Naked City* became the inspiration for the movie.

A world apart from Weegee, Times Square offered a glamorous touch in the stage shows at the great movie palaces along Broadway—the Paramount, Palace, Roxy, Capitol, Loew's State, and Strand. At Rockefeller Center, the cavernous Radio City Music Hall featured the celebrated Rockettes and the world's largest theater pipe organ. In May 1942, it presented the premiere of Alfred Hitchcock's thriller *Saboteur*, which famously included a shootout at the very same Radio City, the prelude to the wrongly accused Robert Cummings confronting the villainous Norman Lloyd at the crown of the Statue of Liberty.

A Brooklyn boy named Woody Allen, treated by his father to occasional visits to Times Square, developed a "romantic fascination" for it.

You'd ride the subway for a half hour from Brooklyn, then walk up into Times Square and look in every direction, and there would be marquees from movie houses. It was just one house after another, all lit up, a number of them with stage shows, and the streets were jammed with soldiers and sailors. There would be the guys with the apparently stringless dancing dolls that they were selling, and sailors picking up girls at, you know, papaya stands. It was just amazing to look at it.

The Paramount, with almost 4,000 seats, had been booking the top big bands since the Depression days. On December 30, 1942, Benny Goodman and his band headlined the stage show. As an "Extra Added Attraction," the Paramount presented a skinny young man from Hoboken given to oversized bow ties who had recently sung with the Tommy Dorsey and Harry James bands. During the next eight weeks, Frank Sinatra became a pop-culture phenomenon, the bobby-soxers arriving early in the morning and staying into the night, watching show after show and swooning in their seats over "Frankie."

In the fall of 1943, Sinatra played the Wedgwood Room of the Waldorf-Astoria, but he returned to the Paramount, and the bobby soxers' frenzy boiled over in the "Columbus Day Riot" of 1944. Thousands of girls snaked in the lines for blocks around the Paramount and jammed Times Square, smashing store windows, trampling passersby, and overwhelming hundreds of policemen called in from duty at the Columbus Day Parade.

Abel Green, the editor of *Variety*, thought Sinatra made his fans feel he was just like them, and one girl who wrote to *Down Beat* magazine agreed.

"Frankie has that certain something that makes every girl think he's singing just for her," she explained.

"If the bobby-soxers were a little older, much of it might be explained, at least partly, in terms of wartime frustration, with 11 million young men away in uniform," Bruce Bliven wrote in the *New Republic*.

Bliven observed that "our civilization no doubt seems wonderful to the children of half-starved, dictator-ridden Europe" but he suggested that the bobby-soxers had been left with "a hunger still unfulfilled: a hunger for heroes."

Sinatra seemed bemused by the mass love affair, the chaos. He told a reporter about one girl "who's always in the audience" and seemed to represent all his fans.

When I look accidentally in her direction, she lets out an awful yell. And sometimes she gets hysterical. The other morning she got that way and they told her they'd let her come up and see me. When I saw her, she was still crying. After a while she promised she'd be a good girl if I'd just give her my bow tie—you know girls have started to wear bow ties. So I did and she promised to be quiet. The next day I got out on the stage and there she was yelling worse than before.

CHAPTER 22

THE LATIN BEAT

The dimout took its toll on Times Square's theater and movie marquees, but the lavish nightclubs were thriving.

"New York became the market town of anybody on the Eastern Seaboard with a 100-dollar bill to spare," noted Alistair Cooke, who saw the city as "Tijuana on the Hudson."

"The nightclubs minted fortunes unmatched even in the lunatic 20s. As the cost of living went higher, more and more girls seemed to have mink and silver fox to wear."

For a night on the town, the Copacabana and the Latin Quarter were the hottest of the hot spots.

In the basement of an old hotel on East 60th Street, off Fifth Avenue, the Copa sprang from the imagination of Monte Proser, a onetime Hollywood press agent who had worked for the silent-film comic Harold Lloyd and sported horn-rimmed glasses that gave him something of a Lloyd look.

Proser had owned the La Conga nightclub in Hollywood, then opened a string of nightspots with a South Sea Island motif, among them the Beachcomber in Manhattan, featuring a tropical décor with sarong-clad girls.

His greatest success arrived when he switched to a South American theme, drawing on the popularity of dances like the rumba, the samba, and the conga, in imitating the nightlife of Rio de Janeiro's Copacabana district at his new Manhattan club.

Opening in October 1940 at the site of the old Villa Vallee restaurant, a Prohibition-era spot that featured the crooning of Rudy Vallee, Proser's brassy Copa moved into a slice of the Upper East Side that bespoke old money and a certain stuffiness. The Copa's neighbors included the Sherry-Netherland, Pierre, and Savoy Plaza hotels and the Harmonie, Colony, Union, and Metropolitan clubs.

The décor of the Rudy Vallee era disappeared when the Copa arrived. The mirrors that lined the walls of the Villa Vallee were stripped and the walls painted green and white. Four large concrete columns were reinvented as white palm trees, adorned by coconuts and reddish-brown leaves. A newly installed bar flashed a long, illuminated mirror depicting Rio's harbor by night.

While the Copa relied on Latin acts in its early days, Proser eventually signed big names like the comedian Joe E. Lewis and Sophie Tucker, "the last of the red hot mammas." Jimmy Durante, his comedic career in eclipse, staged a comeback at the wartime Copa, and Perry Como, having put away his barber's tools in Canonsburg, Pennsylvania, made his Copa singing debut in spring 1943.

Proser recruited chorus lines first known as the Samba Sirens and then, more famously, the Copa Girls, getting his dancers from modeling agencies, Broadway shows, and beauty pageants. Invariably in upswept hairdos and attired by leading designers, they earned up to $75 a week strutting on a 24-square-foot parquet dance floor.

They were supposedly eighteen years old and up. But that wasn't quite the case for Joan Wynne of Brooklyn's Sheepshead Bay section, who modeled as a young teen, then became a Copa Girl in 1945. Her mother had noticed an item in Walter Winchell's column reporting that four Copa Girls were fired for their involvement in a fight somewhere over their rivalry for the affections of the pre-Lucy Desi Arnaz, another of the Latin celebrities of the day. Since that melee presumably left four openings at the Copa, Joan's mother sent her there to audition. She was sixteen years old and petrified.

She arrived at the Copa, then waited outside until she figured the auditions were over for that day, assuming she would be told she was too late. She could then tell her mother she had been rejected.

She ran into Monte Proser.

He said, "Can you dance?"
I said, "No."
He said, "Can you walk?" He had me walk around in a circle.
He asked me, "How old are you?"
I told him, "Sixteen."
He said "Nobody's sixteen."
He told me to go home and get documentation from my father stating I was eighteen and to have my mother put henna in my hair—make me a redhead.

She did it, and he hired her.

When Joan took the Copa floor for the first time, she said, "I was paralyzed from fear. My hands gripped the columns made up to look like palm trees. The dance director got down on his hands and knees. He freed up one hand. But the other one stayed put. When he freed up the other hand, the first one went back."

But she overcame her stage fright, and Proser liked her so much he kept her on for two years although Copa Girls usually stayed for only three months, the length of a single show. "He took me places," she recalled. "He used to buy me a Pink Lady, but I never drank it. But he was a gentleman. He never made a pass at me."

The Copacabana's trademark was a turban-topped Copa Girl, the image appearing on its awning, matchbook covers, and advertising posters. The girl in the turban was, in fact, a member of the Copa chorus line—Emily Jewell, self-described as a "wide-eyed kid from Kansas City," chosen by Proser from the dance line in 1943. With the turban came the adulation that Emily had surely never envisioned back home. Al Jolson, she said, once bought her a $10,000 compact and got down on his knees begging her to marry him. But as she told it, "My mother thought he was too old for me."

For a young woman seeking a career in show business, the night club chorus lines meant a nice paycheck but also the possibility of entrée toward a Broadway or Hollywood role.

Fresh from the Midwest, like Emily Jewell, a show-business hopeful named Julie Wilson joined the wartime chorus lines of both the Latin Quarter and the Copacabana.

During her first semester at the University of Omaha, Wilson appeared in *The Earl Carroll Vanities* when it played the Orpheum Theater in Omaha, her hometown. She made it to New York in 1943 when the show came to the Loew's State. Overwhelmed yet enthralled by Manhattan, she wasn't about to return to Nebraska. A nightclub show booker she knew got her a job at the Latin Quarter.

"I was so scared to be in New York," Wilson recalled. "I had no money, I had nothing. Just to be alive and keep going was an amazing thing. Just to be in a top nightclub was the most thrilling thing in my life."

She also tried for the life of a fashion model and got an appointment with John Robert Powers, the head of the prestigious Powers modeling agency.

But I wasn't built to be a model. I was about five feet six-and-one-half inches. They're all close to six foot tall and weigh about ninety-five pounds and they have little-boy hips. There must have been forty of them going through in the three hours I was there.

I was lucky. Powers introduced me to Curly Harris, a publicist, who said: "You're working seven nights a week and you're getting fifty bucks for the week. Why don't you come over and I'll introduce you to Monte

Proser at the Copacabana? They get seventy-five a week." I thought that was a wonderful idea. Monte said, "We'd like to have you."

Wilson became a Copa girl, but her talents went beyond dancing. "Because I could carry a tune I got to be one of the production singers and sang with a very attractive boy from down south called Bob Johnson. We introduced, 'They've Got an Awful Lot of Coffee in Brazil.' Sinatra later recorded it. It was a tremendous hit."

The gravelly voiced comic Joe E. Lewis, wandering a nightclub stage with a whiskey tumbler in one hand and a microphone in the other, became the biggest star of the wartime Copa. That he even lived to make it there was remarkable. During Prohibition-era Chicago, Lewis had been attacked by gangsters after switching from one mob-run nightclub to another. His tongue and face were slashed and he lay near death for weeks, leaving him with a voice likened to two pieces of sandpaper rubbed together.

As Wilson remembered it: "He was always a favorite, the No. 1 guy. His fans were there, from all over the world and all over the country. The drunker he got—he drank a lot—the funnier he was. But he was never obscene, he was never vulgar, he was just fun. He had a twinkle in his eye, like a mischievous little boy."

When the last of the three nightly shows ended, Wilson and her fellow showgirls often went to Lindy's and wound up their night with breakfast there. And then the glamour faded, at least until the following night. Wilson would "get on my little subway, which was a nickel, and I'd be going to my little apartment." That happened to be in Queens.

The Copa did its bit for the war effort. In October 1944, it played host to more than 500 wounded sailors from St. Albans Naval Hospital in Queens. Wilson was part of a troupe of eight Copa Girls who entertained GIs in France and Germany under USO sponsorship, following V-E Day. At the performances in Nice and Cannes, "there'd be 50,000 boys sitting on the ground in these hills, and down at the bottom they'd put up a floor for us for a stage and we'd do our show."

After the war, Wilson returned to the Copa as a featured performer, appeared in musical theater, and became a leading figure on the Manhattan cabaret scene.

The Copa's wartime chorus line also included the future Hollywood star June Allyson, who was appearing in Broadway's *Panama Hattie* and *Best Foot Forward* while making the late-night Copa shows. Jane Ball, another Copa Girl, went on to Hollywood with roles in *Winged Victory*, *The Keys of the Kingdom*, and *Forever Amber*. Monte Proser, who once said he knew thousands of showgirls, decided she was the one for him and married her in 1945.

Beyond the nightclub flash, a dark issue surrounded the Copa—the question as to who really owned the place. Proser was listed as the Copa's president and major shareholder, but Jules Podell, one of his partners, oversaw the daily operations, assisted by Jack Entratter, the general manager and No. 1 "greeter." The unspoken name was that of Frank Costello.

Podell, who grew up in Brooklyn's Sheepshead Bay, a son of Jewish immigrants from Russia, had once owned the Kit Kat Club in New York and had been a part of the nightclub scene since the early days of the Depression. He was an omnipresent and, for the staff, often-feared figure, who helped pick the talent and supervised the kitchen and the waiters.

When Podell demanded service for himself, he made emphatic use of the onyx ring he wore on his pinkie finger. As the singer Peggy Lee recalled it:

> Jules was relatively short and strongly built. His neck was short; in fact, he seemed almost all of one piece, one solid muscle. He drank a lot, but he always knew exactly what he was doing. If Jules wanted attention, he would knock his big ring on the table and everyone would come running. Tough? They don't come any tougher.

But the toughest guy of them all was Frank Costello (Francisco Castiglia), the mob boss and an influential figure in the Democrats' Tammany Hall machine who was presumed to be a silent partner in the Copa. La Guardia maintained that Costello and the bookmaking kingpin Frank Erickson were among what he called "the tin horns and gamblers" who were the actual owners of the leading New York nightclubs. In 1945, the Copa paid a $10,000 installment on more than $37,000 in back taxes the city claimed, and it agreed to sever any connection it may have had with Costello without admitting that a connection actually existed.

Costello, or at least a girlfriend of his, maintained a presence in the Podell household during the immediate postwar years. The girlfriend babysat for Podell's daughter Mickey, who was born at war's end. Mickey would recall how her mother once told her, "Those mob guys, they really know how to treat a lady, and the biggest gentleman I ever met was Frank Costello."

The prime competition for the Copacabana came from the Latin Quarter at Broadway and 48th Street, the inspiration of Lou Walters, the London-born son of a tailor who came to Boston with his family when he was fifteen. Walters started out as an office assistant in an agency booking show-business acts. Soon he was signing acts on his own for vaudeville and nightclubs, and in 1937 he opened his first club.

He had seen the movie *Gold Diggers in Paris*, starring Rudy Vallee as a

Paris nightclub owner presenting a chorus line he had transported from America. One of the songs in the movie was "Latin Quarter." Walters took the name for his Boston club. It flourished, and in 1940 he bought Earl Carroll's Palm Island club near Miami Beach, offering a Latin theme there as well.

As Walters told it, he was sitting by himself in his South Florida nightspot on New Year's Day 1941 when a press agent named Irving Zussman asked him if he would like to open a nightclub in the Times Square area. Zussman said a space was available for a ten-year lease. E. M. Loew, the owner of a movie-house circuit where Walters had booked vaudeville acts, would provide the financial backing.

The space had previously housed nightclubs variously known as the Cotton Club (a post-Harlem version), the Palais d'Or, the Palais Royal, and the Gay White Way. It held 600 seats, and Walters figured that if his Latin theme could work in Boston and South Florida, why not Times Square?

In April 1942, with financial assistance from Loew, Walters opened the New York Latin Quarter. Walters was a soft-spoken man given to conservative blue suits, white shirts, and tinted glasses and a taste for fine art. But the image he conjured was all flamboyance.

Barbara Walters remembered her father's New York Latin Quarter as the ideal night spot for turbulent times. As she put it: "The opulent fantasy world my father had created—red-velvet-lined walls, a thickly quilted pink ceiling, fountains spouting colored water, mirrors on the staircase, and indirect lighting seeping through ostrich feathers—turned out to be the perfect antidote to the harsh, wartime world outside the club's mauve double doors."

Lou Walters's credo: "Everything in a nightclub should be a little bit better than you can afford." As for the customers: "Fill them full of food and take the breath away. Don't let them relax and feel normal for a minute. The man who goes to a nightclub goes in the spirit of splurging, and you've got to splurge right along with him."

CHAPTER 23

CAFÉ SOCIETY

They were the wealthy and ostensibly well bred, and their ranks included the émigré royalty of Europe. Of late, they were crowded by the newly rich of the boom times brought by war. They gathered to be seen and to be written up by the society columnists. They frequented restaurants like the Colony and "21," nightspots like the Stork Club and El Morocco, and the public rooms of the grand hotels—the Plaza, the Waldorf, the St. Regis, the Ritz-Carlton, and the Sherry-Netherland. Maury Paul, the Cholly Knickerbocker of the Hearst press, called them Café Society.

Notwithstanding the war somewhere out there, New York's social set was not about to defer its nights out. But Café Society might have lost some of its exclusivity. Lucius Beebe, the *Herald Tribune*'s authority on fine food and high style, sneered at what he saw:

> There were rich French refugees with manners which would have outraged a Colorado mining camp in gold-rush days. There were the camp followers of the Federal government in Washington full of idealism about milk for the Hottentots and more practical visions of champagne for themselves, and there were members of the armed forces from Elko, Nevada, and Cedar Rapids, Iowa, who had always hoped to see New York and be shoved around in the Astor Bar but had never dreamed of doing it at the expense of the taxpayers.
>
> And super-added were regiments of shipyard workers and war contract hands and their wives.

They still had money to spend, he observed, after "having filled the front parlor with enough Grand Rapids furniture to stock Sears Roebuck for a decade."

Chambord, a Third Avenue restaurant patronized largely by French refugees, listed Strasbourg foie gras as an hors d'oeuvre on its 1944 menus, which included mallard duck and fine cognacs. The Fifth Avenue jewelry firm Rubel mounted a necklace of square-cut emeralds priced at $80,000 and quickly sold it. The Ellen Gray shop on Madison Avenue offered what was reputed to be the world's finest caviar at $20 a pound.

The high spenders of Café Society packed the shows at the tony hotels.

The "incomparable" Hildegarde, having honed her cabaret flair in Paris (by way of Wisconsin, where Hildegarde Loretta Sell grew up, the daughter of a grocer), charmed the crowds at the Plaza. Tinkering at the piano, the picture of grace in her long white gloves and fluttering lace handkerchief, she serenaded them with "Lili Marlene," "The Last Time I Saw Paris," and "Darling, Je Vous Aime Beaucoup."

As she recalled it: "Headwaiters at the Persian Room were given anywhere from twenty to fifty dollar tips for a table. War money flowed. So did champagne. And I drew a champagne crowd."

Hildegarde complemented her glamour with a comedic touch. "I introduced generals to privates, admirals to sailors. 'Now, will you salute this enlisted man please?' I would ask, and the officers all played along."

Hildegarde lived in a ten-room suite at the Plaza with her longtime business manager Anna Sosenko, who had written "Darling, Je Vous Aime Beaucoup." Following her late shows she invited friends in the audience to take in the suite's pink marble fireplace and glistening chandelier. The nights were all glitz, but Hildegarde worked for the war effort by day, hawking war bonds at Bonwit Teller and Saks Fifth Avenue, where she once sold a $25,000 bond in return for a rendition of "The Last Time I Saw Paris."

At the Waldorf-Astoria, Café Society gathered in the Peacock Alley bar and jammed the Wedgwood Room and the Starlight Room for late-night entertainment, dinner, and dancing. Adjoining the hotel proper, the Waldorf Towers was reserved for permanent apartments, its roster including the Duke and Duchess of Windsor and Herbert Hoover. Hollywood portrayed the hotel's elegance as a backdrop to the tumultuous comings and goings of wartime when Van Johnson and Ginger Rogers passed through in *Week-End at the Waldorf.*

Benny Goodman and his band held forth at the Terrace Room of the Hotel New Yorker. "Appearances at Carnegie Hall and other cultural centers have marked his transition from the rowdy stage and mellowed him, at least in the eyes of his followers, who are no longer given to tearing off his buttons for souvenirs," the *New Yorker* observed.

Guy Lombardo presented "the sweetest music this side of heaven" at the Hotel Roosevelt, where the Arthur Murray faculty held dance contests, often bestowing a first-prize bottle of champagne on a fast-stepping serviceman.

The Colony Restaurant on East 61st Street, off Madison Avenue, occupying an unremarkable gray-stone building, its pink-walled dining room conservatively furnished, attracted scores of Café Society regulars. Gene Cavallero, the senior partner but once its second-in-command headwaiter, greeted the guests in a manner "suave and imperturbable," *Life* magazine reported in a February 1944 photo spread. Cavallero, the son of an Italian innkeeper, saw to it that the choicest celebrities were seated near the entrance since "the center pillar marks the great divide," *Life* explained.

On the day that *Life* visited, Cavallero was chatting with Kitty Carlisle at a center table. *Life* noted that Prince René de Bourbon Parme was also among the guests, but it didn't say whether he was seated on the desirable side of the "great divide."

Lucius Beebee told how "at El Morocco, where Champagne is $25 a bottle, the pockets of Carino, the maitre d'hotel, were leaking banknotes donated by hopefuls in search of table space."

The Stork Club was the supreme arbiter of Café Society. More prized than dinner and dancing, it offered exclusivity. To pass the gold chain, to gain a nod from Sherman Billingsley to the blue-uniformed doorman allowing entry, became a rite of social passage.

Billingsley, a New Yorker by way of Oklahoma, opened his first Stork Club during Prohibition, a West Side speakeasy that plied the Broadway columnists with free food and drink and garnered a plug from Walter Winchell as "New York's New Yorkiest place on West 58th Street."

In 1934, with America no longer officially dry, Billingsley opened a legal Stork Club on East 53rd Street, off Fifth Avenue. By the time America went to war, the club's mirror-paneled main room was playing host to the international society set that fled Europe, show-business and sports celebrities, debutantes, and servicemen whose dress uniforms were an acceptable substitute for evening wear. They snapped up the Stork's black-and-white signature ashtrays for souvenirs.

Billingsley broke through the bar area to create the Cub Room, so named by Winchell for no evident reason. It became the truly exclusive outpost at the Stork, its guests including the Duke and Duchess of Windsor, J. Edgar Hoover, the Kennedys, the Harrimans, Damon Runyon, Frank Costello, and most important, Winchell, who oversaw all at table 50.

The Stork Club photographers made the rounds, supplying the newspapers with shots for the gossip columns. And Billingsley had a house organ as well, *Stork Club Talk*, which in March 1943 inexplicably turned up in the mail arriving in New Guinea for the Army's E. J. Kahn Jr., late of the *New Yorker*.

"Cut off from the news of the rest of the world, are we?" Kahn wrote in his review of *Stork Club Talk* for the *New Yorker*. "Nonsense. We know that the new chef is Henri Geib, that pretty Pat Foster sat with Sammy Smith at his usual table, that Mrs. Cornelius Vanderbilt had tea with the Countess Mercati, that Mrs. Darryl Zanuck is another short-dinner-dress addict, hers being black and spangled and topped off with a 'little-girl bow' on her blonde head, and that the saltines George Jean Nathan pilfers from the table aren't for him at all but for Julie Haydon's pooch."

Winchell, meanwhile, became a lieutenant commander in the Navy reserves. From his duty station at the Stork Club, he flaunted his mastery of naval terminology in a January 1942 column: "Billy de Wolfe and Eve Whitney are Piping Each Other Over the Side . . . Barbara Evans and Spencer Martin are Standing Watch Together . . . Ralph Forbes and Kitty Carlisle are Anchors Aweigh . . . James Cromwell and Dolly de Milhau are Full Speed Ahead . . . Pretty Jinx Falkenburg and Charles Chaplin have been Using the Same Gangway."

In 1941, America's last prewar year, the Stork Club grossed $900,000. Two years later, it grossed $1.25 million, averaging 2,000 guests on weeknights and 3,000 on weekends. In 1945, the Stork Club made it to Hollywood. Paramount paid Billingsley $100,000 to shoot scenes there for its movie *The Stork Club*, starring Betty Hutton as a warmhearted hat-check girl.

In the autumn of 1943, Café Society endured a slice of notoriety when the battered body of twenty-two-year-old Patricia Burton Lonergan was found one Sunday afternoon in the bedroom of her brownstone, triplex apartment on East 51st Street. Her estranged husband, Wayne Lonergan, was charged with her murder in a case that captivated New Yorkers eager for a break from the war news.

Lonergan, a tall, handsome, and charming Canadian, had come to New York in 1939. He worked as a bus dispatcher at the World's Fair while gaining invitations to parties and ingratiating himself in prized social circles through his personality and good looks. He met Patricia and her father, Bill Burton, the heir to a brewery fortune, at a dinner in the George Washington Hotel in Manhattan and expressed sympathy when Patricia pouted about the night she and her father had been refused entrance to the Stork Club. Lonergan's social climbing had gained him entrée at the Stork. He took Patricia there that very night and they were gladly passed through the gold rope.

Soon Lonergan was dating Patricia and also playing in card games with Burton, who was living at the Ritz Tower on Park Avenue. The talk in New York's social set had it that Lonergan was not only Patricia's boyfriend but her dad's as well.

Wayne married Patricia in 1941 following her father's death. They were a familiar couple at the Stork Club, El Morocco, and "21," the former speak-easy on East 52nd Street with its distinctive New Orleans–style iron fence and hitching posts with the likenesses of jockeys clad in the silks of thoroughbred racing's blueblood owners.

A baby, Wayne Jr., came along, but Wayne and Patricia began quarreling; they separated in July 1943, and Patricia cut Wayne out of her will. Wayne had been turned down by the United States Army after telling medical examiners he was homosexual, supposedly on the advice of a doctor he knew who said it was a sure way to beat the draft. But he returned for a time to his native Toronto and enlisted as a cadet in the Royal Canadian Air Force.

Wayne was in Manhattan on a forty-eight-hour pass the weekend Patricia's nude body was found in her bed, two blood-soaked brass-and-onyx candlesticks beside her. By the time the police arrived, he had returned to Toronto. He was picked up there, taken back to New York, and confessed to beating Patricia with the candlesticks and choking her, saying he became enraged when she told him he would never again see their baby, his remaining link to the Burton brewery fortune.

When Lonergan went on trial in March 1944, the New York press had a grand time with snide references to his sexual preferences at a time when such matters were unlikely candidates for breakfast-table patter.

Thyra Samter Winslow of the *Mirror*, who claimed to have been friends with the Lonergans, wrote how Bill Burton "always had with him at least one and sometimes several good looking young men" and that Patricia "accepted her father's companions without question.

"Wayne was bi-sexual. He was known not to be completely homosexual. He liked girls, too . . . Patsy is supposed to have said of Wayne . . . if he was good enough for my father, he's good enough for me."

The *Journal-American* described Lonergan as "the sex-twisted, 25-year-old Café Society playboy with the crew hair-cut and the easy sneer."

Lonergan declined to testify at his trial but his lawyer maintained that his confession was coerced. He was convicted of second-degree murder and sentenced to thirty-five years in prison.

With good housing exceedingly scarce, the Lonergans' spacious apartment at 313 East 51st Street became a prized catch. A young publishing executive and his wife rented it furnished, then found they had to get by with only one night-table candelabra. The other one was retained by the police as the bloody evidence. And the Lonergans had an antique double bed that wasn't of standard size. The apartment's new occupants couldn't find a replacement mattress until the war was over.

With time off for good behavior, Wayne Lonergan was released from state prison in 1965 and deported. Returning to Toronto, he met a well-known Canadian actress named Barbara Hamilton, a member of a socially prominent family, and once again lived in fine style. He died in 1986, his charm evidently undiminished by the years at Sing Sing.

"He was handsome—handsome as a prince," said Barbara Hamilton. "Fourteen years we were together. He was the most kind, gentle and wonderful person I have ever known. I loved him very much."

PART SIX

THE TENSIONS

CHAPTER 24

THE FUEHRER OF YORKVILLE

It was hardly the trial of the century, but the would-be fuehrer who set up his headquarters on Manhattan's Upper East Side made headlines enough.

Two and a half months after Germany's invasion of Poland, Fritz Kuhn, the leader of the German-American Bund (or, as he called himself, the Bundesfuehrer), went on trial in Manhattan's General Sessions Court, accused of being nothing more than a common crook. Spiced with appearances on the witness stand by La Guardia and Manhattan District Attorney Thomas E. Dewey, and the reading of the Bundesfuehrer's love letters, the trial became a farce. It nonetheless played out against the unsavory sight of imitation storm troopers in the heart of the world's most Jewish city.

The bund had its roots in the aftermath of World War I. Enthralled by Hitler's ascension to power, capitalizing on the resentments arising from persecution of German-Americans during and after the war, a German immigrant named Heinz Spanknoebel founded the Friends of New Germany in July 1933 and set up shop in Manhattan's largely German Yorkville section.

Modeled on the Nazi party, appealing to images of racial purity, Spanknoebel's militaristic band may have had 5,000 or so members. It staged a rally to back German rearmament and supported the German-born Bruno Hauptmann during his trial for kidnapping the Lindbergh baby.

Congressional pressure and a looming grand jury investigation in Manhattan, combined with a disavowal of support by Nazi officials wary of anti-Hitler sentiment in America, brought an end to Friends of New Germany—but only in name.

The organization reconstituted itself under Kuhn, a beefy, bespectacled German-born chemist. A native of Munich, Kuhn served in the German infantry during World War I, joined the fledging Nazi party in 1921, then graduated from the University of Munich with a degree in chemical engineering. Newly married, he left a devastated Germany in 1922 and went to Mexico, then entered the United States in 1928, settling in Detroit and working as a chemist at the Henry Ford Hospital and the Ford Motor Company. He became the leader of the Friends of New Germany outpost in Detroit, then took over its national leadership just as it collapsed.

In April 1936, speaking to a cheering crowd of 1,500 at a German beer hall in Manhattan, Kuhn announced creation of a successor organization, the German-American Bund. He pledged to lead a fight against "Jewish Marxism and Communism" and declared "so long as there's a swastika, there'll be no hammer and sickle in this country."

Two months later, Kuhn toured Germany with fifty fellow Bundsmen and secured a brief audience with Hitler, complete with a photo to bring home. The Nazis also gave Kuhn propaganda material to take back but considered him little more than a nuisance who, like the leader of his predecessor group, would only inflame American passions against the Third Reich.

Over the next three years, Kuhn harangued for the Nazi cause in his heavy Germanic accent, setting up national headquarters in Yorkville at 178 East 85th Street. His followers, awash in jack boots and swastikas, turned out for rallies in the Yorkville Casino, Ebling's Casino in the Bronx, and Schwaben Hall in Brooklyn.

Not far from the Army's Camp Upton in Yaphank, Long Island, the bund set up Camp Siegfried, which included the von Hindenburg Athletic Field. The camp, costing $14 a week, advertised itself as a place to "swim and play, develop strong bodies and minds under conditions that preclude dissenting opinions."

The bund proclaimed itself a national organization, but most of its followers came from German immigrant enclaves in the Northeast. Its total membership was essentially impossible to track, but the Justice Department told the House Un-American Activities Committee in April 1939 that it had some 6,600 followers, the majority in the New York metropolitan area.

The bund's biggest moment came on February 20, 1939, when it staged a mass rally for "True Americanism" and a celebration of George Washington's birthday that drew a capacity turnout of 20,000 at Madison Square Garden. The arena was bedecked with a large poster of Washington, American flags, and the German, Italian, and bund flags, along with a banner proclaiming "Wake Up America—Smash Jewish Communism." Speakers denounced Roosevelt (pronounced "Rosenfeld"), the Jews, the Communists, and racial mixing.

La Guardia turned down demands that he bar the bund from the Garden, saying that even the Nazis were entitled to free speech. To make sure that matters didn't go beyond that, 2,000 policemen were on hand inside the arena and outside it, where demonstrators carried signs reading KEEP THE NAZIS OUT OF NEW YORK. Scattered fights erupted among the 10,000 protesters in the streets. All was peaceful inside the Garden until Kuhn's speech winding up the night. A young man named Isadore Greenbaum, presumably looking Aryan enough to get inside, tried to rush at Kuhn only to be beaten by his bodyguards before the police hustled him away.

A month later, District Attorney Dewey's office raided the bund's headquarters and seized its records, looking for evidence that it had not paid New York City taxes on the sale of its merchandise at the Garden. Undaunted, the bund threw a party soon afterward at Ebling's Casino to celebrate Hitler's 50th birthday.

Later in April, the Warner Brothers film *Confessions of a Nazi Spy*, based on the breaking of a German espionage ring in New York, opened at the Strand. With Roosevelt's approval, but without the knowledge of J. Edgar Hoover, Jack Warner had sent one of his contract writers, Milton Krims, to New York to work with an FBI agent, Leon Turrou, who was investigating Nazi spy activities. Krims turned up at bund meetings, posing as a sympathizer, to gather material for the movie, which starred Edward G. Robinson as Turrou.

The film wasn't much of an artistic success but it aroused the ire of the German government, which lodged protests in Washington. Kuhn was none too pleased either, and he filed a $5 million libel suit, contending that the movie falsely linked him to German espionage. Hollywood was back at the war's end with *The House on 92nd Street* (William Eythe and Lloyd Nolan), dramatizing the FBI's cracking of a Nazi spy ring based in Yorkville.

In August 1939, Kuhn was summoned to testify before Congressman Martin Dies's House Un-American Activities Committee. When Congressman Joe Starnes of Alabama suggested to Kuhn that the bund wanted to establish a Nazi-like government in America, Kuhn banged his fist on the witness table and shouted, "It's a lie." Starnes shouted back "don't you call me a liar," leaped from his seat, and stormed through photographers to get at Kuhn, who had risen from the table. Two Capitol policemen got in between them to avert a fistfight. Dies pounded his gavel and yelled, "Sit down, Joe." He did.

For all its odious nature, its echoing of Nazi party doctrine, and its virulent anti-Semitism, the bund did not publicly advocate the forcible overthrow of the United States government and it was little more than a fringe group

Law enforcement authorities could, however, go after the Bundesfuehrer. Dewey brought an indictment in spring 1939 accusing Kuhn of stealing more than $14,500 in bund funds. His passport was confiscated and he went on trial in November.

Judge James Garrett Wallace threw out some of the charges, leaving two accusations for the jury to consider. According to the prosecution, Kuhn had spent $717.02 he raised for the bund's legal defense on moving the furniture of his girlfriend, Florence Camp (known as "Mein Camp" in the press), from Los Angeles to bund headquarters in Yorkville. Kuhn was also accused of keeping $500 in bund funds earmarked for a lawyer, James D. C. Murray, who was defending the operators of Camp Siegfried against charges they were violating New York State's civil rights laws.

Kuhn testified that he had paid for the furniture out of his personal funds while maintaining nonetheless that he could do as he pleased with the bund's money since he was, of course, the Bundesfuehrer. At any rate, he said, Camp was interested in bund activities, entitling her to a courtesy or two.

What Kuhn didn't know when he took the witness stand was that Camp had turned on him when she learned he was married and presumably had no intention of taking her as a second wife. She gave prosecutors three love letters from him, one of them proposing marriage, and denied she was ever a bund member or even a sympathizer.

The mash notes inspired the newspaper headlines "L'Affaire Fritz" and "The Love Life of the Hotsy-Totsy Nazi."

Among the samples of Kuhn's tortured English professing his ardor:

- "So you gained 15 lbs.—do I love that? Yes, sweetheart, I like it, of course it makes not difference to me how heavy you are and how you look—I love you and that is all."
- "You know I believe somewhat in astrology so I looks yours and my horo-skop and found many interesting things—After all I have discovered some of it and I have talked to you about this thing quite a lot—you should not start anything until June 25."
- " . . . darling angel—week after next I am coming to Los Angeles to see you and your family and drive you to Reno, then I'm going to Detroit to get my teeth fixed . . . the dentist in Detroit is a friend of mine and make everthing before."

Maintaining that Kuhn was being victimized by a political conspiracy, his lawyer, Peter Sabbatino, called Dewey and La Guardia to the witness stand.

Sabbatino asked Dewey if he had any personal antipathy toward Kuhn.

Dewey responded: "Never having seen the man or ever having had any acquaintance with him, it would have been impossible for me to have any personal animus, and yet, on the other hand, I must say that I regarded him as a nuisance to the community and probably a threat to civil liberties and the proper preservation of the American system if he should become more important than he was."

Sabbatino wanted to ask La Guardia if he had ever written to the State Department about Kuhn's passport. Judge Wallace, repeatedly irritated by Sabbatino's objections, and likening him to a "pebble in a shoe," ruled the question immaterial, and La Guardia left the witness stand without saying a word.

The jury convicted Kuhn of grand larceny and forgery and he was sentenced to up to five years in prison. In March 1943, in America's first mass denaturalization trial, a federal judge deprived Kuhn and ten other bund leaders of the American citizenship they had acquired, citing the bund's acceptance of the Hitler "leadership principle" and its un-American character. After serving three and a half years in state prison, Kuhn was transferred to a federal internment camp in Crystal City, Texas, as an enemy alien. He was deported to Germany in September 1945.

The bund went into eclipse with Kuhn's imprisonment, but New York hadn't seen the last of anti-Semitic harangues. In the fall of 1940, Joe McWilliams, a former tool company worker from Texas and a failure as a small-time inventor, made a bid for Congress in the district that included Yorkville. McWilliams had formed the American Destiny Party, an offshoot of the German-American Bund and Father Coughlin's fascistic Christian Front, but he ran in the Republican primary.

Setting up headquarters in two small rooms above the Franziskaner Restaurant on Second Avenue and running on a platform that inspired Walter Winchell to dub him "Joe McNazi," McWilliams held nightly rallies in Yorkville, speaking from a horse-drawn covered wagon supposedly representing the pioneer spirit. At one rally, chants of "Jew stooges, Jew stooges" rang from the crowd, and a group of women sold pamphlets titled "Roosevelt's Jewish Ancestry."

Just about everywhere McWilliams went, he encountered a heckler—a West Point graduate named Harry Dalton who offered to fight McWilliams and his bodyguard at the same time. But at six feet and 225 pounds, Dalton was unable to persuade McWilliams or any of his henchmen to scrap with him. McWilliams was trounced in the primary by the Republican organization's candidate, James Blaine Walker Jr., and he lost as well in the twenty-two election districts in Yorkville, trailing Walker by 568 votes to 242.

An editorial in the *New York Times* suggested that Yorkville residents should be grateful to the victorious Walker. "He gave them a good chance to show their loyalty to American principles—and a good chance was all they needed."

McWilliams sought to run in the general election under his American Destiny Party banner, but his candidacy was tossed out by the Board of

Elections in late October on grounds he had an insufficient number of valid signatures. By then he was in the city workhouse, serving a sentence of eighty-six days for violating laws on freedom of speech and assembly after having been ordered to Bellevue's psychiatric ward for a sanity hearing, which he managed to pass.

Nazi propaganda received a warm reception among some people in Yorkville as late as May 1941, when the German film *Sieg im Western (Victory in the West)*, a compilation of official Nazi footage showing the advance of German troops through the Low Countries and France, played at the Ninety-sixth Street Theatre. Pickets, including members of a group called the German-American Congress for Democracy, demonstrated against the film, but inside the theater the images of Panzer troops accompanied by martial music made a rousing impression.

"The applause in the theater is amazing," Arch Mercey, an official of the United States Office of Government Reports, an agency producing films on national defense, wrote to his chief, Lowell Mellett. "Hitler naturally enough draws the most applause, but there is plenty for the parachutists, dive bomb pilots and advance guards."

In the fall of 1941, bundsmen could still be spotted on Yorkville's streets. Francis Chinard, a young physician who was the son of French parents, and a witness to the sorrow of their countrymen at France's World's Fair Pavilion, was startled one day by the uniforms he saw.

I can remember walking down First or Second Avenue and passing in the opposite direction were people dressed as storm troopers. That was a shock because we knew what was happening in Germany. Here were people with swastikas on their arms in full uniforms and totally undisturbed.

A week after America went to war, Treasury Department agents seized the bund offices on East 85th Street. Copies of the last issue of the bund's weekly newspaper were still on a few newsstands in Yorkville though anti-Nazi German-language papers were the publications of choice.

Whatever the private thoughts of some in Yorkville, the public face supported the war against Hitler. The Garden Theatre on East 86th Street took down posters publicizing the German-language movies it had been showing. "We will show no more German pictures," an employee said.

The national council of the Steuben Society of America, a leading German-American organization, issued a statement declaring, "Our country, first, last and all the time."

CHAPTER 25

THE CATHOLICS AND THE JEWS

Stoked at first by the stresses of the Depression and the rantings of the Jew-hating Detroit radio priest Father Charles Coughlin, inflamed by the isolationists who charged that Jews were dragging America into Europe's war, and abetted by long-accepted social conventions, anti-Semitism was on the rise in America during the late 1930s.

The America First isolationists and the German-American Bund may have been silenced when America entered the war, and Coughlin's radio broadcasts ceased in 1942, but the anti-Semitic drumbeats intensified. An oft-repeated theme portrayed Jews as war profiteers whose sons shirked combat.

A national survey in June 1944 asked: "What nationality, religious or racial groups in this country are a menace to Americans?" Twenty-four percent of the respondents cited Jews.

Beneath the façade of homefront unity, religious and racial tensions in New York burst into the public eye. Jewish children were attacked with increasing frequency, particularly in neighborhoods where Irish-American youngsters were presumably egged on by anti-Semitic elements of the Catholic Church.

The Anti-Defamation League of B'nai B'rith issued a report in late December 1943 listing nineteen anti-Semitic incidents in the predominately Irish-American and Jewish Washington Heights neighborhood of Upper Manhattan. It found that "nearly every synagogue has been desecrated. Building walls have been marked with the swastika and pornographically hateful descriptions of the Jews."

The ADL reported that boys who seemed no older than fourteen "roam the streets looking for little Jewish boys to assault." And it said that at least two Protestant churches in the neighborhood had been defaced.

The police seemed none too disturbed. Inspector Joseph Bannon, who oversaw the area, said "the situation is much exaggerated. Things are very calm and collected in Washington Heights."

Police Commissioner Lewis Valentine ordered an increase in patrols of the neighborhood but seemed to shrug off any real concern. As he put it, "Anti-Semitism is always a problem in a large, heterogeneous city such as New York."

In the fall of 1938, when public demonstrations against Hitler were on the rise in the city following news of the Kristellnacht—the Nazis' smashing of Jewish businesses and homes—La Guardia had taken an imaginative step in his use of the police. He assigned an all-Jewish squad of policemen, led by Captain Max Finkelstein, president of the Shomrim Society, the department's organization of Jewish police officers, to protect German officials and German property in the city.

But the Washington Heights attacks, enveloping Jewish organizations and a police department accused of indifference if not anti-Semitic leanings, left La Guardia defensive. And the turmoil gained national attention when *Time* magazine wrote of it under the headline "Christian Action," an account of how a Protestant minister in Washington Heights was organizing an interfaith drive to combat anti-Semitism.

The Christian Front, founded by Coughlin and envisioned as a national organization battling Communism and what it perceived as unchecked Jewish influence in American life, began assembling in secret in New York in 1938, then spread to Boston, Philadelphia, and midwestern cities. The front claimed hundreds of supporters in New York's police department, and it trained and armed itself under the guise of sporting clubs.

In the fall of 1939, a pair of policemen were involved in an incident in Brooklyn involving the street-corner anti-Semitic incitements of the Christian Mobilizers, an offshoot of the Christian Front. A man named Joseph Schwartz was passing a Mobilizers rally when he heard the speaker proclaim that the only good Jews were in cemeteries. Schwartz shouted that he was a good Jew and most definitely alive. A patrolman assigned to keep the peace at the rally arrested Schwartz for disorderly conduct. At the court hearing, the patrolman admitted that he acted unjustly but said he was following the orders of his captain. The magistrate hearing the case said he found it hard to believe "that things of this kind can occur in the streets of this city."

In January 1940, eighteen men identified as Christian Front members were arrested on charges of participating in a ring based largely in Brooklyn that conspired to overthrow the government.

FBI agents seized twelve rifles, eighteen cans of explosives, and 3,500 rounds of rifle ammunition in their raids. J. Edgar Hoover maintained that the Christian Front men had talked of blowing up bridges, seizing utility plants, bombing the *Jewish Daily Forward* newspaper, and ultimately setting up a Nazi-style government in America and eradicating all Jews in the country. But federal prosecutors were unable to convince a jury that the plot actually existed. Nine of the thirteen men who went to trial in April 1940 were acquitted and the others were set free when the jury couldn't reach a verdict.

Acting at the behest of La Guardia and Commissioner of Investigation William Herlands, the Police Department sent a questionnaire to nearly 17,000 of its members asking if they belonged to the Christian Front or "any subversive, Communist, bund or fascist club or organization." Four hundred and seven policemen acknowledged past or present membership in the Christian Front.

That internal police inquiry evoked the wrath of the Brooklyn Roman Catholic Diocese's weekly newspaper, the *Brooklyn Tablet*, which demanded to know why La Guardia had targeted the Front. "Yes, he may say . . . that some of the members of this organization are anti-Semitic," said the *Tablet*. "Well, what of it? Just what law was violated?"

Suspicions of involvement by New York policemen in subversive plots or anti-Semitic movements resurfaced in May 1943 with the suspension of a patrolman named James Drew who was assigned to a stationhouse in Brooklyn's East New York neighborhood.

A fifty-four-page report submitted to La Guardia by Herlands accused Drew of associating with "persons who were engaged in un-American and anti-war activities and who were pro-Hitler and anti-Semitic." Herlands named Joe McWilliams, the anti-Semitic congressional candidate of 1940, as one of Drew's associates, and investigators reported finding thousands of anti-Semitic pamphlets and stickers in the garage of Drew's home.

But in December 1943, Police Commissioner Valentine reinstated Drew with full pay after a departmental trial cleared him. Herlands branded Valentine's exoneration of Drew as "a major defeat on the home front," and Congressman Emanuel Celler of Brooklyn, a fixture in New York politics, sought a re-examination of the evidence.

Soon after that, the Anti-Defamation League told of the attacks on Jews in Washington Heights, and then Herlands issued a report, more than a year in preparation, on anti-Semitic disturbances throughout the city. Although he found no specific conspiracies behind the episodes, Herlands cited the impact of the Christian Front's street corner orators and the persistent rumors that Jews were war shirkers, and he was highly critical of the police response.

Among the incidents described by Herlands beyond those in the Anti-Defamation League report:

- Someone broke into Congregation Shaaray Tefila in Far Rockaway, Queens, during the overnight hours and scrawled "Jew boys" and "Hitler Here I Come" over the honor roll listing of twenty-five sons of temple members in military service.
- Teenage boys, deciding to "go to Jewtown," beat up two youngsters near the Amalgamated Clothing Workers housing development in the Bronx. Two of the assailants were arrested and admitted they were seeking out Jews, but the police report described the attacks as "not a case of anti-Semitic vandalism but really a fist fight among boys."
- Two Parks Department watchmen at the Inwood Recreation Center in Upper Manhattan complained to the police of anti-Semitic attacks, one of them involving a gang brandishing Nazi salutes and shouting "Heil Hitler," only to be told by police officers that it would take machine guns to get rid of the vandals.

Following up his attack on Valentine in the Drew matter, Herlands denounced the police for often regarding anti-Semitic incidents as nothing more than "boyish pranks, ordinary mischievousness and neighborhood hoodlumism."

Eager to defend the reputation of the police department, but pressured in the Drew matter, La Guardia appointed a board composed of two former judges and a former police commissioner to review the police department's investigation of Drew. The panel unanimously upheld the police commissioner's reinstatement of the policeman, prompting La Guardia to invite Drew to appear with him during one of his weekly radio talks. Given the microphone by the mayor, Drew described himself as a law-abiding American and a good Christian. He said that as a policeman, he had been in close contact with "people of the Jewish faith," and "I do not entertain any evil antagonism toward any of these good people."

La Guardia brought policemen representing Jewish, Protestant, and Catholic officers on the radio program to assert their belief that there was no religious intolerance in the department. Valentine followed up with an order formally forbidding policemen to associate knowingly with persons engaged in subversive activities or to join organizations that fostered racial or religious hatred.

A few weeks later, Herlands left the La Guardia administration. He denied departing over the Drew controversy, saying simply that he was entering private law practice.

The issue of anti-Semitism may have made for headlines in the New York press, but La Guardia's reluctance to speak out in the face of police inaction, and in some cases possible police complicity, mirrored national sentiment. Although playwrights like Robert Sherwood and Lillian Hellman exploded the nature of tyranny, wartime popular culture largely ignored domestic anti-Semitism and the Nazis' slaughter of the Jews.

In an exception to that silence, a March 1943 pageant at Madison Square Garden, *We Will Never Die,* pleaded for the Allies to try to save Europe's Jews. The production, conceived and written by Ben Hecht, directed by Moss Hart, and produced by Billy Rose and the German émigré director Ernst Lubitsch, with music by another German refugee, Kurt Weill, drew 40,000 spectators to two performances. The narrators included Jewish actors like Paul Muni, Edward G. Robinson, and John Garfield, and non-Jewish personalities as well, among them Frank Sinatra, Ralph Bellamy, and Burgess Meredith. But its emotional centerpiece came not from show business but the rabbis who recited the Kaddish, the Jewish prayer for the dead, beneath towering tablets engraved with the Ten Commandments.

The unspoken acceptance of anti-Semitism occasioned Arthur Miller's 1945 novel *Focus.* When his first Broadway play, *The Man Who Had All the Luck,* closed in November 1944 after four performances, Miller resolved never to write another play. Rather, as he once put it, he hoped to put in "novelistic form" what he saw all around him—fear to speak out on behalf of Europe's Jews, arising, at least among American Jews and those sympathetic to their cause, from a belief that they could unleash a wave of anti-Semitism in America.

But Miller was skeptical at the prospect of getting a publisher. "No one I talked to could think of any fiction on the subject, although the widespread existence of anti-Semitism, from the universities on down through the large corporations and professions, was of course known to everyone," Miller would recall. "It was like some sort of shameful illness that was not to be mentioned in polite society, not by gentiles and not by Jews."

The publishing house Reynal & Hitchcock (also the publisher for the French émigré Antoine de Saint-Exupéry) took a chance on Miller.

Set in a Brooklyn neighborhood near the war's end, *Focus* told of a church-based neo-fascist movement called the Union Crusaders, based on Father Coughlin's Christian Front. A neighborhood resident named Lawrence Newman, who worked as a personnel manager, was not an active member of the front but in his mild-mannered way he accepted the conventions of anti-Semitism. Eventually, Newman himself became the target of prejudice when he bought a pair of eyeglasses that made him look Jewish. He was demoted with no explanation, resigned, then tried to find another job but was repeatedly spurned.

As Miller described *Focus*, its "central image is the turning lens of the mind of an anti-Semitic man forced by his circumstances to see anew his own relationships to the Jew."

Reflecting on the novel long afterward, Miller wrote that it was inspired in part by his experiences as a shipfitter at the Brooklyn Navy Yard. Miller remembered "the near absence among the men I worked with 14 hours a day of any comprehension of what Nazism meant. It was by no means an uncommon remark that we had been maneuvered into this war by powerful Jews who secretly controlled the Federal Government."

In the aftermath of V-E Day, the newsreels at movie theaters and the images in the press revealed the horrors of the Nazi death camps.

As Miller put it: "Not until Allied troops had broken into the German concentration camps and the newspapers published photographs of the mounds of emaciated and sometimes partially burned bodies was Nazism really disgraced among decent people and our own casualties justified."

CHAPTER 26

HARLEM SEETHES

With the coming of springtime 1943, racial violence wracked the nation. Sailors attacked Mexican youths in Los Angeles in the Zoot Suit riot, and white shipyard workers rampaged against black workmen in Mobile, Alabama, and Beaumont, Texas. Then came one of the bloodiest urban disturbances in American history, the Detroit race riots of late June, bringing the deaths of twenty-five blacks (many of them shot by white policemen) and nine whites.

Roosevelt said little, declining to employ the moral suasion of his office. All his energies were devoted to the war, and statements expressing sympathy with black people would anger the Southern Democratic bloc in Congress.

In the second week of June 1943, an aspiring writer named James Baldwin returned to his home in Harlem. Baldwin had been working at war plants in New Jersey over the previous months, but any sense of patriotic achievement had fallen victim to his rage. When he entered the restaurants near the factories, too many times he had been told, "We don't serve Negroes." Now Baldwin, his nineteenth birthday almost upon him, was back with his family, awaiting the death of his terminally ill father while his mother awaited the birth of a child. "All of Harlem, indeed, seemed to be infected by waiting. I had never known it to be so violently still," he would write a decade later in his essay "Notes of a Native Son."

Baldwin had noticed the tension on the streets.

Reports of muggings, stabbings, and gang wars had brought an increased police presence. "I had never before been aware of policemen, on foot, on horseback, on corners, everywhere, always two by two," he recalled.

And he had never before seen so many knots of people on street corners, on stoops, in hallways—church matrons, girls in "sleazy satin," older men, "sharpies," all of them together. They didn't appear to be saying anything to each other but "on each face there seemed to be the same strange, bitter shadow."

It seemed to Baldwin that they shared a "hopeless bitterness" over the abuse of their loved ones in the segregated Army and "the ghetto's instinctive hatred of policemen."

Wartime lynchings in Mississippi, Florida, Texas, Missouri, and even Arizona brought anguish to Harlem. A cartoon in the *Amsterdam News* in June 1941 depicted Hitler reading about atrocities committed against blacks in the South. "And they've got the nerve to tell me how to run my business," he exclaimed.

Two weeks after Baldwin came home, La Guardia called upon the black poet and writer Langston Hughes, spending the summer at the Yaddo writing colony in upstate New York, to help develop a series of radio programs titled "Unity at Home—Victory Abroad." The programs would tell of New York's history and people, and, as the mayor put it, make a case for preserving the city's "peace and neighborliness." The Writers' War Board, promoting scripts to enhance patriotism, wrote to Hughes in support of the unity theme. It put the case more starkly than La Guardia had: The radio programs would stress unity "so there will be no danger of race riots in New York."

La Guardia sent two policemen, one black and one white, to Detroit in the aftermath of the riot there to learn some lessons that might avert violence in New York. They reported that Detroit's police department had been out of control and recommended tighter supervision of New York's police officers. La Guardia called black leaders to Gracie Mansion to hear their report and he promised to deal with miserable housing at high rents and unconscionable food costs in Harlem.

Although dismayed by what he considered radio's avoidance of any serious dramatic approach revealing the problems of black people, Langston Hughes promised to deliver a couple of radio scripts stressing the "unity" theme.

But it would take much more than that to temper the simmering rage in Harlem so vivid to James Baldwin.

Harlem had been hit by a riot in 1935, when an incident involving a white store manager and a young Hispanic shoplifter led to three deaths, more than 200 injuries, and widespread arrests and property damage.

A biracial commission appointed by La Guardia defined the ills that plagued Harlem, and the mayor worked for improvements in housing, health, and municipal hiring. But Harlem—for all its vibrant culture, its glamorous nightspots—remained mired in poverty during the World War II years, and racial discrimination persisted in New York whatever a black person's station in life.

A position of authority did not necessarily bring respect, as a black police officer named James Sloan discovered when Roosevelt was concluding a campaign trip to New York in the last days of his bid for a third term. Sloan was guarding the president's train before its departure from Penn Station when he was assaulted by FDR's press secretary, Steve Early, who was having trouble getting through the police lines. Sloan accused Early of kicking him in the groin in what became a front-page story in view of the possible impact on the black vote. Early, a Virginian and a descendant of the Confederate Civil War general Jubal Early, acknowledged only that he "kneed" Sloan and issued a vague apology.

The uproar came and went, but the lack of employment opportunities for blacks in wartime New York became a persistent and vexing issue.

The charismatic Adam Clayton Powell Jr., successor to his father as pastor of the huge Abyssinian Baptist Church in Harlem, emerged in the forefront of protests over racial discrimination, drawing on the pulpit, picket lines, his "Soap Box" column in the *Amsterdam News,* his election to the City Council in 1941, his founding of the newspaper the *People's Voice* the following year, and his election to Congress in 1944.

When the 1939–40 World's Fair opening grew near, Powell set up picket lines outside the Empire State Building, where the fair's executives were based, to demand jobs for blacks at Flushing Meadows. Some 700 were eventually hired out of a work force of 7,000, but mostly as laborers. Powell helped launch a boycott in spring 1941 against the Fifth Avenue Coach Company and the New York Omnibus Corporation, which together provided 95 percent of Manhattan's bus service, to protest their refusal to employ blacks except as porters. The boycott brought the hiring of blacks as bus drivers and mechanics.

When he became the first black City Councilman, Powell introduced a resolution demanding an end to racial discrimination in hiring at the municipal colleges, which did not have a single black person among more than 2,000 permanent faculty members. The presidents of City College, Brooklyn, Hunter, and Queens insisted that appointments were made on merit, and the resolution failed by 18–2, its lone backers being Powell and Peter Cacchione, a Communist councilman from Brooklyn.

Detroit and Southern California turned out tanks and planes, but New York City, aside from its shipyards, depended largely on finance, garment work, electronics, small manufacturing, printing, and publishing to fuel its economy. War contracts didn't flow into the city to any great extent until midway through the war, and that came about only after La Guardia pleaded with Washington for help. Even when jobs were in the offing, blacks were usually shunned. The Atlantic Basin Iron Works, a Brooklyn shipyard, refused to hire black workers until persuaded to do so by the federal Fair Employment Practices Commission.

The FEPC was created by Roosevelt in June 1941 in the face of pressure from civil rights leaders, most notably A. Philip Randolph, the Florida-born son of a preacher who arrived in New York in 1911, made it his permanent home, and became a force in organizing black workers.

Tall, handsome, and dignified, Randolph captivated audiences with a speaking style drawing upon his recitations of Shakespeare in Oxford-style English as a young man. In 1937, he capped a long union organizing drive when the Pullman Company agreed to recognize his International Brotherhood of Sleeping Car Porters. Early in 1941, Randolph began advocating a march on Washington for jobs in defense plants and an end to segregation in the military, and he organized a Madison Square Garden rally in mid-June to press his demands. Roosevelt thwarted the march, scheduled for July 1, by signing an executive order banning racial discrimination in defense work and creating the FEPC to enforce it. The agency's influence was limited but it did open up many defense jobs to blacks.

Apart from discrimination in hiring, the mistreatment of black servicemen at the hands of southern drill sergeants and red-neck sheriffs outside the vast training bases of the South angered black people in New York and indeed throughout the nation. For GIs from the north, racial discrimination was nothing new, but most had never encountered blatant segregation, and they told of their anguish and fear in letters back home.

Black leaders preached the "Double V," calling upon their communities to support the war against fascism abroad while continuing to fight for victory over discrimination at home. But maintaining that credo could be a trying affair.

Sadie and Bessie Delany, inseparable sisters, each accomplished in their own right—Sadie a teacher and Bessie a dentist—were living together on Harlem's Edgecombe Avenue in the fashionable Sugar Hill section and doing their part for the homefront.

"When the government asked people to grow Victory Gardens to help the war effort, we were only too happy to oblige," they would recall in a best-selling memoir. There wasn't any space for a Victory Garden on the grounds of the Delanys' six-story apartment building, so they planted on a vacant lot next to their cousins' home in the Bronx, what they proudly called "the best Victory Garden in the neighborhood."

As they put it:

We Delanys were as patriotic as anyone. We were Americans! Our blood and sweat was invested in this land, and we were ready to protect it. As bad as things were for Negroes, you wouldn't have wanted to live anywhere else in the world, that's for sure.

And yet . . .

Their brother Manross, who had settled in North Carolina, was a career soldier, and his all-black unit helped build the Burma Road. Manross saved a white soldier's life. That soldier was also from North Carolina, and he asked Manross to visit his family when he came home. As the Delany sisters told it: "When poor Manross got there, he knocked on the door, but those white folks wouldn't let him in. They didn't want their neighbors to see a Negro coming in the front door. They told him to go around to the back."

The humiliation left Manross "very bitter, very angry."

Some servicemen passing through New York on their way to the war-fronts presumably considered the city an extension of hometowns where blacks were little more than servants or laborers. Even a celebrated figure might feel the sting.

Dizzy Gillespie, the trumpet player at the forefront of bop, the modern-ization of jazz, recognizable for his trademark goatee, beret, and large black-frame glasses, was profiled in *Life* and other mass circulation magazines. In 1944, Gillespie and the bassist Oscar Pettiford led the first bop quartet playing outside of Harlem when they appeared at the Onyx Club on "Swing Street" in midtown. But that hardly gave them immunity from racial hate.

One evening, Gillespie and Pettiford were on Sixth Avenue, near the 50th Street subway station, chatting with a black nightclub hostess known as Madame Bricktop, when trouble arrived.

As Gillespie told the story: "A sailor came by: 'What you niggers doin' talkin' to this white woman?' Bricktop with her red hair! Under those lights, she did look light. Oscar was drunk. He swung at the guy and fell flat.

"I wasn't going to let that sailor kick Oscar. So I straddled him. I had my horn in one hand and a knife in the other—one of those knives with a hooked end for cutting linoleum. Oscar finally got up. By that time three or four other sailors came along. They all went for Oscar. I just swished at them with my knife and caught one. I just cut his uniform. A little more and I would have cut him up."

Gillespie and Pettiford jumped into a cab for an escape to Harlem, but the driver refused to take them. They fled into the subway station with the sailors in pursuit. The knife had slipped out of Gillespie's grasp, so he smashed one of the sailors in the face with his horn. The other sailors began to beat him, but he got away, and moments later the Shore Patrol arrived and arrested the Navy boys. Gillespie took the subway back to Harlem.

The leading black performers enjoyed acclaim from white audiences beyond the nightclubs. Duke Ellington, who had gained his signature num-ber, Billy Strayhorn's "Take the 'A' Train," in 1941, debuted at Carnegie Hall in January 1943 with "Black, Brown, and Beige," which he called "a tone parallel to the history of the Negro in America." Paul Robeson took ten opening-night curtain calls at the Shubert Theatre in October 1943 for his role in Shakespeare's *Othello*.

But the British jazz critic Leonard Feather recalled how in the early 1940s, "Swing Street" was "just as discriminatory and Jim Crow as any place in town, in spite of the number of musicians that were black." Club owners would hire white groups over black groups, he observed, until 1943 or so, when the racial lines in bands became blurred. (Benny Goodman, playing with Lionel Hampton, Teddy Wilson, Gene Krupa, and Roy Eldridge, had provided a notable exception with his racially mixed band.)

Feather resented the clubs' exclusion of black customers. One night in 1939, when he was dating a black woman named Louise McCarroll, a featured vocalist in the Don Redman band, they went to the Famous Door to hear Woody Herman.

As Feather recounted it: "We were stopped at the door. It really was a traumatic experience for both of us. I was from England, and though I knew about things like that, they had never happened in my presence. It was quite a while before black people were generally accepted as regular customers."

The Savoy Ballroom, Harlem's largest dance hall, its bandstands graced by show-business icons, was shut down by the La Guardia administration in April 1943. The city and military authorities claimed that many servicemen had contracted venereal diseases from women they met there, and police plainclothesmen had made several arrests for prostitution. Perhaps more to the point, the Savoy, an entertainment landmark in Harlem since the mid-1920s, attracted many white patrons, and interracial dancing was commonplace. As the NAACP's Roy Wilkins put it in the *Amsterdam News*: "Chiefs of police, commissioners, captains, lieutenants, and plain rookie cops get purple in the face at the very thought of Negroes and whites enjoying themselves socially together."

Protests from the NAACP, Adam Clayton Powell Jr., and other black leaders were to no avail. In mid-summer 1943, while tension rose in Harlem, the Savoy's doors remained closed.

The Navy's refusal in the early war years to accept black women at Hunter College's training base for the newly created Waves was yet another source of anger for the city's black communities. Complaints that the city was abetting racial discrimination by allowing a municipal college to be host for the program were turned aside by La Guardia, who cited Washington's preeminence in running the war.

The mayor had no such excuse when it came to housing, but here, too, racism bred resentment. The Metropolitan Life Insurance Company had received tax exemptions from the city for sponsoring its huge Stuyvesant Town apartment complex on the Lower East Side, but it refused to accept blacks as tenants. The Met Life president, Frederick H. Ecker, was quoted by the *Amsterdam News* as saying that blacks and whites weren't ready to mix and that if black tenants were accepted in Stuyvesant Town, "it would depress all the surrounding property." La Guardia, eager to obtain private backing for sorely needed housing, had supported the Stuyvesant Town project although it did not contain a nondiscrimination clause.

The Met Life contract with the city was signed on August 4, 1943. By then, Harlem's businesses lay in ruin.

CHAPTER 27

THE RIOT OF '43

It began with a fight at a seedy hotel.

The Braddock on West 126th Street had long been a trouble spot, a "raided premises" in police parlance. On the evening of Sunday, August 1, 1943, Police Officer James Collins had been assigned to the lobby, on the lookout for narcotics and prostitution, part of a round-the-clock police presence.

The details of the episode that unfolded there were murky, but the consequences proved vast.

A thirty-five-year-old black woman named Marjorie Polite got into an argument in the lobby with Collins—the origin of the dispute is unclear—and was reported to have become boisterous and profane. When Collins tried to quiet her, she supposedly pleaded with other guests at the hotel to "protect me from this white man."

It would have been an insignificant affair except for what happened next: the intervention of a black GI.

Private Robert Bandy, a twenty-six-year-old native of Alabama, on leave from his all-black Army military police battalion in Jersey City, had been spending the weekend in New York. He had brought his fiancée to the hotel for breakfast with his mother, Florine Roberts, a domestic-service worker for a Middletown, Connecticut, family, who had checked in to the Braddock to see her son. They had all gone to church that morning and then to a movie before returning to pick up the mother's luggage for her return home.

Bandy, who witnessed the argument between Collins and Polite, demanded that the policeman release the woman, and when he didn't do so a fracas erupted. Bandy's mother was alongside him and may have been involved in the dispute as well. At some point, Bandy got ahold of Collins's nightstick, and according to the policeman's account the soldier struck him in the head, then began to run. The officer shot Bandy, grazing him in the left shoulder, then brought him to Sydenham Hospital a block away.

Collins was treated there for head cuts, and Bandy was transferred to the prison ward at Bellevue Hospital.

Although Bandy's wound was minor, Harlem was swept by a report—its origin untraceable—that a white policeman had shot and killed a black soldier who was seeking to protect his mother. As James Baldwin put it long afterward, "the effect, in Harlem, of this particular legend was like the effect of a lit match in a tin of gasoline."

Angry crowds converged at the Braddock, at Sydenham, and at a nearby police station, and at 10:30 p.m. windows began to shatter. By the early morning, looting and vandalism were in full swing, centered on West 125th Street and extending for thirty-five blocks, mostly along Lenox Avenue and Seventh and Eighth avenues. Gangs ripped away iron gates and broke into stores, carting off what they could carry and smashing what they couldn't grab. Teenagers roamed the streets, throwing stones.

A youngster named Claude Brown, asleep in his Harlem tenement, was awakened by the tumult, "thinking that the Germans or the Japs had come and that the loud noises I heard were bombs falling."

He squeezed in between his mother and father at the front window, wondering why the air-raid sirens hadn't been turned on and the street lights turned off. "This ain't no air raid, just a whole lotta niggers gone fool," his father told him. "And git the hell back in that bed."

But the screaming in the streets and the falling of plate-glass windows kept Claude awake. "I imagined bombs falling and people running through the streets screaming," he would write in his memoir *Manchild in the Promised Land*.

"I could see mothers running with babies in their arms, grown men running over women and children to save their own lives, and the Japs stabbing babies with bayonets, just like in the movies."

The next morning, Claude ran into the street to check on the excitement, only to be knocked back into his hallway by a big man carrying a ham under his coat. Seconds later, more men ran into the hall, carrying cases of whiskey, sacks of flour, and cigarette cartons. As Claude started out the door once more, he was bowled over by a policeman with a gun in his hand, racing after the looters. On his third attempt, he got out of the building.

"But I wasn't sure that this was my street. None of the stores had any windows left, and glass was everywhere. It seemed that all the cops in the world were on 145th Street and Eighth Avenue that day."

He went around the corner to his friend Butch's house, and there he found another friend, Kid, sitting on the floor with his hand in a gallon jar of pickled pigs' ears while his buddy Danny cooked bacon on a stove. Butch kept busy hiding something.

"It looked as though these guys had stolen a whole grocery store. While I joined the feast, they took turns telling me about the riot."

Soon after, Claude got into a pawnshop gutted by fire. A policeman yelled at him to get out.

Stopping next at a looted seafood store, Claude and his friends stole shrimp and oysters. Then Claude grabbed two loaves of bread from a grocery. Running through a back yard to escape from a policeman who had spotted him, Claude lost all his oysters. That left him with two loaves of bread and two shrimp in his pocket. He cooked the shrimp at Butch's house, and when he couldn't find any lard he put the shrimp into a frying pan, greasing it with Vaseline hair pomade. He took it out when it was black and smoking and made a sandwich.

It was the first time he had eaten shrimp. "A few years later, I found out that the shrimp were supposed to be shelled before cooking. I ate half of the sandwich and hated shrimp for years afterward."

As the violence spread, the black writer Ralph Ellison was asked by the *New York Post* to report on the riot from Harlem's perspective. Ellison took the subway down to the 127th Street station from his home in upper Harlem and when he came up the stairs at 3 a.m. he heard gunfire and "an unending sound of burglar alarms." Then "the fire trucks came, the hook and ladders, with red headlights flashing, the bells ringing, going swiftly through the dark streets."

He saw men and boys running with rolls of linoleum, mattresses, and clothing. Pawnshops and grocery stores were the main target, but instructions were shouted to the mobs on which stores to attack. Most of the black merchants who got to their stores in time had posted signs identifying themselves and it seemed that many of the rioters were leaving them alone. A street hustler named Malcolm Little would remember how the owner of a Chinese restaurant "didn't have a hand laid on it because the rioters just about convulsed laughing when they saw the sign the Chinese had hastily stuck on his front door: 'Me Colored Too.'"

White-owned stores were the prime targets, but the rioters, in their frenzy, weren't always choosy. One man broke into a black-owned tavern and was shot and killed by the bartender.

Malcolm Little, the future Malcolm X, was coming down St. Nicholas Avenue when he saw looters running. He would tell of one who gained the nickname "Left Feet." He had stolen five women's shoes from a store, but all of them turned out to be for the same foot.

Police officers began to break up the looting, firing their revolvers in the air, but they were outnumbered at first.

Ellison spotted a sound truck from the municipal radio station WNYC.

The speaker, from a civil rights group called the Negro Victory Committee, asked the rioters to go home. He told them that the soldier had not been killed and that La Guardia had promised a fair investigation. Ellison saw how "the crowd applauded and cheered, then returned to its looting."

A man who was about to throw an ash can through a window told Ellison that he made a good living as a longshoreman, but "I'm doing this for revenge." To Ellison, "this whole incident was a naïve, peasant-like act" of retribution.

But it wasn't simply blind revenge, as Ellison recognized. He spoke with the people in the streets and concluded "they were giving way to resentment over the price of food and other necessities, police brutality and the general indignities born by Negro soldiers."

The NAACP's executive secretary, Walter White, had gone to bed at his apartment on Edgecombe Avenue early that Sunday evening, weary from three speaking engagements. He had asked his wife, Gladys, that he not be disturbed if the phone rang. A few minutes later, a staff member called to tell of the riot. No sleep would come for White this night. He dressed quickly, and as he was about to head out, La Guardia phoned, asking White to meet him at the West 123rd Street police station.

White's chief aide, Roy Wilkins, and his wife, Minnie, also lived in the Edgecombe Avenue apartment building. They were returning home when a brick smashed through a window of their bus at Seventh Avenue and West 116th Street. Another missile injured a woman on the bus, and the driver delivered her to Sydenham Hospital, then continued on his route.

Wilkins and his wife returned home shaken. Then came a phone call from White, saying he was en route to join La Guardia in an effort to quell a riot. Wilkins intercepted White in the lobby of the apartment building. His first concern: "Walter was as white as La Guardia; how long either of them could last on the streets of Harlem was anyone's guess." The two NAACP officials set out for the riot area in a taxi. They heard the smashing of plate-glass windows and the shouts of the mobs. And they saw some blacks attempting to attack white people in cars who had driven into Harlem unaware of the violence.

White might have been attacked as well, but the taxi made it through safely since Wilkins was unmistakably a black man.

Walter White's skin was white, his eyes were blue, his hair was blond. His father, mother, five sisters, and an older brother were all light-skinned, but in the parlance of the day they were indeed Negroes. White had grown up in a frame home in a largely black Atlanta neighborhood, his father a mailman. When a riot broke out during the race-baiting Georgia gubernatorial campaign of 1906, Walter White and his father had crouched with guns drawn behind the front window of their home, ready to open fire if torch-bearing men who were descending on their neighborhood from Peachtree Street should step foot on their lawn. The mob never got that far, but the Atlanta race riot seared Walter White's psyche. He grew tense whenever he thought of it.

White could easily have gone through life passing as a white man but devoted himself to working for his people. He had been living in Harlem since 1918 and he had held the NAACP's top post, executive secretary, since the early 1930s, having been best known for his exposes on lynching.

When White and Wilkins arrived at the West 123rd Street police station, they learned that La Guardia had sent 6,000 policemen into Harlem, a third of the force. Some 8,000 New York State Guardsmen (reserves for the homefront, separate from the New York State National Guard) were standing by at armories. But mindful of the wanton firing upon blacks by white policemen in the June 1943 riot that had torn Detroit, La Guardia ordered that the police use force only as a last resort.

The mayor asked the Army authorities at Governors Island to send military police into the area to evacuate black servicemen home on leave, lest they be caught up in the rioting. The first arriving MPs were white. Fearing that the mobs would attack them, White suggested that La Guardia phone again and ask for black MPs and the creation of racially mixed military patrols. That was done, and there were evidently no assaults on the MPs in the hours to come.

White and Wilkins took La Guardia on a tour of the riot zone. As White watched the shouting and cursing rioters, many in shabby clothes, he thought of the stories he had read about the mobs emerging from the slums and sewers of Paris in the French Revolution. When the police car carrying the mayor and the NAACP leaders drove up Lenox Avenue, they heard the crashing of a brick against a storefront, and La Guardia told the driver to take them there. By the time they arrived, a minute or two later, a fire had broken out inside the store. La Guardia jumped from the police car and screamed at the rioters. White wasn't sure if they realized that the man yelling at them was the mayor, but his shouts startled them into quieting down and moving on.

"He had his Italian up," Wilkins recalled. "He rushed on bands of rioters, ordering them to cease and desist, and most were too startled by the sight of the red-faced mayor to do anything but obey."

White suggested that La Guardia bring sound trucks in and enlist black celebrities to ride on them and ask the rioters to go home. White and Wilkins got on the phone but learned that the men they most wanted—Duke Ellington, Cab Calloway, Adam Clayton Powell Jr., and Joe Louis—

were out of the town. They did secure a few well-known if far less glamorous Harlem figures. White rode along Eighth Avenue aboard a sound truck with Ferdinand Smith, secretary of the National Maritime Union, telling the mobs that the black soldier shot by the policeman had not been killed and was, in fact, only slightly wounded. But as their truck moved along the streets dense with rioters, White began hearing a "rat-tat-tat" on its roof. Rocks and bottles were being hurled from tenement windows and rooftops.

Wilkins secured a small victory from his pleas on another sound truck. "Out on the curb an old man had plunked down his loot: a gallon can of vanilla ice cream, which he was polishing off as I rode on my rounds."

As the looting grew in Monday's early hours, White was mortified by a scene unfolding at a grocery store—a snapshot of Harlem's poverty and misery. A toothless, emaciated old woman was walking along the edge of a crowd that had smashed a plate-glass window. In one hand she held two grimy and empty pillow cases. In her other hand, she held the arm of a boy, perhaps fourteen or fifteen years old, possibly a grandson. When an opening in the crowd appeared, she climbed through the broken glass into the store to fill the pillow cases with canned goods. When she had finished, she glanced at the police car where La Guardia and White were sitting.

"Exultation, vengeance, the supreme satisfaction of having secured food for a few days, lighted her face," White recalled.

"And then I looked at the sleepy-eyed child by her side. I felt nausea that an abundant society like America's could so degrade and starve a human being, and I was equally sickened to contemplate the kind of man the boy would become under such conditions."

Through the night and into the daylight hours of Monday, La Guardia repeatedly took to the radio. Wary of inflaming a tense city, he assured New Yorkers that the violence wracking Harlem was not a race riot—this was no Detroit, where white mobs set upon blacks.

"It was just hoodlums—men, people with criminal intent—doing violence and stealing, and stealing from their own group and injuring their own people," the mayor insisted in a broadcast from City Hall.

But this was indeed a "race riot" in the sense that looters focused on white-owned stores, many with few black employees, and turned their wrath on the white policemen patrolling the streets. Although there were only a couple of attacks on white passersby or motorists, they presented few targets of opportunity.

As for the mayor's dismissal of the rioters as "hoodlums," well-dressed Harlem residents were among the protesters early on at Sydenham Hospital, and some of the looters seemed to be members of the middle class. About 100 of those arrested were women.

The riot spent itself by Monday morning, when 300 women from Harlem, carrying clubs and wearing special armbands, were put on patrol as volunteers to augment the police presence.

Scores of prisoners were booked at the West 128th Street police station, their looted food, clothing, and furniture piled in its large lobby. More than 550 arrests were made, the prisoner overflow sent to the National Guard Armory at 96th Street and Park Avenue.

Private Robert Bandy, described by Army officers as a "good soldier," was interviewed at the Bellevue Hospital prison ward by Ferdinand Smith, the black labor leader, for the *People's Voice*, Adam Clayton Powell Jr.'s newspaper. Smith asked Bandy whether he had any message for Harlem's people. "Yes," he said. "Tell them if I was out and in uniform, I would not agree to this rioting. In fact, they should cease rioting."

Bandy was turned over to military authorities for presumed disciplinary action. Marjorie Polite was sentenced to one year's probation for disorderly conduct arising from her argument with the policeman that touched off the chaos.

The rioting claimed either five or six lives, the accounts by the press and the police department differing. All of the dead were black. In addition to the man fatally shot by the black bartender, at least two people were shot to death by policemen while looting. Some forty police officers were injured, including Captain Walter Harding, commander of the 28th precinct, who was hit in the eye by a bottle thrown from a roof. Some 570 people, all but twenty or so black, were treated at hospitals, mostly for cuts from broken glass and flying bottles.

The Uptown Chamber of Commerce, representing Harlem businessmen, reported that 1,485 stores were damaged and nearly 4,500 plate-glass windows smashed. It put property damage at $5 million.

As an outgrowth of the riot, La Guardia announced plans for new municipal housing projects in minority areas. The city's Department of Markets stepped up investigations into price ceiling violations by Harlem merchants. The federal Office of Price Administration implemented rent control in New York a few months after the riot and it opened a Harlem office to look into excessive food prices.

There was movement as well on three matters that had especially inflamed the city's black communities. The Navy eventually admitted black recruits to its Waves training program at Hunter College. City officials allowed the Savoy Ballroom to reopen in October 1943. La Guardia said he considered racially discriminatory tenant selections to be unlawful and promised to implement any judicial decision invalidating it at Met Life's Stuyvesant Town.

Langston Hughes, having agreed to write a couple of radio plays for La Guardia's "Unity at Home—Victory Abroad" campaign to promote racial harmony, was still at the Yaddo writing center when the riot broke out. In reflecting on the conditions that spawned it, he chose not to join in the outrage expressed by much of Harlem's professional class.

"The better class Negroes are all mad at the low class ones for the breaking and looting that went on," he wrote to his friend Noel Sullivan. "It seems their peace was disturbed even more than the white peoples'."

Hughes took a wry look at the upheaval, his means of coping with the grim reality, in his "Ballad of Margie Polite," a salute of sorts to the woman who had touched it off.

The ballad's conclusion notes that the day she was taken away by the police, "It wasn't Mother's/Nor Father's—/It were/Margie's Day!"

James Baldwin's father had died in late July, and the funeral was held the day the rioting erupted, Baldwin's nineteenth birthday. Two days later, the funeral procession moved through Harlem on its way to the cemetery.

"The spoils of injustice, anarchy, discontent and hatred were all around us," Baldwin remembered. "Cans of beans and soup and dog food along with toilet paper, cornflakes, sardines and milk tumbled every which way, and abandoned cash registers and cases of beer leaned crazily out of the splintered windows and were strewn along the avenues. Sheets, blankets and clothing of every description formed a kind of path, as though people had dropped them while running.

> I truly had not realized that Harlem *had* so many stores until I saw them all smashed open; the first time the word *wealth* ever entered my mind in relation to Harlem was when I saw it scattered in the streets. But one's first, incongruous impression of plenty was countered immediately by an impression of waste. None of this was doing anybody any good. It would have been better to have left the plate glass as it had been and the goods lying in the stores.
>
> It would have been better, but it also would have been intolerable, for Harlem had needed something to smash.

PART SEVEN

THE HOMECOMING

CHAPTER 28

THE MIRACLE DRUG

They called it the "wonder drug," the "miracle drug," the "magic bullet." When American troops came ashore in Normandy on D-Day, it came with them, 90 percent of it manufactured at a cluster of thirty buildings in a gritty industrial section of north Brooklyn.

It all began with two cousins arriving from Germany, a chemist named Charles Pfizer and a candy maker, Charles Erhart, who set up shop together on Flushing Avenue in Brooklyn's Williamsburg section in 1849. Their plant turned out additives for food, soft drinks, and medicines, but far grander things lay ahead. Charles Pfizer and Company became the focal point for the mass production of penicillin, the drug that saved the lives and limbs of countless American soldiers of World War II. By war's end, Pfizer was turning out more than half of the world's supply of penicillin, most of it used to treat infections from combat wounds.

At the turn of the twentieth century, Pfizer had been thriving with its production of citric acid, a flavoring additive and an ingredient in industrial processes. In the 1920s, it began producing citric acid through fermentation, a process involving the aeration of a filtered mass. The citric acid was derived from fermenting a white-sugar nutrient in shallow pans.

While Pfizer was beginning to solve its production challenges, a medical drama unfolded in a laboratory at St. Mary's Hospital Medical School in London. On an autumn morning in 1928, Alexander Fleming, a specialist in bacterial research, was perusing his rows of glass plates called petri dishes when he noticed how a commonplace green mold, Penicillium notatum, had destroyed a bacteria culture. Fleming had no clue why it was happening, but he was sufficiently intrigued to tell of his experience in a British scholarly journal. His finding caused little stir. The first of the new sulfa drugs was soon introduced, leaving penicillin as nothing more than a barely noticed curiosity.

But nearly a decade later, British researchers at Oxford University led by Howard Florey, a professor of pathology, and his associates Ernst Chain and Norman Heatley, drew on Fleming's finding to extract the antibiotic substance of this green mold. In February 1941, they conducted its first definitive clinical trial. Researchers at Columbia University also made progress in developing penicillin.

The British scientists received assistance from the Rockefeller Foundation in New York, but they were unable to develop a production scheme to mass-produce the penicillin. Enter Pfizer.

In the 1930s, looking for a more efficient way to make citric acid and similar additives, the Pfizer scientist Jasper Kane had induced molds to grow in large, deep tanks, eliminating contamination of the broth from the air. The process, called "deep fermentation," proved a revolutionary achievement.

In October 1941, federal officials familiar with the penicillin research in Britain called executives from three major American drug companies, Pfizer, Squibb, and Merck, to Washington, launching a drive to mass-produce penicillin for war wounds.

Pfizer had mainly devoted itself to production of chemicals rather than drugs, and it had fewer than 800 employees. But it was precisely that background in producing additives like citric acid that had spawned its head start in deep fermentation. John E. McKeen, a key Pfizer executive and later the company president, was convinced that deep fermentation could mass-produce an antibiotic just as it had yielded citric acid, and he became the driving force in the company's mass production of penicillin.

As McKeen put it: "When antibiotics appeared on the horizon, we didn't have to scramble around and start from scratch, the way most of the other houses did. We already had the basic know-how."

Using deep fermentation, Pfizer begin producing penicillin for the armed forces in early 1942. It had 250 workers concentrating on penicillin production by 1944 and had gone beyond its own factory, buying the Rubel Ice Company of Brooklyn to obtain a freezer for drying penicillin crystals.

In surmounting the numerous technical complexities of deep fermentation to produce penicillin on a vast scale, Pfizer drew on improved hardware, a disagreeable marketing chore that had been undertaken in the Midwest and scientific imagination.

The company put aside its 50-gallon tanks in favor of 7,000-gallon behemoths, and it used a new, more productive strain of penicillin, discovered in 1943 under the guidance of a scientist named Kenneth Raper at the Department of Agriculture's research station in Peoria, Illinois. Searching for molds that would yield significant amounts of penicillin, Raper had assigned an assistant to rummage through the waste fruit at a local market. The woman, nicknamed Moldy Mary, came back one day with a rotten cantaloupe that became the source of a new penicillin strain that grew readily via deep fermentation.

Pfizer used that strain, but its process of deep fermentation was extraordinarily complex. It essentially involved shooting sterile air into a tank of broth through a high-pressure nozzle in the bottom of a tank. To keep the mold from gathering entirely on the surface, its natural inclination in its quest to find oxygen, a central shaft with blades like a washing machine was built into the tank. Its violent agitation mixed oxygen into the broth, allowing the mold to breathe everywhere in the tank, increasing the volume of antibiotic it could produce.

The process may have been unfathomable to anyone outside the scientific community, but the arrival of penicillin quickly took on a very human face in New York.

Pfizer's decision to forego some of the profits on its chemical ventures in order to pursue the uncertain prospects of mass-producing penicillin had its roots beyond patriotic values. John L. Smith, Pfizer's vice president and a chemist, had lost a sixteen-year-old daughter to an infection before the development of penicillin. In June 1943, in the face of severe government restrictions over administering penicillin to civilians, Smith turned over dosages being held by Pfizer for research to treat the young daughter of a Brooklyn doctor suffering from endocarditis, a bacterial heart infection. Thanks to the penicillin, the child recovered. The case was reported in the press and laid the ground for another child's treatment that became a major news story.

The hero this time was Paul Schoenstein, the city editor of the *Journal-American*. A few years earlier, Schoenstein had infiltrated the German-American Bund in New York with a reporter-photographer team that produced a series of exposes. In August 1943, he found himself with a hard-to-resist human interest story.

A two-year-old child from Jackson Heights, Queens, named Patricia Malone, being treated at Lutheran Hospital in Manhattan for septicemia, a staph infection, was given hours to live. Her father, told by the girl's doctor that penicillin might save her, phoned the *Journal-American* for help. The paper contacted a Boston physician, Chester Keefer, who had been designated by the federal War Production Board to allocate the limited supply of penicillin available for civilian use. After getting a go-ahead from Keefer, Schoenstein and his reporters arranged for the Squibb drug company to rush a supply to the girl from its laboratory in New Brunswick, New Jersey. Patricia recovered.

This was, however, a story with a sad ending. The little girl died two months later of a heart infection. Schoenstein and his reporters nonetheless received the Pulitzer Prize for local reporting in May 1944.

The human dimension of Pfizer's penicillin triumph resonated far beyond the sick beds of the few seriously ill children who were fortunate enough to receive the drug. For the soldiers who previously depended on sulfa drugs to treat infections, the arcane chemical processes developed in the deep fermentation tanks at Pfizer's Brooklyn laboratories played out in military hospitals abroad and at home.

Like his fellow GIs in the Fifth Infantry Division, the Red Diamond division of General George S. Patton's Third Army, Private First Class Sumner Glimcher had never heard of penicillin. But he would come to know why it was called the "miracle drug."

It was Christmas Day 1944, a Sunday, and by time night had fallen, it seemed that it would be the last day in the life of the twenty-year-old infantryman from the north shore of Massachusetts outside Boston.

Glimcher had been in combat for two months when his unit was called north to reinforce troops that were being overwhelmed by the Germans' surprise counterattack in the Ardennes region of Belgium, the Battle of the Bulge.

When word came that Glimcher's platoon was to attack, the men went around a ledge. As they came into an open field, they were met with a barrage from mortars, rifles, and rocket launchers fired by Germans hidden in a clump of woods.

Glimcher heard the whistling of a shell coming toward him. He dropped to the ground on his right side and threw his left arm over his head. An 88-millimeter shell hit a tree above him and exploded. He felt a heavy weight on his left leg. He tried to stand, but he fell. His foxole buddy and his lieutenant grabbed him, one under each arm, and dragged him back to the protection of overhanging rocks.

Another GI had a chest wound and he was wheezing. A third soldier had been hit three times, one bullet through his shoulder, one through his arm, and one through his neck, and he was bleeding profusely. Glimcher's lieutenant told him that the unit would move on to pursue the Germans, but he promised to summon the medics.

As Glimcher told the story six decades later:

It was very cold. I looked at my watch. It was 5 o'clock, and dead silence prevailed. We were lying in the snow. I thought: "You're never gonna live through the night. Nobody will ever find us." The other two had passed out. I passed out and came to several times. I was in shock. But because it was so cold, the bleeding diminished. The blood congealed.

I had been given a small packet for medical supplies that contained a sulfa drug. They told you if you were wounded to plug that into the wound. It was sub freezing, but we had gloves. I opened this sulfa package and sprinkled it on my wound, but there was dirt and grime and blood and no fresh water. It would have been surprising if the wound had not become infected.

It was a moonlit night. At one point I heard a rustle in the bushes, and thinking it might be Germans, I grabbed my M-1 although I was in no shape to do anything with it. And then I saw the most miraculous sight that I could imagine. Two U.S. medics appeared with a stretcher coming out of the woods. They had received a radio message from the lieutenant and through some miracle of navigation found the coordinates he had specified, climbed this hill in freezing weather at midnight and found the three of us.

They took the two badly wounded guys out first. Each trip took an hour. At 2 o'clock they took me down and I could feel the branches whipping past my face as we slid down. At the bottom of the hill was a jeep with three stretchers, and they strapped me in. I passed out and I woke up the next morning in a field hospital, a tent with a dirt floor, and I was pulling out of an operation. The surgeon told me he had removed shrapnel from my leg and my arm.

Glimcher was taken to Paris for treatment, then flown to a hospital in Wales.

I had had four big chunks of shrapnel in my leg. The wound was very large—it ran from below my knee to well up into my thigh. It was all infected. The doctor said: "You're probably going to have your leg amputated. But before we do that, there's some kind of a new medication that fights infection. So we're going to try it out on you. It's called penicillin."

I had never heard of it. It was a brand new word. I didn't know how to spell it. I don't think any of the soldiers had heard of it. But anything that might prevent my leg from going was okay with me. For the next two weeks, every four hours a nurse would come and stick me. I got an injection of this new penicillin. At the end of two weeks, the infection had totally cleared up. And the doctor said, "You're gonna keep your leg."

I spent the first month in bed, the second month in a wheelchair, the third month on crutches, and the fourth month they taught me how to walk again. I began going out with the Welsh girls.

Glimcher was sent back to his unit, but marked for limited service—his combat days were over. He could speak and understand some German, and at war's end he became a military interpreter in Bavaria, questioning suspected Nazis prior to the Nuremberg trials. He went on to graduate from Harvard, then came to New York City, headed the film department of New York University's School of Continuing Education, and produced documentaries.

The Battle of the Bulge left him with one leg shorter than the other, and over the years the impairment in his walking and even the way he stood took a toll on his body. He suffered from severe sciatica, stenosis of the spine, and ankle pain from a loss of cartilage.

But reflecting on Christmas in the Battle of the Bulge, he marveled at his good fortune.

"Penicillin was certainly a miracle drug. I figure I had a couple of miracles occur. I should have died Christmas Day 1944 but I didn't. To save my leg from being amputated, it was a miracle. I've had a pretty good outlook on life since then. Because I figure every day since then has been a gift."

CHAPTER 29

"DON'T STARE
AND DON'T ASK QUESTIONS"

The dancing with the junior hostesses, the bantering with the show business stars, continued in full sway at the Stage Door Canteen in the months following the D-Day invasion. But amid the gaiety on West 44th Street, a somber undertone prevailed.

The Broadway producer Brock Pemberton, a leading figure in the canteen's volunteer management, saw the changes in the aftermath of rising casualties in Europe and the Pacific.

"For two years this was a meeting place for eager, pink-cheeked boys on their last liberty before marching up the gangplank," Pemberton noted. "Now some of these same men are back, lean and bronzed, ribbons and clusters of leaves and stars telling stories of deeds they will not talk about. All too many of them, on crutches and in casts, are brought in ambulances by the Red Cross from casualty hospitals."

The volunteer registered nurses at the canteen, who had little to do early on, were busy re-dressing wounds, and the *Canteen News*, the staff publication, cautioned hostesses in an August 1944 issue to "Think Before You Speak." To underline the point, it told of an encounter between a hostess and a serviceman returning from the war.

He was a sailor. He sat there silent and morose, unbending. Everywhere around him there was laughter and gaiety. A canteen worker, trying to bring him out of himself, remarked, "I'd give anything to have the Purple Heart you're wearing."

"I'd like to have your left eye," he replied. Only then did the canteen worker realize that the serviceman had lost the use of one optic. His loss made him embittered. He felt that he had no right to marry the girl back home. As he said, "I'm only a one-eyed bum now."

A senior hostess named Blanche Kimball talked to the sailor, and according to the newsletter "before the evening was over, he was dancing, and if his laughter was not loud, at least it was laughter."

In its October 1944 issue, the newsletter carried the item "How the Boys Feel About It."

"Veterans who are fighting to return to a normal civilian life after losing an arm or leg in combat overseas have two simple 'don'ts' for people who meet them on the street. 'Don't stare' and 'don't ask questions.' "

Sono Osato was shaken by what she saw outside the theater where she was starring as Miss Turnstiles in *On the Town*.

"I remember crossing Fifth Avenue, and coming toward me was a Navy officer. He didn't wear sunglasses. His face had been completely reconstructed. He must have been in a fire. He had a frightening face; it was all patched together."

Of all the show business personalities entertaining the grievously wounded, none could forge a more visceral connection than the tap dancer known as Peg-Leg Bates. Clayton Bates was twelve years old, growing up in Greenville, South Carolina, when he was struck by an automobile that dragged him for fifty feet. The next day, his left leg was amputated above the knee. An uncle carved a pair of crutches, but the boy kept busting them, and finally the uncle devised a peg leg. Clayton Bates began entertaining on the streets of Greenville with dance steps for small change, then tap-danced in shows. He made it to Broadway in *Blackbirds of 1928*, then became a featured attraction as Peg-Leg Bates in nightclubs and vaudeville.

Living in Corona, Queens, when he wasn't on stage in the war years, he visited military hospitals in New York and began his time with the soldiers and sailors by telling his story. "I just talk everyday logic," he told an interviewer. "I say it can happen to anyone and there's no such thing as a handicap."

In those hospital visits, he invariably broke into a song he had written:

> Don't look at me in sympathy
> I am glad that I am this way.
> For I feel good, and I am knocking on wood
> As long as I can say that I am Peg-Leg Bates
> The one-leg dancing fool.

Then he would go into a vigorous dance routine and break up his audience by telling the veterans: "Why should I mind breaking one little leg? I've got some more in the dressing room." In fact, he had a dozen peg legs.

They were made of white oak and hickory and they were not only his show-business trademark but a fashion statement. They came in various colors to match his suits, and he showed them off, never letting his trouser leg hang down over them when he went about his everyday life.

But for all the efforts by show business personalities to cheer the wounded servicemen, the very sight of the most severely damaged might prove too disturbing for New Yorkers so far as the city's Parks Department and its powerful commissioner, Robert Moses, saw it.

On the Fourth of July weekend 1945, the Parks Department denied permission for volunteers at the Army's large Halloran General Hospital on Staten Island to escort twenty-two wheelchair-bound servicemen along an 800-foot stretch of the boardwalk at South Beach in order to reach a Coast Guard pier for an outing.

When the volunteers complained about the rebuff to the press, phone calls and letters expressing outrage poured into the office of Staten Island's borough president, Joseph Palma. "The citizens are up in arms about this," Palma said. "The people over here live with these veterans and are very close to them."

The way Moses explained it, the Parks Department had no specific rule excluding veterans in wheelchairs from its facilities. But "the idea back of the experiment was that these veterans should mingle with public crowds in the face of the fact that they are seriously wounded cases requiring constant attention of a large number of nurses and doctors. Under these circumstances, the parks officials must find means of protecting them from curiosity seekers, small children, etc."

The outing was switched to the secluded and privately owned Midland Beach, which offered a swimming pool, picnic facilities, and, presumably, assurances that no curiosity seekers or young children would be present.

Notwithstanding Moses's comments, signs on city boardwalks had barred any type of vehicle other than baby carriages. The furor over the South Beach incident brought a change in mid-July of 1945. The signs were altered to read: "Prohibited Use—Any Vehicle Except Baby Carriages and Wheelchairs for Invalids."

In contrast to the fearful Parks Department, a measure of emotional comfort was offered at Grand Central Terminal, jammed with servicemen going to and from stateside posts. A baggage handler named Ralston Crosbie Young provided a personal touch amid the frenzy. Known as the Redcap Preacher, he presided over trackside prayer sessions at noon on Mondays, Wednesdays, and Fridays. Young was profiled by *Reader's Digest* for its "most unforgettable character" feature, inspiring letters of gratitude. One came from a wounded veteran who wrote:

I had just arrived from overseas. I was trying to quell my hatred of people when you suddenly said, "Captain, you gotta forgive some of these people." It wasn't so much what you said, although it explained every bit of my feelings. Your words, and the way you said them, were more valuable to me than any other thing.

The more seriously wounded servicemen returning home included prisoners of war who were released when certified as unable to ever return to combat. Many of them arrived in New York aboard the Swedish ship *Gripsholm,* which carried out prisoner exchanges between the Americans and the Germans. On February 21, 1945, the *Gripsholm* brought 463 disabled POWs to New York. A tugboat carrying an Army band and a welcoming party of Wacs and Red Cross women drew alongside, and a loudspeaker on the tug broadcast the Bing Crosby recording "Don't Fence Me In," which brought laughter from the former prisoners. But there were poignant notes as well. An ex-POW wearing dark glasses was guided to the *Gripsholm's* rail by a friend. "When we go by the Statue of Liberty, just tell me," he said.

Many of those wounded went to Halloran General Hospital, the source of that tempest over the wheelchairs. Volunteers, like those pushing the paralyzed vets on the boardwalk, tended to the many needs of the wounded. Their ranks included the future Brooke Astor, who would place her stamp on New York in the decades to come through her extraordinary philanthropy.

She was Brooke Marshall in the war years. Her father, General John H. Russell, was a retired Marine Corps commandant, living in Coronado, California, and her son, Tony, was a marine officer who took part in the invasion of Iwo Jima. Her husband, Charles Marshall, known as Buddie, was overage for the draft and tending to his law practice, which had lost many members to the armed forces. With the military presence in her family, and time to pursue patriotic endeavors, she sought a way to contribute to the war effort.

At first she helped at the USO offices on Park Avenue, but there were more than enough volunteers there. So she joined a Red Cross training class and took a job delivering books from the Halloran library to the patients' bedsides, working five days a week. Early each morning she left her apartment on Sutton Place, rode the Third Avenue El to the Battery, then took the ferry to the Staten Island slip, where a Red Cross car transported the day's volunteers to the hospital. She became one of the Gray Ladies, volunteers who wore gray linen dresses with white collars and cuffs and a gray veil.

Halloran General Hospital, named for Colonel Paul Stacy Halloran, a former Army medical officer, opened in the fall of 1942 on a 383-acre site in Staten Island's Willowbrook section that had been intended for use by New York State as a facility for mentally handicapped children. Obtaining the property for the duration of the war, the Army converted it into one of the largest military hospitals in the nation, with a capacity of 3,000 beds. A compound of what Brooke Marshall called "ugly red brick buildings," Halloran offered treatment in all medical areas, but it specialized in spinal-cord injuries.

Marshall found the wounded men to be "optimistic, cheerful and grateful to be alive," and she was impressed by their varied reading tastes, everything from comic books to *Studs Lonigan* and Shakespeare.

"The paraplegics were great readers. They had to be flat on their backs, then were turned over to lie flat on their stomachs. Their beds were hard, straight cots and when they lay on their stomachs there was a piece of the cot cut out so that their face was out, not pressed against the cot. Their hands were free, so lying face down they could hold a book in their hands and read. Usually they were totally immobile from the waist down, and the smell of urine from the bottles by their beds was overpowering."

One soldier in his early twenties had a big grin when she approached one day. He took her hand and pressed the nail of one of her fingers against his stomach. "I certainly feel that," he exclaimed in a small triumph. For months, he had been without any sensation from the chest down.

But there were moments of despair as well, especially when the young men who had married hurriedly before going overseas, now invalids, were visited by young wives, who, as Marshall saw it, were often incapable of thinking about anything except their own plight. Marshall and the other volunteers were often asked to stay on after the wives' visiting hours to try to bolster the men's spirits.

For all the presumably fine medical care, Marshall found the patients' spirits darkened by Halloran's dress code. Only officers were allowed to wear their uniforms. The enlisted men were required to wear maroon pajamas and bathrobes. Walking around like that made the men mentally and physically sloppy, she thought. Many of the men did not shave as often as they should have, they sometimes left their bathrobes open, and eventually "they spent more and more of their time playing cards and cursing the hospital."

She continued working at Halloran into the fall of 1945, when the war was over and most of the wards had emptied out, leaving behind men from the New York area, some of them bitter paraplegics. When she tried to interest them in a book, she would hear: "Go away. We don't want you here. The Red Cross stinks."

She found that the men "were still in the same old bathrobes and spent the days gambling. Discipline had totally disappeared and some of the personnel were not a very healing or decent influence."

In March 1943, the Navy opened the 1,500-bed St. Albans Naval Hospital in Queens. It treated marines as well, among them Sergeant Barney Ross, the former lightweight and welterweight boxing champion who had come home to a hero's welcome after receiving the Navy Cross, the Marine Corps' highest award for valor after the Medal of Honor, for his exploits on Guadalcanal.

At the Brooklyn Navy Hospital, outside the Navy Yard, morale was fine, so far as Sheldon Mike Young, a corpsman from Cleveland, could see.

When Young arrived at the hospital in June 1945, many of the recuperating servicemen were awaiting assignment to the anticipated invasion of Japan. "I don't recall that they talked about the action they had seen," Young reflected years later. "I thought they were very upbeat. Those guys had smiles on their faces. I don't recall seeing anybody who was down. I think the morale was pretty damn good."

Shortly after V-J Day, Young was transferred to a convalescent center the Navy had opened at the former Monterey Hotel in Asbury Park, New Jersey, and he saw how the psychological effects of combat could be more troubling than physical injuries.

"It was largely for patients who were psychotic, who had suffered what we'd now call post-war syndrome. Two of the worst cases I saw were there. Two sailors who had been on North Atlantic duty for four years. They were still suffering from sea sickness, even on land."

Young remembered how many of the men at the convalescent center "were literally uncontrollable."

"I had night duty once and I tried to silence the people on the ward because if we didn't do that we'd be put on report. One guy came out when I tried to do that and he had a heavy cast on his arm. And I could see that cast coming down on my head fifteen times and I had to apologize to him."

In August 1944, the Navy opened a convalescent center with a notorious past, taking over the former Half Moon Hotel in Coney Island. Back in November 1941, Abe Reles, a hit man for Murder, Inc., plunged to his death from an upper story of the Half Moon while guarded by six New York City detectives who were supposed to make sure he remained alive as a witness in mob trials. An investigation yielded no plausible explanation as to how Reles came to fall out of the window. When the United States Senate's committee on organized crime chaired by Tennessee's Estes

Kefauver, held hearings in New York in 1950, Reles's mysterious death was pursued anew, once more with no answers. By then the convalescing sailors were gone from the Half Moon, and the GIs, the Navy boys, and the marines were discharged from Halloran and St. Albans, making their way in the postwar world.

CHAPTER 30

COLONEL SMITH'S LAST MISSION

For all the air-raid drills, the anti-aircraft guns, the warnings from City Hall that New York presented the prime target for an Axis strike on America, the city had remained untouched and evidently invulnerable through three and a half years of war. But in the summer of 1945, the heart of Manhattan was finally shaken from the skies.

Just before 9 o'clock on the morning of Saturday, July 28, Lieutenant Colonel William Franklin Smith Jr., twenty-seven years old, a cocky West Point graduate from the farming community of Latham, Alabama, wound up a brief reunion with his wife, Martha, and their year-old son, Billy, and lifted off from the Army Air Forces field in Bedford, Massachusetts.

He headed down the New England coast on a dreary morning, bound for Newark Airport to pick up three officers he had flown to the New York area a few days earlier for leave from the Sioux Falls Army Air Field in South Dakota. Smith and his fellow officers would be returning there to continue preparations for the anticipated invasion of Japan.

Smith had flown more than 500 hours of bombing missions over France and Germany, piloting B-17 Flying Fortresses that were often shot up but never shot down, and he had risen to deputy commander of the 457th Bombardment Group.

Now he was flying an unarmed B-25 Mitchell bomber, the twin-engine model named in honor of Colonel Billy Mitchell, the father of Army air power.

The B-25s were best known for carrying Lieutenant Colonel Jimmy Doolittle and his seventy-nine airmen from the aircraft carrier *Hornet* to the skies over Japan in the storied bombing raid of February 1942 that electrified an American homefront reeling from the Pearl Harbor attack. But the Mitchell bomber that Smith was flying this particular Saturday had never left the United States, inspiring the inscription painted in red on the fuselage, "Old John Feather Merchant."

Feather merchants were mythical little people who preferred a life of laziness to hard work. Pilots applied that term to an airplane that had never seen combat. The officer in charge of aircraft maintenance at Smith's base in the Dakotas was Captain John Kemp.

Colonel Smith had two passengers on his hour-long flight.

Sergeant Christopher Dimitrovich, thirty-one years old, a native of the industrial town of Granite City, Illinois, conducted Old John Feather Merchant's mechanical checks, then sat alongside Smith, acting as his flight engineer. In September 1944, Dimitrovich had been riding as a crewman in a C-47 transport dropping paratroopers over Holland in the massive Operation Market Garden when German antiaircraft fire raked the cockpit, killing the pilot and copilot. Dimitrovich bailed out over Eindhoven, made contact with the Dutch underground, then kept a step ahead of German troops as he was guided back to the Allied lines.

There was little for him to do in the cockpit of Old John Feather Merchant on its flight to Newark. Smith was not only the pilot on this day but he was the copilot and the navigator.

His other passenger was Navy Machinist's Mate Albert Perna, a graduate of New Utrecht High School in Brooklyn's Bensonhurst section and three days shy of his twentieth birthday. Stationed with a radar unit at the Bedford air field, he scrambled aboard Smith's plane at the last minute— a hitchhiker. His brother, Anthony, a crewman on the destroyer *Luce*, had been killed in a kamikaze attack off Okinawa. Albert was going home to grieve with his two sisters and his parents, owners of a furniture store in Queens.

In the moments before Smith said good-bye to his wife that morning, she had been gripped by a premonition of disaster. The weather was terrible all along the coastline—rain, fog, mist, low-hanging clouds. But the self-assured Smith remained nonplussed. He would get to Newark to fetch those fellow officers and he would arrive when directed—precisely at 10 a.m.

Fifty minutes into the flight, Old John Feather Merchant—or Army 0577, the flight's designation for controllers—reached a point fifteen miles east of La Guardia Field. The weather remained exceedingly poor; the ceiling, or cloud cover, was perhaps 600 feet. The La Guardia tower directed Smith to land, but he radioed a request to continue on to Newark Airport, saying he had urgent business there.

In the moments that followed, controllers at three separate consoles in the La Guardia tower—the man directly responsible for La Guardia traffic, the controller overseeing takeoffs and arrivals throughout the New York metropolitan area, and an Army Air Forces controller—debated just what to do about Army 0577.

The presence of military planes over New York vying for airspace with commercial liners had proved vexing for controllers. On the afternoon of February 15, 1945, a B-29 bomber with a crew of ten was on a flight from Long Island's Mitchel Field to Florida. The pilot was Major Billy Southworth Jr., a veteran of twenty-five bombing raids over Europe. A minor league outfielder before the war, he was the son of the St. Louis Cardinals' manager. The plane developed engine trouble. Southworth tried for an emergency landing at La Guardia Field, but the bomber bounced off a runway and crashed and burned in Flushing Bay, killing Southworth and four of his crewmen. In that case, a mechanical failure brought disaster, but air controllers, busy enough, hardly welcomed all those military planes with pilots accustomed to dodging flak but unfamiliar with New York's flight rules.

Smith's Army 0577 was refused an instrument approach to Newark, the poor weather having backed up commercial planes heading there. Eager to be rid of this intruder in a crowded airspace over Queens, the controllers finally allowed Smith to continue on to Newark under visual flight rules. But he was directed to maintain three miles visibility or make an immediate return for a La Guardia landing. Victor Barden, the chief controller at La Guardia, warned Smith, "unable to see the top of the Empire State Building."

As he crossed the East River, heading west toward Newark, Smith passed over Welfare Island and its hospital buildings. At that point, Old John Feather Merchant's wheels began to drop. Smith's battle with the rain and the fog, his unfamiliarity with New York's geographical landmarks, had propelled him into a fatal blunder. He had evidently mistaken Welfare Island and its cluster of high rises for midtown Manhattan. In his final seconds over the East River, he evidently believed he had cleared Manhattan and was approaching Jersey City.

Instead, he was about to pass over the luxury apartment buildings of Sutton Place on Manhattan's Upper East Side. His altitude: 500 feet.

Smith suddenly turned into a diagonal path, heading southwest. At that moment, he almost surely realized that he had not crossed the Hudson River, that he was most certainly not over Jersey City. Snapping the controls to raise his landing gear, he revved his engines, banked left, and tried to climb. Manhattan's skyscrapers, their tops barely visible in the mist, loomed before him, seconds away.

Old John Feather Merchant cleared Rockefeller Center's International Building by twenty-five feet and headed down Fifth Avenue. The scattered pedestrians out on a rainy Saturday morning, the midtown motorists, hotel guests, and the men and women working a six-day week gasped as the engines roared, the bomber traversing an incomprehensible path.

The sports announcer Stan Lomax had stopped for a light at Fifth Avenue and 45th Street on his way to the WOR Radio studio. He jumped onto his auto's running board and shouted, "Climb, you damn fool, climb."

Old John Feather Merchant climbed to 700 feet, but its landing gear wasn't entirely up, and Smith fought the drag. He passed astride the Chrysler Building and barely cleared the roof of the Salmon Tower at Fifth Avenue and 42nd Street.

He continued down Fifth, and at 35th Street he began turning east, his bomber's nose in a slight climbing attitude as he searched for a route around the skyscrapers that would take him back to Queens and a runway at La Guardia Field.

Too late.

Traveling at 250 miles an hour, Old John Feather Merchant crashed into the north face of the Empire State Building between the 78th and 79th floors, 975 feet above Fifth Avenue and 34th Street, its nose almost vertical, its right wing vaulted perpendicular to the façade in an extreme left bank. It was 9:55 in the morning.

For the twenty or so men and women working on the 79th floor, much remained to be done in the wake of Europe's devastation. They were employees of the War Relief Services section of the National Catholic Welfare Conference, and they had given up their Saturday to pursue their humanitarian tasks.

Therese Fortier, nineteen years old, a graduate of Andrew Jackson High School in Queens, still living with her family in the St. Albans section, had joined the agency a few months earlier when a priest told her about an opening for a secretary.

"I was working with a woman named Mary Kedzierska," she recalled. "She was in charge of the Polish section. They were trying to connect people. They were all over the place and didn't know where their families were."

From early on, Therese had been awed by the view from her space in the world's tallest building. "We were equipped for air conditioning but we didn't have it put in yet. The first day I went to work for Miss Kedzierska, she had the window opened about six inches or so. It looked like smoke, but there were little puffs of clouds coming in the window. My eyes bugged out of my head."

On this particular Saturday, there wasn't much of a view for Therese. "It was a misty day, foggy and overcast. From my office, you couldn't see anything outside except when the winds would blow the clouds away. But that would be momentary." She remembered:

I had just gotten up from my desk. Miss Kedzierska had asked me to take some dictation. I took my book, and as I got up the building shook.

There were six desks there, facing the service door; it was smoked glass. There was fire on the other side of it. One of our workers, Mr. Fountain, was walking through the office—he must have just passed the main corridor—and he was on fire. I thought it could have been a bomb. We were still at war with Japan.

Old John Feather Merchant ripped through the War Relief Services office, tearing a hole twenty feet across in the Empire State Building's limestone façade, the cockpit crushed and the right wing sheared off in pieces. The plane's fuel tanks burst, spewing hundreds of gallons of gasoline.

One of the plane's motors and part of the landing gear careened into an elevator shaft and fell nearly 1,000 feet to a cellar. The other engine hurtled across the 78th floor, its offices under renovation and unoccupied, and smashed through the south wall. It landed on the roof of a West 33rd Street office building, tearing apart a penthouse apartment-studio owned by Henry Hering, a sculptor. Hering was up in Scarsdale, playing golf despite the bad weather, and his wife emerged from the wreckage unhurt.

Flaming gasoline rained down on the streets together with a fifty-eight-pound piece of the bomber's tail and a portion of the landing gear. Shards of glass shattered on the sidewalks. But the fiery debris killed no one on the ground, the worst of the injuries there amounting to cuts and bruises.

On the 79th floor, the bomber's impact claimed six lives in the first seconds. Colonel Smith, his two passengers, and two of the Catholic agency's employees, John Judge and Jeanne Sozzi, were crushed by the impact of the fuselage. Paul Dearing, a reporter for a Buffalo newspaper working part-time for the agency in public relations, was swept out a closed window onto a 72nd floor landing.

And then the plane's gas tanks exploded, the fire trapping Mary Kedzierska and six fellow workers—Patricia O'Connor, Mary Lou Taylor, Anne Gerlach, Maureen Maguire, Margaret Mullins, and Lucille Bath.

Flames rose as high as the 86th floor observatory, where forty sightseers had spent a frustrating morning, hoping for a glimpse of the misty skyline. The observatory guide took them down, some by elevator, some by the stairs. The 102nd floor observation deck had only two visitors, Lieutenant Allen Aiman, an Army Air Forces veteran of the Pacific campaign, and his wife, Betty. They, too, emerged unscathed.

Therese Fortier, five of the women working with her, and the severely burned Joseph Fountain found refuge in the office of Father Edward E. Swanstrom, the agency's assistant executive director, who had been walking along 34th Street en route to work when the plane struck.

"It was the furthest place we could go," Fortier remembered. "And we closed the door. One of the women had collapsed and a couple of them were suffering smoke inhalation. I guess they got too hysterical. I found I could handle myself in a crisis very well. I had a handkerchief in my pocket. Those were the days when we didn't walk around with tissues. I put that across my face to try to filter out the smoke. But most of the time we couldn't see. Every once in a while a breeze would come and blow the fog and the smoke out of the way, but the smoke was black, it was acrid."

Joseph Fountain, a forty-seven-year-old father of four, tried to buck up the women's spirits despite his excruciating burns, and he remained conscious as the survivors waited, holding little hope for a rescue.

Catherine O'Connor, thirty-seven, of Manhattan, one of the women huddled in the room, told how Fountain, "burned beyond recognition," managed to open a jammed window to bring in some air amid "a holocaust of unbearable thick, black smoke."

Ellen Lowe, twenty-seven, of Floral Park, Long Island, recounted how Fountain "kept his head and he kept his sense of humor, and he kept us all from going crazy while we were trapped together."

When Lowe considered jumping to a ledge five stories below, Fountain deflected that idea with black humor, saying he would have written a note with their room number on it and dropped it to the street "if only someone had thought to bring a pencil."

"He kidded me out of it," Lowe said.

"We prayed," Fortier recalled. "We tried to keep each other calm. We said the Act of Contrition. I don't think we thought we'd come out of it alive so we wanted to be ready to meet God if that was all we were going to have for our lives."

Fortier tossed her two rings out the window, one of them a friendship band with a red stone from her boyfriend, George Willig, an Army ordnance man serving in the Pacific. The other was her high school ring.

"I figured, if I'm not coming out alive, what's the sense of having those rings burned so I took them off and I threw them down."

But the women at the windows had been spotted.

Harold Smith, an employee of the War Assets Administration recently discharged by the Army, was at his desk on the 62nd floor, facing to the north, when he heard the sound of revving engines. Glancing into the worst fog he had ever seen, he spotted the shadow of an airplane for an instant. The plane was ascending, and a second later it hit the building.

Smith went to the south side of his office, looked up, and spotted three women leaning out of a window, surrounded by flames and smoke. He counted to seventeen windows above him, then began racing up the stairs.

Someone blocked him and told him he must go back, he was only heading for trouble. But soon he started up again, and this time he encountered Lieutenant Edward Buchanan of Engine Company 54 and his fellow firefighters.

"He looked in my eyes and he read me," Smith remembered. "He didn't stop me. I led them to where the fire was. I wanted to go in, and it was too hot to touch. There were two other firemen, one with an axe and one with a hose from a standpipe. They broke the door in and they wet me down and I went in first because I knew where I had to go. I picked up the first girl . . . passed out in my arms. I took her to the east end of the building and laid her on the desk. Her nylon blouse was melted."

Smith made two more trips and rescued two more women. And then he was shoved from the scene.

"I was standing with the girls, trying to make them comfortable, and Mayor La Guardia came into this little office and actually physically pushed me on the side so that he could have his picture taken with the girls."

Firemen carried Therese Fortier and the six others from Father Swanstrom's office down a few flights of stairs, then transferred them to an elevator.

One floor above the Catholic agency's office, Betty Lou Oliver, a twenty-year-old elevator operator from Arkansas, was parked at her post when the bomber hit. Severely burned, she was being taken down in another elevator by its operator when its weakened cables snapped at the 75th floor, plunging them into a sub-basement.

When the bomber hit, a seventeen-year-old Coast Guard hospital apprentice named Donald Molony, sightseeing while on leave from his Groton, Connecticut, base, ran into a Walgreens drug store across the street from the Empire State Building, got morphine, needles, and syringes, tubes of first-aid ointment, bandages, and alcohol, and headed for the lobby.

"Just as I got to the elevators I heard a crash in the basement and a girl scream," he recounted. It was Betty Lou Oliver. Firemen cut a hole in the elevator shaft, and since Molony was the smallest one on the scene, they pushed him through it. He pulled Oliver and the male elevator operator with her out of the wreckage. Both survived. Molony went up to the 79th floor after that to provide first aid.

On the floors below the crash, office workers scrambled down the stairs. The 56th floor housed the USO, where a young woman named Gloria Pall was working as a file clerk. She had wanted to work higher up in the building, and an elevator captain she had approached to inquire about job openings had told her there were two spots available. One was for War Relief Services. But, as Pall would recall it, the agency turned her down because she was Jewish. On her lunch hours she would go up to the observation deck with a friend and they would train their binoculars on the ships returning from the war. They used their purse makeup mirrors to reflect the sun, gaining the attention of the soldiers on deck, who flashed back with their shaving mirrors.

The crash hurtled Pall against a desk, injuring an arm. A fellow worker screamed: "It's the German buzz bomb. They tricked us. They didn't really surrender."

Showered with broken glass and plaster, Pall and her coworkers made it to the street. A nurse put Pall's arm in a sling, and then she encountered La Guardia, who asked if she was okay. Moments later, Pall's boss pushed through the crowd. "You ought to come in next Saturday," he told her. "You didn't even work two hours today."

The crash took fourteen lives—the three men aboard the bomber and eleven employees of War Relief Services. The last to die was Joseph Fountain, who succumbed to his burns at Bellevue Hospital.

On Monday morning, two days after the crash, the Empire State Building reopened. Its facades were fireproof and its integrity remained intact. War Relief Services opened temporary offices at Catholic Charities, across the street from St. Patrick's Cathedral, then returned to the Empire State Building a few months later in offices just below the 86th floor observation deck.

For Therese Fortier, the shock lingered at war's end. "I would hear a plane, and forget it. I couldn't sleep. My doctor put me on phenobarbital." She visited friends in Loveland, Ohio, simply to get away from New York. "On the way out to Ohio on the train, I threw the phenobarbital down the toilet. I didn't want to get addicted. The trip calmed me down."

She had thrown away the ring from her boyfriend in those frantic moments on the 79th floor, but in October 1946 she married him. Therese and George Willig raised six children. They named their first son George.

In May 1977, George Willig Jr. climbed the 110-story south tower of the World Trade Center on a lark. He ascended 1,362 feet—more than a hundred feet higher than the top of the Empire State Building—and they called him the "human fly."

"He reached the top of that building around the same time of day as the plane had hit the Empire State Building," his mother remembered.

George Jr. was arrested, but the city settled for fining him $1.10, a penny for each story of the World Trade Center he had climbed, a light-hearted conclusion to an episode of irretrievable innocence.

CHAPTER 31

"FOR A WORTHY CAUSE"

Anthony Casamento, Thomas J. Kelly, Joseph F. Merrell, George Peterson, John James Powers, Charles W. Shea, and Kenneth Walsh: Collectively their names personified the diversity of New York, and each of them received the Medal of Honor.

Three of those citations were awarded posthumously. On May 8, 1942, in the Battle of the Coral Sea, Navy Lieutenant Powers, a dive-bomber pilot from Manhattan, was shot down while attacking a Japanese warship at a perilously low altitude to insure a direct hit. On March 30, 1945, Army Staff Sergeant Peterson, from Brooklyn, silenced three German machine-gun positions although severely wounded, but he was killed while aiding a fallen comrade. On April 18, 1945, Army Private Merrell, a native of Staten Island, killed twenty-three Germans single-handedly during the drive toward Nuremberg before he was cut down.

Staff Sergeant Meyer Levin, from East 33rd Street in Brooklyn's Flatlands section and a graduate of Brooklyn Tech High School, was hailed back home for a bombing run that thrilled the nation three days after the Pearl Harbor attack.

Levin was the bombardier of the B-17 Flying Fortress piloted by Captain Colin Kelly that was said to have sunk the Japanese battleship *Haruna* off the northern Philippines. The bomber crashed after being jumped by Japanese fighters on its return to Clark Field in the Philippines. After his fellow crewmen bailed out, Kelly went down with his plane and became a national hero.

Levin went on take part in some fifty bombing raids in the Pacific. In November 1942, 2,500 neighborhood residents gathered outside the Levin family's house to present a plaque to the airman's father, Sam, a clothing inspector for the Navy, and his mother, Leah.

On January 7, 1943, Meyer Levin's bomber ran out of fuel in bad weather off New Britain Island after tracking a Japanese convoy. Levin managed to remove a life preserver from the plane, tossing it to the other crewmen.

They climbed aboard, but Levin was knocked unconscious and drowned. Army Chief of Staff Marshall sent a personal note of condolence to the Levin family.

Colin Kelly's plane had not, in fact, destroyed a battleship. It damaged a cruiser, according to later reports, but Kelly and Levin would long be remembered.

Five months after the Pearl Harbor attack, the Japanese overran the Philippines. In the tunnels of Corregidor, the remnants of the American forces under General Jonathan Wainwright, driven from the Bataan Peninsula, were in the last throes of their holdout, waiting for the Japanese onslaught.

Their final words were tapped out on May 5, 1942, by the son of a Brooklyn tailor, a twenty-two-year-old Signal Corps operator named Irving Strobing.

> General Wainwright is a right guy and we are willing to go on for him, but shells were dropping all night, faster than hell. Damage terrific. Too much for guys to take. The jig is up. Everyone is bawling like a baby. They are piling dead and wounded in our tunnel.
>
> My name Irving Strobing. Get this to my mother, Mrs. Minnie Strobing, 605 Barbey Street, Brooklyn, N.Y. They are to get along o.k. My love to Pa, Joe, Sue, Mac, Garry, Joy and Paul. God bless you and keep you.

Private Strobing's radio message was picked up in Hawaii by an Army radio technician named Arnold Lappert, who happened to be a New Yorker as well—a Manhattan boy. Lappert relayed Strobing's words to the American mainland, and they were read on *The Army Radio Hour* and printed in newspapers, touching the emotions of the homefront.

On September 6, 1945, Strobing was released from a prison camp in northwest Japan where he had labored in a quarry, subsisting on barley three times a day, together with plant leaves and a few ounces of meat a week. "It was work or starve, or probably both," he told reporters.

Strobing and Lappert each returned to New York in October 1945 and they reenacted the events of springtime 1942 at a Madison Square Garden pageant telling of the contributions American Jews had made in all the nation's wars.

New Yorkers were also proud of the four Breen brothers of Brooklyn, all in the Navy. Their father, John Joseph Breen, an oiler on a cargo ship, lost his life in June 1942 when it was torpedoed in the Caribbean. His son William was already in the Navy, and the other three boys, John Jr., James, and Martin, joined up as well. When their mother, Catherine, marked her fifty-sixth birthday on March 24, 1943, all her sons obtained leave to be with her.

"My husband is still the No. 1 war hero to me," said Catherine Breen.

In the sports world, the New York Giants football team lost Jack Lummus, the end who was awarded the Medal of Honor posthumously for heroism on Iwo Jima, and Al Blozis, a tackle who died in the Vosges Mountains of France. Dudley (Red) Garrett, a defenseman for the New York Rangers, lost his life while serving with the Royal Canadian Navy off Newfoundland.

New York's publishing houses issued a host of titles relating the exploits of servicemen from throughout the nation. Private Marion Hargrove's missteps in basic training, *See Here, Private Hargrove*, sold more than two and a half million copies. John Hersey's *Into the Valley* told of a marine skirmish on Guadalcanal. Ernie Pyle's *Brave Men* presented the stories of the men in the foxholes. Captain Ted Lawson, who lost a leg in the crash of his bomber in the Doolittle Raid, wrote *Thirty Seconds over Tokyo*.

Publishers shipped millions of small, paperbound books to servicemen overseas through the nonprofit Armed Services Editions. Soldiers and sailors could put the war aside for a few moments with titles like *The Fireside Book of Dog Stories*, while the more literary types could immerse themselves in the woes of the previous decade with *The Grapes of Wrath*.

The face of New York on the battlefront captured the imagination of Hollywood, which saw the personification of the citizen soldier, the "everyman" in the foxhole, in boys from Brooklyn. *Guadalcanal Diary* told of the doomed Marine corporal Taxi Potts (William Bendix), a onetime cabbie who yearned to be back in the stands at Ebbets Field. The infantry squad slogging through Italy in *A Walk in the Sun* was lucky to have Private Tranella (Richard Benedict), an immigrant's boy fluent, as the narrator put it, in "Italian and Brooklyn."

The Breens of the Navy lived in Brooklyn's Crown Heights section. The city that sent more than 800,000 men and women to war was a sea of neighborhoods, notwithstanding the glitter of midtown Manhattan. Readers of The *Bronx Home News,* the *Brooklyn Eagle*, and the *Long Island Press* and *Long Island Star-Journal* of Queens were eager for the "local angle" in the war.

Mark Marchese delivered the *Bronx Home News.*

They never let their readers forget the Bronx's role in the war. I remember photos of young men being sworn in for the armed forces and they would be captioned, "Bronx residents among the first to respond." They'd show you military planes flying and it would read "planes fly over Bronx in search for Nazi subs." And there were pictures of GIs all over the world. They'd be in North Africa, say, and they'd have signs like "Grand Concourse" or "Pelham Bay."

But not everyone who was physically able went off to war. The poet Robert Lowell, living in New York, was sentenced to a year in federal prison for refusing induction in order to protest the killing of civilians in Allied bombing raids. While at the West Street jail in Lower Manhattan before being transferred to the federal penitentiary in Danbury, Connecticut, Lowell encountered "Lepke," the racketeering kingpin Louis Buchalter, who was awaiting execution for the murder of a Brooklyn trucker. *Memories of West Street and Lepke* became one of Lowell's better-remembered poems. He wrote of Lepke: "Flabby, bald, lobotomized, he drifted in a sheepish calm where no agonizing reappraisal jarred his concentration on the electric chair hanging like an oasis in his air of lost connections." (Lepke died in the Sing Sing electric chair in March 1944.)

By spring 1945, the Americans and British were closing in on Berlin from the west, the Russians from the east. On April 12, the bulletins arrived telling of Franklin D. Roosevelt's death. He was the only president most of the troops had known.

At the Stage Door Canteen, Beatrice Lilly was preparing to present *The Seven Lively Arts Show* when the director signaled for the orchestra to stop. He raised his hand, asking for quiet. "I have a terrible announcement to make," he said, "but out of respect for the president of the United States this show cannot go on."

The audience seemed puzzled. "The president has just died," the director explained. Some of the servicemen wept, and they all filed into the street.

Corporal Sid Frigand of Brooklyn was operating a mortar with an Army patrol in Germany.

We were in a town. We were walking single file and there were kids sitting on a stone fence. And they were ridiculing us. They said, "Your president is dead." We didn't know that Roosevelt had died. One of the officers got confirmation on his phone. We knew Harry Truman was vice president, but we didn't know anything about him.

"Today's List of Casualties" in the next day's *New York Post*—the daily and seemingly endless columns of New York's missing and dead on all the battlefronts—began:

Washington, Apr. 13—Following are the latest casualties in the military services, including next of kin.

ARMY-NAVY DEAD

ROOSEVELT, Franklin D. Commander-in-Chief, wife, Mrs. Anna Eleanor Roosevelt, the White House.

On May 8, 200,000 people gathered in Times Square to celebrate Germany's surrender. A national "brownout" to conserve coal supplies, imposed in early February and darkening Times Square far beyond the "dimout" restrictions that had already been lifted, came to an end on V-E Day. The New York Stock Exchange observed two minutes of silence and confetti rained down on Wall Street. Prayer services were held throughout the city.

In Brooklyn, V-E Day proved an opportunity for one youngster to try something unthinkable only the day before.

Maury Allen's family, having moved from Bensonhurst, was living three blocks from one of Flatbush's busiest shopping streets.

A friend and myself walked down to Kings Highway. People had noise-makers, and they were beating pots and pans, and everybody was yelling. I was now 13½ years old and my hormones were turning up. There were a lot of girls there who looked to me like college girls, but they were probably high school girls. I was still in junior high school.

We see these guys running up to these girls and kissing them. All of a sudden I got the nerve to walk up to this one girl and I just grabbed her and gave her a little kiss—I bent her over like they do in the movies—and the sweat started to run down my forehead and on my face, I was so nervous. I had done something so dramatic. I think she was mostly laughing because I was pretty young. She might have been 15.

On June 19, General Dwight D. Eisenhower, the supreme allied commander, home on leave, rode in a motorcade through thirty-seven miles of New York streets, cheered by 4 million. A General Electric noise meter calculated the roars of the crowd as the equivalent of 3,000 simultaneous peals of thunder. Police Commissioner Lewis Valentine remembered the city's reception for Admiral Dewey following the Spanish-American War's Battle of Manila Bay and he certainly recalled the ticker-tape parade for Charles Lindbergh in 1927, but "this beats them all," he said.

La Guardia presented Ike with the city's Gold Medal at a ceremony in City Hall Park, and Eisenhower thanked New York as the gateway to Europe's battlefronts for more than 3 million servicemen, among them hundreds of thousands of the city's own. Marveling at the outpouring of affection on this day, he couldn't resist a folksy note: "New York simply can't do this to a Kansas farmer boy and keep its reputation for sophistication."

On the following day, the *Queen Mary* arrived in New York with 15,526 soldiers, sailors, airmen, and Army nurses who were welcomed by military vessels, tugs, city ferries, and a water-spouting municipal fireboat. Those servicemen did not expect to be home for good. Many would presumably be bound for the Pacific and the invasion of Japan, the casualties envisioned as immense.

Then came Hiroshima and Nagasaki.

At 7:03 p.m., Tuesday, August 14, the electronic sign winding around the Times Tower proclaimed: "Official. Truman Announces Japanese Surrender."

By 10 o'clock, two million people had jammed the Times Square area, sounding noisemakers, tossing hats in the air, waving American flags. On First Avenue in Brooklyn's Bay Ridge neighborhood, effigies of Emperor Hirohito were hung from lampposts and burned. In Chinatown, a dragon dance snaked along Mott and Pell streets.

Sheldon Mike Young, getting a few hours off from his corpsman's duties at the Brooklyn Navy Hospital, found himself in Chinatown at one point as he made the rounds of the city to celebrate with his buddies. "I wound up getting a Coke at a shop where Chinese were playing mah-jongg at a table set up in the doorway. Someone pushed me onto a cushion, set a stack of bills in front of me and took my hand to move the tiles into play. Someone made bets for me and shoved dollar bills into my blouse pocket. I found myself held up by two blondes as we went marching in a parade preceded by teen-agers carrying Chinese and American flags."

For all the guys and all the girls joined in fleeting embrace, one image endures: the sailor and the nurse in Times Square, captured most famously by *Life* magazine's Alfred Eisenstaedt but also photographed by a Navy man.

Eisenstaedt grew up in Berlin, his father a retired department store owner, and when he was thirteen an uncle gave him an Eastman Kodak camera. Soon he was developing and printing his own pictures in the family's bathroom, turned into a darkroom. By the early 1930s he had become an accomplished freelancer. He photographed Joseph Goebbels, Hitler's propaganda minister, scowling at his camera during a League of Nations meeting in Geneva in 1933, and Hitler meeting Mussolini for the first time, at a Venice airport in 1934.

Eisenstaedt came to New York in 1935, joined Henry Luce's newly created *Life* in 1936, and teamed with the renowned Margaret Bourke-White and two others as the magazine's first full-time photographers. On V-J Day, he was in the midst of countless embraces when his moment arrived.

I saw a sailor running along the street grabbing every girl in sight. I was running ahead of him with my Leica looking back over my shoulder. Whether she was a grandmother, stout, thin, old, didn't make any difference. Then suddenly, in a flash, I saw something white being grabbed. I turned around and clicked the moment the sailor kissed the nurse. I took exactly four pictures. It was done within a few seconds. People tell me that when I am in heaven they will remember this picture.

"The Kiss," *Life*'s cover photo for its V-J Day issue, became the most recognized image in the history of the magazine. The same embrace was captured at a slightly different angle by Lieutenant Victor Jorgensen, a Navy photographer, whose caption told how "they threw anything and kissed anybody in Times Square." Jorgensen's picture, though overshadowed by Eisenstaedt's photo, appeared in the *New York Times*.

Neither Eisenstaedt nor Jorgensen got the names of the sailor and the nurse, but it didn't matter—they symbolized a moment of overwhelming joy and relief.

In the months following V-J Day, the servicemen returned to the Port of New York by the hundreds of thousands, and the war brides followed. Reunions played out for couples like Francis and Jo Chinard.

Following his medical internship at Columbia-Presbyterian Medical Center in the war's early years, Francis Chinard became a flight surgeon with the Eighth Air Force. He was living in High Wickham, an English town of 15,000, when he met Jo.

The Red Lion Hotel was a watering place. I was sitting at a table alone, smoking a pipe, and I noticed a young woman sitting with a glider pilot. She was extremely attractive. To my surprise, after I'd been there about twenty minutes, a chap gets up and comes over to me and introduces himself as lieutenant so and so. Would I mind very much if he introduced me to his companion because he had to go to the men's bar with mates of his outfit who were celebrating. We were introduced properly— I was supposedly his old friend—but I had never met him before. We sat down and talked. Her name was Jo. She ate sardines and we talked politics and the war for about two hours. At the end of the evening I was absolutely smitten.

Francis and Jo were married in England in June 1943.

At war's end, Francis was stationed at Randolph Field near San Antonio, Texas. In September 1945, Jo arrived in New York. Many of the war brides came to America later on the grand ocean liners. But Jo had secured an early passage in exchange for a more modest means of transportation: a Liberty ship called the *Benjamin Hill*, its main cargo 20,000 bottles of scotch whiskey.

"There were only two passengers," Jo remembered, "myself and an elderly lady who was going to be a nanny for some family. She was Scotch.

"We were approaching the Statue of Liberty. The purser was a nice old man, an American, though we had a Dutch captain. He looked after me. He knocked on my cabin door and said 'immigration will be onboard.' "

Jo wasn't exactly familiar with American vernacular.

I said, "Have somebody knock me up." And he looked at me shocked. In a kind manner, he said, "Don't ask people to do that." In the old days in England, when they had young people working in the mills, they used to have professional knocker-uppers. They would go and knock on the windows and get people out of bed, get them up early to work.

Like her choice of words, Jo's wardrobe was appropriate for England but not so much for New York. "I thought it would be nice fall weather but it was like ninety degrees and the humidity was beyond belief. And I had a tweed suit on and a felt hat."

Francis's father, teaching at Princeton, tried to find out where the *Benjamin Hill* was docking so he could meet his daughter-in-law. But as Francis remembered it: "They refused to tell him because they didn't know whether he was interested in the passenger or in the whiskey. So Jo had to get here on her own."

Jo's Liberty ship docked in Brooklyn, and "the old purser put me in a cab to Penn Station where they had travelers' aid."

There was joy for most, but everywhere the toll had been felt.

A service flag bearing a gold star had graced the front window of the Breen family's brownstone apartment on Brooklyn's Lincoln Place to honor the father of the four sons in the Navy. A blue star signified that somebody from a home was in military service. A gold star meant that a family member had been killed in action.

For a teenager like Mark Marchese, a student at James Monroe High School growing up as a subway motorman's son in a blue-collar South Bronx neighborhood where "the focal point was the candy store" and "if your father was a police lieutenant that was high status," a gold-star family was treated with reverence.

Everybody knew everyone else in the neighborhood, When a gold star went in the window there was a good chance you knew the person. It commanded a quiet respect. The kids would place their hands over their heart when they went past a gold star, or they blessed themselves. In some cases the kids would address their absent friends.

I had a friend named Harold Chesser. He had a part-time job with Western Union. He wore a uniform, and he had a leather thing that you wore around your legs to prevent your trousers getting caught in the drive section of a bicycle. Just the sight of him struck terror in the hearts of a lot of women in the neighborhood. They were fearful of a telegram. If he showed up, it was awful. If he rang a bell, he would shout out if it was good news, "I've got a birthday telegram." They had singing telegrams in those days. So the people would know immediately.

During the war years, Bess Myerson lived with her family in the Sholom Aleichem Cooperative housing in the Bronx, named for the Yiddish writer whose tales of Tevye the milkman would inspire *Fiddler on the Roof*. She attended Hunter College, first at its Bronx campus and then, when the Waves' training station opened there, at its Manhattan classrooms. In September 1945 she became the first Jewish woman to win the Miss America contest.

She remembered "the horror of passing Gold Star mothers on the stairs of the Sholom Aleichem, women who had once looked on me and my sisters as potential wives for their dead sons."

Moments after Truman's V-J Day announcement was flashed in Times Square, a fifty-four-year-old widow from Harlem named Esther Luciano fainted in front of the Times Tower. She was treated at Bellevue Hospital, where the police found a letter from the War Department in her possessions. Dated three days earlier, it notified her that her son Technical Sergeant Charles Luciano, twenty-four, had been killed in action on January 15 fighting with the infantry in Belgium. Mrs. Luciano was told that he had received the Silver Star and Bronze Star. She could go to Governors Island to pick them up, the War Department said.

For the family of Albert Perna, the sailor who perished as a passenger aboard the Army bomber that crashed into the Empire State Building, the aftermath of V-J Day brought deeper sorrow.

Albert was coming home to Queens to mourn with them over the loss of his brother, Anthony, in a kamikaze raid. Now both were gone.

Their sister Teresa could hear her parents sobbing in their bedroom night after night. Then came an unanticipated blow. As Teresa Arnesen recalled it long afterward: "We lived in an attached house, and the people next door also had two sons, who also were named Anthony and Albert. When the servicemen were coming home, our next door neighbors staged a welcome party for their sons and put up a huge banner across the street. It said, 'Welcome Home—Anthony and Albert.' "

Sam Kramer, the shipfitter at the Brooklyn Navy Yard who worked alongside Sylvia Honigman, one of the pioneering female welders, then married her, had written home frequently after going into combat with the 78th

Infantry Division in the war's final months. And then his letters stopped. On May 2, 1945, a telegram arrived: Sam had been killed in action. On the day FDR died, Sam's jeep was ambushed outside the German town of Remscheid. He died of a bullet wound to the chest.

On December 3, 1944, Sam had written a letter to Sylvia for deliverance if he were killed in action. He entrusted it to one of his unit's officers, who passed the letter on to Sylvia a few weeks after Sam's death.

"Having died I at least tasted of the full measure of happiness," he told Sylvia, and he concluded, "I had no remorse for having died for a worthy cause."

CHAPTER 32

FINALE FOR LA GUARDIA

When New York's servicemen came home, they found their city in urgent need of just about everything. Federal funds had flowed to New York in the New Deal days, but wartime Washington had neither the money nor the inclination for municipal public works and social service programs.

Most new construction envisioned for New York had been shunted aside, leaving the modernistic municipal asphalt plant alongside the East River Drive at 90th Street, completed in 1944, as the city's most notable wartime project. Consisting of exposed concrete cast over parabolically arched steel frames, it housed a single large room with an adjacent storage building illuminated by natural light to turn out paving materials for city streets. Robert Moses ridiculed the design as "a Cathedral of Asphalt with a nearby corrugated shoebox," but the Museum of Modern Art and *Architectural Forum* magazine lauded it. Thirty-five years later, the architecture critic Paul Goldberger hailed it as "New York's great piece of mid-twentieth century industrial architecture."

The city's housing stock was in such short supply during the war that more than 165,000 families were doubling up. The subway and elevated rail lines (Manhattan's Third Avenue El was still standing at war's end) had been consolidated into a unified, municipally owned system in 1940, but the nickel fare was politically untouchable, preventing long needed improvements.

The Brooklyn Battery Tunnel remained unfinished, a casualty of Moses's empire building. Back in 1942, La Guardia had named Moses to head the city's collection of industrial-grade scrap metal for war needs. Moses resigned after several weeks in the post, but not before recommending that the federal War Production Board requisition the tunnel's lining segments, which he said were made of steel, melt them down for war use, and halt further work on the tunnel for the war's duration. The lining was in fact composed of cast iron unsuitable for armaments, as La Guardia and an official of the New York City Tunnel Authority pointed out. Moses, already overseeing the toll bridges of his Triborough Bridge Authority, had been unable to gain control of the tunnel unit as well. By persuading the federal government to halt construction of the Brooklyn Battery Tunnel with a baseless argument, he gave himself time to take it over in the postwar years.

Fiorello La Guardia, the dynamo who had inspired and entertained, who had spoken for the downtrodden through the Depression, became irritable and frustrated as the war dragged on.

After his unhappy stint as director of the national Office of Civilian Defense, La Guardia looked beyond City Hall again. In July 1942, he began taping fifteen-minute broadcasts in Italian from City Hall, urging the people of Italy to overthrow the Germans and Mussolini, his voice heard at first on short-wave transmissions sent by NBC but later carried by the federal Office of War Information. The fascists took notice. In October 1942, the Italian agency Stefani retorted via Radio Rome with a broadcast of its own: "That false Italian and authenticated Jew Fiorello La Guardia clears his throat every night on Radio New York to launch in his bad Italian language appeals to the Italian people to sabotage the war and the German-Italian alliance. Émigré La Guardia tries to pass for an Italian to better exploit Italians in New York."

La Guardia pleaded for a military commission—as a brigadier general, he hoped—to help oversee the eventual reconstruction of Italy. As he put it in a letter to Roosevelt in February 1943: "I still believe that Genl Eisenhower can *not* get along without me and am awaiting your order (but as a soldier) . . . Let me know . . . *Con amore*, Fiorello."

Roosevelt seemed willing, but Secretary of War Henry Stimson and Army Chief of Staff Marshall counseled against giving La Guardia the sensitive post. Newbold Morris, the City Council president and a La Guardia ally, would speculate that Stimson "probably had visions of the mayor suddenly popping up on some foreign shore and shooting off his pistol in advance of the American army, throwing the carefully laid plans of the diplomats into confusion."

And La Guardia became mired in spats and embarrassing situations of his own making.

An uproar arose after a minor government official in Pozzuoli, Italy, named Fabio Scinia wrote a letter to La Guardia in May 1944 seeking his help in punishing a sailor named Frederick Brooks who he claimed had seduced his twenty-year-old daughter with a promise of marriage before returning to the United States without so much as a good-bye. La Guardia passed the note on to the Secretary of the Navy, saying he understood that the Navy "does not countenance conduct of this kind." He asked to be informed of what action would be taken so he could "send a word of comfort to the unhappy family."

Brooks, a twenty-one-year-old petty officer who lived on Long Island, was arrested by the Navy in January 1945 and was to be returned to Italy for a general court martial. But the Navy didn't reckon with Brooks's nineteen-year-old wife, Grace, who contacted the newspapers, claiming that her husband, who maintained his innocence of what didn't seem to be much of a crime in the first place, was being railroaded by La Guardia and naval officials. Under the headline "Married Sailor Faces Shotgun in Italy," the *Daily News* described the affair as a "weird war drama." The City Council demanded that the mayor apologize for his intrusion, and letters of outrage descended on City Hall, including one that urged La Guardia to "try to do your job well before worrying about incidents that are none of your business." The affair ended in March 1945 when the Navy dropped charges against Brooks.

La Guardia was evidently still in a snit over being denied a commission as a brigadier general when he defied Washington over a request he could have easily gone along with. When the War Production Board urged a midnight curfew at restaurants and nightclubs throughout the country in March 1945 to preserve coal supplies, La Guardia decreed that New York's nightspots could remain open until 1 a.m., presumably to accommodate servicemen. (The regular closing time had been 4 a.m.) When the Army and Navy threatened to dispatch the MPs and the shore patrol to eject men still out on the town in the early hours, the proprietors agreed to shut down at midnight notwithstanding La Guardia's protests.

"I'm running the city," he said in insisting on a 1 a.m. closing time. "I tried to run the Army, but they wouldn't let me."

While La Guardia fumed at City Hall, fellow New York political figures got into uniform to help administer Italy. William O'Dwyer, the Brooklyn District Attorney who won headlines for prosecuting Murder, Inc., then lost to La Guardia as the Democratic candidate in the 1941 mayoral race, and Charles Poletti, briefly serving as governor of New York, were given the kind of jobs that La Guardia coveted.

O'Dwyer, on leave from his district attorney's post, received an Army commission. In late June 1944, some three weeks after the liberation of Rome, he was named as the ranking American official in the economic sector of the Allied Control Commission for Italy, a civilian and military unit taking over its administration. He was promoted to brigadier general soon afterward, and in January 1945 he was appointed executive director of the War Refugee Board, aiding Holocaust survivors and other victims of Nazi Germany.

Poletti, the son of an Italian immigrant stonecutter, a Harvard Law School graduate, a former member of a prestigious New York law firm, and a judge, had moved up from lieutenant governor of New York when Herbert Lehman resigned to direct American war-relief efforts in Europe in early December 1942. Poletti was governor for only twenty-nine days before giving way to the newly elected Thomas E. Dewey but he had become the first person of completely Italian ancestry to serve as the governor of any state.

In January 1943, Poletti was named a special assistant to Stimson, and he received an Army commission three months later. Landing in Sicily with American troops in July 1943, he became a senior officer in the Allied military government. As British and American troops swept through Italian regions in their drives northward, Lieutenant Colonel Poletti followed, overseeing restoration of water supplies, transport, and electricity and providing equitable food supplies in the face of widespread black-market operations.

Directing civil affairs operations in Naples, Rome, and Milan, the occupation period described by John Hersey in his novel *A Bell for Adano*, Poletti joked in Italian and drank wine while listening to the pleas of Italians visiting his offices, much in the mold of Hersey's sympathetic occupation officer Major Victor Joppolo.

Poletti once found himself as the only American in the Sicilian city of Favara, which American troops had taken moments before, then abandoned. He went to the chief of police and told him what he needed.

"Then I made a speech to a mass of people crowded around City Hall and explained that there would be no difficulty if they obeyed the military regulations," he told an Associated Press correspondent. "They applauded and cheered as I drove away. It was just like a political meeting back home."

It was the kind of political panache that La Guardia could have shown if given the chance.

But La Guardia's misadventures and disappointments in his quest for a significant war role paled beside a family tragedy. His sister, Gemma, and her husband, Herman Gluck, a Hungarian Jew, were living in Budapest when they were rounded up by the Nazis in June 1944. Gemma was sent to the Ravensbruck concentration camp and later jailed in Berlin together with her daughter and infant grandson. La Guardia did not learn of their whereabouts until they were liberated by the Russians in May 1945. Gemma's husband and son-in-law were killed by the Nazis.

Early in May 1945, La Guardia announced he would not seek a fourth term.

On the afternoon of Sunday, July 1, he enjoyed one of the final flourishes in his mayoralty.

La Guardia was making another of his Sunday *Talk to the People* broadcasts from City Hall on the municipal radio station WNYC, a weekly staple since January 1942 opening with the "Marines' Hymn" and closing with his favorite expression, "patience and fortitude." He told the children in his audience to gather round their radios. He wanted to tell them about Dick Tracy.

The newspaper deliverymen had gone on strike, depriving the youngsters of the jut-jawed detective and all their other comic-strip favorites. La Guardia enjoyed the comics, and now he was coming to the aid of the children. Impersonating the characters, he related Dick Tracy's latest exploits in the *Daily News*. And he promised that someone from WNYC would read from the comics daily while the strike continued. "Listen, Morris, every afternoon I want you to pick the time, and do not tell me that you do not have time . . . because you know that all of your programs are not so hot," the mayor said, enjoying a little joke at the expense of Morris Novik, the head of WNYC.

When La Guardia went on the radio the following Sunday, five newsreel cameras were rolling. Word of his tour de force had spread, and now La Guardia was really hamming it up. He told of a $50,000 stash in the latest Dick Tracy installment that was "dirty money." The moral for the children: "Dirty money always brings sorrow and sadness and misery and disgrace."

La Guardia would be remembered for reading from the comics long after his many deeds modernizing New York and wiping out pervasive corruption had faded into the haze of history.

William O'Dwyer was elected mayor in November 1945, returning the Democrats to City Hall for the first time since 1933.

The war was over, but the tasks were daunting. "Not a single hospital had seen a paintbrush in the 16 years prior to my swearing-in ceremonies," O'Dwyer would say. "In the meantime, the city's population had increased by a million residents, and each department was woefully undermanned. The smoke was choking New Yorkers, and the raw sewage had long ago discouraged fish in the bay or in the North River and had rendered our beaches dangerous for bathing. Veterans were returning home with no place to live. The rapid transit system, once our pride and joy, was falling apart."

La Guardia, wife, Marie, and their children "retired" to their home in the Riverdale section of the Bronx. La Guardia continued to make radio broadcasts, and Truman sent him to Brazil as the American representative at the inauguration of its new president.

Three months after leaving office, La Guardia gained a world stage when Truman named him to succeed Herbert Lehman as head of the United Nations' relief organization.

He embarked on a tour of European capitals, but interrupted that mission for a reunion in Copenhagen with Gemma whom he had not seen in twenty years. He had helped her get to Denmark while her plea for entrance to the United States was being processed, but he told her that she would have to wait her turn for a visa. She came to the United States in 1947.

Charged with feeding the remnants of the Holocaust and all the other displaced people of Europe, La Guardia witnessed misery far exceeding anything he had encountered at City Hall in the depths of the Depression.

"I thought I had seen some pretty hard and difficult situations but there is nothing I have been through . . . where so many people were facing death through starvation," he said.

Touring Russia, Poland, Yugoslavia, Italy, Greece, Germany, and Austria, he spoke with the desperate survivors and issued orders for food allocations. At an Italian orphans' home, he was presented with children's art and essays, one of them titled "A Fiorello La Guardia Nostro Amato Protettore (Our Beloved Protector)."

La Guardia became enraged by what he saw as insensitive administration of displaced persons' camps by the American military. He called for the United States to admit tens of thousands of refugees, and as the Cold War dawned, he battled against the Truman administration's reluctance to provide humanitarian aid to countries falling under Soviet control. He denounced the United States for abandoning humanitarian principles—it is "morally wrong; it is wicked."

It was La Guardia's last battle. He emerged from it exhausted and he looked haggard. But this was more than the consequence of an insurgent's life, of decades raging against injustice and political foes. La Guardia had pancreatic cancer. He died at his Bronx home on September 20, 1947, at age sixty-four.

When his black safe-deposit box was opened, his assets, besides his mortgaged home in Riverdale, amounted to $8,000 in war bonds.

As Truman put it in a telegram to Marie La Guardia: "He was as incorruptible as the sun."

EPILOGUE

WORLD CAPITAL

·

Herbert Lehman, Fiorello La Guardia, William O'Dwyer, and Charles Poletti placed a New York accent of sorts on postwar Europe.

In working to rebuild the continent's war-ravaged economies and feed its people, they reflected a larger picture as well.

With London yet to recover from the blitz and the buzz bombs, Paris still emerging from the long German occupation, and Berlin and Tokyo in ruin, physically unscathed New York reigned as the preeminent international city.

In October 1945, Sixth Avenue was renamed Avenue of the Americas, as first proposed by V. Clement Jenkins, president of the Sixth Avenue Association business group when the avenue's blight-inducing El was torn down in 1939. Jenkins envisioned redevelopment of the avenue into "the commercial capital of the Western Hemisphere." A month after the name change became official, plans were announced for a forty-seven-story Good Neighbor Building. Nothing came of those particular visions, and Sixth Avenue would remain just that in the minds of New Yorkers, whatever the street signs and the Post Office said. But a point was made: New York had grand plans for a presence far beyond the Hudson.

The city's international ascendancy was underscored in March 1946, when delegates from the eleven member countries of the fledgling United Nations Security Council convened at Hunter College in the Bronx, scene of the Navy's wartime training program for the Waves. Their meeting place: the unlikely confines of the gymnasium, which had been converted to a conference hall with acoustical tile sheathing the rafters, thick carpeting glued to the planked floor, and 3,500 yards of fabric attached to the brick walls to muffle sound. In October 1946, the U.N. General Assembly met in the New York City Building at Flushing Meadows Park, the site of the World's Fair.

As 1946 came to a close, the United Nations voted to establish its permanent headquarters along the East River in the forties, on a tract still occupied by slaughterhouses. The land had been bought up for a futuristic urban development by the real estate investor William Zeckendorf, but the Rockefeller family paid him $8.5 million for it, clearing the way for the United Nations' arrival.

The deal was completed on December 11, 1946, reportedly at Zeckendorf's unofficial offices in the Monte Carlo nightclub, which he owned. When the architect Wallace Harrison, the planning director for the U.N. buildings, signed the final papers, he telephoned Nelson Rockefeller at his Rockefeller Center office with the news. Rockefeller shouted into the phone: "Wally, that calls for a celebration. See if you can't bring back a bottle of champagne." Harrison went into a liquor store for something worthy of the occasion. In the wallet of his inside pocket, he had the executed papers for the $8.5 million deal and two one-dollar bills for the champagne.

All through the war, New York's great rail stations were bursting with servicemen heading to training camps, with war-plant workers en route to out-of-town jobs, but there remained a touch of glamour. Grand Central Terminal boasted the Twentieth Century Limited, which departed on its nonstop journey to Chicago every evening at 6:01 from a platform known as "the quay," the passengers having strolled upon red-and-gray carpeting bearing its illustrious name to enter its stainless steel, air-conditioned cars. Penn Station offered the Broadway Limited to Chicago, and its waiting room served as a backdrop in the 1945 Hollywood movie *The Clock*, telling of a lonely soldier (Robert Walker) who finds love in New York (Judy Garland), then departs for the battlefront.

The age of the railroads still had a ways to go and ocean liners were again arriving and departing at Manhattan's piers when peace arrived. But international air travel loomed, and New York was getting ready.

A vast airport was arising on the south shore of Queens, astride Jamaica Bay, eclipsing La Guardia Field on the borough's north shore. The city had begun filling in marshy tidelands in 1942, envisioning a 1,100-acre airport on the site of Idlewild Golf Course. It became the greatest construction project in New York's history.

New York International Airport—known simply as Idlewild—began serving foreign airlines on July 9, 1948, when a Peruvian International Airways D-4 touched down with thirty-three passengers. The airport was formally dedicated on July 31 in a ceremony attended by President Truman.

"It will be the front door for the United Nations," Truman said. "Men and women from the far corners of the earth will land here in their search for peaceful solutions to their countries' difficulties."

On that day, Idlewild had grown to 4,900 acres, or 7.1 square miles, about the size of Manhattan from the Battery to 42nd Street. Foreign carriers were already touting their tourist and business destinations from offices on Fifth Avenue. Air France was the first one on the avenue, in 1946, followed two years later by Britain's BOAC, KLM Royal Dutch Airlines, and Swissair.

The United Nations and Idlewild Airport were the most visible symbols of New York's burgeoning international presence. But the city was placing its imprint overseas in all manner of ways.

New York was still the manufacturing citadel and busiest port in America in the immediate postwar years. Surveying the city's statistical wonders in December 1946, the *New York Times Magazine* reported that more people were employed in New York's garment trades than were making autos in Detroit or steel in Pittsburgh. The war-ravaged countries of Europe needed everything. New York could meet their demand for garments, machinery, electronic products, and shipping laden with food. And unlike Detroit, where the auto plants built tanks and planes during the war, New York didn't have to retool.

British visitors were struck by New York's vibrancy.

Cyril Connolly, who arrived from London in 1946 to work on a special American issue of his magazine *Horizon* and to report on the art scene, found "an unforgettable picture of what a city ought to be; that is, continuously insolent and alive, a place where one can buy a book or meet a friend at any hour of the day or night, where every language is spoken and xenophobia almost unknown, where every purse and appetite is catered for, where every street and every quarter and the people who inhabit them are fulfilling their function, not slipping back into apathy, indifference, decay."

"If Paris is the setting for romance," he said, "New York is the perfect city in which to get over one, to get over anything."

Following his visit to New York in 1947, J. B. Priestley made it clear that he was hardly enamored of New York's lust for commerce, the city's hallmark since the days of the Dutch. He remarked on how many objects of high value offered in its fine stores had been made by craftsmen in the great cities of Europe and even China. But he marveled nonetheless at its splendid offerings.

"Coming from a half ruined Europe, I saw, more sharply than ever, this fabulous city as Nineveh and Babylon piled on Imperial Rome. All the rich loot of civilization now rushing into oblivion, except for the textbooks of history, is to be seen in the shops of Fifth Avenue and the neighboring streets numbered among the Fifties."

The British writer Beverley Nichols, visiting New York in 1948, found a stark contrast with London:

More than ever before, as the shop windows filed past in a glittering parade, there was the sense of New York as the great international city to which all the ends of the world had come. London used to be like that, but somehow one had forgotten it . . . so many aeons since the tropical fruit had glowed in the Bond Street windows. Coming from that sort of London to America in the old days, New York had seemed just—American; not typical of the continent, maybe, but American first and foremost. Now it was the center of the world.

New York's great banking institutions and the major American corporations based in the city thrived at war's end. They gained opportunities for international trade and investment from the Bretton Woods system, created at an international conference in 1944 in New Hampshire that established the American dollar as the world's prime currency in place of Britain's sterling and founded GATT (the General Agreement on Tariffs and Trade), the International Monetary Fund, and the World Bank.

The New York foreign policy elite, having played a major role in running the war, put its mark on the Truman administration. Secretary of State Dean Acheson and John McCloy, New York lawyers, and Averell Harriman, Robert Lovett, and James Forrestal, figures from the city's powerful investment banks, took part in creating the Defense Department, the National Security Council, the Central Intelligence Agency, the Marshall Plan, and NATO.

New York's advertising agencies, "Madison Avenue," essentially marked time during the war, turning to public service announcements or promises of a bountiful future once the Germans and Japanese were disposed of. When peace arrived, the opportunities seemed limitless, abroad as well as at home. The multinational Lever Brothers, known for its soap products, had considered Chicago for a new headquarters building. But in April 1950, when it unveiled plans for Lever House, an innovative skyscraper playing light and shadow on glass, it chose Manhattan, selecting a site on Park Avenue in the fifties. As a Lever Brothers representative put it, "the price one pays for soap is 89 percent advertising . . . and the advertising agencies of America were there."

And New York became the cultural capital of the west.

Paris no longer reigned as the world's art center. The modernist artists fleeing occupied Europe for the safety of New York—figures like André Breton, Marcel Duchamp, Max Ernst, and Fernand Léger—had continued to paint in the wartime city. Their presence presumably inspired, but also created a spirit of rivalry, among the rising stars of American art, the Abstract Expressionists, also known as the New York School.

Many artists who were aided during the Depression by FDR's Works Progress Administration lived in New York. They got to know each other, and in the postwar years they gathered in Greenwich Village at spots like the Artists Club and Cedar Tavern. For the most part, with the notable exception of Barnett Newman, the Abstract Expressionists weren't native New Yorkers. Among the elder figures, Willem de Kooning had arrived in the United States from Holland in 1926, and Hans Hofmann, a renowned artists' mentor who settled in New York in 1932, was a Bavarian. Jackson Pollock, the most celebrated of the younger Abstract Expressionists, known for his "drip" style, in which he dripped paint onto flat canvases in a spontaneous expression of his psyche, came from Wyoming and had studied with the western artist Thomas Hart Benton.

But they joined with figures like Robert Motherwell, Mark Rothko, Arshile Gorky, and Jack Tworkov in an awakening of the New York art scene during the war. And Abstract Expressionism endured as America's first truly international art form.

As defined by the Polish-born Tworkov:

Post World War II painting in New York moved against two repressive experiences—the rhetoric of social realism, preached especially by the artists and ideologues on the arts projects of the thirties, and the hegemony of Paris in modern art. The response was an art that stood against all formula, an art in which impulse, instinct and the automatic, as guides to interior reality, were to usurp all forms of intellectualizing.

Pollock had his first one-man show at Peggy Guggenheim's Art of This Century gallery in 1943. The Abstract Expressionist works were also displayed during the war at the Museum of Modern Art; at the Whitney, which was then on West 8th Street, and at the Museum of Non-Objective Painting on East 54th Street, the forerunner of the Guggenheim. When World War II ended and the Cold War heated up, the Abstract Expressionists extended their reach overseas. The State Department sponsored international exhibitions of their paintings as a reflection of American cultural freedom.

New York garnered the international fashion spotlight as well.

Paris had continued to turn out fashions during the German occupation, but editors at the prestigious American magazines like *Vogue* and *Harper's Bazaar* were unable to see the designs. The magazines, newspaper fashion columnists, and publicists turned their attention to the New York fashion shows. Virginia Pope, the fashion editor of the *New York Times*, originated an annual show, "Fashions of the Times," in 1942. Eleanor Lambert, a publicist whose clients included Norell, Adrian, and Trigere, trumpeted New York's style offerings to newspapers around the country. The American Fashion Critics Award, known as the the Coty for its sponsor, was inaugurated in 1943. Looking to seize the moment in order to supplant Paris, La Guardia created a committee to plan a World Fashion Center for postwar New York.

In an August 1943 issue, *Life* magazine found French designs arriving in America to be "vulgar exaggerations of famous silhouettes" in contrast to the trim and figure-enhancing designs conceived in New York.

The wartime New York fashion scene boasted Mainbocher, the American expatriate who returned to the United States in 1940 after running a leading Paris couture house for the previous ten years, its creations having included the pale blue wedding dress worn by the American-born Wallis Simpson when she became the Duchess of Windsor.

A native of Chicago, Mainbocher was born Main Rousseau Bocher, his first name derived from his mother's Scottish maiden name and his surname of French Huguenot derivation. After serving in World War I, he had worked as a fashion artist for *Harper's Bazaar* in Paris, then became editor in chief of *French Vogue* before opening his design house. (His first and last names, run together, were pronounced MainBocker.)

Mainbocher opened what became Manhattan's most exclusive couture house on East 57th Street, adjoining Tiffany off Fifth Avenue. His evening dresses, shortened in the light of fabric rationing and known for their elegant and subdued look, averaged $750 a pop. He also designed uniforms for the Waves, the women marines, and the American Red Cross, and outfitted Mary Martin for her Broadway musical *One Touch of Venus*.

Christian Dior, whose "new look" unveiled in Paris in 1947 heralded a resurgence of the French fashion scene, hailed Mainbocher. And Dior was evidently impressed as well with the new-found prowess of the New York fashion scene. Attending a dinner with fellow European designers, Dior was said to have remarked: "We are all equals, but Mainbocher is really in advance of us all because he does it in America."

Elsewhere in New York's wartime fashion world, Hattie Carnegie employed a thousand people at her tony East 49th Street store. Special clients had their own mannequins, made to their measure. As *Life* magazine put it in a November 1945 issue, "to rate your own dummy at Hattie Carnegie's is probably the financial equivalent of supporting a race horse."

New York's rise as an international fashion center was buttressed by more than the wartime absence of significant French design, as Caroline Rennolds Milbank, a fashion writer who had headed the costume department at Sotheby's, viewed it long afterward.

What rendered New York so important was its demonstrated competence, skill, and ingenuity; the clothes it produced were stylish, appropriate for Americans, and well made even in the thousands. The difference that the war years made was that this was finally recognized. Ready-to-wear was no longer considered a necessary evil; it was modern, it was democratic, and New York had proved that it was stylish.

There were, of course, shadows to come.

New York's manufacturing base would erode, as the garment trades fell victim to nonunion labor in the South and ultimately to Third World sweatshops. The piers that dispatched all those men and all those armaments to the European war fronts fell into disrepair. The cities of what became known as the Sun Belt gained economic clout and political influence. Returning servicemen would forsake their crowded New York neighborhoods to raise families in suburban Levittown and its like.

And a nuclear catastrophe could erase everything. New York schoolchildren of the postwar decade, whose GI fathers joined with the Russians in crushing Hitler, scrambled beneath their desks in the Cold War's equivalent of the World War II air-raid drills, fanciful protection from a Soviet atomic strike.

In his essay "Here Is New York," written not long after the servicemen came home, E. B. White pondered New York's vulnerability in the atomic age:

A single flight of planes no bigger than a wedge of geese can quickly end this island fantasy, burn the towers, crumble the bridges, turn the underground passages into lethal chambers, cremate the millions.

White nonetheless saw hope in the U.N. headquarters that would rise on the East Side of Manhattan, and he viewed the world body's impending presence as emblematic of a triumphant New York.

Along the East River, from the razed slaughterhouses of Turtle Bay, as though in a race with the spectral flight of planes, men are carving out the permanent headquarters of the United Nations—the greatest housing project of them all. In its stride, New York takes on one more interior city, to shelter, this time, all governments, and to clear the slum called war. New York is not a capital city—it is not a national capital or a state capital. But it is by way of becoming the capital of the world.

———

At 9 o'clock in the morning, Sunday, October 26, 1947, the gray-and-tan transport *Joseph V. Connolly*, her ensign at half mast, a single coffin enveloped by an honor guard of servicemen on her deck, emerged from a haze and entered the Narrows of New York Harbor. The destroyers *Bristol* and *Beatty*, the Coast Guard cutter *Spencer*, and five New York City fireboats escorted her into the Upper Bay.

On the Bristol's fantail, Marine Corporal Carroll Ridley raised his trumpet and sounded Church Call. The destroyers' sailors lifted floral displays in the forms of a nine-foot cross, a large Star of David, and an American flag and tossed them into the waters. Chaplains recited the Twenty-third Psalm, the words drowned out by an escort of hovering aircraft. Cannon volleys sounded from Fort Wadsworth on the Staten Island shore, from Fort Hamilton on the Brooklyn oceanfront.

More than 3 million servicemen had departed from New York Harbor for the World War II battlefronts. Now the return of the war dead had begun.

The *Joseph V. Connolly* carried 6,248 coffins in its hold, most with the remains of servicemen who died in the Battle of the Bulge. It berthed at Pier 61, along West 21st Street. The signs reading "Welcome Home" or "Well Done" that had been placed on that pier to greet the returning soldiers and sailors of months past had been painted out or had faded away. "They came in too late," an ensign on the *Bristol* remarked of the fallen.

At 12:45 p.m., the flag-draped coffin on the *Connolly*'s deck, bearing the body of a Medal of Honor recipient, his identity withheld as he represented all 6,248, and indeed all of the war dead, was placed aboard a caisson. The coffin was attached to an armored car. A soldier from the Second Armored Division and another from the 82nd Airborne Division stood in the turret at attention, facing the coffin.

To the beat of muffled drums, the armored vehicle and the coffin led a procession of men and women from all the branches of the armed forces on a sunlit day, temperatures rising into a record-breaking mid-70s.

Some 250,000 New Yorkers lined the streets in silence as the line of march made its way to the Eternal Light in Madison Square Park, a memorial to the dead of World War I—"the war to end all wars." General Courtney Hodges, whose First Army fought in the climactic battles for Europe, placed a wreath upon the marker.

The procession moved up Fifth Avenue to the pealing of bells from St. Patrick's Cathedral, Marble Collegiate Church, and St. Thomas Protestant Episcopal Church. It entered Central Park and halted at the Great Meadow, where a crowd of 150,000 had gathered. The coffin was placed upon a catafalque draped in purple and black. At the north end of the meadow, West Point artillery boomed a salute, the blue smoke rising from the trees. Politicians spoke and chaplains offered prayers. A West Point bugler sounded

Taps. A military honor guard carried the flag-draped coffin back to its caisson and placed it behind the armored car once more. It rolled southward out of the park, the United States Army Band sounding the British World War I tribute to the fallen, "The Vanished Army (They Never Die)," as twilight descended on a golden autumn's day.

ACKNOWLEDGMENTS

When I heard Seymour Wittek tell of April 24, 1943, in the Port of New York, the day he joined with fellow coastguardsmen in fighting a fire on an ammunition boat that threatened to touch off a massive explosion, World War II didn't seem so distant. Mr. Wittek seemed equally proud of his days in wartime New York when he took out a photograph from June '43: Seymour of the Bronx in his Coast Guard dress uniform, Anne of Brooklyn in wedding-dress white.

Francis Chinard gave me a copy of his membership card in France Forever, from the days when he rallied to the cause of the Free French. He was a medical intern in Manhattan back then, and his father, a professor at Princeton, was among the first members of the French community in America to publicly back Charles de Gaulle. And Dr. Chinard had another card to show me, this one with his photograph: "The City of New York Citizens' Defense Corps: Emergency Medical Service." If bombs were to drop on New York, he was "subject to call."

Marie O'Hare Walsh also had a photo for me, this one from a newspaper of May 2008, taken at the Rocky Hill Veterans Hospital in Connecticut, where she joined with the women of her generation in Waves National Connecticut Yankee Unit 42 at their monthly meeting. She had been among the pioneering women of the Navy, a member of the Waves' training class at Hunter College in the Bronx during World War II, and she remained devoted to the Waves, marching in the veterans' parades in the Hartford area.

Whatever their achievements over the years, and the joys of family life, the men and women who shared their memories of World War II New York with me regarded that time as an enduring marker in their lives. I'm grateful to all of them for their reflections.

I appreciate the efforts of K. T. Sullivan, Stephen Downey, Robert Kimball, and Joy Brown in helping me contact members of the wartime show-business world. Douglas Di Carlo of the La Guardia Archives, at La

ACKNOWLEDGMENTS

Guardia Community College in Queens, hunted down material for me. William J. vanden Heuvel provided me with a copy of his talk recounting the campaign of the Century Association's internationalist members to win support for embattled Britain in the pre-Pearl Harbor months. John Rousmaniere guided me through the New York Yacht Club archives. Mike Mania and John McDonald of the USS *Turner* Association aided me in telling the largely forgotten story of a winter's dawn when the destroyer *Turner* exploded and sank in New York Harbor.

I'm grateful to Martin Beiser, my editor at Free Press, for saying yes to this story and providing his incisive counsel, and to Paul Bresnick, my agent, for his hard work and enthusiasm.

My wife, Nancy Lubell, was there as always with her love and encouragement. She happens to be the daughter of a Coast Guard ensign in World War II. But so much for the New York angle—her dad patrolled the waters off Boston.

NOTES

INTRODUCTION

ix *"perpetual New Year's Eve"*   Carlos Romulo, *My Brother Americans*, p. 146.

ix A total of 3,283,678 members of the armed forces left for overseas from the Port of New York between 1941 and 1945, according to the New York State War Council, Keith Drew Hartzell, *The Empire State at War*, p. 327.

x *"adventure in the streets"*   Betty Comden and Adolph Green, "When N.Y. Was a Helluva Town," *New York Times*, Oct. 31, 1971.

x "the American branch of the Fermi family"   Laura Fermi, *Atoms in the Family*, p. 139.

xi "Upwards of 800,000 men and women" from New York City were in military service during World War II, according to the New York City Municipal Reference Library's *New York Advancing, Victory Edition*, p. xvi.

xi *"belongs to the world"*   J. B. Priestley, "Priestley Appraises New York," *New York Times Magazine*, Jan. 4, 1948 (transcription of the BBC broadcast).

CHAPTER 1

3 *"greets the World of Tomorrow"*   *New York Times*, May 1, 1939.

5 *"This looks like the real thing"*   *New Yorker*, Aug. 18, 1945, pp. 15–16.

6 *"the world was headed for grief"*   William Lanouette, with Bela Silard, *Genius in the Shadows*, pp. 186–87.

6 *"extremely powerful bombs"*   Ibid, p. 205.

6 *"a football squad at Columbia"*   Richard Rhodes, *The Making of the Atomic Bomb*, pp. 396–97.

7 *"it would all disappear"*   Ibid, p. 275.

7 New York locations in atomic bomb project cited by Robert S. Norris, "Manhattan Project Sites in Manhattan," *The Manhattan Project*, pp. 219–22.

7 *"a new engineer district"*   Robert S. Norris, *Racing for the Bomb*, p. 170.

8 *"the most famous occupant"*   William J. vanden Heuvel, "Franklin Delano Roosevelt: A Man of the Century," address to the Century Association, April 4, 2002.

8 *"victory itself is doubtful"*   *New York Times*, May 24, 1941.

10 *"I did not have too much"*   August Heckscher, *When La Guardia Was Mayor*, p. 302.

10 *"the next four years will be hell"*   George Martin, *CCB*, p. 464.

CHAPTER 2

11 *"there were public address announcements"*   Carlo DeVito, *Wellington*, p. 100.

12 *"What the hell are they talking about?"*   George Franck, author interview.

12 *"You got me on that Martian stunt"*   Richard M. Ketchum, *The Borrowed Years*, p. 776.

12 *"It was complete disbelief"*   Seymour Wittek, author interview.

13 *"we are at war with Japan"*   Daniel Okrent, *Great Fortune*, p. 408.

13 *"What if someone throws something?"*   Sono Osato, author interview.

14 *"the world would never be the same again"*   K. D. Richardson, *Reflections of Pearl Harbor*, p. 109.

14 *"he told me about Pearl Harbor"*   Robert Satter, author interview.

14 *"Everybody was stunned"*   Kay Travers Langan, author interview.

15 *"Do you know what has happened?"*   Ray Hoopes, *Americans Remember the Homefront*, p. 33.

15 *"committed national hari-kari"*   *New York Herald Tribune*, Dec. 8, 1941.

16 *"an air attack approaching New York?"*   Marcia Davenport, *Too Strong for Fantasy*, p. 286.

16 *"murder by surprise"*   *New York Times*, Dec. 8, 1941.

16 *"unfortunate situation"*   Ibid.

16 *"they say on the radio"*   Kristin Downey, *The Woman Behind the New Deal*, p. 319.

16 *"Why the cabinet meeting tonight?"*   Frances Perkins, *The Roosevelt I Knew*, p. 378.

17 *"He had Texas pride"*   Franck, interview.

18 *"a damn good end"*   Bill Ross, *Iwo Jima: Legacy of Valor*, p. 309.

CHAPTER 3

20 *"It was idiotic of him"*   Robert Satter, author interview.

21 *"I realized it was a drill"*   Sid Frigand, author interview.

22 *"The FBI showed up at Saks"*   Lucetta Berizzi Drypolcher, "Orders to Take Him Away," *Una Storia Segreta*, p. 219.

23 *"ridiculous"*   *New York Times*, March 14, 1942.

23 *"misinterpreted as disrespectful"*   *New York Times*, Dec. 11, 1941.

23 *"Won't somebody catch hell"*   Associated Press, Dec. 11, 1941.

25 *"swivel chair scribes"*   *New York Times*, Jan. 2, 1942.

CHAPTER 4

26 *"three or four very rapid explosions"*   *New York Times*, Mar. 14, 1942.

27 *"able to keep a secret"*   Eleanor Roosevelt column "My Day," cited in *The Target*, publication of Auxiliary Aircraft Warning System, Emeline Roche papers, Box 1, Folder 8.

29 *"We called them Victory Tomatoes"*   Maury Allen, author interview.

30 *"He never missed a blackout"*   *New York Times*, June 29, 1943.

30 *"Complete confusion"*   *New York Times*, Sept. 16, 1943.

30 *"bombs must not be allowed to be dropped"*   Margaret Case Harriman, "Bombs on the Melting Pot," *New Yorker*, Feb. 7, 1942.

31 *"New Year's Eve without lights"*   *New York Times*, May 1, 1942.

33 *"If the Nazi planes ever came"*   Dave Anderson, author interview.

34 *"forgive me now"* . . . *"All is forgiven"*   *New York Times*, Jan. 14, 1944.

34 Statistics for wardens cited by Keith Drew Hartzell, *The Empire State at War*, p. 332.

34 *"I don't even deny it"*   Andy Rooney, "Did They Try to Bomb New York?" *Harper's Magazine*, Mar. 1947.

34 *"we've got rid of all the lightweights"*   *New Yorker*, Dec. 23, 1944, p. 15.

CHAPTER 5

36 *"bomb could be made from Chiclets"*   *New York Times*, Sept. 18, 1941.

37 *"typically American boy"*   *New Yorker*, July 25, 1942, pp. 8–9.

37 *"joined the Coast Guard instead"*   Alice Cullen, author interview.

38 *"Shut up you damn fool"*   Eugene Rachlis, *They Came to Kill*, p. 101.

38 *"made me suspicious"*   W. A. Swanberg, "The Spies Who Came in From the Sea," *American Heritage*, April 1970.

38 *"I wouldn't want to have to kill you"*   *New York Times*, July 16, 1942.

41 *"many people there we didn't even know"*   Cullen, interview.

42 *"enjoying the whiskey"*   Erich Gimpel, *Agent 146*, p. 111.

43 OSS drug experiments cited by John F. Crewsdon and Jo Thomas, "Files Show Tests for Truth Drug Began in U.S.," *New York Times*, Sept. 5, 1977.

CHAPTER 6

45 *"this extraordinary quality"*   Jennet Conant, *The Irregulars*, p. 295.

46 Arrival of Admiral Godfrey and Ian Fleming in New York, and photograph of Godfrey, cited by John Pearson, *The Life of Ian Fleming*, pp. 96–99.

46 *"magnetic personality"*   Ian Fleming, foreword to H. Montgomery Hyde, *Room 3603*, p. x.

47 *"it took eleven secretaries"*   Kenneth Roman, *The King of Madison Avenue*, p. 71.

48 *"published by Winchell as it stood"*   British Security Coordination, p. 126.

48 *"WS's [William Stephenson's] intermediary"*   Ernest Cuneo, the New York lawyer and presumably the intermediary referred to, had been an aide to La Guardia when he served in Congress and was later a counsel to the Democratic National Committee. Cuneo was the liaison between the White House, the United States Office of Strategic Services, and Stephenson's agency. Cuneo's wife, Margaret, like Stephenson a native of Manitoba, worked for him at Rockefeller Center. Hyde, p. 186; *New York Times*, Margaret Cuneo obituary, Aug. 17, 1976.

49 *"Mr. Shaw will be back to work soon"*   *New York Times*, July 29, 1944.

49 *"an obvious eccentric"*   British Security Coordination, p. 400.

50 *"I have a message from Julius"*   Sam Roberts, *The Brother*, p. 92.

50 *"I just listened"*   Ibid, p. 101.

51 *"she knows about her husband's work"*   John Earl Haynes and Harvey Klehr, *Venona*, p. 310.

51 *"call my wife a liar?"*   Roberts, p. 484.

NOTES

CHAPTER 7

55 Shipyard and storage particulars for the wartime port cited in "Port in a Storm: the Port of New York in World War II," New York State Museum, Joseph F. Meany Jr., principal investigator.

55 *"every ship afloat"*   "Gateway to the World," *Popular Mechanics,* April 1942.

56 *"I knew I'd found the answers"*   Nelson Metcalf Jr, "The Story Behind 'The Kid in Upper 4,' " in Julian Lewis Watkins, *The 100 Greatest Advertisements,* p. 149.

56 Camp Kilmer construction cited in "A Historical Sketch of Camp Kilmer," National Archives & Records Administration, Northeast Region, New York.

57 *"first look at Camp Shanks"*   Camp Shanks Museum, Orangeburg, New York.

57 *"haunting remembrance"*   Ibid.

58 Statistics for cargo and petroleum shipments from New York Harbor were compiled by the Port of New York Authority. Cited in Keith Drew Hatzell, *The Empire State at War,* p. 327.

58 *"The bay was filled with ships"*   Dave Anderson, author interview.

59 U-boat 123's ventures near New York Harbor cited by Clay Blair, *Hitler's U-Boat War: The Hunters, 1939–1942,* pp. 302, 460–61.

61 *"embarrassment to the Navy"*   Rodney Campbell, *The Luciano Project,* p. 17.

62 Testimony in Herlands inquiry, Ibid, pp. 126–27.

62 *"herded like cattle"*   Robert Tessmer, "Life Aboard a Troop Transport," www.100thww2.org.

63 *"I got a sick feeling"*   Guy Charland, "Boarding the Troopship SS Dominion Monarch," www.tankbooks.com.

CHAPTER 8

65 *"he had about three minutes"*   Margaret Truman, *Harry S. Truman,* p. 159.

65 *"an avenger to the barbarians"*   *New York Times,* Jan. 30, 1944.

65 *"the quietest launching"*   Ellen Snyder-Grenier, *Brooklyn: An Illustrated History,* p. 127.

67 *"The yard was vastly overmanned"*   Arthur Miller, *Timebends,* p. 200.

68 *"they had never seen a woman there"*   Billie Cohen, "Torch Songs," *Brooklyn: A State of Mind,* p. 342.

69 *"you would think we came from Mars"*   Ibid, p. 343.

69 *"the rabbis told us we should work"*   Snyder-Grenier, p. 127.

70 *"a flag-raising ceremony"*   Ibid, p. 131.

70 *"it was like 'Dante's Inferno,' "*   Ibid, pp. 129–30.

70 *"they want to go to Sands Street"*   Carson McCullers, "Brooklyn Is My Neighborhood," *Vogue,* 1941.

71 *"couldn't shoot more rivets"*   *New Yorker,* Aug. 15, 1942, pp. 10–11.

71 *"out of our chaos and incompetence"*   Miller, p. 202.

CHAPTER 9

74 *"whiffed this smoke"*   *New York Times,* Feb. 10, 1942.

75 *"The ship was listing"*   Stanley Franks, author interview.

76 *"through the police and Navy lines"*   Coleman Schneider, *The Voyage of the S.S. Jeremiah O'Brien*, p. 95.

78 *"Your* Normandie *is burning"*   Harvey Ardman, *Normandie*, p. 326.

79 *"There is no evidence of sabotage"*   Harvey Ardman, "The Ship That Died of Carelessness," *American Heritage*, Dec. 1983.

CHAPTER 10

82 *"The alarm bell rang"*   Seymour Wittek, author interview.

82 *"that guy's crazy"*   North Clarey, "They Saved New York," *Saturday Evening Post*, May 13, 1944.

83 *"through the soles of my shoes"*   Ibid.

83 *"The flames came right at us"*   Harry Biffar, *Fireboats of 9/11 video.*

84 *"like it was another job"*   Biffar, author interview.

84 *"imminent danger of an explosion"*   *New York Times*, Apr. 25, 1943.

84 *"This lamp belongs on the ship"*   Clarey, *Saturday Evening Post.*

84 *"you get the hell off"*   Wittek, interview.

85 *"thank God we got through it safely"*   *New York Herald Tribune*, April 26, 1943.

86 *"thought it was an earthquake"*   *New York Times*, Jan. 4, 1944.

87 *"burned all the clothes off me"*   John McDonald, author interview.

87 *"I heard screams"*   Robert Freear, "Survivor Tales of the USS Turner," www.USSTurner.org.

88 *"a handful of burned flesh"*   Leon Fredrick, *Hooligan Sailor*, p. 23.

88 *"explosion split her in two"*   Seymour Freiden, "50 to 60 Feared Killed as Blast Sinks Destroyer off Rockaway," *New York Herald Tribune*, Jan. 4, 1944.

89 *"had to feel our way around"*   Thomas Beard Barrett, *Wonderful Flying Machines*, p. 49.

90 *"endangering the Statue of Liberty"*   Ibid, p. 67.

CHAPTER 11

91 *"All I have, I have with me"*   *New York Times*, July 13, 1940.

91 *"there is no Maeterlinck in it"*   *New York Times*, Aug. 25, 1940.

91 *"Bluebirds are the symbol of happiness"*   Jeffrey Mehlman, *Émigré New York*, p. 47.

92 *"home of the homeless"*   Alistair Cooke, *The American Home Front, 1941–1942*, p. 281.

93 *"It is the refugee's voice"*   Simeon Strunsky, *No Mean City*, pp. 11–12.

93 *"I am haunted by longing"*   Colin W. Nettlebeck, *Forever French*, p. 27.

95 *"saving the world"*   Stacy Schiff, *Saint-Exupéry*, p. 364.

96 *"however touching the appeal"*   Ibid, p. 391.

97 *"artistic patrimony of humanity"*   Nettlebeck, pp. 52–53.

97 *"Piscator lifted up the trapdoor"*   Marlon Brando, *Songs My Mother Taught Me*, p. 88.

98 *"the international avant-garde"*   Hilton Kramer, "Glamorous Character," *New York Times Book Review*, Dec. 23, 1979.

99 *"teasing along toward the strip"*   Edward Alden Jewell, "31 Women Artists Show Their Work," *New York Times*, Jan. 6, 1943.

99   *"he watched over me"*   Dorothea Tanning, *Between Lives*, p. 64.

100 *"pleading her ignorance"*   Peggy Guggenehim, *Art of This Century*, p. 285.

100 *"most colossal spectacle"*   Associated Press, July 20, 2008.

101 *"heard from no more"*   Tanning, p. 74.

CHAPTER 12

106 *"dancing is desirable"*   E. J. Kahn Jr., "Midshipmen's Country," *New Yorker*, May 10, 1941.

106 *"killed on a destroyer"*   Robert Satter, author interview.

107 *"truly memorable scam"*   Edward J. Keyes, "Navy Days."

107 *"as good as the regular officers"*   Satter, interview.

109 *"violently opposed to calling women"*   Virginia Gildersleeve, *Many a Good Crusade*, p. 271.

109 *"a lot of disparaging remarks"*   Kay Travers Langan, author interview.

110 *"comfort the older admirals"*   Gildersleeve, p. 273.

110 *"was simply horrified"*   Ibid, p. 277.

111 *"may suffer some inconvenience"*   *New York Times*, Jan. 11, 1943.

112 *"to be ordering face powder"*   *New Yorker*, Feb. 20, 1943, pp. 8–9.

113 *"The shoes were so heavy"*   Olive Osterwise O'Mara, "My Service in the Waves, World War II." Oren Heritage Advisory Commission, January–February 2006.

113 *"The inspectors would come in"*   Marie O'Hare Walsh, author interview.

114 *"you keep your chin up"*   *New York Times*, June 17, 1943.

CHAPTER 13

116 *"better than commandos"*   *New York Times*, July 28, 1942.

116 *"walk around the gym"*   Collingwood Harris, "U.S. Coast Guard Oral History Program," Oct. 18, 1984.

116 *"threw me against a wrestling mat"*   Walter E. Lafferty, "America's Greatest Generation: Coast Guard Heroes," Sep. 2002.

117 *"it felt patriotic"*   Jack Dreyfus, *A Remarkable Medicine Has Been Overlooked*, pp. 77–78.

118 *"barracks with only black men"*   Christopher Evanson, "A Veteran Remembers Coast Guard Desegregation," Cox News Service, Nov. 18, 2007.

118 *"an efficient use of manpower"*   Morris J. MacGregor Jr., *Integration of the Armed Forces, 1940–1965*, p. 18.

119 *"jarring anybody's sensibilities"*   Pete Peterson, "The Mariners," *American Legacy*, spring 2005.

120 *"brotherhood and freedom"*   Ibid.

CHAPTER 14

122 *"only thing I can't pick up is a dinner check"*   Harold Russell, *Victory in My Hands*, p. 151.

122 *"amputees had nothing to hide"*   Ibid, p. 159.

122 *"I'm a soldier"*   Ibid, p. 161.

124 *"I'd take candid photographs"*   Ray Fisher, author interview.

124 *"practice shooting in the back lot"*   Robert Wandrey, "Photo School," www.ascen
dantimage.com.

125 *"Private Cortez, this is an order"*   Gerald Hirschfeld, "Wrap Shot," www.ascendan
timage.com.

CHAPTER 15

133 *"the wind that's blowing through the world"*   Carl Rollyson, *Lillian*, p. 205.

133 *"that you make your point"*   Deborah Martinson, *Lillian Hellman*, p. 186.

134 *"repeated blasting"*   *New York Times*, May 19, 1942.

135 *"struggling to make a new world"*   Otis L. Guernsey Jr., *Broadway Song and Story*, p. 223.

136 *"sense of romance"*   John Van Druten, *Playwright at Work*, p. 50.

137 *"static for being a Nazi"*   Skip Homeier, author interview.

CHAPTER 16

139 *"the guilt we all suffered"*   "The American Theatre Wing During World War II," www.americantheatrewing.org/about/history.

140 *"my mother's track winnings"*   Ellis Nassour, "Antoinette Perry Makes a Name," www.theatermania.com (May 29, 2000).

140 *"chief cook and bottle washer"*   Jared Brown, *The Fabulous Lunts*, p. 297.

141 *"Will you shake hands with me?"*   *Canteen News*, Jan. 8, 1944.

141 *"I talked. I laughed"*   Jane Cowl papers, Box 31, Folder 15.

142 *"I will never forget you"*   Landon Chambliss, *Canteen News*, Jan. 8, 1944.

142 *"war was a fiction to me"*   Lauren Bacall, *By Myself*, p. 41.

142 *"the girls here overwhelm me"*   *Canteen News*, Sept. 18, 1944.

143 *"I took the hint"*   Robert F. Gallagher, "World War II Story," www.gallagher.com/ww2.

143 *"have complained bitterly"*   Minutes, Stage Door Canteen executive committee, Dec. 21, 1942, Emeline Roche papers, Box 1, Folder 17.

CHAPTER 17

146 *"we'll finish Commander Gilmore's battle"*   *New Yorker*, Aug. 21, 1943, pp. 16–17.

146 *"On Time"*   Cited in "The Lunchtime Follies," www.americantheatrewing.org/about/history.

148 *"Get out of my way, Cuddles"*   Ethel Merman, with George Eels, *Merman*, p. 124.

149 *"Save your boos for the end"*   Steven Bach, *Dazzler*, p. 257.

149 *"Some of those boys were disfigured"*   Ibid, p. 258.

150 *"the girls they were leaving behind"*   Sono Osato, *Distant Dances*, p. 224.

CHAPTER 18

153 *"the band at Camp Upton"*   Phil Kraus, author interview.

154 *"bulletproof perfection"*   Josh Logan, *Josh*, p. 190.

154 *"no one is to talk to the press"*   Alan Anderson, *The Songwriter Goes to War*, p. 74.

155 *"Some of those guys were absolutely gorgeous"*   *New York Times*, May 10, 1982.

NOTES

156 *"in an old doughboy's uniform"*   Mary Ellin Barrett, *Irving Berlin*, p. 203.

156 *"He loved to sing"*   Laurence Bergreen, *As Thousands Cheer*, p. 406.

156 *"He still hated to get up in the morning"*   Anderson, p. 66.

157 *"flowers, candies and cookies"*   *New York Times*, May 10, 1982.

157 *"we were a snappy looking bunch"*   Anderson, p. 69.

157 *"check for venereal disease"*   Bergreen, p. 406.

158 *"And Burl Ives comes running out"*   Seymour Greene, author interview.

160 *"My prayer now"*   Anderson, p. 339.

CHAPTER 19

162 *"the general wasn't in show business"*   Irving Lazar, with Annette Tapert, *Swifty*, p. 71.

163 *"I learned more about my country"*   Moss Hart, "A Winged Victory," *New York Times*, Nov. 14, 1943.

164 *"He took us to a back office"*   Ramon Blackburn, author interview.

165 *"All of a sudden Glenn Miller showed up"*   Norman Leyden, author interview.

165 *"turns a director into a father figure"*   Lazar, p. 77.

165 *"that civilian was Moss Hart"*   Steven Bach, *Dazzler*, p. 246.

166 *"they marched us to the hotel"*   Eugene Shepherd, author interview.

166 *"overemphasized"*   Jared Brown, *Moss Hart*, p. 252.

167 *"after the war he became Mario Lanza"*   Karl Malden, *When Do I Start?* p. 137.

169 *"92nd Street Commandos"*   *The Gremlin*, Jan. 8, 1944.

169 *"That's what this play is all about"*   *New York Times*, Nov. 28, 1943.

170 *"a flag-waving production"*   Emery Battis, author interview.

170 *"to repair the ravages"*   Brown, p. 259.

CHAPTER 20

172 *"an American flavor"*   Richard G. Hyland, *Richard Rodgers*, p. 141.

172 *"before they went overseas"*   Myrna Katz Frommer and Harvey Frommer, *It Happened on Broadway*, p. 105.

172 *"rowdy, noisy GIs"*   Lillian Ross, "Enchanted Evening," *New Yorker*, Apr. 7, 2008.

173 *"a score you could hum"*   George S. Irving, author interview.

173 *"financial resistance"*   Richard Rodgers, "Reflections on a 'Four-Year-Old,' " *New York Times*, March 30, 1947.

173 *"these naïve kids"*   Myrna Katz Frommer and Harvey Frommer, p. 100.

174 *"the glow was like the light"*   John Steele Gordon, "Oklahoma!" *American Heritage*, Feb.–March 1993.

174 *"the audience was screaming"*   Meryle Secrest, *Somewhere for Me: A Biography of Richard Rodgers*, p. 255.

174 *"dreamy girls don't deliver"*   Carol Easton, *No Intermissions*, p. 203.

175 *"shipping out for Europe"*   Ethan Mordden, *Rodgers & Hammerstein*, p. 45.

175 *"went around in threes"*   Amanda Vaill, *Somewhere: The Life of Jerome Robbins*, p. 90.

176 *"on the prowl for girls"*   Humphrey Burton, *Leonard Bernstein*, p. 127.

176 *"We were uprooted"*   Marshall Berman, *On the Town: One Hundred Years of Spectacle in Times Square*, pp. 67–68.

177 *"a real braiding"*   Vaill, p. 103.

NOTES

178 *"a whole lifetime into a day"* Betty Comden and Adolph Green, "When N.Y. Was a Helluva Town," *New York Times*, Oct. 31, 1971.

179 *"the enormous love"* Vaill, p. 108.

179 *"filled with soldiers, sailors, and airmen"* Sono Osato, author interview.

179 *"a half-Japanese as an all-American girl"* Sono Osato, *Distant Dances*, p. 243.

180 *"preciousness of our todays"* Ibid, p. 235.

CHAPTER 21

184 *"I didn't really like cigarettes"* Tama Starr and Edward Hyland, *Signs and Wonders*, p. 141.

185 *"at the street level it was all lit"* Farnsworth Fowle, author interview.

185 *"still a good deal brighter"* E.J. Kahn Jr., "Somewhere in New York," *New Yorker*, May 29, 1943.

187 *"Coney Island was not fun"* Sid Frigand, author interview.

187 *"restlessness as they wandered"* Robert Coates, "Big Night," *New Yorker*, May 27, 1944.

187 *"drunken kind of flying wedge"* Meyer Berger, "Times Square Diary," *New York Times Magazine*, Sept. 3, 1944.

188 *"not a vice crusade"* *New York Times*, Jan. 23, 1944.

188 *"Charlie didn't know"* *New York Times*, Jan. 24, 1944.

188 *"vulgar and perniciously poisonous"* Andrea Friedman, *Prurient Interests*, p. 90.

188 *"my cruising partner"* Tennessee Williams, *Memoirs*, pp. 52–53.

189 *"all smaller and shorter"* George S. Irving, author interview.

189 *"About drives I am ignorant"* Philip Hamburger, "The Bard in the Delicatessen," *New Yorker*, March 18, 1944.

189 *"a carnation a day"* "Broadway," *Life* magazine, Nov. 13, 1944.

190 *"crime is my oyster"* Leonard Wallock, "New York: Culture Capital of America, 1940–1965," p. 65.

190 *"jammed with soldiers and sailors"* Woody Allen, "Playing It Again," New York, April 6, 1998.

191 *"she gets hysterical"* Arnold Shaw, "Sinatrauma: The Proclamation of a New Era," in *Sinatra: Twentieth-Century Romantic*.

CHAPTER 22

192 *"Tijuana on the Hudson"* Alistair Cooke, *The American Homefront*, pp. 281–82.

193 *"make me a redhead"* Joan Wynne, author interview.

194 *"wide-eyed kid from Kansas City"* *New York Times*, Oct. 15, 1976.

195 *"They've Got an Awful Lot of Coffee in Brazil"* Julie Wilson, author interview.

196 *"They don't come any tougher"* Mickey Podell-Raber, *The Copa*, p. 116.

196 *"Those mob guys"* Ibid, p. 42.

197 *"harsh, wartime world"* Barbara Walters, *Audition*, pp. 43–44.

CHAPTER 23

198 *"shoved around in the Astor Bar"* Lucius Beebe, *Snoot If You Must*, pp. 3–4.

199 *"War money flowed"* Hildegarde, *Over 50—So What!* p. 73.

199 *"transition from the rowdy stage"* *New Yorker*, Dec. 26, 1942, p. 39.

200 *"suave and imperturbable"*   "Life Visits the Colony," *Life* magazine, Feb. 7, 1944.

200 *"were leaking banknotes"*   Lucius Beebe, "Gotham on a Spending Spree," *American Mercury*, May 1944.

200 *"New York's New Yorkiest place"*   Ralph Blumenthal, *Stork Club*, p. 9.

201 *"Mrs. Cornelius Vanderbilt had tea"*   E. J. Kahn Jr., "Word From Mr. Billingsley," *New Yorker*, March 6, 1943.

201 *"Ralph Forbes and Kitty Carlisle Are Anchors Aweigh"*   *New Yorker*, Jan. 10, 1942, pp. 9–10.

202 *"Wayne was bi-sexual"*   Hamilton Darby Perry, *A Chair for Wayne Lonergan*, pp. 117–18.

202 *"the sex-twisted 25-year-old"*   Wolcott Gibbs, "Five Days Wonder," *New Yorker*, Nov. 6, 1943.

202 Renting out of the Lonergan apartment cited by Walter Gray in "A Once-Notorious Haunt Still Stands," letter to the editor, *New York Times*, July 21, 1995.

203 *"I loved him very much"*   Susan Kastner, "Barbara Hamilton Looks Back," *Toronto Star*, July 3, 1994.

CHAPTER 24

208 *"so long as there's a swastika"*   Susan Canedy, *America's Nazis*, p. 73.

209 *"It's a lie"*   *New York Times*, Aug. 18, 1939.

210 Excerpts from Fritz Kuhn's letters, *New York Times*, Nov. 23, 1939.

210 *"I regarded him as a nuisance"*   *New York Times*, Nov. 18, 1939.

211 *"Jew stooges"*   Robert Lewis Taylor, "The Kampf of Joe McWilliams," *New Yorker*, Aug. 29, 1940.

212 *"Hitler naturally enough draws the most applause"*   Richard Lingeman, *Don't You Know There's a War On?* p. 173.

212 *"people dressed as storm troopers"*   Francis Chinard, author interview.

212 *"no more German pictures"*   *New York Times*, Dec. 12, 1941.

CHAPTER 25

213 *"a menace to Americans?"*   Leonard Dinnerstein. *Anti-Semitism in America*, p. 131.

213 *"hateful descriptions of the Jews"*   *New York Times*, Dec. 30, 1943.

213 *"Things are very calm"*   "Christian Action," *Time* magazine, Jan. 10, 1944.

214 *"Anti-Semitism is always a problem"*   *New York Times*, Dec. 30, 1943.

214 *"things of this kind can occur"*   Thomas Kessner, *Fiorello H. LaGuardia and the Making of Modern New York*, p. 523.

215 *"pro-Hitler and anti-Semitic"*   *New York Times*, May 21, 1943.

215 *"a major defeat"*   *New York Times*, Dec. 21, 1943.

215 Incidents recounted in "Investigation of Anti-American and Anti-Semitic Vandalism"   La Guardia Papers, Departmental Correspondence, Box 3333, Roll 583, New York City Municipal Archives.

216 *"people of the Jewish faith"*   *New York Times*, Jan. 17, 1944.

217 *"not to be mentioned in polite society"*   Arthur Miller, "Shattering the Silence, Illuminating the Hatred," *New York Times*, Oct. 22, 2001.

218 *"any comprehension of what Nazism meant"*   Arthur Miller, "The Face in the Mirror: Anti-Semitism Then and Now," *New York Times Book Review*, Oct. 14, 1984.

NOTES

CHAPTER 26

220 *"the ghetto's instinctive hatred of policemen"*   James Baldwin, "Notes of a Native Son," *Harper's*, Nov. 1955.

222 *"as patriotic as anyone"*   Sarah Delany and A. Elizabeth Delany, *Having Our Say*, pp. 172–73.

223 *"I just swished at them with my knife"*   Arnold Shaw, *The Street That Never Slept*, pp. 258–59.

224 *"just as discriminatory"*   Ibid, pp. 279–80.

224 *"Negroes and whites enjoying themselves"*   Nat Brandt, *Harlem at War*, p. 171.

CHAPTER 27

226 *"protect me from this white man"*   Walter White, *A Man Called White*, p. 234.

227 *"a lit match in a tin of gasoline"*   James Baldwin, "Notes of a Native Son," *Harper's*, Nov. 1955.

227 *"None of the stores had any windows left"*   Claude Brown, *Manchild in the Promised Land*, p. 13.

228 *"Me Colored Too"*   Alex Haley and Malcolm X, *The Autobiography of Malcolm X*, p. 117.

230 *"the red-faced mayor"*   Roy Wilkins, *Standing Fast*, pp. 183–84.

231 *"degrade and starve a human being"*   Walter White, *A Man Called White*, p. 238.

231 *"It was just hoodlums"*   *New York Times*, Aug. 3, 1943.

232 *"I would not agree to this rioting"*   Nat Brandt, *Harlem at War*, p. 205.

233 *"The better class Negroes"*   Arnold Rampersad, *The Life of Langston Hughes, Vol. II*, p. 75.

233 *"Ballad of Margie Polite"*   Ibid, pp. 76–77.

233 *"Harlem had needed something to smash"*   Baldwin, *Notes of a Native Son*.

CHAPTER 28

237 Penicillin supplies for D-Day invasion cited by Pfizer in PR Newswire, Jan. 4, 1999.

238 *"We already had the basic know-how"*   Berton Roueche, "Something Extraordinary," *New Yorker*, July 23, 1951.

240 Combat recollections by Sumner Glimcher, author interview.

CHAPTER 29

243 *"are brought in ambulances"*   Brock Pemberton, "The Canteen Grows Up," *New York Times*, Feb. 25, 1945.

243 *"to have the Purple Heart"*   *Canteen News*, Aug. 3, 1944.

244 *"He had a frightening face"*   Sono Osato, author interview.

244 *"no such thing as a handicap"*   *New Yorker*, Nov. 20, 1943, pp. 19–20.

245 *"live with these veterans"*   *New York Times*, July 4, 1945.

246 *"you gotta forgive"*   John Belle and Maxinne Rhea Leighton, *Grand Central*, pp. 81–82.

246 *"When we go by the Statue of Liberty"*   *New York Times*, Feb. 22, 1945.

247 *"The paraplegics were great readers"*   Brooke Astor, *Footprints*, p. 201.

248 *"I thought they were very upbeat"*   Sheldon Mike Young, author interview.

CHAPTER 30

252 *"unable to see the top of the Empire State Building"*   *New York Times*, July 29, 1945.

253 *"Climb, you damn fool, climb"*   Arthur Weingarten, *The Sky Is Falling*, p. 197.

253 *"the building shook"*   Therese Willig, author interview.

256 *"I led them to where the fire was"*   Robert McCabe, "51 Years Ago, B-25 Hit N.Y. Skyscraper," *Fort Lauderdale Sun-Sentinel*, July 28, 1996.

256 *"Her nylon blouse was melted"*   National Public Radio, July 28, 1995.

256 *"a crash in the basement"*   Walter Arm, "Apprentice, 17, in Coast Guard Helped Victims," *New York Herald Tribune*, July 29, 1945.

257 *"You didn't even work two hours today"*   Gloria Pall, "The Day a B-25 Bomber Crashed Into the Empire State Building," *Van Nuys Aviation & Business Journal*, July 2001.

CHAPTER 31

259 *"They are piling dead and wounded"*   Associated Press, May 30, 1942.

259 *"It was work or starve"*   Associated Press, Sept. 18, 1945.

260 *"the No. 1 war hero"*   *New York Times*, Mar. 25, 1943

261 *"the president has just died"*   New York Times, April 13, 1945.

261 *"didn't know anything about him"*   Sid Frigand, author interview.

262 *"to a Kansas farmer boy"*   *New York Times*, June 20, 1945.

263 *"carrying Chinese and American flags"*   Sheldon Mike Young, "Former Sailor Recounts Blissful Exuberance of 50 Years Ago," *Columbus Dispatch*, Aug. 13, 1995.

264 *"the moment the sailor kissed the nurse"*   Cited by Ray Zone, Peter Fetterman Gallery, Santa Monica, CA, http://artscenecal.com, and *The Digital Journalist*, www .digitaljournalist.org

264 *"I was absolutely smitten"*   Francis Chinard, author interview.

265 *"he looked at me shocked"*   Jo Chinard, author interview.

266 *"the sight of him struck terror"*   Mark Marchese, author interview.

266 *"the horror of passing Gold Star mothers"*   Susan Dworkin, *Miss America, 1945*, p. 54.

266 *"also were named Anthony and Albert"*   Ed Lowe, "The Arrows of Fate," *Newsday*, Aug. 16, 1998.

267 *"I had no remorse"*   David Everitt, *Remembering Sam*, pp. 115–16.

CHAPTER 32

268 *"corrugated shoe box"*   Robert A. M. Stern, Thomas Mellins and David Fishman, *New York 1960*, p. 855.

268 *"New York's great piece"*   Ibid, p. 855.

268 Brooklyn Battery Tunnel dispute cited by Robert Caro, *The Power Broker: Robert Moses and the Fall of New York*, pp. 689–90; *New York Times*, Oct. 6, Oct. 31, 1942.

269 *"authenticated Jew Fiorello La Guardia"*   Radio Rome broadcast cited in *New York Times*, Oct. 29, 1942.

269 *"am awaiting your order"*   Ralph Martin, *CCB*, p. 474.

269 *"shooting off his pistol"*   Newbold Morris, *Let the Chips Fall*, p. 192.

270 *"a word of comfort"*   "Brooks Case," La Guardia Papers, Departmental Correspondence, Box 3333, New York City Municipal Archives.

NOTES

270 *"none of your business"* Ibid.
270 *"I tried to run the Army"* *New York Times*, March 22, 1945.
271 *"like a political meeting back home"* Richard Goldstein, "Charles Poletti Dies at 99," *New York Times*, Aug. 10, 2002.
272 *"pick the time"* WNYC broadcast, July 1, 1945, La Guardia Archives.
272 *"dirty money"* WNYC, July 8, 1945, Ibid.
272 *"each department was woefully undermanned"* Sam Roberts, "New York 1945," *New York Times*, July 30, 1995.
273 *"death through starvation"* Thomas Kessner, *Fiorello H. La Guardia and the Making of Modern New York*, p. 581.
273 *"it is wicked"* Ibid, p. 587.
273 *"as incorruptible as the sun"* *New York Times*, Sept. 21, 1947.

EPILOGUE

274 *"the commercial capital"* Stern, Mellins and Fishman, *New York 1960*, p. 394.
275 *"that calls for a celebration"* Ibid, p. 607, citing Howard Meyers, "A Letter From the Publisher," *Architectural Forum*, Feb. 1947.
275 *"the quay"* Jan Morris, *Manhattan '45*, p. 174.
275 *"front door for the United Nations"* *New York Times*, Aug. 1, 1948.
276 *"what a city ought to be"* Jared Perl, *New Art City*, pp. 37–38.
276 *"this fabulous city"* J.B. Priestley, "Priestley Appraises New York," *New York Times*, Jan. 4, 1948 (transcription of BBC broadcast).
276 *"the great international city"* *The American Experience: The Center of the World*, www.pbs.org/wgbh/amex/newyork/timeline.
277 *"advertising agencies of America were there"* *New York 1960*, p. 339.
278 *"Post World War II painting in New York"* Leonard Wallock, *New York: Culture Capital of America, 1940–1965*, p. 136.
279 *"in advance of us all"* Gilbert Millstein, "Mainbocher Stands for a Fitting," *New York Times Magazine*, March 25, 1956.
279 *"What rendered New York so important"* Caroline Rennolds Milbank, *New York Fashion*, p. 143.
280 *"becoming the capital of the world"* E. B. White, *Here Is New York*, p. 52.
281 *"they came in too late"* Meyer Berger, "400,000 in Silent Tribute as War Dead Come Home," *New York Times*, Oct. 27, 1947.

SOURCES

INTERVIEWS

Maury Allen, Dave Anderson, Emery Battis, Harry Biffar, Ramon Blackburn, Francis Chinard, Jo Chinard, Alice Cullen, Sono Osato Elmaleh, Ray Fisher, Farnsworth Fowle, George Franck, Stanley Franks, Sid Frigand, Sumner Glimcher, Seymour Greene, Skip Homeier, George S. Irving, Phil Kraus, Kay Travers Langan, Norman Leyden, Mark Marchese, John McDonald, Robert Satter, Eugene Shepherd, Marie O'Hare Walsh, Therese Fortier Willig, Julie Wilson, Seymour Wittek, Joan Wynne, Sheldon Mike Young

BOOKS

Anderson, Alan. *The Songwriter Goes to War.* Pompton Plains, NJ: Limelight, 2004.

Ardman, Harvey. *Normandie: Her Life and Times.* New York: Franklin Watts, 1985.

Astor, Brooke. *Footprints.* Garden City, NY: Doubleday, 1980.

Atkinson, Brooks. *Broadway.* New York: Macmillan, 1970.

Bacall, Lauren. *By Myself.* New York: Knopf, 1978.

Bach, Steven. *Dazzler: The Life and Times of Moss Hart.* New York: Perseus, 2002.

Baggelaar, Kristin. *The Copacabana.* Charleston, SC: Arcadia, 2006.

Barrett, Mary Ellin. *Irving Berlin: A Daughter's Memoir.* New York: Simon & Schuster, 1994.

Barrett, Thomas Beard. *Wonderful Flying Machines: A History of U.S. Coast Guard Helicopters.* Annapolis, MD: Naval Institute Press, 1996.

Beebe, Lucius. *Snoot If You Must.* New York: D. Appleton-Century, 1943.

Belle, John, and Maxinne R. Leighton. *Grand Central: Gateway to a Million Lives.* New York: Norton, 2000.

Bergreen, Laurence. *As Thousands Cheer: The Life of Irving Berlin.* New York: Viking, 1990.

Berman, Marshall. *On the Town: One Hundred Years of Spectacle in Times Square.* New York: Random House, 2006.

Blair, Clay. *Hitler's U-Boat War: The Hunters, 1939–1942.* New York: Random House, 1996.

Blum, John Morton. *From the Morgenthau Diaries.* Vol. 2. Boston: Houghton Mifflin, 1967.

Blumenthal, Ralph. *Stork Club.* Boston: Little, Brown, 2000.

Brando, Marlon, with Robert Lindsey. *Songs My Mother Taught Me.* New York: Random House, 1994.

Brandt, Nat. *Harlem at War.* Syracuse: Syracuse University Press, 1996.

Brown, Jared. *The Fabulous Lunts.* New York: Atheneum, 1986.

———. *Moss Hart: A Prince of the Theatre.* New York: Back Stage Books, 2006.

SOURCES

Burton, Humphrey. *Leonard Bernstein.* New York: Doubleday, 1994.

Campbell, Rodney. *The Luciano Project.* New York: McGraw-Hill, 1977.

Canedy, Susan. *America's Nazis.* Menlo Park, CA: Markgraf, 1990.

Capeci, Dominic J. Jr. *The Harlem Riot of 1943.* Philadelphia: Temple University Press, 1977.

Caro, Robert. *The Power Broker: Robert Moses and the Fall of New York.* New York: Knopf, 1975.

Conant, Jennet. *The Irregulars: Roald Dahl and the British Spy Ring in Wartime Washington.* New York: Simon & Schuster, 2008.

Cooke, Alistair. *The American Home Front, 1941–1942.* New York: Atlantic Monthly Press, 2006.

Davenport, Marcia. *Too Strong for Fantasy.* Pittsburgh: University of Pittsburgh Press, 1967.

Delany, Sarah, and A. Elizabeth, with Amy Hill Heath. *Having Our Say: The Delany Sisters' First 100 Years.* New York: Kodansha America, 1993.

Dinnerstein, Leonard. *Anti-Semitism in America.* New York: Oxford University Press, 1994.

Distasi, Lawrence, ed. *Una Storia Segreta: The Secret History of Italian-American Evacuation and Internment During World War II.* Berkeley, CA.: Heyday, 2001.

Downey, Kristin. *The Woman Behind the New Deal: The Life of Frances Perkins, FDR's Secretary of Labor and His Moral Conscience.* New York: Doubleday, 2009.

Dreyfus, Jack. *A Remarkable Medicine Has Been Overlooked.* New York: Landmark Books, 2000.

Dworkin, Susan. *Miss America, 1945: Bess Myerson and the Year That Changed Our Lives.* New York: Newmarket, 1987.

Easton, Carol. *No Intermissions: The Life of Agnes de Mille.* Boston: Little, Brown, 1996.

Everitt, David. *Remembering Sam: A Wartime Story of Love, Loss and Redemption.* Chicago: Ivan R. Dee, 2008.

Fermi, Laura. *Atoms in the Family: My Life with Enrico Fermi.* Chicago: University of Chicago Press, 1954.

Fredrick, Leon. *Hooligan Sailor: The Saga of One Coast Guardsman in World War II.* Ozark, MO: Hazelwood, 2005.

Friedman, Andrea. *Prurient Interests: Gender, Democracy and Obscenity in New York City, 1909–1945.* New York: Columbia University Press, 2000.

Frommer, Myrna Katz, and Harvey Frommer. *It Happened on Broadway.* New York: Harcourt Brace, 1998.

Gallagher, Dorothy. *All the Right Enemies: The Life and Murder of Carlo Tresca.* New Brunswick, NJ: Rutgers University Press, 1988.

Gildersleeve, Virginia. *Many a Good Crusade.* New York: Macmillan, 1954.

Gimpel, Erich. *Agent 146.* New York: St. Martin's Press, 1957.

Goldstein, Richard. *Spartan Seasons: How Baseball Survived the Second World War.* New York: Macmillan, 1980.

Guernsey, Otis L. Jr., *Broadway Song and Story.* New York: Dodd, Mead, 1985.

Guggenheim, Peggy. *Out of This Century.* New York: Universe Books, 1979.

Haley, Alex and Malcolm X. *The Autobiography of Malcolm X.* New York: Ballantine, 1964.

Hamilton, Charles V. *Adam Clayton Powell Jr.: The Political Biography of an American Dilemma.* New York: Atheneum, 1991.

Hartzell, Karl Drew. *The Empire State at War: World War II.* The State of New York, 1949.

Haynes, John Earl, and Harvey Klehr. *Venona: Decoding Soviet Espionage in America.* New Haven: Yale University Press, 1999.

SOURCES

Heckscher, August. *When La Guardia Was Mayor.* New York: Norton, 1978.

Hildegarde, with Adele Whitely Fletcher. *Over 50—So What!* Garden City, NY: Doubleday, 1963.

Hoopes, Ray. *Americans Remember the Home Front.* New York: Hawthorn, 1977.

Hyde, H. Montgomery. *Room 3603: The Story of the British Intelligence Center in New York During World War II.* New York: Farrar, Straus, 1962.

Hyland, William G. *Richard Rodgers.* New Haven: Yale University Press, 1998.

Jackson, Lawrence. *Ralph Ellison: Emergence of Genius.* New York: John Wiley, 2002.

Kelly, Cynthia D., editor. *The Manhattan Project.* New York: Black Dog & Leventhal, 2007.

Kessner, Thomas. *Fiorello H. La Guardia and the Making of Modern New York.* New York: McGraw-Hill, 1989.

Ketchum, Richard M. *The Borrowed Years, 1938–1941.* New York: Random House, 1989.

Lanouette, William, with Bela Silard. *Genius in the Shadows: A Biography of Leo Szilard.* New York: Scribner's, 1992.

Lazar, Irving, with Annette Tapert. *Swifty: My Life and Good Times.* New York: Simon & Schuster, 1995.

Lingeman, Richard R. *Don't You Know There's a War On? The American Home Front, 1941–1945.* New York: Putnam's, 1970.

Logan, Josh. *Josh: My Up and Down, In and Out Life.* New York: Delacorte, 1976.

Lowell, Robert. *Life Studies.* New York: Farrar, Straus, 1959.

MacGregor, Morris J. Jr. *Integration of the Armed Forces, 1940–1965.* Washington, DC: Center of Military History, United States Army, 1985.

Malden, Karl. *When Do I Start?* New York: Simon & Schuster, 1997.

Martin, George. *CCB: The Life and Century of Charles C. Burlingham, New York's First Citizen.* New York: Hill and Wang, 2005.

Martinson, Deborah. *Lillian: A Life With Foxes and Scoundrels.* New York: Counterpoint, 2005.

Mehlman, Jeffrey. *Émigré New York: French Intellectuals in Wartime Manhattan, 1940–1944.* Baltimore: Johns Hopkins University Press, 2000.

Merman, Ethel, with George Eels. *Merman: An Autobiography.* New York: Simon & Schuster, 1978.

Milbank, Caroline Rennolds. *New York Fashion: The Evolution of American Design.* New York: Harry N. Abrams, 1989

Miller, Arthur. *Timebends: A Life.* New York: Grove Press, 1987.

Mordden, Ethan. *Rodgers & Hammerstein.* New York: Harry N. Abrams, 1992.

Morris, Jan. *Manhattan '45.* New York: Oxford University Press, 1986.

Morris, Newbold. *Let the Chips Fall.* New York: Appleton-Century-Crofts, 1955.

Nettlebeck, Colin W. *Forever French: Exile in the United States, 1939–1945.* Oxford, UK: Berg, 1991.

Norris, Robert S. *Racing for the Bomb.* South Royalton, VT: Steerforth Press, 2002.

Okrent, David. *Great Fortune: The Epic of Rockefeller Center.* New York: Viking, 2003.

Osato, Sono. *Distant Dances.* New York: Knopf, 1980.

Pearson, John. *The Life of Ian Fleming.* New York: McGraw-Hill, 1966.

Perkins, Frances. *The Roosevelt I Knew.* New York: Viking, 1946.

Perl, Jed. *New Art City: Manhattan at Mid-Century.* New York: Knopf, 2005.

Perry, Hamilton Darby. *A Chair for Wayne Lonergan.* New York: Macmillan, 1972.

Pfeffer, Paula F. *A. Philip Randolph, Pioneer of the Civil Rights Movement.* Baton Rouge, LA: Louisiana State University Press, 1990.

SOURCES

Podell-Raber, Mickey, with Charles Pignone. *The Copa: Jules Podell and the Hottest Club North of Havana.* New York: HarperCollins, 2007.

The Post's New York. New York: HarperResource, 2001.

Rachlis, Eugene. *They Came to Kill.* New York: Random House, 1961.

Rampersad, Arnold. *The Life of Langston Hughes. Volume II, 1941–1967, I Dream a World.* New York: Oxford University Press, 1988.

Rankin, Rebecca B., ed. *New York Advancing: Victory Edition.* New York: Municipal Reference Library, 1945.

Rhodes, Richard. *The Making of the Atomic Bomb.* New York: Simon & Schuster, 1986.

Richardson, K. D. *Reflections of Pearl Harbor.* Westport, CT.: Praeger, 2005.

Robbins, Michael W., and Wendy Palitz. *Brooklyn: A State of Mind.* New York: Workman, 2001.

Roberts, Sam. *The Brother: The Untold Story of Atomic Spy David Greenglass and How He Sent His Sister, Ethel Rosenberg, to the Electric Chair.* New York: Random House, 2001.

Rollyson, Carl. *Lillian Hellman.* New York: St. Martin's Press, 1988.

Roman, Kenneth. *The King of Madison Avenue: David Ogilvy and the Making of Modern Advertising.* New York: Palgrave Macmillan, 2009.

Romulo, Carlos. *My Brother Americans.* Garden City, NY: Doubleday, Doran, 1945.

Ross, Bill D. *Iwo Jima: Legacy of Valor.* New York: Vanguard, 1985.

Russell, Harold, with Victor Rosen. *Victory in My Hands.* New York: Creative Age Press, 1949.

Schiff, Stacy. *Saint-Exupéry.* New York: Knopf, 1994.

Schneider, Coleman. *The Voyage of the S.S. Jeremiah O'Brien: San Francisco to Normandy, 1994.* Tenafly, NJ: privately printed, 1994.

Secrest, Meryle. *Somewhere for Me: A Biography of Richard Rodgers.* New York: Knopf, 2001.

Shaw, Arnold. *Sinatra: Twentieth-Century Romantic.* New York: Holt, Reinhart and Winston, 1968.

———. *The Street That Never Slept: New York's Fabled 52nd Street.* New York: Coward, McCann and Geoghegan, 1971.

Shefter, Martin, ed. *Capital of the American Century: The National and International Influence of New York City.* New York: Russell Sage Foundation, 1993.

Snyder-Grenier, Ellen M. *Brooklyn! An Illustrated History.* Philadelphia: Temple University Press, 1996.

Starr, Tama, and Edward Hayman. *Signs and Wonders.* New York: Doubleday, 1998.

Stephenson, William, ed. *British Security Coordination: The Secret History of British Intelligence in the Americas, 1940–1945.* St. Ermin's Press, Britain, 1998. New York: Fromm International, 1999.

Stern, Robert A., Thomas Mellins, and David Fishman. *New York 1960.* New York: Monacelli Press, 1995.

Strunsky, Simeon. *No Mean City.* New York: E. P. Dutton, 1944.

Tanning, Dorothea. *Between Lives: An Artist and Her World.* New York: Norton, 2001.

Truman, Margaret. *Harry S. Truman.* New York: Morrow, 1973.

Vaill, Amanda. *Somewhere: The Life of Jerome Robbins.* New York: Broadway, 2006.

Van Druten, John. *Playwright at Work.* New York: Harper, 1953.

Wallock, Leonard, ed. *New York: Culture Capital of the World, 1940–1965.* New York: Rizzoli, 1988.

Walters, Barbara. *Audition: A Memoir.* New York: Knopf, 2008.

Watkins, Julian Lewis. *The 100 Greatest Advertisements.* New York: Moore Publishing, 1949.

Weingarten, Arthur. *The Sky Is Falling.* New York: Grosset & Dunlap, 1977.

SOURCES

Wertheim, Albert. *Staging the War: American Drama and World War II.* Bloomington, IN: Indiana University Press, 2004.

White, E. B. *Here Is New York.* New York: Harper & Row, 1949.

White, Walter. *A Man Called White.* New York: Viking, 1948.

Wilkins, Roy, with Tom Mathews. *Standing Fast: The Autobiography of Roy Wilkins.* New York: Viking, 1982.

Williams, Tennessee. *Memoirs.* Garden City, NY: Doubleday, 1972.

Wouk, Herman. *The Caine Mutiny.* Garden City, NY: Doubleday, 1951.

ARTICLES

Allen, Woody. "Playing It Again." *New York*, Apr. 6, 1998.

Ardman, Harvey. "The Ship That Died of Carelessness." *American Heritage*, Dec. 1983.

Arm, Walter. "Apprentice, 17, in Coast Guard Helped Victims." *New York Herald Tribune*, July 29, 1945.

Baldwin, James. "Notes of a Native Son." *Harper's*, Nov. 1955.

Beebe, Lucius. "Gotham on a Spending Spree." *American Mercury*, May 1944.

Berger, Meyer. "400,000 in Silent Tribute as War Dead Come Home." *New York Times*, Oct. 27, 1947.

———. "Times Square Diary." *New York Times Magazine*, Sept. 3, 1944.

Bliven, Bruce. "The Voice and the Kids." *New Republic*, Nov. 6, 1944.

"Broadway: New York's Wonderful Big Street Is Busier Than Ever." *Life* magazine, Nov. 13, 1944.

"Christian Action." *Time*, Jan. 10, 1944.

Clarey, North. "They Saved New York." *Saturday Evening Post*, May 13, 1944.

Clarke, Maureen. "The Wing Takes Off." *Back Stage*, Dec. 16, 1994.

Coates, Robert A. "Big Night." *New Yorker*, May 27, 1944.

Cohen, Billie. "Torch Songs," in Michael W. Robbins and Wendy Palitz, eds. *Brooklyn: A State of Mind.* New York: Workman, 2001.

Comden, Betty, and Adolph Green. "When New York Was a Helluva Town." *New York Times*, Oct. 31, 1971.

Crewsdon, John F., and Jo Thomas. "Files Show Tests for Truth Drug Began in U.S." *New York Times*, Sept. 5, 1977.

Drypolcher, Lucetta Berizzi. "Orders to Take Him Away," in *Una Storia Segreta*, edited by Lawrence Distasi. Berkeley, CA: Heyday, 2001.

Evanson, Christopher. "A Veteran Remembers Coast Guard Desegregation." Cox News Service, Nov. 18, 2007.

Freidin, Seymour. "50 to 60 Feared Killed as Blast Sinks Destroyer off Rockaway." *New York Herald Tribune*, Jan. 4, 1944.

"Gateway to the World." *Popular Mechanics*, April 1942.

"Gateway to Victory." *Collier's*, Jan. 20, 1945.

Gibbs, Wolcott. "Five Days Wonder." *New Yorker*, Nov. 6, 1943.

Goldstein, Richard. "Charles Poletti Dies at 99." *New York Times*, Aug. 20, 2002.

Gordon, John Steele. "Oklahoma!" *American Heritage*, February–March 1993.

Haberman, Clyde. "Time Ebbs for the Heroes Who Saved the Harbor." *New York Times*, May 27, 2008.

Hamburger, Philip. "The Bard in the Delicatessen." *New Yorker*, March 18, 1944.

Harriman, Margaret Case. "Bombs on the Melting Pot." *New Yorker*, Feb. 7, 1942.

SOURCES

Hart, Moss. "A Winged Victory." *New York Times*, Nov. 14, 1943.

Jenkins, Philip. "Home-Grown Terror." *American Heritage*, Sept. 1995.

Jewell, Edward Alden. "31 Women Artists Show Their Work." *New York Times*, Jan. 6, 1943.

Joslin, John. "Facts and Figures That Tell the Unique Story of Our Incredible City." *New York Times Magazine*, Dec. 22, 1946.

Kahn, E. J. Jr. "Midshipmen's Country." *New Yorker*, May 10, 1941.

———. "Somewhere in New York." *New Yorker*, May 29, 1943.

———. "Word From Mr. Billingsley." *New Yorker*, Mar. 6, 1943.

Kastner, Susan. "Barbara Hamilton Looks Back." *Toronto Star*, July 3, 1994.

Kramer, Hilton. "Glamorous Character." *New York Times Book Review*, Dec. 23, 1979.

"Life Visits the Colony." Life magazine. Feb. 7, 1944.

Lowe, Ed. "The Arrows of Fate." *Newsday*, Aug. 16, 1998.

McCabe, Robert. "51 Years Ago, B-25 Hit N.Y. Skyscraper." *Fort Lauderdale Sun-Sentinel.* July 28, 1996.

McCullers, Carson. "Brooklyn Is My Neighborhood." *Vogue*, Mar. 1, 1941.

Miller, Arthur. "The Face in the Mirror: Anti-Semitism Then and Now." *New York Times Book Review*, Oct. 14, 1984.

———. "Shattering the Silence, Illuminating the Hatred." *New York Times*, Oct. 22, 2001.

Millstein, Gilbert. "Mainbocher Stands for a Fitting." *New York Times Magazine*, Mar. 25, 1956.

Munch, Janet Butler. "Making Waves in the Bronx: The Story of the U.S. Naval Training School (WR) at Hunter College." *Bronx County Historical Society Journal*, Spring 1993.

Naczi, Robert F. "Tragedy Strikes in New York Harbor." *Naval Institute Proceedings*, Dec. 1995.

Norris, Robert S. "Manhattan Project Sites in Manhattan." *The Manhattan Project*, Ed. Cynthia D. Kelly. New York: Black Dog & Leventhal, 2007.

O'Hara, Tom. "400,000 Bow in Rites Here For War Dead." *New York Herald Tribune*, Oct. 27, 1947.

Pall, Gloria. "The Day a B-25 Bomber Crashed Into the Empire State Building." *Van Nuys* (Calif.) *Aviation & Business Journal*, July 2001.

Pemberton, Brock. "The Canteen Grows Up." *New York Times*, Feb. 25, 1945.

Peterson, Pete. "The Mariners." *American Legacy*, Spring 2005.

Roberts, Sam. "New York 1945: The War Was Ending, Times Square Exploded. Change Was Coming." *New York Times*, July 30, 1995.

Rodgers, Richard. "Reflections on a 'Four-Year-Old.'" *New York Times*, Mar. 30, 1947.

Rooney, Andy. "Did They Try to Bomb New York?" *Harper's*, Mar. 1947.

Ross, Lillian. "Enchanted Evening." *New Yorker*, Apr. 7, 2008.

Roueche, Berton. "Something Extrordinary." *New Yorker*, July 23, 1951.

Smith, Gene. "Bundesfuhrer Kuhn." *American Heritage*, Sept. 1995.

Swanberg, W. A. "The Spies Who Came in From the Sea." *American Heritage*, Apr. 1970.

Taylor, Robert Lewis. "The Kampf of Joe McWilliams." *New Yorker*, Aug. 29, 1940.

Willing, Richard. "The Nazi Spy Next Door." *USA Today*, Feb. 27, 2002.

Winkler, David F. "Port Security—A Mission Renewed." *Sea Power*, Aug. 1, 2002.

Young, Sheldon Mike. "Former Sailor Recounts Blissful Exuberance of 50 Years Ago." *Columbus Dispatch*, Aug. 13, 1995.

Vanden Heuvel, William J. "Franklin Delano Roosevelt: A Man of the Century." Address to the Century Association, Apr. 4, 2002.

SOURCES

REPORTS, WEB SITES, ORAL HISTORIES, INTERVIEWS, BROADCASTS, VIDEO

The American Experience: The Center of the World. www.pbs.org/wgbh/amex/newyork/ timeline.

"The American Theatre Wing During World War II." www.americantheatrewing.com.

"Brooks Case." New York City Municipal Archives. Office of the Mayor, Fiorello H. La Guardia. Subject Files, 1934–1945. Roll 0013.

Browning, Robert M. Jr. "Captains of the Port." United States Coast Guard Historian's Office, Washington, DC, January 1999.

Camp Shanks Museum, collections, Orangeburg, New York.

Canteen News, publication of Stage Door Canteen. Billy Rose Collection, Library of Performing Arts, New York Public Library.

Charland, Guy. "Boarding the Troopship SS Dominion Monarch, Port of Embarkation, New York." www.tankbooks.com/charland/charland1.html (2003)

Cowell, Jane. Papers. Billy Rose Collection, Library of Performing Arts, New York Public Library.

Cressman, Robert J. "Lafayette." Dictionary of American Naval Fighting Ships. Department of the Navy, Naval Historical Center, Washington, DC, May 2007.

Fireboats of 9/11. Dreamtime Entertainment, 2003.

Freear, Robert. "Survivor Tales of the USS Turner DD-648." www.USSTurner.org.

Gallagher, Robert F. "World War II Story." www.gallagher.com/ww2.

The Gremlin, publication of *Winged Victory* cast. Billy Rose Theater Collection, Library of Performing Arts, New York Public Library.

Harris, Collingwood. "Reflections." U.S. Coast Guard Oral History Program, Oct. 18, 1984.

Herlands, William B. "Investigation of Anti-American and Anti-Semitic Vandalism." City of New York Department of Investigation. New York City Municipal Archives. La Guardia Papers, Departmental Correspondence, 1934–1945. Box 3333, Folder 1, Roll 583.

Hirschfeld, Gerald. "Wrap Shot." www.ascendantimage.com.

"Historical Sketch of Camp Kilmer," National Records and Archives Administration, Northeast Region, New York.

Keyes, Edward J. "Navy Days: Anti-Submarine Warfare in the Atlantic WWII." New York Yacht Club archives.

Lafferty, Walter E. "Dad's War." America's Greatest Generation: Coast Guard Heroes. http://carol_fus.tripod.com/cg_hero_welafferty.html (September 2002).

Meany, Joseph F., Jr. "Port in a Storm: The Port of New York in World War II." Museum of the State of New York.

"Lunchtime Follies." www.americantheatrewing.org/about/history.

Nassour, Ellis. "Antoinette Perry Makes a Name," www.theatermania.com (May 29, 2000).

O'Mara, Olive Osterwise. "My Service in the Waves, World War II." Veterans' Oral Histories Preservation Project, Orem (Utah) Heritage Advisory Commission, January–February, 2006.

Priestley, J. B. "Priestley Appraises New York." Transcription of BBC broadcast in *New York Times Magazine,* Jan. 4, 1948.

Randolph, David, and Harold Smith, interviews, Empire State Building plane crash. National Public Radio, "Morning Edition," July 28, 1995.

Roche, Emeline. Papers, Billy Rose Collection, Library of the Performing Arts, New York Public Library.

SOURCES

Satter, Robert. Interview, Rutgers University Oral History Archives. Sept. 20, 2006.

Souder, Jeff. "The Army Pictorial Service's Films as Information-Operations Tool in World War II." www.gordon.army.mil/ocos/ac.

The Target, publication of Auxiliary Aircraft Warning Service, First Fighter Command. Billy Rose Collection, Library of the Performing Arts, New York Public Library.

Tessmer, Robert. "Life Aboard a Troop Transport." www.100thww2.org.

"33 Members of the Duquesne Spy Ring." www.fbi.gov/libref/historic/famcases/spyring.

"Velvalee Dickinson Doll Woman." www.fbi.gov/libref/historic/famcases/dickinson.

Wandrey, Robert, "Photo School," www.ascendantimage.com.

WNYC Radio. La Guardia broadcast texts, July 1, July 8, 1945. La Guardia Archives. Fiorello H. La Guardia Community College, Long Island City, New York.

INDEX

INDEX

INDEX

ABOUT THE AUTHOR

Richard Goldstein writes for the *New York Times*, where he also worked as an editor. His previous books include *America at D-Day*, *Desperate Hours: The Epic Rescue of the Andrea Doria*, *Spartan Seasons: How Baseball Survived the Second World War*, and *Mine Eyes Have Seen: A First-Person History of the Events That Shaped America*.